WORLD YEARBOOK
OF EDUCATION 1999

INCLUSIVE EDUCATION

Supporting Inclusion in Education Systems

Edited by
Harry Daniels and Philip Garner
Series editors: David Coulby and Crispin Jones

KOGAN PAGE

First published in 1999
First published in paperback in 2000

Kogan Page Limited
120 Pentonville Road
London
N1 9JN
UK

Stylus Publishing Inc.
22883 Quicksilver Drive
Sterling
VA 20166-2012
USA

© Harry Daniels and Philip Garner, 1999

British Library Cataloguing in Publication Data

A CIP record for this book is available from the British Library.

ISBN 0 7494 2237 8 (hbk)   ISBN 0 7494 3454 6 (pbk)

Typeset by Kogan Page
Printed and bound by Biddles Ltd, Guildford and King's Lynn

Contents

SECTION I: DEFINING SPECIAL EDUCATION IN A DEMOCRACY – INCLUSIVE EDUCATION

SECTION II: DILEMMAS FOR INCLUSIVE EDUCATION

SECTION III: DIALOGUES ON INCLUSIVE EDUCATION

Contributors

Ms Maria Baez, University of Newcastle, England
Professor Len Barton, University of Sheffield, England
Professor Christopher Blake, Towson University, Maryland, USA
Professor Marie Cerná, St Charles University, Prague, Czech Republic
Professor Pam Christie, University of the Witwatersrand, Johannesburg, South Africa
Dr Magda Damiani, University of Pelotas, Rio Grande de Sul, Brazil
Professor Harry Daniels, University of Birmingham, England
Mr John Dwyfor Davies, University of the West of England, Bristol, England
Professor Zlatko Dobrev, University 'St Kliment Ohridsky', Sofia, Bulgaria
Professor Alan Dyson, University of Newcastle, England
Peetjie Engels, Student in Care-Giving for the Elderly, Schinnen, The Netherlands
Dr Peter Evans, Organization for Economic Co-operation and Development, Paris
Professor Lynn Fuchs, Vanderbilt University, USA
Roberta Garbo, Vice President, Association of People with Downs Syndrome, Milan, Italy
Dr Philip Garner, Brunel University, London, England
Professor Alan Gartner, Graduate School and University Center, City University of New York, USA
Professor Paul Ghuman, University of Wales, Aberystwyth, Wales
Professor Anders Gustavsson, University of Stockholm, Sweden
Professor Michael Hardman, University of Utah, USA
Professor Jesper Holst, University of Copenhagen, Denmark
Professor Jo Lebeer, University of Antwerp, Belgium
Professor Gerald LeTendre, Penn State University, USA
Professor Dorothy Kerzner Lipsky, Graduate School and University Center, City University of New York, USA
Professor Margaret McLaughlin, University of Maryland, USA
Dr Cor Meijer, Institute of Educational Research SVO, The Hague, The Netherlands
Professor Angeles Parrilla, Universidad de Sevilla, Spain

Dr Sip Jan Pijl, Institute for Educational Research, University of
  Groningen, The Netherlands
Professor Hidetada Shimizu, Northern Illinois University, USA
Professor Roger Slee, University of Western Australia, Nedlands, Australia
Professor Gary Thomas, University of the West of England, Bristol,
  England
Professor Sally Tomlinson, Goldsmith's College, University of London,
  England
Dr Diana Tzokova, University 'St Kliment Ohridsky', Sofia, Bulgaria
Annet De Vroey, Co-ordinator, 'Project Mentor', Antwerp, Belgium
Professor Margret Winzer, University of Lethbridge, Canada

Acknowledgements

A number of people have assisted in the compilation of this book. First of all, however, we would like to thank our contributing authors and those who have informed their writing. The production of chapters frequently has to take second place to other official duties and we are grateful that each of our contributors has found the time to write, thus providing a set of chapters which illustrate the range and complexity of Inclusive Education. Indirectly, too, we thank the diverse populations who are the focus of this book.

We would also like to express gratitude to various colleagues within our own institutions who have offered assistance at a variety of levels: administrative, intellectual or emotional. Amongst these, special thanks must be offered to Jac Eke, who reformatted the initial contributions, and to Adrian Ellis, who freely gave his expertise on PCs and email when requested. Moreover, we wish to recognize that our own institutions have provided each of us with the necessary flexibility in our academic commitments to work on this volume.

Finally, our gratitude is extended to the Series Editors, Crispin Jones and David Coulby, for their advice and encouragement and, in the latter stages of our own editing, for their patience in awaiting the final draft of the manuscript. More importantly, we wish to acknowledge their foresight in identifying Inclusive Education as a title within the Yearbook series and their commitment to the project.

Series editors' introduction to the paperback edition

David Coulby and Crispin Jones

The World Yearbook of Education is probably the longest running publication of its kind, the first volume being published as far back as 1933. In 1981, Dr Bob Cowen, himself later to be the editor of a volume, estimated that the volumes published by that date marked a significant monument to scholarship, not least in their sheer quantity, as he estimated they totalled more than three million words. Twenty years and many volumes later, the total would be much greater.

The first editor of the Yearbook was Lord Eustace Percy, but Sir Percy Nunn, the then Director of the Institute of Education, London University, was closely involved, an involvement that other Directors of the Institute maintained until 1974. Indeed, one of the editors of a forthcoming volume (*Values, Culture and Education*, 2001) Professor Denis Lawton, was also a Director of the Institute. As the Yearbook's coverage became less Euro-focussed and more international, a close relationship was built up with staff at Teachers' College, Columbia; a fruitful collaboration that lasted until the early 1970s. In 1974, the Yearbooks ceased to be published by Evans Brothers, the series resuming in 1979, at this point being published by Kogan Page, still the current publisher.

The aim of the Yearbook since its inception has been to treat current educational concerns in as thorough and current manner as is possible. More recently, the globalization of educational concern has made these international surveys a fascinating and valuable comparative resource for educationists around the world.

The publication of the1999 volume in paperback marks its particular success. This was due partly to the outstanding field of international scholars on whom the editors were able to draw. But also on their own conceptualization of Inclusive Education in the widest sense being an essential of schooling in a democracy.

This paperback publication of a Yearbook is a new venture for us and for Kogan Page. We hope that it draws the attention of a wider readership to this important, international series.

Introduction to the paperback edition
Inclusive Education: challenges for the
new millennium

Harry Daniels and Philip Garner

Our introduction to the original Yearbook on inclusion was written in the middle of a time of great changes in the education system in our own country, events which had their parallels in many of the locations described in the book. Looking back over the relatively short period of time that has elapsed since our comments were made, it is clear to us that there has been a discernible shift in the way in which educational and social inclusion is being considered. For most people, the 1990s represented a period of gradual familiarization with what the term inclusion actually meant. Frequently it was defined as a 'different' policy approach in comparison with 'integration' or 'segregation'. This phase was also characterized by a developing understanding that it was a term that sought to assert individual rights in ways other than by policy directives from governments. Moreover, this relatively immature phase saw the concept of inclusion being to some extent 'bolted on' to pre-existing initiatives, whether in education, health or social care. It was only towards the end of the decade, and sporadically on a global scale, that central governments appeared to pursue formal policy agendas that were inclusive. Even where this happened the tendency was to emphasize inclusive ideology and its principles rather than substantive practical initiatives. In short these policies attained what could at best be regarded as rhetorical status. A further theme, which was indicative of this first, formative phase, was that inclusive approaches were frequently characterized by marginalized communities and individuals having inclusion 'done to them': the related concept of self-advocacy was also in its infancy.

We have now entered a more mature phase of inclusive thinking and action. In this the concept has become a central component of social and educational policy on a more consistent and widespread global canvas. Collaborative efforts involving international agencies are increasingly directing efforts towards developing educational inclusion as an embedded element of quests for more general social inclusivity. Individual governments now pursue overt and highly specific inclusion policies across many aspects of their administration. Moreover, such policies are now having practical impacts, as has been demonstrated by the shift from philosophy in *Excellence for All Children* (1997) to concerted innovation and change in *A Programme of Action* (1998) in England. Initiatives forthcoming within the European Union (EU) provide good examples of ways in which governments, acting collaboratively in the interest of a particular region or country, have begun to highlight inclusion as a major strategy to secure economic and social cohesion.

These and other policy shifts have also involved a greater degree of participation in policy making on the part of those formerly marginalized. Such an approach requires that those with disability or learning difficulty be given a central role in decision-making. This is now of vital importance, given that the 'equal opportunities' movement has presented the field of special needs education with a number of dilemmas and challenges. Not least of these is that policies which are designed to ensure equality of opportunity may easily slip to become practices which are oriented to notions of 'sameness'. Our suggestion is that policy should be oriented to promoting equity through difference. This is a more fundamental component of 'full inclusion', although it is fraught with both conceptual misunderstanding and operational difficulty.

Difference is lived at multiple levels. It has material, social, cultural, symbolic and emotional dimensions. It adheres in teachers' different orientations to pupils (Connolly 1998; Duffield 1998) and pupils' different orientations to schooling and learning (Kramarae and Treichler 1990).

Solstad (1994) suggests that the concept of equity may be embedded in two distinct sets of referents. Equity, on the one hand, may be referenced to equality, and the principle may be realised through centralized and centralizing actions by agencies such as the state. Alternatively, the principle of equity may be referenced to diversity, and realized in particular settings, regions and localities. Evans (1995) provides an extended discussion of this matter in the context of feminist theory. She contrasts the equality–difference controversy with a sameness–difference analysis:

> We might then want to see 'equality', 'sameness', and 'difference' as forming not a continuum, but three corners of a triangle. Then the notion of 'equality in difference' enters in. (This is the idea that we merit equal though not identical treatment; equal in the sense of 'equally good, and appropriate to us'.) Though so does 'equality through difference', as opposed to 'equality through sameness'.
>
> (Evans, 1995, p 3)

Evans proposes that to treat people equally it is not necessary to treat them in exactly same way. On the contrary, 'To treat people as equals may *require* that they not be treated the same way'(Evans, 1995, p 4). However, it is essential that they be treated fairly. The data suggest that girls and boys are not treated in the same way, in that more boys are sent to special schools. But this is not to say that more girls should be sent to special schools, or to suggest that girls are being treated fairly, because in fact their needs may be being ignored. Nor is it to suggest that special schools do not have an important role to play in the in-clusion process. What it does do, however, is suggest that if questions con-cerning equity are to be engaged with, then there is a requirement for appropriate tools or categories of analysis. These tools will need to be suffi-ciently sophisticated to encompass the complexity of issues surrounding the term equality.

The principle of self-advocacy is deeply enshrined within the development stage of statutory frameworks. Arguably the most distinctive feature of the phase of 'mature' inclusion, however, is the increasing recognition of the need to engage in vigorous debate on the conceptual issues and practical matters which are its co-determinants. Equally, this latter period is being character-ized by the adoption of a more circumspect, critically reflective and yet sup-portive, stance regarding the pressures and conflicts, which always seem to go hand-in-hand with policies which introduce new orientations in thinking. Consequently, we now appear to be in a period in which a broad spectrum of view is being actively sought at each of the three different levels of our admit-tedly crude categorization in the original Yearbook. These debates are already fascinating, and will undoubtedly impact further on thinking and practice as the decade unfolds.

It is not our intention here to rehearse the full extent of the polarities and di-lemmas, which characterize such debates. Nor is it our intention to attempt a comprehensive mapping of these emerging issues. So, just as inclusive educa-tion needs to be viewed as a dynamic process rather than an end-product, there should be an in-built expectation that new dilemmas will present them-selves at various chronological points and spatial locations as education sys-tems attempt to adopt a more fully inclusive orientation. Indeed, this Yearbook has already provided ample illustration of such considerations in a range of national locations. However, it may be useful to summarize some of the most recent and ongoing challenges to policy-makers, practitioners and for those for whom inclusion holds the utmost personal relevance–whilst emphasising the cautionary rider that for each issue identified several others might also demand our attention.

The challenge of the knowledge society

The World Health Organisation is developing a new system of classification (ICIDH-2). In this new scheme functioning and disablement are viewed as outcomes of an interaction between a persons physical and metal condition and a social and physical environment. The classification speaks of interven-tions concerned with impairment, activity limitations and participation re-striction. One fundamental question here concerns the kind of activity and the form of participation that will be required as schools attempt to prepare young people for the 'knowledge society'.

Schools encounter great difficulties when they attempt to become learning organizations. From the point of view of those concerned with schools as organizations there is a need to shift schools from positions of passive compliance and/or resistance to change and ask how best they might be transformed. The answer has been sought in the development and supervision of new management structures, formal standards and curriculum development. Alternatively and arguably more realistically (given the new economic and communications reality) schooling should be more responsive to the demands of whatever the 'knowledge society' becomes.

Scardamalia and Bereiter (1991,1996) suggest that the kind of education that will best prepare students for life in a knowledge society should foster:

- flexibility;
- creativity;
- problem-solving ability;
- technological literacy;
- information-finding skills;
- lifelong readiness to learn.

As Scardamalia and Bereiter argue, the idea of students as participants, along with teachers and perhaps others, in a collaborative enterprise has been around at least since Dewey, but has been taking a more definite shape over the past decade in various experimental programmes. The new approaches are all to some extent based on the model of the scientific research team. Brown and Campione (1990, 1994) have used the term 'fostering communities of learners' to characterize the very impressive approach they have developed. In it, teaching and learning are closely intertwined. In a typical activity, different groups of students research different aspects of a topic and then prepare materials that they use to instruct the members of the other groups. A robust application of the scientific research team model is in what Bereiter and Scardamalia call 'collaborative knowledge building' (Bereiter and Scardamalia, 1992; Scardamalia, Bereiter, and Lamon, 1994). (after Bereiter and Scardamalia 1991, 1996).

Therefore, if the future lies in schools as knowledge building organizations we need to rethink teaching by examining the relationships between cognition and context and between learning and knowledge production. International research is already highlighting the advantages of a combined focus on cognition, context and knowledge in research on pedagogy. This research has lead to the following three premises:

(i) *Learning occurs through engaged participation in the activities of knowledge Communities.*
    Participation involves both the use and production of knowledge and a disposition to engage. The current policy agenda, aimed at social inclusion through economic participation in a knowledge-based economy,

calls for a pedagogy which addresses students' self-beliefs and knowledge use and production in and out of school (Osin and Lesgold, 1996;
Bentley, 1998; Brighouse and Woods, 1998).

(ii) *Teaching involves informed interpretations of and responses to students' orientations to knowledge.*

Teaching is therefore a complex activity, which demands that teachers
interpret students' constructions of opportunities for engagement and
select responses that assist that engagement. Effective teaching is
informed by knowledge of pupils, knowledge of disciplines and knowledge of pedagogy. But how that knowledge is used and produced
remains contested (Wells, *in press*). In discussions of pedagogy, moreover, we lack those 'middle level concepts' (Bereiter, *in preparation*) with
which teachers' knowledge might be shared, used and developed. However, if these middle level concepts are to be developed, this is most likely
to occur at the sites of practice in conversations about practice (Greeno,
Collins and Resnick, 1996; Hirst, 1996).

(iii) *Schools, as sites of teachers' knowledge use and production, need to understand
the range of orientations to knowledge held within them and how they originated.*

Understanding relationships between historically formed institutional
knowledge and the pedagogies of practitioners will assist the implementation innovatory practices. We therefore need to know more about how
schools interpret and respond to the situational affordances of their internal and their wider communities as they work to engage students as
learners. It is clear that pedagogies which respond to the shifting
demands of a fast moving knowledge economy will best be developed in
schools which are capable of using and producing new knowledge.
(Edwards, Daniels and Ranson, 2000).

In classrooms that adopt the collaborative knowledge building approach, the
basic job to be done shifts from learning to the construction of collective
knowledge. The nature of the work is essentially the same as that of a professional research group, with the students being the principal doers of the work.
Thus, in the ideal case, there is a complete shift from students as clients to students as participants in a learning organization. The primary function of
schooling shifts from learning to the construction of collective knowledge in
'problem-based learning' and 'project-based learning'. There is an emphasis
on the distinction between knowledge content residing in people's minds and
knowledge as resource or knowledge as product. The job of a school class that
takes a knowledge building approach is to construct an understanding of the
world as they know it. (after Bereiter and Scardamalia, 1996).

If schools of the future are to become sites for the construction of collective
knowledge rather than sites where prescribed outcomes are 'delivered' then
we must rise to the challenge of understanding the kinds of interventions that
will facilitate successful participation by all. This is not to deny the need for

tools for learning and participation (eg literacies and numeracies). If the 'mainstream' is to become the place where young learners are prepared for a knowledge building future then appropriate supportive interventions must be available. The danger is that systems of support retain a focus on outdated knowledge and competence.

Schooling faces the challenges of a changing society. Preparing young people for new patterns of communication and knowledge production calls on us to reconsider the purposes and methods of schooling. As changes take place in schooling we must face the challenge of rethinking the best means of supporting participation in these new forms of educational activity. More of the same will not be sufficient.

The challenge of conceptual preparedness

Alongside such new, inclusion-sensitive reorientations in knowledge, cognition and pedagogy, there is an attendant struggle to articulate and operationalize a set of cultural requirements which might best create inclusive systems. Fundamentally this involves change at three levels. Governments must firstly embed the concept of lifelong professional and personal development within inclusion policy. Those professionally and personally involved in the process will inevitably comprise the initial grouping who initiate development. They can only be equipped to do this with significant fiscal commitment to the process on the part of governments, acting singularly or in collaboration.

Furthermore, the nature of such development must be located in the process of addressing the increasing number of questions which have arisen regarding inclusion during the period of maturation in our thinking. Any understanding of the practical implications of these will not be achieved exclusively within a heavily prescriptive, time-bound and formal arena of debate. Ideally, given the conceptual complexities inherent in some of these issues, those involved professionally will, be encouraged to engage as 'cultural workers' (Hooks, 1994). Operating in this way it may be more possible to develop the conceptual understanding, which can lead to procedural coherence in educational practice. In this the concept of inclusion has to be seen as one which is more able to secure entitlement, social justice and individual rights across all human operations.

Many of the conceptual questions remain either completely unanswered or unexplored, or at best only partially so. Indeed, it could be argued that such lack of closure is a signal of the health and vitality of the debate on inclusive education. For instance, our example of some of its parameters (Figure 1) is both incomplete and fraught with issues of conceptual and terminological acuity. But this is the kind of mapping that needs to take place in order that a real debate is maintained. Inclusion is not a fixed state, more a dynamic process: the discussion must reflect this.

CONCEPTUAL ISSUE

Human Rights

Issues of:
- empowerment;
- enablement;
- social justice;
- equity & equality.

Inclusive Technologies

Issues of:
- knowledge;
- pedagogy;
- management;
- location/placement;
- resources.

A Curriculum for All

Issues of:
- matching need;
- assessment;
- inspection and quality assurance;
- preparation of personnel.

Figure 1   Some conceptual arenas for challenge, conflict and resolution in inclusive education

We must, however, be cautious in making assumptions that these debates are both widespread and inclusive. The case of teacher education in England and Wales – as in some other post industrial democracies – presents a sobering example of the way in which policy-rhetoric can move in advance of grass-roots understanding. Many courses of teacher preparation, still do not provide direct input on conceptual and practical issues relating to inclusion (Robertson, 1999). Basic questions remain virtually unanswered, for example, what is inclusion? What maps it as entirely different from integration? To what extent can 'one size fit all' (Hornby, 1999) – and so on. It is our belief that such questions – and even more complex concerns relating, for example, to the interface and contradiction between a centrally-driven inclusion policy and in-dividual rights – need to be presented to newly qualifying teachers (and others) preparing to work with those who are seen as educationally, culturally, socially and medically 'different'.

Finally, a repertoire of more local exemplars must be developed. These should demonstrate inclusion to be a culturally and socially sensitive process, which empowers local workers at the point of engagement. On a global canvas there are signals that cases of good, transferable practice are becoming more increasingly available, and there is an expanding literature on this (see, for example, Armstrong, Armstrong and Barton, 2000; Booth and Ainscow, 1998). What such work demonstrates is that inclusion needs to be articulated as a bottom-up, 'lived' experience. Whilst the efforts of governments and international agencies are important in securing a pathway towards inclusive thinking, it is only at the site of local 'struggle' that its efficacy can be gauged.

The challenge of efficacy and effectiveness in a market culture

To what extent is inclusion likely to result in a significantly enhanced range of educational opportunities and, subsequently, an increase in the extent and quality of the life chances of those who have disability and learning difficulty? One of the major threats to the inclusive movement, identified by Feiler and Gibson (1999), are the assumptions that: there is a prevailing and widespread belief that inclusion is being demanded by all; that it is unilaterally beneficial for all; and that those involved as professionals automatically embrace its core principles and practices.

There is little in the way of empirical evidence in support of any of these assumptions, Feiler and Gibson note '…an alarming absence of such empirical evidence', commenting that 'many who currently advocate inclusion do not underpin their arguments with research'. What little research that has been done suggests that a more cautious stance is adopted, and certainly one which is less strongly driven by ideological conviction. Thus, Ward and Le Dean (1996) found that student teachers demonstrated no consensus in favour of inclusion. Moreover, experienced teachers show an equally circumspect attitude regarding its efficacy (Garner, 1998), whilst studies of parents and carers and of advocates working on behalf of children with disabilities suggest that the position is at best unclear (Cuckle, 1997). A summary of the position, therefore, prompts us to suggest that an evidence base needs to be developed if the effectiveness of inclusion is to be understood and generally accepted. Such 'effectiveness' can only be measured in terms of the educational and social reality of those who have disabilities. At the present time, as Salend and Duhaney (1999) remark, the impact on such students is, at best, mixed.

Lunt and Norwich (1999) have sought to explore further the link between inclusive schools and school effectiveness. Their analysis provides one example of the complexity that faces education systems in the 21st century as they seek to find a common ground in what may well be best described as highly polarized dimensions of schooling. In particular, they delineate further what has been an emerging dilemma for individual schools as accountability to 'consumers' (children and parents), and to investors (government, acting on behalf of taxpayers) has become the driving for of the school effectiveness movement. Lunt and Norwich put this dilemma quite simply: is it possible for schools to be both effective and inclusive?

Their prognosis is not encouraging. They observe that schools who are most successful in securing high positions in the 'league tables' of public examination results in England tend to have fewer pupils who have registered special educational needs than those who are less successful by that measure. The difference is considerable, according to Lunt and Norwich: the former have an average of 8 per cent of their pupil roll having SEN, whilst the latter have an average of 33 per cent. In attempting to respond to their own self-posed dilemma, the authors conclude that 'in the dominant conception of effectiveness, we cannot answer in the affirmative to the question of whether effective schools can be inclusive schools' (p 84). Nor are such discussions limited to England. Similar debates are ongoing in widely diverse educational contexts, on a global scale: USA (Goldhaber and Goldhaber, 2000) and Sweden (Persson, 2000), to name but two locations.

It would seem that, whatever the political complexion of a particular administration, the influence of some form of neo-liberal market is to be seen at work. An ongoing tension between excellence as promoted through the market and equity as promoted through inclusion is manifest in many of the policy struggles that exist in most of the states represented in this book. The excellence–inclusion tension has also given rise to a tension in the balance between the values that underpin social and moral regulation and the emphasis on the 'marketable' commodities of performance.

Recent critics of the 'School Effectiveness' movement have suggested that the emphasis on what Bernstein (1981) refers to as 'instructional discourse' has subverted attention to the 'regulative discourse 'of schooling (Slee, Weiner, and Tomlinson, 1998).

'School effectiveness is largely silent on or under theorises matters of equity' (Sammons, Hillman, and Mortimore, 1995). Equity is submerged within the rhetorical exhortation of the achievement in test scores. Test scores become ends. Questions of student destinations have no truck in this genre of research and writing. Explicit discussions of values and type of society to which schools articulate/adhere are ignored (Slee, 1998,p 111).

The interplay between matters of inclusion, excellence in the market, performance against narrowly defined indicators that serve market purposes, and the promotion of attitudes and values fit for an inclusive society, continue to ricochet through the field.

And a good many of the recent commentaries and critiques of inclusive education have found their way back to the broad social and educational concerns that have consistently regaled education systems world-wide – and have done so irrespective of the stage of inclusive education development that a country might find itself in.

The challenge of 'new' pedagogy

There has been a rapidly developing view, during recent years, that the mechanisms by which children are thought to be best 'mainstreamed' – for instance, differentiation, accelerated learning, individual education plans (IEPs), 1:1 teacher inputs and so forth – might themselves be exclusionary or non-inclusive. By equal measure, some have sought to advance a view that pedagogy for those with learning difficulties might simply mean 'good teaching', or that such pupils will be recipients of 'more of the same'.

In keeping with the selective approach of this chapter, we stop short of even a sketch of the core issues of teaching activity with special needs populations. However the following themes seem to encapsulate the breadth of debate currently occurring in this most practical manifestation of inclusion. Although some are characteristic of the emergent 'knowledge society', referred to earlier in this chapter, each one is indicative of the degree to which the technology of inclusive education, rather than its policy or ideological standpoint, is of most concern to critical end-users: pupils and teachers. So, within this sub-section, a series of questions can be posed, all of which have the utmost bearing on practice. At the same time responses to these questions will be revealing of the extent to which the 'inclusion debate' is embedded in the process and product of teaching.

- Can practices which are directed exclusively to separate school populations (eg differentiated learning programmes, separate groupings or classes) be regarded as being located within an inclusive paradigm?
- Does allegiance to a standardised 'national' curriculum reveal nothing other than educational piety, or even moral vanity, given that those pupils who are termed as having 'severe' learning difficulties can rarely proceed beyond the most basic level of performance?
- To what extent does discrete professional development in pedagogy for SEN-specific personnel militate against full educational inclusion?
- Are there common sets of pedagogic principles applicable to all children, irrespective of their level of performance? In other words, is there (or not) a set of SEN-specific pedagogies?
- Why is such are such principles and approaches not articulated within the initial training regimes of teachers?
- To what extent will access to new technology, particular in respect of information and communications, becomes a key element of curriculum access? And to what extent will teachers be able to maximise its potential with special needs populations?

Conclusion

These challenges, alongside others, provide the tapestry or backdrop against which inclusive practices in the 21st century are most likely to be played out. Contributors to the original 1999 Yearbook have been prophetic in sketching many of these, and therein lie the continuing value of their critiques. Inclusive education comprises a vibrant, global movement, which is located within a humanistic educational struggle. This effort is currently proceeding in an international and national climate of economic accountability and individual rights – most definitely conflicting standpoints within the debate. Such polarities add, at a simplistic level, colour to the discussion. More importantly, however, they result in widespread inventiveness and risk-taking on the part of those most closely involved in the quest to ensure that inclusive education becomes practical reality.

References

Armstrong, F., Armstrong, D. and Barton, L. (2000) *Inclusive Education. Policy, Contexts and Comparative Perspectives*, David Fulton Publishers, London

Bentley, T. (1998) *Learning Beyond the Classroom: education for a changing world*, Routledge, London

Bereiter, C. and Scardamalia, M. (1996) 'Rethinking learning' in D. Olson and N. Torrance (eds) *Handbook of Education and Human Development: New models of learning, teaching and schooling,* (pp. 485–513), MA: Basil Blackwell, Cambridge

Booth, T. and Ainscow, M. (eds.) (1998) *From Them to Us. An International Study of Inclusion in Education*, Routledge, London

Brighouse, T. and Woods, D. (1998) *How to Improve your School,* Routledge, London

Brown, A. L., and Campione, J. C. (1990) 'Communities of learning and thinking, or a context by any other name', *Human Development*, 21, pp108–26

Brown, A. L., and Campione, J. C. (1994) 'Guided discovery in a community of learners', in K. McGilley (ed) *Classroom Lessons: Integrating cognitive theory and classroom practice* pp 229–70 MA: MIT Press, Cambridge

Connolly, P (1998) *Racism, Gender, Identities and Young Children: Social relations in a multi-ethnic inner city primary school*, Routledge, London

Cuckle, P. (1997) 'The school placement of pupils with Down's syndrome in England and Wales', *British Journal of Special Education*, 24 (4), pp175–79

Duffield, J. (1998) 'Unequal Opportunities or Don't Mention the [Class] War', paper presented at the Scottish Educational Research Association [SERA] Conference, Dundee September 24-26th.

Edwards, A., Daniels, H. and Ranson, S. (2000) *Knowledge Building*, Mimeograph University of Birmingham

Evans, J. (1995) *Feminist Theory Today*, Sage, New York

Feiler, A. and Gibson, H. (1999) 'Threats to the inclusive movement', *British Journal of Special Education*, 26 (3), pp147–52.

Garner, P. (1998) '*Dragging the Horse to Water: Secondary school subject teachers and special needs*', European Conference on Educational Research, Llubljana, September.

Goldhaber, D. and Goldhaber, J. (2000) 'Education for all young children', in C. Brock & R. Griffin (eds) *International Perspectives on Special Educational Needs*, John Catt Educational Limited, Saxmundham

Greeno, J. Collins, A. and Resnick, L. (1996) 'Cognition and learning', in D. Berliner and R. Calfee (eds) *Handbook of Educational Psychology*, Macmillan, New York,

Haddock, L and Malcolm L. (1992) '"Make trouble: get results": provision for girls in support services' *Educational Psychology in Practice*; Vol.8, No.2.

Hooks, B. (1994) *Teaching to Transgress*, Routledge, New York

Kramarae, C. and Treichler, P. A. (1990) 'Power relationships in the classroom', in S.L.Gabriel and I. Smithson (eds) *Gender in the Classroom: Power and pedagogy*, University of Illinois Press, Urbana and Chicago

Hornby, G. (1999) 'Inclusion or delusion: can one size fit all?', *Support for Learning*, 14 (4), pp 152–57

Lunt, I. and Norwich, B. (1999) *Can Effective Schools Be Inclusive Schools?* Institute of Education, University of London, London

Osin, L. & Lesgold, A. (1996) 'A proposal for the reengineering of the educational system', *Review of Educational Research*, 66 (4) pp 621–56

Persson, B. (2000) 'Special Education in today's Sweden – a struggle between the Swedish model and the market', in F. Armstrong, D. Armstrong and L. Barton, (eds) *Inclusive Education. Policy, Contexts and Comparative Perspectives*, David Fulton Publishers, London

Robertson, C. (1999) 'Initial teacher education and inclusive schooling', *Support for Learning*, 14 (4), pp 169–73

Salend, S. & Duheney, L. (1999) 'The impact of inclusion on students with and without disabilities and their educators', *Remedial and Special Education*, 20, pp 114–26

Sammons, P., Hillman, J. and Mortimore, P. (1995) 'Key Characteristics of Effective Schools: a review of school effectiveness research', *A Report by the Institute of Education for OFSTED*. Institute of Education and University of London, London

Scardamalia, M., and Bereiter, C. (1991) 'Higher Levels of Agency for Children in Knowledge-Building: A Challenge for the Design of New Knowledge Media', *The Journal of the Learning Sciences*, 1(1), 38

Scardamalia, M., Bereiter, C., and Lamon, M. (1994) 'The CSILE project: Trying to bring the classroom into world 3', in K. McGilly (ed) *Classroom Lessons: Integrating cognitive theory and classroom practice*, pp 201–28,MA: MIT Press, Cambridge

Scardamalia, M. and Bereiter, C. (1996) 'Student communities for the advancement of knowledge', *Communications of the ACM*, 39 (4), pp 36–37

Slee, R., Weiner, G. and Tomlinson, S. (1998) *School Effectiveness for Whom? Challenges to the School Effectiveness and School Improvement Movements*, Falmer Press, London

Solstad, K. J. (1994) *Equity at Risk: Schooling and change in Norway*, PhD thesis Norway National Education Office, Nordland Office

Ward, J. and Le Dean, L. (1996) '"Student teachers"' attitudes towards special education provision', *Educational Psychology*, 16 (2), pp 207–18

Introduction

Harry Daniels and Philip Garner

This book is concerned with the relationship between the theory and practice of inclusion, and the broader social and political contexts to which the concept has been applied. It explores a range of matters in relation to the spatial and incremental differentiation by which the development of inclusive practices can be mapped across an international context. The reader is provided with a glimpse of the complexity of the issues that confront educationalists, and those who work alongside them, who seek to foster the process of inclusion in a wide range of political, economic, cultural and social settings. The aim is to contribute to a debate that is arguably still in its infancy, and that is defined by paradox or axiom, in the relationships between democracy and disability. More particularly, the collection of essays seeks to explore comparative interpretations of those individual rights and freedoms by which people with disabilities, difference and special educational needs[1] are supported within education systems.

The development of democracy, by definition, involves increasing levels of participation in social and political life. To subscribe to some form of democratic ideal is, then, to have an aim to include all people in the development of civil society. Whilst much has been written about inclusion in relation to education, particularly in the United States and in Western Europe, the term may be constructed to assume a broader focus than disability and difficulty in education alone. Processes of what may be seen as inclusion may be associated with large-scale political, economic and social change, as in the context of oppressed and disfranchised groups in countries such as South Africa, Brazil, Germany or Australia. A similar conceptualization might be applied to many of the emergent democracies in the central and eastern parts of Europe. Defined in these terms, the concept of 'inclusion' may be viewed as applicable in a global dimension, irrespective of the 'stage of development' reached by a country; this may be designated against a set of operative criteria or dimensions.

Whether the focus is within education or beyond, the term 'inclusion' implies a form of change that is different from that implied by the term 'integration'. There remain tensions and dilemmas – between a focus on changing individuals to fit existing systems, and changing systems in order that endemic and often subliminal practices of exclusion and marginalization are avoided. For example, if a system is changed in order to avoid exclusion, it may not necessarily be adept at reintegrating those who have formerly been excluded; indeed, there is adequate evidence, at local, regional, national and international levels, that the promise of such endeavours results in little more than the re-definition, followed rapidly by the re-marginalization, of the target group(s). Processes of exclusion and marginalization create and sustain ways of being that are both social and deeply personal, whilst remaining distinctly resistant to ideological and structural change. Thus, within the local-state, practitioners may articulate a reality gap between their own grassroots aspirations and those of policy-makers. The belief-systems and operations of the practitioners themselves may, to an even greater extent, be isolated or fractured from those of the fundamental actors in the scenario – the marginalized or disengaged individuals and groupings themselves. The unique consequences of the experience of marginalization carry with them challenges for the creation of a more inclusive system. And they will have a differential impact on all those involved, irrespective of their level of commitment.

An important element in the political discourse of education in many countries is concerned with the development of accountable systems. Discussions of cost-effectiveness may be cast against particular goal frames relating to national policy. But, increasingly, globalization is ensuring that such localized initiatives are required to be placed within an internationalist framework. At the same time, they are required to ensure that the individualistic requirements of the post-modern nation-state remain intact. In part, this book is concerned with how those goal frames – the local political, cultural, social, moral and economic imperatives – achieve definition and microcosm within education. Goal frames may have a macro or micro focus, and the tensions inherent in systems that are overly dependent on either of these orientations have become apparent within special education since the publication of the 1993 *World Yearbook* (Mittler, Brouillette and Harris, 1993). Arguably, the tumultuous political developments in Central and Eastern Europe, and the recognition that financial irregularities in another hemisphere have certain predictable impacts on economic systems previously seen as immune to international perfidy, have subsequently provided a counterbalance to 'global individualism'. Thus, whilst emergent or established nation-states have sought to define their unique qualities against globally determined sets of indicators, they have done so in recognition of the contexts within which they function. As in other policy formulations, those countries that conceptualize, construct and subsequently operationalize inclusive education on a narrow or parochial dimension may ultimately find that the grassroots effect may be nominal, or even counter-productive.

Irrespective of scale or location, however, the means by which the boundaries between those who are able to exercise some control over their life, and those who cannot, reflect relations of power. It is the readjustment of these relations of power that is often so difficult – both to conceptualize and to operate. Superficial adjustments may infer power shifts and subsequent re-directions of policy and practice. However, all too often, observation of actual practices suggests that many 'adjustments' assume a rhetorical position, and lack impact. Such rhetoricism is equally apparent on an international and national dimension. Thus, successive resolutions within global conventions designed to protect individual rights and autonomy have been unilaterally recognized on a global dimension. At a more local level, such innovative and ultimately praiseworthy initiatives bear little cause for close scrutiny. The lack of voice leading to marginalization and social exclusion is witnessed too often in systems that announce a commitment to empowerment, but lack the political will to ensure that rhetoric becomes reality. Token and rhetorical responses to initial concerns, leading to policy statements that make little or no impact on the lives of children, are all too frequent. This applies equally to countries at very different stages of development, and is by no means the sole domain of those nations seeking to establish a political and economic footing within the global order of things. A particular example of this may be seen in the general difficulty in including children in debates about possibilities for their own education, a process that the education system of England and Wales, for example, has only recently begun to recognize as an indicator of its effectiveness. Whether in 'systems in transition', 'in change' or 'in development', there is much talk of 'listening to children', but much evidence of official 'hearing impairment'.

Globally, such remarks are descriptive of many systems of general education, but it is within special education that these arguments are most vibrantly circulating; and they have been doing so since the beginning of the 1990s. The concept of 'inclusion' is by no means new (Thomas, Walker and Webb, 1998) – its roots have been sown by a succession of educationists and philosophers throughout the twentieth century – but it is the recent widespread and increasingly vociferous demand to establish individual rights as a central component in policy-making that has provided the impetus to place inclusion firmly on the agenda of social change.

Whilst, in some locations policies of supposed 'inclusion' fail to progress beyond rhetoric, others creditably may be seen to contradict parallel aspects of national social policy. One example of such a contradiction between individual social policy directions occurs in Romania. There, attendance at special school carries with it a number of welfare benefits, such as allowances for transport and clothing. These economic benefits act as a significant disincentive to parents who, given a more advantageous economic framework, would prefer to see their children educated in a mainstream setting; this situation is replicated in numerous other countries, frequently irrespective of their stage of development. The perceived benefits of local community schooling have to be weighed against the costs of loss of benefits and social support. This is just one example indicating the complication of the often contradictory messages presented by legal and welfare systems to parents, children, and to those who are in a position to formulate policy.

There are, of course, limits to the extent to which inclusion can be seen as a context-independent movement. There is an inextricable link with economic, political and cultural underpinnings, and this will readily be apparent in the reading of this volume. The book draws on the experience of a diverse range of nations, each with its own strengths and dilemmas. The writers are located in very different political contexts and thus express different concerns and dimensions regarding some of the constituent elements of inclusion as a social and educational movement.

The diversity of the country-specific descriptions is itself an indication of the necessity for the term 'inclusion' to be constructed within a framework of pre-existing conditions. At the same time, however, the ultimate goal may be something approximating to the framework given definition within the *Salamanca Statement* (UNESCO, 1994). What is also clear is that, even in the majority of post-industrial nations, the actual practice of inclusion is often only an adumbration of the ideal state charted in that resolution.

Within this book, this embedding in local discourse is relayed in the terms used by the various contributors, which vary as a function of linguistic difference and/or social/political contexts. For example, 'handicapped' is used by Scandinavian writers as a term embodying the social consequence of disability, rather than a term of denigration, with a focus on individual deficiency. It is important to recognize that semantic confusion can lead to misunderstanding; similarly, English-language translations may obfuscate the real issue. It has not been our wish, as editors, to restrict or condition by standardization the terminology of our contributors. Indeed, the cultural and historical antecedents of the development of particular forms of political correctness are a subject of study in their own right, although outside the immediate remit of this book (Corbett, 1995).

We have chosen a structure of three parts:

1. Part One: Defining Special Education in a Democracy – Inclusive Education;
2. Part Two: Dilemmas for Inclusive Education; and
3. Part Three: Dialogues on Inclusive Education.

Part One is concerned directly with the interplay between political and economic environment and the possibilities for the development of the concepts of special and inclusive and inclusion education. In the last *World Yearbook* concerned with special education, Chapter 20 was entitled 'The future of special education: who will pay the bill'. Ron Brouillette's discussion of economic constraints and incentives prompted us to think about the need for an extended discussion of the ways in which cultural forms such as special and inclusive education enter into the local official discourses concerning the welfare state and the 'market' (Brouillette, 1993). The conditions of democracy and post-industrial economic life, which provide the context in which so much of the discussion of 'inclusive education' takes place, are by no means universal. The development of democracy itself may be seen to condition the possibilities for, and imperatives of, what was special education, and what may become universal inclusive education.

The development needs of newly emergent democracies relate as much to democratic goals themselves as to the economic conditions that underpin development. Changes in economic circumstances certainly affect resource capabilities, and may well affect the perceived desirability of particular forms of social action. Alan Gartner and Dorothy Kerzner Lipsky explore the wider implications of this theme in the opening chapter. The implication, from their writing, is that democratic operations are the essential premise for establishing inclusivity – including the capacity to vote for financial policies that will ensure its practical operation. That the process of inclusion is embedded in national policy orientation is a requirement amplified by Margaret McLaughlin, Lynn Fuchs and Michael Hardman, who make pointed reference to the somewhat prophetic OECD indicator that 'There should be only one comprehensive social policy'. To define a different set of statutes for those with disability, they argue, serves only to illustrate and expose exclusivity.

Alan Dyson argues a theory of 'multiple inclusions', based on a set of contrasting discourses. The reader will recognize the difficulties inherent in Dyson's challenge. On the one hand, we are at a relatively early stage in defining and articulating inclusive practices – however long its philosophical pedigree might be. Yet, contrastingly, there has been a reinforcement of post-modern individuality based upon culture and history. The tension between establishing newly inclusive operations in erstwhile exclusive societies will, crucially, be conditioned by national identity and future vision. As Dyson suggests, broad and open debate must ensure that inclusion does not become simply a slogan.

Democratic principles have most recently become conditioned by economic reality in a number of locations world-wide. Individual expression, personal freedoms and the rights that provide a framework for their realization have been placed in jeopardy in a new era of economic angst. The global growth of a commitment to inclusive education has corresponded with a rise in self-doubt and financial uncertainty in many countries. Preservation of the old order required a revisionist intake of breath and a major question mark over resource direction. This provides the theme for Len Barton's chapter, which concludes the opening part of the book.

In Part Two we have invited our contributors to outline and provide commentary on what they regard as the key issues and national concerns of attempts to formulate and promote inclusive practice. Our selection of contributors was, in part, driven by an, albeit crude, categorization of educational contexts, as follows:

Systems in reformulation: countries where there has been a tradition of universal education in mainstream and special schools, and there are debates about the development of inclusive education, which relate to the reformulation of national educational provision for those with learning difficulties. A component of such debates is the shift away from segregated provision and the emergence of education as a market-led component of social policy. Within the latter, reformulation brings to these countries and regions an ever-increasing need to justify expenditure on welfare and education, with a commensurate discourse underpinned by the twin imperatives of financial expediency and political pragmatism.

Systems in change: countries that are undergoing significant political, social and/or educational change. Again, in these locations, universal education has long been established, with provision in mainstream and special schooling. What identifies this grouping as distinct is the far-reaching ideological and structural change that has taken place during the last few years, and their initial exposure to education and welfare systems demarcated by individual rights and freedoms.

Systems in development: countries that are in the process of developing schooling for all. Here, formal educational provision for those with learning difficulty remains separate, and the debate concerning inclusion is taking place at a time when state systems are trying to realize effective basic, segregated provision. These are countries and regions that, as a result of economic and political factors, usually relating to their spatial location, are in the process of a bilateral definition of special education, in terms of the reality of ensuring provision *per se*, and future conceptual planning that recognizes the principles of inclusion.

These groupings provide for something beyond a country-by-country treatment of the national characteristics of inclusive education. In a broad sense, it is a fairly intuitive and highly personalized attempt to suggest that the term inclusion can often be paradoxical, and that, in many ways, discontinuities are not always a configuration of a country's location, ideology or infrastructure; and, further, that in each grouping there is ample evidence of successful inclusionary practice. This may suggest that one of the positive impacts of globalization is the refinement, within special education practice, of transmission models: the traditional concept of 'borrowing', as applied particularly when considering north and south hemispheres or, more regionally, East and West Europe, or North and South America, has changed. Whilst there is a contradictory argument, powerful indications exist to suggest that the movement towards inclusion is premised by collaborative development, particularly that promoted by international or regional agencies. Arguably, this is one of the defining characteristics of the movement; other educational or welfare initiatives may accrue marked benefit from examination of it.

The comparative study of disability in an educational context has had a very short pedigree. In many ways this volume represents a first major shift in direction in international studies, by confirming the movement away from a special education *per se* focus to one that explores inclusive education. The brief period of development of comparative study in the former area was, arguably, heralded by Barton and Tomlinson (1984), who called for an extension of interest in studies of this kind, with a neatly prophetic advisory note to future authors that '…it is important to analyse changes and developments in special education in some kind of a comparative perspective, to avoid assuming that developments in one country are the norm' (p 5). Certainly, this advice remains essentially current, with particular regard to post-industrial nations, whose inclination is to assume that the level to which they have refined, for instance, issues of service delivery, are far more appropriate and effective in meeting identified need. Whilst there may be a notional case for this assumption, our experience is that many countries falling outside, for example, the OECD, can often provide exemplars of inclusive practice, a feature demonstrated by Booth and Ainscow (1998).

The fifteen years following Barton and Tomlinson's observation have seen a gradual but steady rise in an interest amongst academics and theorists in drawing parallels and comparisons in special education on an international scale. Thus, volumes containing collections of accounts of special education practice from a range of countries have become more widespread: Mazurek and Winzer (1994), Mittler and Daunt (1995), and Artiles and Hallahan (1996) have all made significant contributions to this developing field. Moreover, it has become increasingly common for writers to use international comparisons when exploring policy issues in special education, as classically illustrated by Fulcher (1989). These developments were paralleled by a perceptible increase in contributions from special educationists to international conferences and to comparative education journals. The continued popularity and influence of such dedicated special education journals as the *European Journal of Special Needs Education* in the 1990s, as well as the further growth of international or regional associations (of both professionals and advocates), is further evidence of the vitality of this area of study. Most recently, there has also been some re-orientation in comparative studies of special education: in keeping with national trends, and influenced by the global move towards claiming empowerment and individual rights, inclusive education *per se* has become firmly established in a comparative context. Pijl, Meijer and Hegarty (1997) and Booth and Ainscow (1998) exemplify this shift, and there is now a dedicated academic periodical in the field, the *International Journal of Inclusive Education*.

It is one of our anticipations in the construction of this volume that it might provide further '…new insights from international comparisons that will assist in the process of finding solutions for common problems' (Pijl, Meijer and Hegarty, 1997). However, in attempting this, we have exhorted our contributors to move beyond what can best be summarized as 'level one' comparison, in which descriptions (of legislation, organization and practice) are accompanied by a (usually) neo-conservative commentary. Studies like this, as Pijl,

Meijer and Hegarty (1997) have pointed out, generally offer little that is surprising and are inclined to be repetitive, almost as if devoid of context. This volume seeks to avoid this by asking chapter-authors, in Part Two, to identify an overall theme around which the dilemmas and potentials of inclusion can be discussed, whilst making particular reference to the ideological embedding that proscribes them. Thus, there will be only a notional treatment of the structural features of national educational systems, and the special provision available within them.

In sum, writers have been given an open brief to provide an intuitive response to those concerns regarding inclusion that are currently apparent in their own location. The resulting commentaries take us back to a broadening view of the term inclusion, the chapters representing diverse constructions of its principles, meanings, practical impacts and future relevance.

The selection of countries included in Part Two was based on a very loose interpretation, at the planning stage of this volume, of the perceived current conceptual and practical position obtaining in a given country location. Somewhat perversely, moreover, there was no intention at the outset to provide an 'inclusive' treatment, even at a regional level. This was a pragmatic decision, based on what might be seen as the locational uniqueness of an inclusive practice. Indeed, we have already highlighted the dangers of homogeneity in a matter which, as Alan Dyson has described in this volume, is as theoretically diverse as inclusion. For many of the countries in Part Two, the selection was accomplished in an almost context-free manner. However, each of us has some familiarity and previous or ongoing professional involvement with colleagues, institutions or government agencies in many of the others.

Within Part Two the reader will encounter a diverse set of themes mapped on a national or regional basis. Some of these will be highly particularized, as with the tensions between federalism and nationalism (Canada, Spain), the inclusion of specific minorities (gypsy children in Bulgaria), and new majorities (South Africa). Elsewhere, there is evidence of the debate between securing democracy and the economic cost of sustaining it (for example, the Czech Republic), and of the tension between the individual and the state (Japan, United States of America). Thus, whilst individual authors in this part of the book write from a national perspective, the collective, it could be argued, broadly defines the terms of reference for the ongoing ideological debate concerning the efficacy of inclusion.

In Part Three we asked individual authors to take up a position in respect of the relationships and tensions emerging from Parts One and Two. Again, in recognition of the broad framework within which we have considered inclusion, the selection of themes is almost inevitably incomplete. Nevertheless, the chapters offer insights into concerns that, as the country reports illustrate, are dynamic and are spatially constructed. The dilemmas inherent in balancing welfare intervention against personal advocacy are considered by Jesper Holst, who gives recognition to one of the frequently overlooked, and certainly underwritten, concepts underpinning inclusive practice in education. This is the concept that those towards whom policy has traditionally been directed are a resource, and need to be accommodated centrally within policy formulation. Such is the importance of this aspect of inclusion that we have chosen to identify it as the concluding theme of this *Yearbook*.

Roger Slee examines the nature and implications of the gap between inclusive policy and its implementation. In particular, he explores aspects of the context-bound nature of inclusion, thereby echoing Dyson's overview of the multidimensional nature of the term. Importantly, Slee sees the debate as essentially one in which the characteristics of 'inclusions' might be pro-actively established around a set of propositions. Defining each term, therefore, is more about refining what it is, rather than what it is not.

In contrast, Paul Ghumann particularizes the dilemmas inherent in such an interpretation; he considers the extent to which one frequently marginalized population might be the recipient of forms of 'multiple exclusions' – racial, social, educational and economic – so that a non-inclusive identity is maintained or consolidated. In some senses, we hope that a focus on the underachievement–ethnicity interface illustrates that inclusion itself cannot be viewed as the particular domain of those with learning difficulties *per se*. Peter Evans articulates this notion in his commentary from an international perspective, arguing that, whilst the work of such organizations as the OECD is guided by a philosophy of 'human rights and social justice', its focus and application vary according to location.

Can the movement towards inclusion in education act as an agent of social change? This question is central to Sally Tomlinson's thesis. Inasmuch as education is projected as a mirror of the society of which it is a function, such reflexivity may extend to education (and notably inclusive education) as a model for redefining individual actions to secure social justice.

Finally, some of the practical implications of including children, young people and adults with learning difficulties are mapped by Jo Lebeer and his co-contributors. In identifying this theme as a concluding chapter we encountered a dilemma. Does its own inclusion, as a discrete chapter, resemble both the exclusive practice and unwanted tokenism that this *Yearbook* seeks to critically examine? The message it contains, we believe, far outweighs the sensibilities of two editors.

The fledgling debate about inclusive education has provided ample evidence of the need to adopt approaches that are flexible, dynamic and responsive to individuals within localized spatial contexts. This presents a huge challenge. Inclusion has to be viewed in a multidimensional way (in spite of the broad sweeps provided by policy statements by international organizations), which allows for individual autonomy within corporate, national actions. The very fluidity required to accommodate these variants as a global movement may prove to be counter-productive and not in the best interests of those with disabilities. Initiatives based upon personally articulated statements of need are as central a part of inclusion as are the policies and structures that are most commonly used to define it. As we approach the beginning of a new century, it would seem essential that the educational debate should be broadened from its somewhat parochial origins (as viewed by participating professionals). Thus, not only is there a need to define its terms of reference from a point beginning with those most pivotal to and affected by the process, but also this involvement should be quantifiable in terms of 'outputs': that one of these indicators might be the removal of the prefix 'inclusive' from education might signal a more substantive and democratic application of the term.

Endnote

1. We recognize that such terms are problematic. Throughout the text we, as editors, have retained those terms which individual contributors regard to have a local legitimacy.

References

Artiles, A. and Hallahan, D. (eds) (1996) *Special Education in Latin America: Experiences and Issues*, Praeger, Westport, Conn., and London

Barton, L. and Tomlinson, S. (eds) (1984) *Special Education and Social Interests*, Croom Helm, Beckenham

Booth, T. and Ainscow, M. (1998) *From Them to Us. An International Study of Inclusion in Education*, Routledge, London

Brouillette, R. (1993) 'The future of Special Education: Who will pay the bill?', in P. Mittler, R. Brouillette and D. Harris (eds) *The World Yearbook of Education. Special Needs Education*, Kogan Page, London

Corbett, J. (1995) *Bad Mouthing: The Language of Special Needs*, Falmer Press, London

Fulcher, G. (1989) *Disabling Policies? A Comparative Approach to Education Policy and Disability*, Falmer Press, London

Mazurek, K. and Winzer, M. (eds) (1994) *Comparative Studies in Special Education*, Gallaudet University Press, Washington

Mittler, P. and Daunt, P. (eds) (1995) *Teacher Education for Special Needs in Europe*, Cassell, London

Mittler, P., Brouillette, R. and Harris, D. (eds) (1993) *The World Yearbook of Education. Special Needs Education*, Kogan Page, London

Pijl, S. J., Meijer, C. and Hegarty, S. (eds) (1997) *Inclusive Education: A Global Agenda*, Routledge, London

Thomas, G., Walker, D. and Webb, J. (1998) *The Making of the Inclusive School*, Routledge, London

UNESCO (1994) *The Salamanca Statement and Framework for Action on Special Needs Education*, UNESCO, Paris

Section I
Defining special education in a democracy – inclusive education

1. Inclusive education: a requirement of a democratic society

Dorothy Kerzner Lipsky and Alan Gartner

Introduction

It is not common to address the topic of inclusive education in the context of democracy or within the broad ambit of social policy. We do so in recognition of the limits of our understanding, and particularly of the constraints of our own cultural and ideological perspectives. While we have both had the opportunity to study and work in a number of countries, it is the fact that we are North Americans, and our experience of education in the United States, that shape (and limit) our understanding of the issues.

We urge two cautions in considering comparative analyses of special education reform in a post-industrial society. They have been noted by Artiles and Larsen (1998), and are pertinent to this discussion. They are as follows:

1. that, as special education[1] is increasingly located within general education,[2] these reforms must be examined in the context of broader national educational reform efforts; and
2. that similarities between two nations may be produced by different forces or might serve different functions. (p 6)

The first section of this chapter addresses inclusive education in the broad context of educational reform in the United States, and then turns to inclusive education as a democratic principle in contemporary society.

Inclusive education and educational reform

In the United States, there is no official definition of inclusive education. The term, along with 'inclusion', 'integration' and 'mainstreaming', appears nowhere in the federal legislation – The Education of All Handicapped Children Act, passed in 1975, or its current manifestation, the Individuals with Disabilities Education Act, reauthorized in 1997. Neither does it appear in state statutes.[3] The following concepts of inclusive education are presented in light of the above omissions.

In its *National Study of Inclusive Education* (1994), the National Centre on Inclusive Education and Restructuring (NCERI), defined inclusive education as:

> providing to all students, including those with significant disabilities, equitable opportunities to receive effective educational services, with the needed supplemental aids and support services, in age-appropriate classes in their neighborhood schools, in order to prepare students for productive lives as full members of society. (p 6)

Recently, a New York City school administrator described inclusive education as 'full membership'. While inclusive education has many facets, including those noted above, the phrase 'full membership' captures the essence of the meaning of inclusive education.

The primary perspective of inclusive education must be viewed from that of the student – both the typical student and the student with disabilities. This perspective can be formulated around the following two questions and answers.

Question 1: Is there a clear demarcation that allows for distinguishing between one set of students – those without disabilities – from another – those with disabilities? Are students sufficiently different in their characteristics (and are there measures of sufficient reliability and validity to mark those distinctions)?

Answer 1: In summarizing the most comprehensive review of the evaluation system for determining whether students have disabilities and require special education services, Ysseldyke (1983) characterized it as little better than a flip of the coin.

Three-quarters of a century ago, Walter Lippman wrote a series of essays on the use of the newly developed IQ tests to measure officer candidates to serve in the United States Army in World War I. In remarks prescient of the special education evaluation system, he wrote of his fear that these tests would be used to label children as inferior and, thus, consign them to a second-class life.

> It is not possible, I think, to imagine a more contemptible procedure than to confront a child with a set of puzzles, and after an hour's monkeying around with them, proclaim to the child, or to his parents, that here is a C-minus individual. It would not only be a contemptible thing to do. It would be a crazy thing to do. (Cited in Granger and Granger, 1986, p v)

Question 2: Are there sufficient differences in the needed pedagogic practices so as to allow for a binomial division of children into the permanent categories of disabled/non-disabled or special education/general education?

Answer 2: 'There is no evidence to support the contention that specific categories of students learn differently. Yet, students are instructed in categorical groups on the notion that these groups of students learn differently.' (Ysseldyke, 1983, p 265)

The manner in which we choose to educate students with disabilities is a consequence of the ways in which we view disability. This concept was explored by Hahn.

> The conventional approach...has been shaped by a functional limitations model, which assumes that the principal difficulties of people with disabilities resides within these individuals, and that solutions can be found by surmounting or transcending such deficits to the maximum extent possible. Inspired in part by the growing disability rights movement, however, this orientation has been challenged by a 'minority group' paradigm, which posits that the primary problems facing disabled citizens are external rather than internal, and that remedies can be achieved through efforts to alter the environment in which they live, instead of their personal characteristics. While the field of special education traditionally has been dominated by the former model, which stresses the development of effective methods of instruction compatible with the restrictions imposed upon students with various types of disabilities, the latter construct implies a comprehensive new agenda that promises to introduce significant changes in the content as well as the techniques of elementary, secondary, and higher education. (Hahn, 1989, p 225)

The shift in focus from the individual (and his/her impairments) to the social context was presented by Minow (1990) in her analysis of the options facing a school system when educating a child who is deaf.[4] The school system 'assumed that the problem was Amy's: because she was different from other students, the solution must focus on her'. (Minow, 1990, p 82.) Instead, Minow asserted, one can conceptualize the class as a learning community and Amy as a collaborative 'worker' with her classmates. This shifts the focus from Amy, and means that the problem – and the remedy – involves all of the students.

> After all, if Amy cannot communicate with her classmates, they

> cannot communicate with her, and all lose the benefit of exchange. Moreover, conducting the class in both spoken and sign language would engage all the students in the difficult and instructive experience of communicating across traditional lines of difference. All the students could learn to struggle with problems of translation and learn to empathize by experiencing first-hand discomfort with an unfamiliar mode of expression. It would be educational for all of them to discover that all languages are arrangements of signs and to use group action to improve the situation of the individual. (Minow, 1990, p 84)

Recognizing the social nature of the problem and 'involving classmates in the solution affords a different stance toward the dilemma of difference: it no longer makes the trait of hearing impairment signify stigma or isolation but responds to the trait as an issue for the entire community' (Minow, 1990, p 84). The consequence not only involves the person with disabilities but also has consequences for the learning and perspectives of the students without disabilities.

> When students in the majority avoid the experience of not being understood, or not understanding what others say, they fail to learn about the limits of their own knowledge. By their very comfort in the situation, they neglect the perspective of any student they consider different from themselves. (p 29)

The consequence for children was identified by the parents of a child who had been labeled as learning-disabled. 'Every time a child is called mentally defective and sent off to the special class for some trivial defect, the children who are left in the regular class receive a message: No one is above suspicion; everyone is being watched by the authorities; nonconformity is dangerous' (Granger and Granger, 1988, p xii).

This point is echoed by the parent of a kindergarten student (Minnesota State Education Department, 1993). At a conference with her son's teacher, the parent was told that two students with physical disabilities would be in the child's class. The teacher 'quickly added that there would be a full-time paraprofessional so that their presence would not take away any time from the other students. This statement was made with the best of intentions for my son.' (p 4.) When the parent picked up her son at the end of the first day, he pointed to an adult and said, 'That lady is for the wheelchair people.' (p 4.) The parent commented,

> Today I thought, 'What was Charlie going to learn about people with physical disabilities and other differences that carry the perception of not normal? He could learn that people with disabilities are not competent and need another person to be with them, that they cannot communicate for themselves, that they are always the recipients of help from caregivers.' (p 4)
> I believe that children with disabilities do not take away from other children. They do not diminish the community. I believe, instead, that these children, currently known as the 'wheelchair people', have the potential to contribute enormously to my son's learning and growth – but only if the environment and people take advantage of this opportunity. (p 5)

The practice of inclusive education

Inclusive education is not a reform of special education. It is the convergence of the need to restructure the public education system, to meet the needs of a changing society, and the adaptation of the separate special education system, which has been shown to be unsuccessful for the greater number of students who are served by it. It is the development of a unitary system that has educational benefits for both typical students and students with special needs. It is a system that provides quality education for all children.[5]

Factors included in the rationale for restructuring

Efficacy data
A growing body of data demonstrates the effectiveness of inclusive education programmes (*18th Annual Report*, 1996, 62-6; Lipsky and Gartner, 1997, ch. 14). At the same time, there is little evidence demonstrating that segregated special education programmes have significant benefits for students.

Legal issues
While not a requirement of the federal law, inclusive education has been affirmed as appropriate in the major appellate court decisions (Lipton, 1994), while the grounding of the education of students with disabilities in the general education environment is central to the reauthorized Individuals with Disabilities Education Act, or IDEA ('The 1997 Reauthorization', 1998). For example, the law now requires the following:

1. students are not to be referred for special education if the basis of the referral is the inadequacy of instructional programmes provided;
2. when a student with disabilities is not to be served in the general education environment (with needed supplemental aids and support services), then the particular bases for such exclusion must be explained, and justification provided for such exclusion; and
3. outcome standards for students with disabilities must be drawn from the outcomes expected of students in general, and the results of their performance must be included in the school's overall results.

Procedural issues
The emphasis on formal procedures, especially with regard to the evaluation of students, and to the determination of their eligibility for special education services, has too often been at the expense (in educators' time and school system resources) of instructional activities that directly benefit students.

Population increases
The growing population of students 'identified', especially in the 'learning disability' category, is of increasing concern, because of both its fiscal and pedagogical consequences.

Disjointedness
The current design discourages a unitary system and often precludes a student from participating with his/her peers in general education. Too often, the curriculum taught in segregated special education programmes is separate and different from that taught in the general classroom for typical students. This is true even in the Resource Room programme, which is the least separate of the special education services (Allington and McGill-Franzen, 1992).

Funding

The growing cost of special education services, particularly in the light of the limited effectiveness of the separate design, threatens continuing tax-payer support. Further, the pattern of funding special education has been a disincentive to serving students in the general education environment. The reauthorized IDEA now requires that states adopt funding formulae that are placement-neutral; in other words, the formulas should not provide an incentive for placing a child in a more restrictive setting.

Inclusive schools

While there is no single educational model or approach, inclusive schools tend to share similar characteristics and beliefs (*National Study*, 1995; Lipsky and Gartner, 1997; Stainback and Stainback, 1996). These are detailed below.

School-wide approaches
Inclusion is not a single 'pilot' or special inclusion class. The philosophy and practice of inclusive education is accepted by all stakeholders. As a consequence, the school brings together the full range of students, educational personnel, and fiscal, and other, resources.

All children can learn
Inclusive schools have a belief that all children can learn and that all benefit when that learning is done together.

A sense of community
The belief is that all children belong and that diversity among students is a positive characteristic for the school (and for society). A child does not have to 'prove' his or her way in order to be included.

Services based on need rather than location
Each student is recognized as an individual, with strengths and needs, not as a label or as a member of a category. Further, the response to those needs is seen as the provision of services.

Natural proportions
Students attend their home school, thus assuring that each school (and class) has a natural proportion of students with and without disabilities.

Supports are provided in general education
Schools recognize that all students have special needs. In doing so, they do not equate this with the need for separate programmes. Rather than addressing those needs in separate locations or programmes, in the language of the

federal law, supplemental aids and support services are provided in the general education environment.

Teacher collaboration

Various models enable educators to work collaboratively, for example, as co-teachers, in team teaching, through consultation, and in 'push-in' programmes for special services. Programmes of professional development, as well as time for teachers to work collaboratively, are integral in inclusive schools.

Curriculum adaptation

Drawing from the school's general curriculum, inclusion provides adaptations to enable all students to benefit from the common curriculum.

Enhanced instructional strategies

Inclusive education requires a wide range of instructional strategies, which enable all students to learn in recognition of students' differences in intelligence, learning style, strengths and limitations. These include co-operative learning, peer instruction, hands-on activities, learning outside of the classroom, and the use of instructional technology.

Standards and outcomes

The learning outcome for students with disabilities is drawn from that expected of students in general. Their performance, with necessary adaptations and modifications in the measurement instruments and procedures, is incorporated in the school's overall performance. In other words, everybody counts.

Inclusive education as integral to a democratic society

When the work of a society is manual, rote, and routine, its school system values those who are best prepared for such work. When the nature of the work changes, those who can be prepared for the new work are more valued. Indeed, the structure and shape of the school system become isomorphic with the work. Changes in the society – in the nature of work, the composition of the workforce, or the character of societal values – are both cause and consequence of new designs of education and schooling. At the same time, the conceptualization of disability – as deficit or difference, for example – is affected by society's work and values, and then becomes a factor in the education of those it decides to label as 'disabled'. Meadmore makes this point explicitly:

> The drive to test, categorize and select children for differential treatment in educational institutions has a history, which is inextricably linked with the

provision of state-funded education in Western democracies. Mass schooling often paralleled a need made apparent by industrial capitalism for a
more docile and morally correct workforce. When education was made
available to all children, schools became arenas for competition for life
chances. (Meadmore, 1993, p 27)

Just as the regimen of the production line influenced the shape of public education in the industrial era, the nature of post-industrial society, its work and
values, has a consequence for education of the twenty-first century. Such
work is collaborative, calling more for skills in problem-solving than for existing knowledge, and requiring more flexibility than routine. In the new workplace there is both growing diversity among the workforce, and an increasing
focus on co-operation and teamwork among the workers. In this new climate,
education equity would be viewed, according to Skrtic (1991), as

a pre-condition for excellence in the post-industrial era, for collaboration
means learning collaboratively with and from persons with varying interests, abilities, skills, and cultural perspectives, and taking responsibility for
learning means taking responsibility for one's own learning and that of others. Ability grouping and tracking have no place in such a system. (Skrtic,
1991, p 181)

For a large proportion of the growing population, however, future work opportunities are not promising. Unfortunately, the education system is not
changing sufficiently rapidly to address the problem. In particular, 'special
education is implicated in this problem because, as a form of tracking, it is
uniquely placed within public education to serve the necessary sorting function'. (Skrtic, 1996, p 106.)

Contrasting the characteristics of education in the industrial and information ages, Keating (1996) presents the following table:

Table 1.1

Characteristics	Industrial Age	Information Age
Pedagogy	Knowledge transmission	Knowledge-building
Prime mode of learning	Individual	Collaborative
Educational goals	Conceptual grasp for the few; basic skills for the many	Conceptual grasp and knowledge-building for all
Nature of diversity	Inherent, categorical	Transactional, historical
Dealing with diversity	Selection of elites; basics for broad population	Developmental model of life-long learning for the broad population
Anticipated workplaces	Factory, vertical bureaucracies	Collaborative learning organizations

In the shift to the information age, schooling plays an important role in shaping the future, both economic and political.

Inclusive education and democracy

Ramsey (1993) connects inclusive schooling to its consequence for society.

Such an education, in its inclusivity, would be richer, more diverse and more stimulating education, and a more appropriate preparation for post-school life in an egalitarian community not only for those students who are disadvantaged by the current arrangements, but indeed for all students. (pp viii–ix)

Kunc (1992) argues for inclusive education in the context of the needed changes in attitudes towards persons with disabilities, and then connects this to broader societal development:

The fundamental principle of inclusive education is the valuing of diversity within the human community. Every person has a contribution to offer to the world. Yet, in our society we have drawn narrow parameters around what is valued and how it makes a contribution.

When inclusive education is fully embraced, we abandon the idea that children have to become 'normal' in order to contribute to the world. Instead, we search for and nourish the gifts that are inherent in all people. We begin to look beyond typical ways of becoming valued members of the community, and in doing so, begin to realize the achievable goal of providing all children with an authentic sense of belonging.

As a collective commitment to educate *all* [emphasis in the original] children takes hold and 'typical' students realize that those kids do belong in their schools and classes, typical students will benefit by learning that their own membership in the class and the society is something that has to do with human rights rather than academic or physical ability. In this way, it is conceivable that the students of inclusive schools will be liberated from the tyranny of earning the right to belong. It is ironic that the students who were believed to have the least worth and value may be the ones who can guide us off the path of social destruction. (p 38)

Perhaps Kunc's view was shaped, at least in part, by his own experience as a person with a disability. The voices of persons with disabilities are critical in the development of a unitary education system, yet they are too little heard in the debates.

As French (1993) points out, in the medical models of disability,

which most frequently undergird the use to which technology is put, the purpose of the intervention is to make the person with a disability as normal as possible, i.e., to adapt the individual to the conditions of the society in s/he lives. The challenge that Hakken (1995) presents is full access to the society.

'What should be done to insure…that technology is not substituted for access? [S]supplying people with machines can come to be a way to avoid supplying them with access and an excuse for not making public places accessible.' (p 518)

We have come to understand that full equality and participation requires a recognition of the uniqueness and strengths, in both participants and values if we are to move towards the transformation of society into one of more diversity; the goal is not assimilation into an unchanged society. In the case of students with disabilities, inclusion in the schools of the nation must not result either in any loss of their identity, nor in society's forfeiture of their contributions.

Social policy must, as Boulding (1967) states, be justified by an 'appeal to build the identity of a person around some community with which he [or she] is associated' (p 7). The opposite of alienation, which threatens community, is identity and inclusion. Citing Dewey (1980, 1988), Skrtic (1996) states, 'Because humans must learn to be democratic, social policy – and particularly educational policy – must promote inclusive systems because these are the types of institutional arrangements in which democratic identities, values, and communities are cultivated.' (p 107.)

The Salamanca Statement and Framework for Action on Special Needs Education (1994), adopted by representatives of 92 governments and 25 international organizations, connects its championing of inclusive schools with broader societal goals:

Regular schools with this inclusive orientation are the most effective means of combating discriminatory attitudes, creating welcoming communities, building an inclusive society, and achieving education for all…(p ix)

The trend in social policy during the past two decades has been to promote integration and participation and to combat exclusion. Inclusion and participation are essential to human dignity and the exercise of human rights. (p 11)

We then come back to the premise of this chapter – inclusive education is not merely a characteristic of a democratic society, it is essential to it.

Endnotes

1. We use the term 'special education' to denote those programmes and services provided to students with disabilities. Traditionally, in the United States, these have been separate classes and programmes.
2. We use the term 'general education' to denote those programmes provided to non-disabled students. Increasingly, in the United States, students with disabilities are being served in general education settings, as a result of inclusive education programmes.

3. In the United States, education is a state responsibility. The federal law concerning the education of students with disabilities offers states the opportunity to participate; while some states initially chose not to do so, for the past twenty years all 50 states have elected to participate and, thus, are governed by the strictures of the federal law and its interpretation by the federal courts.
4. The illustration is based upon *Board of Education v. Rowley* (1982), a landmark court case in which the school system argued that the provision of interpreter services for Amy Rowley provided a satisfactory education for her. The US Supreme Court held that the requirements of P.L. 94-142 were met per a standard of educational sufficiency, and that the law did not require maximum benefits for the student.
5. For a comprehensive review of current developments in inclusive education in the United States, see Lipsky and Gartner, 1996; Lipsky and Gartner, 1997.

References

Allington, R.L. and McGill-Franzen (1992) 'Unintended effects of educational reform in New York', *Educational Policy*, 4, pp 397–414

Artiles, A. J. and Larsen, L. A. (1998) 'International perspectives on special education reform', *European Journal of Special Needs Education*, special issue 13 (1), pp 5–133

Boulding, K. (1967) 'The boundaries of social policy', *Social Work*, 12, pp 3–11

Coalition of Essential Schools, *Fall Forum* (1998) Author, Providence, RI

Dewey, J. (1980) [1916], 'Democracy and education', in J. A. Boydston (ed.) *John Dewey: The Middle Works, 1899–1924* (vol 9, pp 1–370), Southern Illinois University Press, Carbondale

Dewey, J. (1980) [1929–1930], 'Individualism, old and new', in J. A. Boydston (ed.) *John Dewey: The later works, 1925–1953* (vol. 2, pp 235–372), Southern Illinois University Press, Carbondale

18th Annual Report to the Congress on the Implementation of the Individuals with Disabilities Education Act, US Department of Education, Washington, DC

Engel, D. M. (1993) 'Origin myths: Narratives of authority, resistance, disability, and law', *Law and Society Review*, 27 (4), pp 785–826

French, S. (1993) 'What's so great about independence?', in J. Swain, V. Finkelstein, S. French and M. Oliver (eds) *Disabling Barriers – Enabling Environments*, Sage, London

Gardner, H. (1983) *Frames of Mind: The Theory of Multiple Intelligences*, Basic Books, New York

Gartner, A., Lipsky, D. K., and Turnbull, A. P. (1991) *Supporting Families with a Child with a Disability: An International Outlook*, Paul H. Brookes Publishing Co, Baltimore, MD

Granger, L. and Granger, B. (1988) *The Magic Feather*, E. P. Dutton, New York

Guttman, A. (1987) *Democratic Education*, Princeton University Press, Princeton, NJ

Hahn, H. (1987) 'Public policy and disabled infants: A sociopolitical perspective', *Issues in Law and Medicine*, 3 (1), pp 3–4, 7–8

Hahn, H. (1989) 'The politics of special education', in D. K. Lipsky and A. Gartner (eds.) *Beyond Special Education: Quality Education for All*, Paul H. Brookes Publishing Co, Baltimore, MD, pp 225–42

Hakken, D. (1995) 'Electronic curb cuts: Computing and cultural (re)construction of disability in the United States', *Science as Culture*, 4, Part 4, (21), pp 502–34

Johnson, L. and Moxon, E. (1998) 'In whose service? Technology, care and disabled people: The case for a disability politics perspective', *Disability and Society*, 13 (2), pp 241–58

Keating, D. P. (1996) 'The transformation of schooling: Dealing with diversity', in J. Lupart, A. McKeough and C. Yewchuck (eds) *Schools in Transition: Rethinking Regular and Special Education*, Thomas Nelson Canada, Toronto

Kunc, N. (1992) 'The need to belong: Recovering Maslow's hierarchy of needs', in R.Villa, S. Thousand, W. Stainback and S. Stainback (eds) *Restructuring for Caring and Effective Education: An Administrative Guide to Creating Heterogeneous Schools*, Paul H. Brookes Publishing Co, Baltimore, MD, pp. 25–39

Lipsky, D. K. (1985) 'A parental perspective on stress and coping', *American Journal of Orthopsychiatry*, 55 (4), pp 614–17

Lipsky, D. K. and Gartner, A. (1996) 'Inclusion, school restructuring, and the remaking of American society', *Harvard Educational Review*, 66 (4), pp 762–96

Lipsky, D. K. and Gartner, A. (1997) *Inclusion and School Reform: Transforming America's Classrooms*, Paul H. Brookes Publishing Co, Baltimore, MD

Lipton, D. (1994) 'The Full Inclusion Court Cases: 1989–1994', *NCERI Bulletin*, 1 (2), pp 1–8

Meadmore, D. (1993) 'Divide and rule', in R. Slee (ed) *Is there a desk with my name on it? The politics of integration*, Falmer Press, London, pp 27–38

Minnesota State Education Department (1993) 'Will our children learn to value diverse community members?', in *Inclusive Education in Minnesota: What's Working?* Author, Minneapolis, pp 4–5

Minow, M. (1990) *Making All the Difference: Inclusion, Exclusion, and American Law*, Cornell University Press, Ithaca, NY

National Study of Inclusive Education (1995) 'New York: the City University of New York', *National Center on Educational Restructuring and Inclusion*

Ramsey, E. (1993) 'Foreword', in R. Slee (ed.) *Is There a Desk With my Name on it? The Politics of Integration*, Falmer Press, London

The 1997 reauthorization of IDEA, *NCERI Bulletin*, spring, 1998

The Salamanca Statement and Framework for Action on Special Needs, World Conference on Special Needs Education: Access and Equality (1994), UNESCO, New York

Skrtic, T. M. (1991) 'The special education paradox: Equity as the way to excellence', *Harvard Educational Review*, 61 (2), pp 148–207

Skrtic, T. M. (1996) 'School organization, inclusive education, and democracy', in J. Lupart, A. McKeough and C. Yewchuck (eds) *Schools in transition: Rethinking Regular and Special Education*, Thomas Nelson Canada, Toronto, pp 81–118

Stainback, S., Stainback, W. and Ayres, B. (1996) 'Schools as inclusive communities', in W. Stainback and S. Stainback (eds) *Controversial Issues Confronting Special Education: Divergent perspectives*, 2nd edn, Allyn and Bacon, Boston, MA, pp 31–43

Stainback. W. and Stainback, S. (1996) *Controversial Issues Confronting Special Education: Divergent perspectives*, 2nd edn, Allyn and Bacon, Boston, MA

Villa, R. A. and Thousand, J. S. (1995) 'The rationales for creating inclusive schools', in R. A. Villa and J. S. Thousand (eds) *Creating an Inclusive School*, ASCD, Alexandria, VA, pp 28–44

Ysseldyke, J. (1983) 'The classification of handicapped students', in M. C. Wang, M. C. Reynolds and H. J. Walberg (eds) *Handbook of Special Education: Research and Practice, Vol. 1: Learner Characteristics and Adaptive Education*, Pergamon Press, New York, pp 253–71

2. Individual rights to education and students with disabilities: some lessons from US policy

Margaret J. McLaughlin, Lynn Fuchs and Michael Hardman

The rights of the individual

To understand the current tensions and ambiguities between individual rights and an educational system based on normative principles, one must consider the evolution of individual rights within democratic societies. All democracies are based on a premise that individuals bear certain rights. Broadly interpreted, this means that the individual has a right to be protected from government interference. In this concept of individual rights, each citizen (a term subject to various definitions) has the right to engage in private actions or enter into contracts. The collective actions on the part of the government are taken only to preserve the rights of the individual citizens.

This *laissez-faire* view of individual rights is reflected in the US Constitution, which established a Bill of Rights applicable to each citizen. Essentially, the original Bill of Rights guarantees each citizen the right to life, liberty and the pursuit of happiness. For the first century and a half of the history of the US, these individual rights were zealously guarded by government and by a system of common courts (Sunstein, 1990).

The protection of the private individual guaranteed open competition and supported 'free markets'. This concept of individual rights assumed that 'all' individuals were created equal and thus would equally enter into, and profit from, the structures and organizations of society. This early interpretation of individual rights in the US argued against government's regulation of economic or social structures, including schools. Citizen self-determination was the expressed norm. Thus, the control of education was constitutionally deferred to the individual states, which, in turn, permitted local towns and other geographical areas to decide when and how, as well as which, children should be educated.

A fundamental shift in this construct of individual rights began to occur in the US during the 1930s, as part of the 'New Deal' policies of the Roosevelt administration. During this time, reformers began to view the system of common law's protection of individual property rights, and the government's neutrality or abstention from interference with the individual, as harmful to many. People of colour, the poor and the disabled were not protected under the earlier concepts of individual rights. In fact, the reformers argued, they were denied access to the same rights that others enjoyed. These ideas were also fuelled by new economic theories, which viewed government spending as a means of spurring economic growth.

A 'second' Bill of Rights was articulated by President Roosevelt. It was designed to protect the individual's right to housing, welfare, employment, education and food. The result of these New Deal policies, and accompanying government actions, was to transfer power from the local level and the private sectors to the central or federal government, which began to act on behalf of individual citizens. The system of federal and state courts began to attack the former system of government *laissez-faire* and, together with the federal administration, ushered in a new era of individual rights. This new view of rights assumed that harm was not just experienced by one individual, but that it was felt equally by a class or collective group. This discourse was used to justify a number of new initiatives, including the civil rights movement, moves to ensure environmental quality and occupational safety, and protection of consumer rights (Sunstein, 1990).

Public education was one of the institutions most powerfully impacted by the shift in interpretation. The crucial 1954 Supreme Court decision, *Brown v. the Board of Education*, established that the right to education was an individual property protected under the US Constitution. Thus, when a state undertakes to provide education to some children, it has established a property interest that cannot be denied to other children without due process of law. The *Brown* decision established both that black children had a right to education, and that they had a right to the same education received by white children. It cited that 'separate but equal' schools were inherently unequal, due to the stigma and deprivation of interaction with children from other backgrounds (Rothstein, 1990). Thus, the US federal courts not only intervened to establish an individual right to an education, but also began to define a uniform and egalitarian form of education. This view of individual rights has led to a variety of affirmative action policies within US education; these policies have had an impact upon admissions policies in universities, as well as upon curriculum organization and opportunities within primary and secondary education.

The effort to enforce equality of treatment in education has focused on ensuring equity in funding and expenditure of resources. It has also raised fundamental public policy questions such as: what constitutes an adequate education? Whom should we educate? What is the purpose of education? Various studies have demonstrated that students of colour and poor students have not had the same curricular experiences nor the same educational outcomes as middle-class white students (National Center for Education Statistics, 1996; Philips, 1997). As such, a fundamental question confronting education policy-makers has been how to ensure that educational opportunities, including challenging curricula and effective instruction, are provided to each individual student.

This premise of equity is an important theme in current reform initiatives in the US, including the creation of *common* standards, challenging assessments, and enhanced accountability for student performance. Central to these reforms is the notion that each student is entitled to instruction that is grounded in a common set of challenging content standards, and that schools and individual students must be held accountable for achieving equally high levels of performance based on these standards.

Current US federal and state education policies reflect a major commitment to this view of standards-based reform. For example, all 50 states have developed content standards that require teachers to teach more complex levels of knowledge and skills, as well as to deliver instruction in new ways. In addition, states and local districts are developing new assessments, to measure how well students are learning the new curricular material. The results are attached to sanctions and/or rewards for schools, teachers, and students.

Major US federal legislation, such as Goals 2000: Educate America Act, Title 1 of the Improving America's Schools Act, and the Individuals with Disabilities Education Act (IDEA), now contains provisions that require states to develop challenging common standards, and to report on how *all* students are meeting these standards. For students with disabilities, the expectation is that they will participate in the standards and accountability systems, and that their educational experiences will be explicitly linked to the general curriculum. The intent of all this legislation is to ensure that no group of students receives differential treatment within schools. The assumption is that each individual student should have an equal opportunity to achieve the same outcome.

'Equal Outcomes and Equal Treatment'

The concept of equal opportunity and equity of treatment, as currently being defined in US education policy, poses some unique challenges to students with disabilities who maintain an entitlement to an individualized educational programme. If these students are to achieve the challenging standards, and reap the rewards of participating in the reforms to which all students are entitled, schools must provide them with instruction that is designed carefully to meet their individual learning requirements.

Effective instruction for individuals with high-incidence disabilities

Three critical features – individually referenced decision-making, intensity and explicit instruction – define effective instruction for students with mild to moderate learning disabilities.

Individually referenced decision-making

Effective practice centres instructional decision-making on the individual student (Fuchs and Fuchs, 1995). Research specifies how to track student progress and how to use the resulting database to formulate ambitious learning goals (Fuchs, Fuchs, and Hamlett, 1989a), and to test alternative hypotheses about which instructional methods produce satisfactory growth rates (Fuchs, Fuchs and Hamlett, 1989b). Over time, the teacher empirically tests and develops an instructional programme tailored for the individual student.

Individually referenced decision-making is perhaps the significant feature of effective practice for individuals with high-incidence disabilities. Individual decision-making fosters high expectations for learning; it requires teachers to reserve judgement about the efficacy of an instructional method for a student, until the method proves effective for that individual; it necessitates a form of teacher planning that incorporates ongoing adjustments in response to the individual student's learning; and it requires knowledge of multiple ways to adapt curricula, modify instructional methods, and motivate students.

A meta-analysis summarized research on individually referenced decision-making with an effect size of .70 standard deviation units (Fuchs and Fuchs, 1986); more recent studies in reading, spelling, and mathematics (Fuchs, Fuchs, Hamlett and Allinder, 1991; Fuchs, Fuchs, Hamlett and Ferguson, 1992; Fuchs, Fuchs, Hamlett and Stecker, 1991) corroborate earlier effect sizes.

Intensity

The second feature of effective practice is instructional intensity. Meta-analyses and narrative syntheses (Cohen, Kulik and Kulik, 1982; Glass, Cahen, Smith and Filby, 1982; Wasik and Slavin, 1993) show that intensive instruction can result in impressive learning for students who would otherwise fail to achieve critical benchmarks (Glass, McGaw and Smith, 1981). Torgesen (1996), for example, has studied students with phonological processing deficits, who had been predicted to experience serious problems in learning to read. Children were assigned randomly to four conditions – a conventional control group and one of three experimental conditions. These represented a range of methods, but shared one feature – one-to-one tutoring delivery that fostered intensive instruction. Preliminary results within a longitudinal design indicated that children in all three intensive instruction treatments achieved comparably, but reliably, better than the control group.

It is important to note that, although one-to-one tutoring may be necessary to achieve instructional intensity, and promote learning within certain domains of functioning, such as reading acquisition, intensive instruction is not synonymous with one-to-one delivery. Rather, intensive instruction refers to a broader set of instructional features including, but not limited to, the following:

1. high rates of active responding at appropriate levels;
2. careful matching of instruction with students' skill levels;

3. instructional cues, prompts, and fading to support approximations to correct responding; and
4. detailed task-focused feedback.

These are all features that may be incorporated into group lessons (see the work of Wolery and colleagues; Lysakowski and Walberg, 1982). In fact, for promoting social development and communicative competence, meaningful participation by students with disabilities among normal, age-appropriate peer groups for instructional activities can be critical (Haring and Reinduce, 1994; Nietupski and Hamre-Nietupski, 1987; Snell and Brown, 1993).

Explicit instruction
A third feature of effective instructional practice for individuals with high-incidence disabilities is explicit contextualization of skills-based instruction. One major philosophical influence in the current education reform movement is constructivism. This views children as active, self-regulating learners who construct knowledge in developmentally appropriate ways, through socially situated, authentic interactions with the world (Harris and Graham, 1995; Pressley, Harris and Marks, 1992). This translates into three essential assumptions about education practice:

1. that the appropriate role for teachers is to guide the construction of knowledge, rather than to direct explicit instruction (Tharpe and Gallimore, 1989);
2. that the curriculum cannot be fractionated into a hierarchy of discrete skills (Harris and Graham, 1995); and
3. that success in basic skills is not a prerequisite to more advanced learning and higher-order thinking (Means and Knapp, 1991).

In sharp contrast to these assumptions, effective practice for individuals with high-incidence disabilities maintains a strong focus on the explicit teaching of basic skills. This traditional focus is based on three findings, which question the tenability of constructivist principles for students with disabilities.

First, the assumption that the appropriate role of the teacher is that of guide rather than provider of explicit instruction appears tenuous in the light of research into students with disabilities. This shows that such students typically cannot be viewed as active, self-regulated learners (Deci and Ryan, 1985, 1986; Garber and Seligman, 1980), and that they necessitate more structured, teacher-directed approaches to learning (Dweck and Leggett, 1988). Research contradicts the assumption that children with disabilities systematically construct knowledge via their natural interactions with the world; in fact, it demonstrates that extensive, structured, and explicit instruction is necessary for these children if they are to develop the processes and understandings that other children learn more easily and naturally (Bransford, Goldman and

Hasselbring, 1995; Brown and Campione, 1990; Harris and Graham, 1992; Kronic, 1990).

The second assumption – that cognitive components cannot be isolated or fractionated, and that the curriculum cannot be taught as a series of discrete skills – also appears fallacious for students with disabilities. In fact, research indicates that analysing and teaching tasks in their component parts is effective, and may, indeed, be necessary for students with disabilities. The primary problem characterizing children with reading disabilities, for example, is a phonological processing deficit that impedes word learning and word recognition (Adams and Bruck, 1993; Gough and Tunmer, 1986; Perfetti, 1985; Siegel, 1993; Stanovich, 1986; Vellutino and Scanlon, 1987). To overcome this deficit, explicit instruction on discrete phonological awareness and word-recognition skills is required (Stanovich, 1995). Analogous research suggests the efficacy of related approaches that analyse and teach reading comprehension and written expression as component strategies (Harris and Pressley, 1991).

Third, the assumption that a command of basic skills is not a prerequisite for advanced learning appears not to relate to students with disabilities. The acquisition of quantitative concepts and their applications seems to be hierarchical: when students fail to acquire early mathematics proficiency, they do not succeed, either within an academic track (which requires high-order, problem-solving applications of earlier maths content), or within a basic track (which requires applications to real-world situations) (Bryan, Bay, Lopez-Reyna and Donahue, 1992). The failure to learn to read undoubtedly puts individuals at risk of a poor outcome within the middle- and high-school curricula, where reading proficiency is assumed and required. Reading and mathematics competence is, moreover, critical as individuals with disabilities make the transition to today's high-tech marketplace (US Department of Labor, 1987).

Together, these three principles of effective practice – individually referenced decision making, intensive instruction and explicit contextualization of skills-based instruction – represent a potent set of instructional methods. These methods have been demonstrated to enhance the learning of, and increase the probability of attainment of challenging standards for students with high-incidence disabilities. The research base on the specific interventions subsumed under these broad principles document effect sizes ranging from .50 to over 1.5 standard deviations (Forness and Kavale, 1996; Swanson, 1996).

Effective instruction for students with severe cognitive disabilities

Individually referenced decision-making, intensive instruction, and the explicit teaching of basic skills are also key components of effective special education practice for students with more severe cognitive disabilities. However, for these students, the focus is less on teaching to high academic standards, and more on preparing for access to, and participation in, appropriate post-school outcomes. Historically, many of the outcomes in human-service programmes for people with severe disabilities, particularly for those with significant cognitive disabilities, were oriented towards protection and care. The objective of such programmes was to protect the individual with disabilities from society – and society from the individual. This philosophy resulted in services that isolated the individual with disabilities, and provided physical care rather than preparation for life in a heterogeneous world.

With the civil rights movement of the past two decades, one aspect of which focused on educating students with disabilities in public schools, traditional outcomes were reconceptualized to the following:

1. employment, useful work and valued activity;
2. access to further education when desired and appropriate;
3. personal autonomy, independence and adult status;
4. social interaction, community participation, leisure and recreation; and
5. participation within the life of the family.

If students with severe disabilities are to achieve the same types of post-school outcomes valued for all students, they need be taught using a curriculum that concentrates on skills that provide opportunity for functioning as independently as possible in home, school and community settings. Brown *et al.* (1976) refer to this approach as 'the criterion of ultimate functioning'. Fredericks and Brodsky (1994) described a functional curriculum as

> the life skills needed by a student in the current environment in which he or she was functioning, the life skills needed in the student's immediate next educational environment, and the skills the student would need after leaving school to function in vocational, residential, and recreational environments. (p 33)

Using the criterion of ultimate functioning as a basis for decision-making, instruction for students with disabilities has evolved into an ecological framework. The ecological approach to instruction is based on creating a match between the needs and functioning level of an individual student and the demands of the environment. Skills are never taught in isolation from actual performance demands. Schalock (1986) described the ecological model as a three-phase process. First, each student's capabilities are assessed in relationship to the environmental demand. Second, 'the goodness of fit' between the student and the environment must be assessed, specifically identifying barriers that prevent the individual's participation in an environment. Third, instruction is directed toward breaking down those barriers through the following:

1. adaptation and accommodations within the environment; and
2. student skill training. Individually referenced instruction is determined from the results of an ecological inventory of those natural routines and activities that are used most frequently by the student across environments.

The process specifies the following:

1. the age-appropriate settings where performance and participation occur;
2. the routines and activities that normally take place in these settings;
3. a short description of the natural sequences of steps for an activity;
4. descriptive features of each activity, such as its duration, social or communicative demands, natural mechanisms of support, materials that are needed, and natural signals or cues; and
5. mobility requirements for the activity and stimulus dimensions of the setting, commonly collected through the use of a teacher-drawn map. (McDonnell *et al.*, 1995, p 204)

Research suggests that, if planned and managed properly, the ecological approach to instruction for students with severe disabilities can result in significant gains in adaptive skills (McDonnell *et al.*, 1995), and increased achievement of IEP objectives (Brinker and Thorpe, 1984; Hunt, Goetz and Anderson, 1986).

One-to-one instruction for students with more severe disabilities is optimal for skill development, particularly in the area of personal management (Billingsley, Liberty and White, 1994). However, as suggested by Reid and Favell (1984), the research also points out that students with severe disabilities are capable of learning certain skills in group settings, often achieving mastery in periods of time comparable to those in one-to-one situations.

There are two primary factors that support the need for students with more severe disabilities to receive at least some of their instructional programming in group settings. First, the acquisition of functional skills, particularly communication and social development, is correlated with meaningful participation and performance by students in normal, age-based routines and settings (Haring and Reinduce, 1994; Sell and Brown, 1993; Nietupski and Hamre-Nietupski, 1987). Second, the criterion of ultimate functioning is based on the premise that effective instruction includes both the content of the skills to be taught (the curriculum), and the situated context (environment) in which learning is most effectively acquired and applied.

Research over the past ten years supports the utilization of the criterion for ultimate functioning to teach valued outcomes for students with severe disabilities. When systematic instruction (such as shaping, cues and prompting, reinforcement, task analysis, etc.) is used within an ecological framework, the results are the following:

1. more meaningful participation and performance in normal, age-based routines (Sell and Brown, 1993; Nietupski and Hamre-Nietupski, 1987); and
2. the development and generalization of social and communication skills that enhance interaction with peers and adults across home, school, and community settings (Haring and Reinduce, 1994; Forest and Pierpoint, 1992; Haring and Lovinger, 1989; Odom and Strain, 1986).

Global directions

There is clearly an important need to foster an education system that promotes high expectations for all students, including those with disabilities. The intended long-term outcomes for students with disabilities should be no different from those for students who are not disabled; schools exist to prepare individuals for life. However, content of the preparation may differ, depending on the needs and abilities of the individual (for example, an academic vs. a functional life orientation). To this end, the evolving notion in US policy, of individual entitlement to the same treatment (such as common standards and curriculum opportunity) versus entitlement to differential treatment (such as individualized goals and instruction), may be at odds. Reconciling these differences requires clarification of the concept of individualization in education. For students with disabilities, individually referenced decision-making is not only empirically sound, but also necessary, given the unique learning characteristics of many of these students. Thus, the concept of common standards and universally applied assessments may need to be carefully interpreted for individual students. Nevertheless, the concept of universal accountability, meaning that public education is responsible for ensuring that each child is progressing towards important outcomes (McDonnell *et al.*, 1997), is a valid one.

As suggested by the Organization for Economic Co-operation and Development (1986), a common set of indicators relative to social policy and service delivery should be in place, and these indicators should apply both to disabled and non-disabled people:

1. There should be only one comprehensive social policy. Policies for those with disabilities should not be separate or merely the consequences of other policies.
2. Integration in the education system cannot be discussed separately from general policies for primary and secondary education.
3. There is a need for coherent objectives for services so that benefits and other provision enhance autonomy and competence.
4. Young people with disabilities have the same human rights as others and thus have a right to adult status. (p 21)

Thus, individual rights for students with disabilities must encompass the universal right to equal access to the same institutions, such as public education and universal public accountability, within the framework of individualized accommodation, programmes and services.

References

Adams, M. J., and Bruck, M. (1993) 'Word recognition: The interface of educational policies and scientific research', *Reading and Writing: An Interdisciplinary Journal*, 5, pp 113–39

Billingsley, F. F., Liberty, K. A. and White, O. R. (1994) 'The technology of instruction', in E. C. Cipani and F. Spooner (eds) *Curricular and Instructional Approaches for Persons with Severe Disabilities*, Allyn and Bacon, Boston, pp 81–116

Bransford, J., Gridman S.R. and Hasselbring T.S. (1995) 'Marrying constructivist and skill-based models: should we and could technology help?', Symposium presented at annual meeting of the American Educational Research Association, San Francisco

Brinker R. P. and Thorpe, M. E. (1984) 'Integration of severely handicapped students and the proportion of IEP objectives achieved, *Exceptional Children*, 51, pp 168–75

Brown, A. L. and Campione, J. C. (1990) 'Interactive learning environments and the teaching of science and mathematics', in M. Gardner, J. Greens, F. Reif, A. Schoenfeld, A. di Sessa and E. Stage (eds) *Toward a Scientific Practice of Science Education*, Erlbaum, Hillsdale, NJ, pp 111–39

Brown, L., Nietupski, J. and Hamre-Nietupski, S. (1976) 'The criterion of ultimate functioning and pubic school services for severely handicapped students', in M. Thomas (ed.) *Hey, Don't Forget About Me: New Directions for Serving the Severely Handicapped*, Council for Exceptional Children, Reston, VA. pp. pp 2–15

Bryan, T., Bay, M., Lopez-Reyna, N. and Donahue, M. (1992) 'Characteristics of students with learning disabilities: A summary of the extant database and its implications for educational programs', in J. Lloyd, A. Repp and N. Singh (eds) *Perspectives on the Integration of Atypical Learners in Regular Education Settings*, Sycamore, DeKalb, IL, pp 143–76

Cohen, P., Kulik, J. A. and Kulik, C. (1982) 'Educational outcomes of tutoring: A meta-analysis of findings', *American Educational Research Journal*, 19, pp 237–48

Deci, E. L. and Ryan, R. M. (1985) *Intrinsic Motivation and Self Determination in Human Behavior*, Plenum, New York

Deci, E. L. and Ryan, R. M. (1986) 'An analysis of learned helplessness: Continuous changes in performance, strategy, and achievement cognition after failure', *Journal of Personality and Social Psychology*, 36, pp 451–62

Dweck, C. S. and Leggett, E. (1988) 'A social-cognitive approach to motivation and personability', *Psychological Review*, 95, pp 256–73

Forest, M. and Pierpoint, I. (1992) 'Families, friends, and circles', in J. Nisbet (ed.) *Natural Supports in School, at Work, and in the Community for People with Severe Disabilities*, Paul H. Brookes, Baltimore

Forness, S. and Kavale, K. (1996) 'Can 700 Studies Be Wrong? Mega-analyses of Special Education Meta-analyses', unpublished paper presented at the annual meeting of the Council for Exceptional Children, Orlando, FL, April

Fredericks, B. and Brodsky, M. (1994) 'Assessment for a functional curriculum', in E. C. Cipani and F. Spooner (eds) *Curricular and Instructional Approaches for Persons with Severe Disabilities*, Allyn and Bacon, Boston, pp 31–49

Fuchs, D. and Fuchs, L. (1995) 'What's "special" about special education', *Phi Delta Kappan*, 76 (7), pp 522–30

Fuchs, L. S. and Fuchs, D. (1986) 'Effects of systematic formative evaluation on student achievement: A meta-analysis', *Exceptional Children*, 53, pp 199–208

Fuchs, L. S., Fuchs, D. and Hamlett, C. L. (1989a) Effects of alternative goal structures within curriculum-based measurement', *Exceptional Children*, 55, pp 429–38

Fuchs, L. S., Fuchs, D. and Hamlett, C. L. (1989b) 'Effects of instrumental use of curriculum-based measurement to enhance instructional programs', *Remedial and Special Education*, 10 (2), pp 43–52

Fuchs, L. S., Fuchs, D., Hamlett, C. L. and Allinder, R. M. (1991) 'Effects of expert system advice within curriculum-based measurement on teacher planning and student achievement in spelling', *School Psychology Review*, 20, pp 49–60

Fuchs, L. S., Fuchs, D., Hamlett, C. L. and Ferguson, C. (1992) 'Effects of expert system consultation within curriculum-based measurement using a reading maze task', *Exceptional Children*, 58, pp 436–50

Fuchs, L. S., Fuchs, D., Hamlett, C. L. and Stecker, P. M. (1991) 'Effects of curriculum-based measurement and consultation on teacher planning and student achievement in mathematics operations', *American Educational Research Journal*, 28, pp 617–41

Garber, J. and Seligman, M. E. P. (1980) *Human Helplessness*, Academic Press, New York

Glass, G., Cahen, L., Smith, M. L. and Filby, N. (1982) *School Class Size*, Sage, Beverly Hills, CA

Glass, G., McGaw, B. and Smith, M. (1981) *Meta-analysis in Social Research*, Sage, Beverly Hills, CA

Gough, P. B. and Tunmer, W. E. (1986) 'Decoding, reading, and reading disability', *Remedial and Special Education*, 7 (1), pp 6–10

Haring, T. and Lovinger, L. (1989) 'Promoting social interaction through teaching generalized play initiation responses to preschool children with autism', *The Journal of the Association for Persons with Severe Handicaps*, 14, pp 58–67

Haring, T. and Reinduce, D. (1994) 'Strategies and instructional procedures to promote social interactions and relationships', in E. C. Cipani and F. Spooner (eds) *Curricular and Instructional Approaches for Persons with Severe Disabilities*, Allyn and Bacon, Boston. pp 289–321

Harris, K. R. and Graham, S. (1995) 'Constructivism: Principles, paradigms, and integration', *The Journal of Special Education*, 28, pp 233–47

Harris, K. and Pressley, M. (1991) 'The nature of cognitive strategy instruction: Interactive strategy instruction' *Exceptional Children* 57, pp 392–404

Hunt, P., Goetz, L. and Anderson, J. (1986) 'The quality of IEP objectives associated with placement on integrated vs. segregated school sites', *The Journal of the Association for Persons with Severe Handicaps*, 11, pp 125–30

Kronick, D. (1990) 'Holism and empiricism as complementary paradigms', *Journal of Learning Disabilities*, 21, pp 425–28

Lysakowski, R. S. and Walberg, H. J. (1982) 'Instructional effects of cues, participation, and corrective feedback: A quantitative synthesis', *American Educational Research Journal*, 19, pp 559–78

McDonnell, J., Hardman, M., McDonnell, A. and Kiefer-O'Donnell, R. (1995) *Introduction to Persons with Severe Disabilities*, Allyn and Bacon, Inc, Boston

Means, B. and Knapp, M. S. (1991) 'Cognitive approaches to teaching advanced skills to educationally disadvantaged students', *Phi Delta Kappan*, 23, pp 8–10

National Center for Education Statistics (1996) *Digest of Education Statistics*, Government Printing Office, Washington, DC

Nietupski, J. and Hamre-Nietupski, S. (1987) 'An ecological approach to curriculum development', in L. Goetz, D. Guess, and K. Stremel-Campbell (eds) *Innovative Program Design for Individuals with Dual Sensory Impairments*, Paul H. Brookes, Baltimore

Odom, S. L. and Strain, P. S. (1986) 'A comparison of peer initiation and teacher antecedent interventions for promoting reciprocal interactions of autistic preschoolers', *Journal of Applied Behavior Analysis*, 19, pp 59–72

Organization for Economic Cooperation and Development (OECD) (1986) *Young People with Handicaps: The Road to Adulthood*, Author, Paris, France

Perfetti, C. (1985) *Reading Ability*, New York, Oxford University Press

Phillips, M. (1997) 'Does School Segregation Explain Why African-Americans and Latinos Score Lower than Whites on Academic Achievement Tests?', paper presented at the Annual Meeting of the American Sociological Association

Pressley, M., Harris, K. R. and Marks, M. B. (1992) 'But good strategy instructors are constructivists!', *Educational Psychology Review*, 4, pp 3–31

Reid, D. H. and Favell, J. E. (1984) 'Group instruction with persons who have severe disabilities: A critical review', *The Journal of the Association for Persons with Severe Handicaps*, 9, pp. 167–77

Rothstein, L. F. (1990) *Special Education Law*, Longman, White Plains, NY

Schalock, R. (1986) *Transitions from School to Work*, National Association of Rehabilitation Facilities, Washington, DC

Siegel, L. S. (1993) 'Alice in IQ land or why IQ is still irrelevant to learning disabilities', in M. Joshi and C. K. Leong (eds) *Reading Disabilities: Diagnosis and Component Processes*, Kluwer Academic, Dordrecht, The Netherlands, pp 71–84

Sell, M. E. and Brown, F. (1993) 'Instructional planning and implementation', in M. E. Sell (ed.) *Instruction of Students with Severe Disabilities*, Merrill Publishing, New York, pp 99–151

Stanovich, K. E. (1986) 'Toward an interactive-compensatory model of individual differences in the development of reading fluency', *Reading Research Quarterly*, 16, pp 32–71

Stanovich, K. E. (1995) 'Constructivism in reading education', *The Journal of Special Education*, 28, pp 259–74

Sunstein, C. R. (1990) *After the Rights Revolution: Reconceiving the Regulatory State*, Harvard University Press, Cambridge, MA

Swanson, H. L. (1996, February) 'Assessing and synthesizing interventions for students with mild to moderate disabilities in regular and special education classrooms', paper presented at the Pacific Coast Research Conference, La Jolla

Tharpe, R. G. and Gallimore, R. (1989) *Rousing Minds to Life: Teaching, Learning, and Schooling in Social Context*, Cambridge University Press, New York

Torgesen, J. K. (1996, January) 'The prevention and remediation of reading disabilities', presented in the John F. Kennedy Center Distinguished Lecture Series, Vanderbilt University, Nashville, TN

US Department of Labor (1987) *Worforce 2000: Work and Workers for the 21st Century*, Washington, DC and Indianapolis, IN., US Department of Labor and Hudson Institute

Vellutino, F. and Scanlon, D. (1987) 'Phonological coding, phonological awareness, and reading ability: Evidence from a longitudinal and experimental study', *Merrill-Palmer Quarterly*, 33, pp 321–63

Wasik, B. and Slavin, R. (1993) 'Preventing early reading failure with one-to-one tutoring: A review of five programs', *Reading Research Quarterly*, 28, pp 179–200

3. Inclusion and inclusions: theories and discourses in inclusive education

Alan Dyson

Global agenda or special education bandwagon?

In recent years, inclusive education has become so central to the education policies of large numbers of countries in both the 'developed' and 'developing' world that commentators have been able to describe it, without exaggeration, as 'a global agenda' (Pijl, Meijer and Hegarty, 1997). At the same time, other commentators have viewed this apparently sudden rise with alarm and have seen inclusion, not as the obvious way forward into the next millennium, but, rather, as a 'special education bandwagon' (Kauffman and Hallahan, 1995).

These mixed reactions are, to a large extent, attributable simply to the different educational – and, ultimately, political and ethical – positions adopted by these commentators. However, it is the contention of this chapter that they are also due to some significant ambiguities in the concept of inclusion itself, such that it makes some sense to talk about different 'inclusions'. Moreover, these ambiguities arise from different discourses, through which different theoretical notions of inclusion are constructed. This chapter seeks to explore these discourses, and the 'inclusions' that they construct. This may not only lend some clarity to the field, but also open up the possibility of a genuine debate between different 'inclusions', so that the field remains dynamic and continues to develop.

The ambiguity of inclusion

In 1994, representatives of 88 national governments and 25 international organizations concerned with education met in Salamanca, Spain, under the auspices of UNESCO and the Spanish Government. Together, they drew up the *Salamanca Statement on Principles, Policy and Practice in Special Needs Education*, together with its accompanying *Draft Framework for Action* (UNESCO, 1994). The former opens with a reiteration of the rights in respect of education, which are enshrined in the *Universal Declaration of Human Rights* (UN, 1948) and the *United Nations Standard Rules on Equalization of Opportunities for Persons with Disabilities* (UN, 1993). It then proclaims five principles that are held to issue from these rights:

1. every child has a fundamental right to education, and must be given the opportunity to achieve and maintain an acceptable level of learning;
2. every child has unique characteristics, interests, abilities and learning needs;
3. educational systems should be designed, and educational programmes implemented, to take into account the wide diversity of these characteristics and needs;
4. those with special educational needs must have access to regular schools, which should accommodate them within a child-centred pedagogy capable of meeting these needs;
5. regular schools with this inclusive orientation are the most effective means of combating discriminatory attitudes, creating welcoming communities, building an inclusive society, and achieving education for all; moreover, they provide an effective education to the majority of children, and improve the efficiency and, ultimately, the cost-effectiveness of the entire educational system. (UNESCO, 1994, par. 2)

The *Salamanca Statement* is currently proving extremely powerful as a means of stimulating educational change. Even the UK Government, not noted for looking beyond its national boundaries for education policies, nor, indeed, for subscribing readily to international proclamations, has recently declared its support for Salamanca, and announced a policy of inclusion (DfEE, 1997). However, despite all its power, the *Salamanca Statement* remains a deeply ambiguous document, constituting a somewhat shaky platform on which to base policy. Some of these ambiguities are evident in the principles quoted above. Much of this text is couched in an absolutist language of rights and moral imperatives – every child has a *right* to education; education systems *should be* designed to take into account children's characteristics; those with special needs *must* have access to regular schools – and so on. This is supported by absolutist characterizations of the human condition – 'every child *has* [not 'can be seen as having'] unique characteristics, interests, abilities and learning needs'.

Such absolutist statements may be perfectly acceptable in the domain of fundamental principles and values. However, the absolutism washes over into the empirical domain, where it may be somewhat less appropriate. For instance, we are told that 'regular schools with [an] inclusive orientation are the most effective means of...' and then there follows a list of what we can expect from inclusive schools – building a better society, offering an effective education to the majority of children, and improving the efficiency of the education system as a whole. These claims may well be true, but they are, of course, claims of a quite different order from the earlier statements of principle; whether inclusive schools actually offer an effective education is, we might think, a matter for empirical investigation in a way that the right of every child to an education is not.

Similarly, assertions are made about the necessity of a 'child-centred pedagogy' if the aims of inclusion are to be realized. Again, there is ambiguity here. The assertion appears to be an empirical one, which demands to be tested; it is at least possible that some other form of pedagogy might prove to be more inclusive. Recently in the UK, for example, there have been assertions that the child-centred approach, which has been characteristic of the UK system for three decades and more, is an inappropriate response to diversity (Reynolds and Farrell, 1996). Moreover, it is far from clear what, precisely, is meant by 'child-centred pedagogy'; there is a multiplicity of pedagogical techniques that can claim to take the individual child as their starting point, but the *Salamanca Statement* declines to specify which of these techniques fall within its definition and which do not.

Much the same could be said of the advocacy of 'schools with [an] inclusive orientation'. What do such schools look like? Which characteristics make schools 'inclusive', and which lead us to categorize them as 'exclusive'? Is the all-important 'orientation' a matter of structure, of practices, or of attitude? And does an inclusive school educate *every* child in its neighbourhood? Or just *most* children? Or *more* children than other schools in its particular education system? Indeed, the very notion of 'inclusion' is ambiguous in the *Salamanca Statement*. We might believe that inclusion as a right applies to all children and, therefore, that all children should be taught in inclusive regular schools. However, *Salamanca* talks about inclusive schools offering an effective education only to a *majority* of children. Where, then, are the minority educated? And what is the 'right' to education? Is it a right to placement in a regular school, or simply the right to be offered an education in a school of *some* sort?

Such ambiguities are, of course, only to be expected in such a document as the *Salamanca Statement*, which is essentially the outcome of political processes and compromises. As a piece of polemic, it is enormously powerful. Its ambiguities would be of little significance if they did not reflect underlying ambiguities within the inclusion movement. It is my contention that these ambiguities arise from the coming together of fundamentally different discourses.

The discourses of inclusion

The 'inclusive education movement' has both stimulated and been stimulated by a wide range of commentary, much of which has taken the form of scholarly analysis. This commentary has tended to be extremely rich, questioning many of the assumptions on which 'traditional' special education has been based, and exploring alternative interpretations of concepts such as 'special need' and 'individual difference'. At the level of individual contributions, this commentary is frequently characterized by sophistication and subtlety, which draws upon a range of theoretical roots, and which cannot sensibly be reduced to one or other theoretical position. Perhaps the most obvious example of this is the work of Tom Skrtic (Skrtic, 1991a, 1995), in which the potential theoretical richness of the inclusion movement is made explicit and is exploited to the full. None the less, I concur with Paul and Ward (1996) in the view that it is possible to see the literature (both academic and otherwise) on inclusion as a whole as being located within a limited number of discourses, which can usefully be disentangled from individual contributions. I agree to a great extent with their suggestion that there are somewhat different discourses, to do with 'ethics' on the one hand, and 'comparison' (which I call 'efficacy') on the other. However, whereas they see these in terms of competing paradigms, I believe it is more useful to see them as poles along a single dimension, since they frequently interact in the work of particular commentators. Moreover, if this dimension is primarily concerned with the *rationale* for inclusion, I believe it is useful to see it as intersected by a second dimension that is concerned with the *realization* of inclusion.

The rationale for inclusion: the rights and ethics discourse

As we have seen in the *Salamanca Statement*, inclusion can be justified by reference to the right of children to 'an education' and, moreover, to an education that is made available alongside the majority of their peers. This is simply part of a much wider discourse, in which inclusion is seen as an inevitable outcome of a commitment either to rights as such, or to some more generalized notion of social justice. Lipsky and Gartner's (1996) assertions that 'equity requires inclusion', or Skrtic's (1991a, 1991b) advocacy of 'equity as the way to excellence', are typical in this respect. However, this position emerges from much more than a simple assertion of children's rights, for it is supported by a critical analysis of traditional (i.e. segregated) forms of special education.

This analysis appears to derive from the structuralist sociology of the 1950s onwards, which began to problematize the notion that universal education was a means of equalizing opportunities and spreading economic and cultural benefits more widely through society. Commentators such as Bourdieu (Bourdieu and Passeron, 1977) and Bernstein (1970) began to theorize the ways in which education systems reproduced rather than removed social inequalities; researchers in the UK began to demonstrate empirically the extent to which the children of already socially advantaged families were able to exercise a stranglehold on educational opportunities (Floud, Halsey and Martin, 1956); and Bowles and Gintis produced their classic analysis of the US education system as a major agent of social reproduction in a capitalist society (Bowles and Gintis, 1976). It was inevitable, therefore, that special education would sooner or later be subjected to similar scrutiny. The classic early analyses in the UK were produced by Sally Tomlinson and Len Barton (Barton and

Tomlinson, 1981, 1984; Tomlinson, 1982, 1985), but their work is simply part of a wide-ranging international critical literature that continues to grow apace (see, for instance, Ballard, 1995; Booth, Ainscow and Dyson, 1997; Fulcher, 1989; Gartner and Lipsky, 1989; Kamin, 1977; Lewis and Vulliamy, 1980; Lipsky and Gartner, 1997; Oliver, 1992a and b; Slee, 1996b; Sleeter, 1986; Susman, 1994; Vlachou, 1997).

According to this analysis, special education presents a benign face as the protector of and provider for vulnerable children. However, it is nothing of the sort. Rather, special education serves the interests of advantaged members of society by maintaining and rationalizing the further marginalization of those whom it claims to help. The establishment of special education creates an alternative location for the education of problematic children whose needs and demands might otherwise challenge the established order of regular schooling. It creates a domain within which special-education professionals (teachers, medics, psychometrists and others) can exercise their expertise and maintain their privileged positions. It legitimates the treatment of children (and hence adults) with disabilities as deviant, removes the imperative for any social restructuring in response to their characteristics, and thus contributes to their 'oppression' (Abberley, 1987). Occasionally, and perversely, it offers a means whereby advantaged families can secure additional resources for their children who find schooling difficult, by 'inventing' forms of disablity, which are at one and the same time perceived as non-stigmatized and needy of resourcing.

It follows from this that the decision to place a child in special education is inseparable from issues of rights and justice. In most cases, such a placement will legitimate the marginalization of that child by enabling first schools and then society as a whole to ignore his/her distinctive characteristics. In a few cases, it may marginalize other children in difficulties, whose difficulties are excluded from the 'prestigious' disability categories, and from whom scarce resources are removed. In any event, maintaining segregated special education is incompatible with the establishment of an equitable education system and hence, ultimately, with an equitable society. It follows, therefore, that only inclusive education can deliver social justice.

The rationale for inclusion: the efficacy discourse

Running alongside and interacting with the rights and ethics rationale for inclusion has been a discourse related to efficacy. As the *Salamanca Statement* argues, inclusive schools can be seen as bringing greater social benefits, as being more effective educationally, and as being more cost-efficient than segregated special education. As with the rights and ethics discourse, a major strand of this discourse is a critical analysis of special education. In the UK at least, this analysis appears to have been focused in the first instance on special education as delivered in semi-segregated settings within mainstream schools.

Much of this provision was focused on the 'remedial' teaching of reading, but increasingly appeared to be somewhat unsuccessful in bringing about the sustained improvements in reading that were expected (Carroll, 1972; Collins, 1972; Lovell, Johnson and Platts, 1962). Moreover, it became apparent that such approaches were too narrowly targeted, both in terms of the numbers of students who were involved, and the range of their difficulties that was addressed. At the same time, international (and especially Scandinavian) studies of the effectiveness of education in special schools were being undertaken, and these showed that children fared no better in special schools than in mainstream schools. Indeed, they seemed perhaps to fare a little worse. (Galloway and Goodwin, 1987.)

Other questions have also been raised about the efficacy of special education. The rationale for segregated provision presumably rests on the notion that something distinctive is provided for students 'with special educational needs' in segregated settings. However, some researchers have sought in vain to identify this distinctive provision (Ysseldyke, Algozzine and Epps, 1983). Moreover, segregated special education is a costly business, which concentrates relatively large resources on a few children, and which requires the maintenance of a separate infrastructure of schools, teachers and administrators. In a number of countries, therefore, questions have been asked about the efficiency of segregated provision and the possibility of delivering similar levels of service more efficiently in regular schools (Audit Commission and HMI, 1992; Coopers and Lybrand, 1996; Lipsky and Gartner, 1997). Although, therefore, the *Salamanca Statement*'s claims about the superiority, in terms of efficacy, of inclusive education over segregated provision may seem extravagant, it is now possible to amass a considerable body of empirical evidence that can support these claims (usefully summarized in Lipsky and Gartner, 1997).

The realization of inclusive education: the political discourse

A second dimension along which the discourses of inclusive education can be categorized might be called the *realization* dimension. Inclusion arises within national education systems that are almost always characterized by the presence of an infrastructure of segregated special education, in terms of institutions, professionals and legislative framework. The implementation of inclusive education has, therefore, to be concerned not only with determining the particular forms that will realize the general principle of inclusion, but also with the transition from a segregated to an inclusive system.

One prominent discourse sees this transition in political terms. Special education is sustained by a range of vested interests (its own professionals, regular educators, parental interest groups, and so on); it is, therefore, necessary to 'struggle' (Vlachou, 1997) against these interests in order to bring inclusive education into being. This struggle may take many forms. It may involve individuals and groups in direct action within their own situations aimed at realizing inclusion (Fulcher, 1993; Skrtic, 1991a, 1995). Such direct action may require those individuals to align themselves with oppressed groups in a wider social struggle, or may even demand that the struggle be handed over entirely to those groups (Ballard, 1994, 1995; Barton, 1994; Oliver, 1992a, b). In addition to 'direct action' of this kind, however, it may also require a critical assault on the conceptual structures – the ideas, the assumptions, the discourses – that sustain and rationalize segregated education, both in society at large and, indeed, even within the mind of the committed individual (Fulcher, 1995; Peters, 1995; Slee, 1995, 1998).

Whatever form it takes, this struggle is an essentially manichaean one between the forces of exclusion and the forces of inclusion; it is the advocacy of the need for struggle and the delineation of segregationist practices and concepts that preoccupy this discourse.

The realization of inclusive education: the pragmatic discourse

This concern with struggle is what marks the political discourse out from what I choose to call the 'pragmatic' discourse. Whilst the former is concerned with the processes of resistance, the latter is concerned with what inclusive education looks like in practice and with how, in practical terms, it can be brought about. Within this discourse, there is a significant strand that is concerned with the nature of inclusive schools as organizations. The assumption tends to be made that inclusive schools (and the local and national systems of which they are a part) have determinate characteristics – systems, structures, practices, 'ethos' – that are distinctively different from the characteristics of non-inclusive schools.

Some commentators have attempted to list these characteristics on the basis of empirical research, in the manner of the effective schools literature (Ainscow, 1997; Rouse and Florian, 1996; Sebba and Sachdev, 1997; Thomas, Walker and Webb, 1998), whilst others – notably Skrtic (1991a, b, c) – attempt to develop middle-range theory to delineate more fundamental differences between inclusive and non-inclusive schools. Similarly, there is within this discourse a concern with delineating an inclusive pedagogy. Again, this can be approached from the point of view of underlying principles derived, for instance, from theories of learning and instruction (Ware, 1995), or can simply be listed as a set of strategies that teachers can follow (Udvari-Solner, 1995; Udvari-Solner and Thousand, 1995).

Given this delineation of the characteristics of inclusive schools and pedagogies, it becomes possible to set out a series of practical steps that practitioners, managers and policy-makers can take to realize inclusion. Hence, there is a proliferation within this discourse of guides, handbooks and commentaries that conclude with series of recommendations (see, for instance, Ainscow, 1994; Sebba and Sachdev, 1997; Stainback and Stainback, 1990, 1992; Villa and Thousand, 1995; Villa et al., 1992). Such guides represent a technicization of what, in the political discourse, is seen as a matter of conflict and struggle. In other words, the realization of inclusion is seen, not (or not simply) as something that has to be fought for, but as something that results from taking the 'right' sort of action at different levels of policy-making and implementation.

Relating the discourses

If this analysis of thinking within the field of inclusive education has any validity, it begs, I believe, an important question – how, precisely, do the different discourses relate to one another? Is there a unified body of inquiry advancing steadily within a coherent field, or do we have, rather, what Paul and Ward (1996) characterize as 'paradigms in conflict' – four separate discourses constructing inclusion in four quite different ways, with chaotic consequences?

My answer to this question is two-fold. At one level, there is no doubt that the literature on inclusion is characterized by a good deal of eclecticism, in that commentators tend to borrow arguments at will from within each of the discourses. Some of this eclecticism is rigorous, in that the arguments are mutually supportive, particularly when they are drawn from different dimensions. It is, for instance, entirely consistent to argue that inclusion is at one and the same time a right, and something that must be realized through political struggle. Similarly, there are a few instances of arguments from opposite poles of the *same* dimension being presented together. In these cases, commentators have to argue that the apparent contradictions between them are illusory. Skrtic's (1991b) argument that 'equity' is 'the way to excellence' – that inclusive schools produce excellent outcomes for all students, because they are prepared to respond to individual characteristics in an equitable manner – is perhaps the *locus classicus* of such thinking.

However, I believe it has to be admitted that there is some eclecticism within the inclusion literature that is of a much less rigorous variety, and generates the sorts of ambiguities identified at the beginning of this chapter. Moreover, there is, I suggest, a danger in all attempts to assimilate the four discourses of inclusion into a single homogenous discourse. Inclusion is different from many other fields of inquiry in that it is premised on an answer rather than a question. That 'answer', of course, is that inclusive education is superior in one or other way to non-inclusive education.

The strength in this position is that it enables a relatively young field to define and advance itself in the face of considerable hostility. Indeed, it is doubtful if inclusion would have made so much impact on the education policies of so many countries if it had been less certain of its answer. The danger, however, is that it becomes all too easy for thinking on inclusion to descend from analysis to polemic, and for certain values and beliefs to become ossified,

ultimately to the detriment of those marginalized groups in whose interests
the inclusion movement claims to act. This is, perhaps, particularly important
since inclusion has differentiated itself from its liberal predecessors (such as
'integration' or 'mainstreaming') by, amongst other things, a particular emphasis on the discourse of ethics and rights (Thomas, 1997). There is, therefore,
a possibility that the ethics and rights discourse will come to dominate other
discourses, within which inclusion might be constructed, and which will thus
effectively stifle debate within this field.

I have argued elsewhere (Clark, Dyson and Millward, 1995) that the way to
avoid this danger is neither to isolate commentary within somewhat separate
discourses, nor to homogenize those discourses through a superficial eclecticism, but rather to seek out rigorous and reputable ways of enabling the different discourses to inform each other. One way to do this is to recognize the
extent to which the different discourses construct different notions of inclusion, and to pursue different implications arising from those notions. It then
becomes possible to interrogate one notion of inclusion in terms of another, in
order to find the limitations of each and open up possibilities for new ways of
thinking. This is not an easy task, since different discourses do not always contain equally explicit notions of inclusion. None the less, it is a first step towards
a mutual interrogation.

Interrogating inclusions

One way to understand the differences between discourses is to consider the
very different questions that they make it possible to ask about schools and education systems. The discourses of ethics and politics, for instance, lead to
questions about whether a particular school or system is an ethical institution,
how far it protects and realizes the rights of its students, and how power is distributed and used within it. Their principal concern is with what Barton
(1997), following Kemmis (1994), calls 'the socially just school'. The discourses
of efficacy and pragmatics, on the other hand, make it possible to ask questions about the outcomes from schools and education systems. Those outcomes may be in terms of pupil attainment, or improved community relations,
or enhanced learning experiences, but they are essentially things that are *produced* by the school rather than what the school inherently *is*.

These differences have a number of implications. First, because they interrogate schools and systems in somewhat different ways, they may well point
towards very different forms of inclusive schooling. Some critics of notions of
inclusion arising out of the ethical discourse, for instance, suggest that its only
concern is with 'place' – in other words, that an inclusive school is one in
which disabled children are *placed*, rather than one in which they receive appropriate services or a stimulating education (Baker and Zigmond, 1995;
Gerber, 1996; Zigmond and Baker, 1995, 1996). Barton (1997) explicitly rejects

this charge, but his defence of an ethics- and rights-oriented version of the inclusive school is illuminating. 'Education for all, ' he argues,

> involves a serious commitment to the task of identifying, challenging and contributing to the removal of injustices. Part of this task involves a self-critical analysis of the role schools play in the production and reproduction of injustices such as disabling barriers of various forms. Schools need therefore to be welcoming institutions. It is more than mere questions of access that are at stake here. It is a quest for the removal of policies and practices of exclusion and the realization of effective participatory democracy. It also involves a wider concern, that of clarifying the role of schools in combating institutional discrimination in relation to, for instance, the position of disabled people in society. (p 234)

Although this position is by no means reducible to a concern simply with 'place', it is, none the less, a definition of the inclusive school that has remarkably little to say about what such schools look like, how they are organized, what pedagogies are deployed within them, and so on. Inclusion is defined not by the *presence* of particular pedagogical practices and organizational forms, but by the *absence* of injustice, discrimination, exclusionary barriers and so on. Such definitions are, of course, quite different from those arising from the efficacy and pragmatics discourses, which, as we have seen, are likely to be highly detailed and prescriptive in the areas where Barton remains silent.

These differences are further highlighted when we see how commentators drawing on different discourses offer different critiques of attempts to realize inclusive principles in schools and education systems. Booth (1995; Booth, Ainscow and Dyson, 1997), for instance, has applied the sorts of 'critical analysis' Barton advocates to apparently inclusive schools, and has powerfully revealed the extent to which exclusionary processes remain constantly at work within such schools. Similarly, a number of commentators have analysed national and local inclusion policies, and uncovered the extent to which the surface appearance of inclusiveness serves only to conceal the continued operation of vested and exclusionary interests (Ballard, 1996; Fulcher, 1989; Sayed and Carrim, 1998; Slee, 1996b).

From a more efficacy-oriented perspective, a series of commentators (Baker and Zigmond, 1995; Diamond, 1995; Fuchs and Fuchs, 1994; Gerber, 1995; Reynolds, 1995; Zigmond and Baker, 1995, 1996) have argued that forms of inclusion that apparently deliver children's rights to inclusion may also, at the same time, provide those children with inferior educational experiences. To take a specific example, Baker and Zigmond's critique of inclusion as mere placement is accompanied by a notion that children with learning difficulties should be provided, not merely with non-exclusive, barrier-free schooling, but also with something that is recognizably 'special'; that is to say, they should be offered a pedagogy and form of school organization that is carefully tailored to their individual characteristics.

These critiques beg the question whether inclusion in the ethical and rights sense is tightly or loosely coupled (Weick, 1976) to inclusion in the efficacy sense. Put crudely, the question is: must a school that is truly 'just' necessarily produce good outcomes for its most vulnerable pupils, and must a school producing those outcomes also necessarily be just? Skrtic (1991b) would argue for this form of tight coupling. However, it is at least possible that the 'ethical' and 'educational' orders of a school (or education system) might be sufficiently loosely coupled for them to have to be addressed distinctly, if not separately, in any move towards inclusion. Under these circumstances, it perhaps makes sense to talk not of inclusion, but of *inclusions*, and to seek not a single form of 'inclusive school' so much as a wide range of practice and organization, which needs constantly to be interrogated in terms of the different notions of inclusion that are available.

This notion of a multiplicity of inclusions gains strength, I suggest, from an examination of the concepts of social justice implied by different forms of inclusion. Barton (1997), in the passage cited above, makes an explicit link between educational inclusion and wider notions of social justice. For him, as for many others drawing on the ethics discourse, the inclusive school is both a microcosm of, and a pathway towards, an inclusive society. Moreover, that society is inclusive not in the sense that a 'normal' majority tolerates the presence of 'abnormal' minorities in its midst. Rather, society is *structurally* inclusive, in the sense that it is a genuinely 'participatory democracy' in which difference is celebrated rather than tolerated, and social arrangements are such that minorities are not excluded at any point from social and political participation.

Not surprisingly, there is less explicit articulation of principles of social justice within the efficacy discourse. None the less, the concern with efficacy itself implies a particular view of the just society. If it matters that children receive an appropriate education, that their attainments increase, that they become part of a welcoming community, and so on, then, by implication, the just society is one which educates its children, in which all amass a certain intellectual capital, and in which all feel a sense of belonging. It may well be that this view of social justice is congruent with that which arises from the ethics discourse; however, this is by no means certain. It appears – without further explication by commentators, appearances are all we have to go on – to be the distributive form of social justice, which is explicitly rejected by some commentators from within an ethical and rights perspective (Slee, 1996a; Thomas, 1997). In other words, the accumulation of social goods, albeit on an equitable basis, is not identical with the creation of a participatory and barrier-free society, which is advocated by Barton and others drawing on an ethical and rights discourse. Be that as it may, the point is that there are multiple versions of social justice that might arise from different discourses within inclusive education, and the current, rather limited attempts to explicate the relationship of inclusion and justice (see, for instance, contributors to Christensen and Rizvi, 1996; Thomas 1997) urgently need to be extended. The issue for us is simply that the relationship between inclusion and social justice is by no means self-evident, and that a debate needs to be had in this area.

The issue of social justice leads on to a final observation in respect of the interaction between discourses: different discourses construct the 'target group' for inclusion differently. In one sense, of course, inclusive education has no target group, since *all* children are to be included in regular schools. However, there are children who are currently excluded from, or at risk of exclusion from, such schools, and these constitute the target group, in the sense that some specific action is needed in order to ensure their inclusion. The way that this target group is defined is, to a significant extent, a function of the different discourses within which it is defined. For instance, if inclusion is seen to be primarily a matter of human rights, then the target group are those whose rights are currently denied. If, on the other hand, inclusion is a matter of efficacy, then the target group are those for whom current educational arrangements are not efficacious. Similarly, if inclusion is realized through political struggle, then the target group are those who can be included as the result of such a struggle. And if inclusion requires some sort of practical educational development, then the target group are those whose inclusion becomes possible through changes in educational practice.

These differing definitions have some important implications. For instance, some commentators have presented the struggle for inclusion as part of the wider struggle by disabled people for their rights, analogous to the struggle by other marginalized groups (such as ethnic and sexual minorities) to secure equal rights in the face of an 'oppressive' society. In the case of disabled children, the discourses of rights and of political struggle may make a great deal of sense. The issue for these children is not that there are insuperable educational problems in the way of educating them in regular schools, but that schools and education systems exclude them as a matter of policy, perhaps in the supposed interests of resource efficiency, or of maintaining the *status quo* of practice and organization in regular education. Given that some schools and systems manage to include these children, their exclusion comes down to a matter of political will and it is, therefore, not unreasonable to assume that a political struggle will put the situation right.

Such considerations, however, do not necessarily hold good for other potential target groups for inclusion. If the central issue in inclusion is one of efficacy, the appropriate target groups are those for whom regular education is not efficacious – that is, those in respect of whom it fails to produce outcomes that are held to be desirable. This certainly includes children who are physically excluded from regular schools by virtue of their disabilities, but it is not restricted to this group. There are many other groups who have a right of access to regular schools, but who receive what one Chief Inspector of Schools in England called a 'shoddy' deal from those schools (Inspectorate, 1990). Such children may be disaffected, or long-term non-attenders, or find learning in regular classrooms difficult, or follow a travelling life-style, or speak a language

other than the language of instruction, or fail to thrive in regular education for
some other reason.

As Booth (1995, 1996, 1998) points out, such groups tend to remain invisible
in discourses of rights and struggle that privilege issues around disability. For
them, the discourse of rights is only partially appropriate. The issue is not that
their right of access to regular schools is denied; rather, it is that the structures
and practices of regular schools fail, for a variety of reasons, to deliver educational experiences in which those groups can fully participate, and from
which they can fully benefit. It follows, of course, that the discourse of political
struggle is also only partially appropriate. Whilst it may be a necessary condition of their inclusion that such a struggle take place, in order that their situation be acknowledged, it is not a *sufficient* condition. A number of genuine
pragmatic issues – issues to do with curriculum, pedagogy, school organization, responses to behaviour difficulties, and so on – have to be resolved if inclusion for these groups is to be meaningful.

Beyond inclusion

I have attempted to show through this analysis that there are different discourses within the inclusive education movement – at least as it is represented
in the literature – and that certain crucial aspects of inclusion are constructed
somewhat differently by these discourses. Particularly significant is the difference between the ethics and rights discourse on the one hand and the efficacy
discourse on the other. The complex differences between the constructions
that emerge from those discourses might be summed up as follows:

1. *The ethics and rights discourse*, particularly when it is joined by the politics
   discourse, tends to operate with a concept of social justice that is based on
   the notion of a participatory democracy in which none are excluded or
   oppressed, and which celebrates difference; it is interested primarily in
   the ethical and political order of the inclusive school as a microcosm of,
   and pathway towards, that society, and has relatively little to say about the
   detail of educational structures and practices; and it focuses attention on
   those social groups that are excluded from full social participation.
2. *The efficacy discourse*, particularly when it is joined by the pragmatics discourse, operates with an implicit model of social justice as equitable access
   to social goods; it is interested in the 'educational' order of the inclusive
   school and has much to say, therefore, about the practical matters of educational organization and practice; and it focuses attention on those
   groups who do not currently have effective access to social goods.

However crude and inadequate this summary is, it has, I suggest, some major
implications for the way we view inclusion, and for the way in which thinking
and inquiry in this field develop. Inclusion is not a monolithic concept; there

are multiple versions of inclusion, so that it makes sense to talk about 'inclusions', in the plural. It follows that some dialogue between these inclusions is necessary if thinking and practice around inclusive education is to become coherent, let alone if it is to develop. Moreover, this dialogue cannot be restricted to single issues, such as the characteristics of 'the inclusive school'. Constructions of inclusion imply different notions, not simply of what schools should look like, but also of what constitutes exclusion, of who are the excluded groups, of the rationale for and purposes of inclusion, and, indeed, of what is meant by the 'just society'. Currently, commentaries generated within different discourses tend to shy away from exploring one or other of these implications. The dialogue needed, therefore, will not only have to be wide-ranging, but will also require commentators to pursue the implications of their ideas to the full, instead of remaining within familiar territory.

Finally, it is by no means certain that such a dialogue will leave thinking about diversity in education at its current resting point, beneath the aegis of 'inclusion'. There is no doubt that inclusion has proved – and continues to prove – a powerful rallying-cry around which commentators, practitioners, policy-makers and users of the education system can unite. Certainly, it has opened up forms of practice and inquiry that might otherwise have remained closed and inaccessible. However, there is, I believe, a real danger that inclusion will become the prison that confines inquiry and practice, rather than the key that releases them. If a dialogue of 'inclusions' does not take place, inclusion may become an empty slogan, reduced, perhaps, to a basic concern with 'place'. It may, moreover, come to be dominated by one or other of its available forms, paradoxically to the exclusion of all others; certainly, this is what some believe is already happening (Fuchs and Fuchs, 1994). In democratic societies, notions of what schools should be like, of what education is for, of who is most vulnerable, and of how social arrangements are made more just are inevitably dynamic. There is, as Skrtic (1995) points out, a democratic process of constructing and reconstructing our responses to these issues, to which the inclusion movement has, thus far, given considerable impetus. We now need to ensure that inclusion itself is deconstructed and reconstructed in such a way that it does not become a barrier to the continuation of that process.

References

Abberley, P. (1987) 'The concept of oppression and the development of a social theory of disability', *Disability, Handicap and Society*, 2 (1), pp 5–19

Ainscow, M. (1994) *Special Needs in the Classroom: A Teacher Education Guide*, Jessica Kingsley Publishers/UNESCO Publishing, London

Ainscow, M. (1997) 'Towards inclusive schooling', *British Journal of Special Education*, 24 (1), pp 3–6

Audit Commission and HM Inspectorate (1992) *Getting in on the Act: Provision for Pupils with Special Educational Needs: the National Picture*, HMSO, London

Baker, J. M. and Zigmond, N. (1995) 'The meaning and practice of inclusion for students with learning disabilities: Themes and implications from the five cases', *Journal of Special Education*, 29 (2), pp 163–80

Ballard K (1994) 'Disability: an introduction', in K. Ballard (ed) *Disability, Family, Whanau and Society*, The Dunmore Press, Palmerston North

Ballard, K. (1995) 'Inclusion, paradigms, power and participation', in C. Clark, A. Dyson and A. Millward (eds), *Towards Inclusive Schools?*, David Fulton, London

Ballard, K. (1996) 'Inclusive education in New Zealand', *Cambridge Journal of Education*, 26 (1), pp 33–45

Barton L (1994) 'Disability, difference and the politics of definition', *Australian Disability Review*, 3 (94), pp 8–22

Barton, L. (1997) 'Inclusive education: romantic, subversive or realistic?', *International Journal of Inclusive Education*, 1 (3), pp 231–42.

Barton, L. and Tomlinson, S. (ed) (1981) *Special Education: Policy, Practices and Social Issues*, Harper and Row, London

Barton, L. and Tomlinson, S. (ed) (1984) *Special Education and Social Interests*, Croom Helm, London

Bernstein, B. (1970, 26 February 1970) 'Education cannot compensate for society', *New Society*, pp 344–7

Booth, T. (1995) 'Mapping inclusion and exclusion: Concepts for all?, in C. Clark, A. Dyson and A. Millward (eds), *Towards Inclusive Schools?* David Fulton, London

Booth, T. (1996) 'A perspective on inclusion from England', *Cambridge Journal of Education*, 26 (1), pp 87–99

Booth, T. (1998) 'The poverty of special education: theories to the rescue?', in C. Clark, A. Dyson and A. Millward (eds) *Theorising Special Education*, Routledge, London

Booth, T., Ainscow, M. and Dyson, A. (1997) 'Understanding inclusion and exclusion in the English competitive education system', *International Journal of Inclusive Education*, 1 (4), pp 337–54

Bourdieu, P. and Passeron, J. (1977) *Reproduction in Education, Society and Culture*, Sage, London

Bowles, S. and Gintis, H. (1976) *Schooling in Capitalist America*, Routledge and Kegan Paul, London

Carroll, H. M. C. (1972) 'The remedial teaching of reading: an evaluation', *Remedial Education*, 7 (1), pp 10–15

Christensen, C. and Rizvi, F. (ed) (1996) *Disablity and the Dilemmas of Education and Justice*, Open University Press, Buckingham

Clark, C., Dyson, A. and Millward, A. (1995) 'Towards inclusive schools: Mapping the field', in C. Clark, A. Dyson and A. Millward (eds), *Towards Inclusive Schools?*, David Fulton, London

Collins, J. E. (1972) 'The Remedial Education hoax', *Remedial Education*, 7 (3), pp 9–10

Coopers and Lybrand (1996) *The SEN Initiative: Managing Budgets for Pupils with Special Educational Needs: Management Summary*, The SEN Initiative, London

Department for Education and Employment (DfEE) (1997) *Excellence for All Children*, DfEE, London

Diamond, S. C. (1995) 'Special education and the great god, inclusion', in J. M. Kauffman and D. P. Hallahan (eds), *The Illusion of Full Inclusion: A Comprehensive Critique of a Current Special Education Bandwagon*, PRO-ED, Austin, TX

Floud, J. E., Halsey, A. H. and Martin, F. M. (1956) *Social Class and Educational Opportunity*, Heinemann, London

Fuchs, D. and Fuchs, L. S. (1994) 'Inclusive schools movement and the radicalization of special education reform', *Exceptional Children*, 60 (4), pp 294–309

Fulcher, G. (1989) *Disabling Policies? A Comparative Approach to Education Policy and Disability*,

Falmer Press, Lewes

Fulcher, G. (1993) 'Schools and contests: a reframing of the effective schools debate?', in R. Slee (ed), *Is there a Desk With My Name On It? The Politics of Integration*, Falmer Press, London

Fulcher, G. (1995) 'Excommunicating the severely disabled: struggles, policy and researching', in P. Clough and L. Barton (eds), *Making Difficulties: Research and the Construction of Special Educational Needs*, Paul Chapman Publishing, London

Galloway, D. and Goodwin, C. (1987) *The Education of Disturbing Children: Pupils with Learning and Adjustment Difficulties*, Longman, London

Gartner, A. and Lipsky, D. K. (1989) *The Yoke of Special Education: How to Break it*, National Center of Education and the Economy, Rochester, NY

Gerber, M. (1996) 'Reforming special education: beyond "inclusion"', in C. Christensen and F. Rizvi (eds), *Disability and the Dilemmas of Education and Justice*, Open University Press, Milton Keynes

Gerber, M. M. (1995) 'Inclusion at the high-water mark? Some thoughts on Zigmond and Baker's case studies of inclusive educational programs', *Journal of Special Education*, 29 (2), pp 181–91

HM Inspectorate (1990) *Standards in Education, 1988–89: The Annual Report of HM Senior Chief Inspector of Schools*, DES, London

Kamin, L. J. (1977) *The Science and Politics of IQ*, Penguin Books, Harmondsworth

Kauffman, J. K. and Hallahan, D. P. (eds) (1995) *The Illusion of Full Inclusion*, PRO-ED, Austin, TX

Kemmis, S. (1994) *School Reform in the '90s: Reclaiming Social Justice*, The Flinders University of South Australia, Adelaide

Lewis, I. and Vulliamy, G. (1980) 'Warnock or warlock? The sorcery of definitions: the limitations of the report on special education', *Educational Review*, 32 (1), pp 3–10

Lipsky, D. K. and Gartner, A. (1996) 'Equity requires inclusion: the future for all students with disabilities', in C. Christensen and F. Rizvi (eds), *Disability and the Dilemmas of Education and Justice*, Open University Press, Buckingham

Lipsky, D. K. and Gartner, A. (1997) *Inclusion and School Reform: Transforming America's classrooms*, Paul H. Brookes, Baltimore

Lovell, K., Johnson, E. and Platts, D. (1962) 'A summary of a study of the reading ages of children who had been given remedial teaching', *British Journal of Educational Psychology*, 32, pp 66–71

Oliver, M. (1992a) 'Changing the social relations of research production?' *Disability and Society*, 7 (2), pp 101–14

Oliver, M. (1992b) 'Intellectual masturbation: a rejoinder to Soder and Booth', *European Journal of Special Needs Education*, 7 (1), pp 20–28

Paul, P. V. and Ward, M. E. (1996) 'Inclusion paradigms in conflict', *Theory into Practice*, 35 (1), pp 4–11

Peters, S. (1995) 'Disability baggage: changing the education research terrain', in P. Clough and L. Barton (eds), *Making Difficulties: Research and the Construction of Special Educational Needs*, Paul Chapman Publishing, London

Pijl, S. J., Meijer, C. J. W. and Hegarty, S. (ed) (1997) *Inclusive Education: A global agenda*, Routledge, London

Reynolds, D. (1995) 'Using school effectiveness knowledge for children with special needs – the problems and possibilities', in C. Clark, A. Dyson and A. Millward (eds), *Towards Inclusive Schools?*, David Fulton, London

Reynolds, D. and Farrell, S. (1996) *Worlds Apart? A Review of International Surveys of Educational Achievement Involving England*, OFSTED, London

Rouse, M. and Florian, L. (1996) 'Effective inclusive schools: A study in two countries', *Cambridge Journal of Education*, 26 (1), pp 71–85

Sayed, Y. and Carrim, N. (1998) 'Inclusiveness and participation in discourses of educational governance in South Africa', *International Journal of Inclusive Education*, 2 (1), pp 29–43

Sebba, J. and Sachdev, D. (1997) *What Works in Inclusive Education*, Barnardos, Ilford

Skrtic, T. M. (1991a) *Behind Special Education: A Critical Analysis of Professional Culture and School Organization*, Love, Denver

Skrtic, T. M. (1991b) 'The special education paradox: equity as the way to excellence', *Harvard Educational Review*, 61 (2), pp 148–206

Skrtic, T. M. (1991c) 'Students with special educational needs: artifacts of the traditional curriculum', in M. Ainscow (ed.), *Effective Schools for All*, David Fulton, London

Skrtic, T. M. (ed) (1995) *Disability and Democracy: Reconstructing (Special) Education for Postmodernity*, Teachers College Press, New York

Slee, R. (1995) *Changing Theories and Practices of Discipline*, Falmer Press, London

Slee, R. (1996a) 'Disability, class and poverty: school structures and policing identities', in F. Rizvi and C. Christensen (eds), *Disability and the Dilemmas of Education and Justice*, Open University Press, Milton Keynes

Slee, R. (1996b) 'Inclusive education in Australia? Not yet!', *Cambridge Journal of Education*, 26 (1), pp 19–32

Slee, R. (1998) 'The politics of theorising special education', in C. Clark, A. Dyson and A. Millward (eds), *Theorising Special Education*, Routledge, London

Sleeter, C. E. (1986) 'Learning disabilities: the social construction of a special education category', *Exceptional Children*, 53 (1), pp 46–54

Stainback, W. and Stainback, S. (eds) (1990) *Support Networks for Inclusive Schooling*, Paul H. Brookes, Baltimore

Stainback, S. and Stainback, W. (eds) (1992) *Curriculum Considerations in Inclusive Classrooms: Facilitating Learning for all Students*, Paul H. Brookes, Baltimore

Susman, J. (1994) 'Disability, stigma and deviance', *Social Science and Medicine*, 38 (1), pp 15–22

Thomas, G. (1997) 'Inclusive schools for an inclusive society', *British Journal of Special Education*, 24 (3) pp. 103–07

Thomas, G., Walker, D. and Webb, J. (1998) *The Making of the Inclusive School*, Routledge, London

Tomlinson, S. (1982) *A Sociology of Special Education*, Routledge and Kegan Paul, London

Tomlinson, S. (1985) 'The expansion of special education', *Oxford Review of Education*, 11 (2), pp 157–65

Udvari-Solner, A. (1995) 'A process for adapting curriculum in inclusive classrooms', in R. A. Villa and J. S. Thousand (eds), *Creating an Inclusive School*, ASCD, Alexandria, VA

Udvari-Solner, A. and Thousand, J. (1995) 'Effective organizational, instructional and curricular practices in inclusive schools and classrooms', in C. Clark, A. Dyson and A. Millward (eds), *Towards Inclusive Schools?*, David Fulton, London

UNESCO (1994) *The Salamanca Statement and Framework on Special Needs Education*, UNESCO, Paris

Villa, R. and Thousand, J. S. (eds) (1995) *Creating an Inclusive School*, Association for Supervision and Curriculum Development, Alexandria, VA

Villa, R. A., Thousand, J. S., Stainback, W. and Stainback, S. (eds) (1992) *Restructuring for Caring and Effective Education: An Administrative Guide to Creating Heterogeneous Schools*, Paul H. Brookes, Baltimore

Vlachou, A. D. (1997) *Struggles for Inclusive Education: An Ethnographic Study*, Open University Press, Buckingham

Ware, L. (1995) 'The aftermath of the articulate debate: the invention of inclusive education', in C. Clark, A. Dyson and A. Millward (eds), *Towards Inclusive Schools?*, David Fulton, London

Weick, K. E. (1976) 'Educational organizations as loosely coupled systems', *Administrative*

Science Quarterly, 21, pp 1–19

Ysseldyke, J. E., Algozzine, B. and Epps, S. (1983) 'A logical and empirical analysis of current practice in classifying students as handicapped', *Exceptional Children*, 50, pp 160–66

Zigmond, N. and Baker, J. M. (1995) 'Concluding comments: Current and future practices in inclusive schooling, *Journal of Special Education*, 29 (2), pp 245–50

Zigmond, N. and Baker, J. M. (1996) 'Full inclusion for students with learning disabilities: Too much of a good thing?', *Theory into Practice*, 35 (1), pp 26–34

4. Market ideologies, education and the challenge for inclusion

Len Barton

Introduction

The topic of this paper is a very serious one and I am conscious of the dangers of approaching it in a sterile, obtuse and dispassionate manner. My stance is, thus, one of anger and moral indignation, and expresses 'an attitude' (Ladwig, 1996). It partly derives from a recognition that the impact of market-ideology on the governance, process and outcomes of education has been to establish a more hierarchical, status-ridden, selective system, in which exclusionary policies and practices have become more prominent. And this question of social exclusion is not solely applicable to the area of education. It is a feature of the welfare and social system generally (Walker and Walker, 1997).

Another factor influencing my stance concerns my critical attitude towards those individualistic within-the-person explanations that have been a powerful force in the field of 'special education'. They have significantly informed policies and practices which legitimate deficit models and dependency-sustaining relations between professional bodies and disabled people. This form of atomized thinking has failed to engage with the deep structural socio-economic conditions and relations of society, which maintain divisive inequalities, discriminations and exclusionary practices. It is important, therefore, to recognize that education cannot be viewed in a vacuum and, as Sultana (1997) contends,

> schooling cannot be divorced from the wider social order, and schools and educators are not and cannot be 'neutral' and 'apolitical' channels for equally 'neutral' and 'apolitical' knowledge. Whatever we make happen in schools – constantly and inevitably – gives messages defining what it means to be 'human', 'good' and 'normal' in particular social contexts. (pp 26–7)

This perspective reminds us that educational issues cannot be adequately understood in merely technical and resource terms. They are fundamentally social questions, involving struggles over, for example, social justice, equity and citizenship (Brown and Lauder, 1992).

New Right ideologies

Under consecutive Conservative governments a cultural and economic revolution has taken place in Britain. A new vision of the 'good society' has been articulated, involving the celebration of individualism, competition and the decentralization of planning and decision-making.

A political language has been developed influenced by free-market ideas and, as Taylor (1990) notes, has been 'constructed around notions of "choice" and the "freedom" of the market and "the rights of the individual" over and above the notions of social justice, the "community" and, indeed, of "welfare" as such' (p 5).

Through, for example, economic advisers and right-wing intellectuals writing and being interviewed on radio and television, and the tabloid press, in particular, this discourse has been tirelessly presented (Taylor, 1990). Central to this powerful discourse have been concerns over issues of policy, provision and practice in relation to questions of cost and efficiency. Coupled with this has been a strong moral component, which has sought to discredit existing social democratic values, presenting alternative ones, as part of a more general intention of introducing a new political and moral leadership in the country (Gamble, 1994).

The influence and comprehensive range of the critiques involved in this market-driven discourse are enormous. For example, the family is presented as being under threat, and its authority is assumed to be breaking down. A commitment to greater equality is viewed as both economically inefficient and morally reprehensible. Schools are depicted in terms of their failure to maintain standards and discipline, thereby reducing the nation's international competitiveness in the market place (Gamble, 1994; David, 1990; Ball, 1994).

Underpinning the drive for change is a belief that market forces are more efficient at allocating resources, more responsive to the needs of individuals, and will inevitably lead to the improvement of standards, and to more public accountability on the part of providers of services. In this new world, markets are viewed as more democratic than democracy itself (Henig, 1994).

Many of these values and intentions had a particular poignancy during the Thatcher administrations; what Hall (1980) has called 'authoritarian populism' led to the means becoming available by which the extensive restructuring of the educational system took place. It was, as Gamble (1994) so shrewdly notes,

> populist because it drew upon popular discontent with many aspects of the social democratic state to win support for a radical right programme. It was authoritarian because in the implication of its programmes it further increased the power of the state and weakened opposition to it. (p 182)

The political strategy entailed confrontational politics, and reflected the determination of a strong government to be victorious over groups, such as trade unions, that sought to question its authority, and develop alternative ideas and practices (Atkinson and Savage, 1994).

It is important to recognize that the contributory factors influencing the powerfulness of the New Right discourse included its accessibility, its self-confirming, self-evident rhetorical style and its capacity to play down questions of the social effects and costs of a market-driven system of provision and practice (Taylor, 1990).

Fundamental to the New Right approach is a belief in a free economy and a strong state. This involves both a paradox, and a reminder that the New Right does not entail a coherent, homogeneous set of ideas. The paradox is, as Gamble (1994) illustrates,

> The state is to be simultaneously rolled back and rolled forward. Non-interventionist and decentralized in some areas the state is to be highly interventionist and centralized in others. The New Right can appear by turns libertarian and authoritarian, populist and elitist. This ambiguity is not an accident. It derives in part from the fact that the New Right has two major stands: a liberal tendency, which argues the case for a freer, more open and more competitive economy, and a conservative tendency, which is more interested in restoring social and political authority throughout society. (p 36)

Both the neo-liberal and neo-conservative elements within the Conservative tradition do share some common interests. They are both critical of egalitarianism and collectivism, which they maintain have encouraged an anti-enterprise and permissive culture. They are also united in their emphasis on such themes as 'authority, tradition, stability, order, the family and morality' (Atkinson and Savage, 1994, p 7). This has provided the basis for warnings about the 'enemies within society', and the demands for returning to 'back to basics' in all aspects of civil life.

Through the activities of the New Right we have seen the mobilization of a new legitimating discourse – that of the market. The emphasis has been on the desirability of creating an enterprise culture based on free-market economic policies. Responsibilities previously equated with the welfare state must now be properly discharged privately by individuals and/or the family. In redefining what is politically acceptable, an emphasis has been given to notions of 'choice', 'efficiency', 'diversity of provision' and 'rights of the individual'. Policy programmes formulated around such concerns have been based on a fundamental assumption that 'success has to be earned through improved competitiveness' (HMSO, 1994, p 8).

It is this commitment that provides the driving force for establishing new ways of thinking about the individual and the state, and about the relationship between the two.

The State

In a paper concerned with research agendas for philosophy of education and, in particular, the contribution that the discipline can make to meta-theoretical debates, Jonathan (1998) argues that education is a peculiar and complex good. It can be understood as both a private and a public issue. In so far as education at an individual level is an exchange value for achievement and, thus, social status in a competitive ethos, it can be viewed as a *private* good. In so far as education is an institutional arrangement that brings 'collective benefit to a society as a whole in enhancing social climate and national economy, it is a *public* good' (p 81). One of the impacts of a system of policy and practice increasingly informed by economic rationality is that education is viewed as a *private* good. In terms of both the public and private dimensions, there are important disputes over the purpose and degree of the role of the state in this process.

One analyst, Neave (1988), examines the development of what he calls the 'evaluative state' through a comparative analysis of the rise of mass higher education in Western Europe. He makes a distinction between evaluation concerned with system maintenance and evaluation for strategic change. The 'evaluative state' represents a fundamental shift in the timing, purpose and location of evaluation. He contrasts *a priori* evaluation with *a posteriori* evaluation. The latter is a new and innovatory form of state activity, which 'works through the control of *product*, not through the control of process' (p 10).

Whilst this approach specifically engages with higher educational issues, it has very important implications for all aspects of the educational system, including schools. They include, first, a much more radical way of *steering* institutions in terms of key goals. Second, by signifying the centrality of *outcome*, the purpose of education in terms of the economy is given a much more privileged position. Finally, this perspective introduces a different way of *conceiving* 'quality' and 'social justice'.

The education context

The system of educational provision and the values underpinning it have been the subject of a most radical transformation. This powerful programme of change has been directed at the governance, content and outcome of all aspects of the educational system. The role of undemocratically elected quangos and extensive legislation have been influential in this process of policy creation and implementation.

The impact of marketization on schools can be seen, for example, in the following changes:

- increased diversity of school provision;
- the introduction of the local management of schools;

- opting-out opportunities;
- the changing nature of governing bodies;
- the published league tables of examination results and low truancy rates;
- the reduction of the role of LEAs in planning and decision-making;
- an emphasis on parental choice;
- changes to the financing of education;
- vouchers for pre-school nursery children;
- the intensification of competitiveness within and across institutions; and
- new forms of assessment and examination.

In research conducted in 1991–94 at the Centre for Educational Studies, at King's College, London, the focus has been on a set of specific educational networks – three clusters of secondary schools (15 in all). The research included monitoring the market behaviour of schools, conducting interviews with parents in such clusters, and collecting from LEAs the overall patterns of parental choice. The findings support the view that the principle of self-interest is increasingly driving the market system, and that existing patterns of inequalities expressed in the cultural capital of parents are influencing patterns of participation and opportunity. These include opportunities for transport, flexibility for moving house, child-care support, and extra coaching for school placement (Ball, 1994). The notion of 'parental choice' from the insights derived from this research becomes highly problematic and obfuscates major inequalities between families.

Inclusive education

Inclusive education is not integration and is not concerned with the assimilation or accommodation of discriminated groups or individuals within existing socio-economic conditions and relations. It is not about making people as 'normal' as possible. Nor is it about the well-being of a particular oppressed or excluded group. Thus, the concerns go well beyond those of disablement. Inclusive education is not an end in itself, but a means to an end – the creation and maintenance of an inclusive society. As such, the interest is with all citizens, their well-being and security. This is a radical conception, not satisfied with piecemeal, short-term reforms. It is ultimately about the transformation of a society and its formal institutional arrangements, such as education. This means change in the values, priorities and policies that support and perpetuate practices of exclusion and discrimination (Barnes, 1991; Oliver, 1995).

The desire for an inclusive society and educational system is motivated by a deeply held, informed conviction that discrimination is a stubborn and long-standing feature of a society based on inequalities and disadvantage. In an analysis of the past two decades in British society, Walker (1997) provides an important definition of social exclusion:

[it is]…the dynamic process of being shut out, fully or partially, from any of the social, economic, political and cultural systems which determine the so-cial integration of a person in society. Social exclusion may, therefore, be seen as the denial (or non-realization) of the civil, political and social rights of citizenship. (p 8)

The collection of papers in Walker's book support the proposition that, during the past two decades, inequalities, discrimination and poverty have been ex-acerbated, and that 'a narrow focus on economic efficiency and economic growth will not solve problems such as poverty and social exclusion but, rather, will make them worse'. (p 11)

This harrowing perspective is a reminder that there is no single, 'quick-fix' solution to these stubborn, long-standing inequalities. Within education, as Mortimer and Whitty (1997) maintain, those who come from families that are disadvantaged, and have most to gain, are those who most experience the stigma and exclusion of failure. Education has a part to play in combating in-justice and discrimination both within and outside the educational system. However, it cannot carry out this task alone; new alliances and creative rela-tionships with parents, the community and wider organizations will be neces-sary if these problems are to be overcome.

The struggle for inclusive education involves an identification, challenge and removal of all forms of barriers to participation, including social, cultural, ideological and physical factors. Armstrong (1998) maintains that schools are crucially involved in the generation and regeneration of social differences and stereotypes. This, she argues, is powerfully exemplified in the ways in which *space* within schools is designed and divided up, and thus contributes to the practice of exclusion based on negative conceptualizations of difference. The curriculum, she contends, is given a particular cultural space, a privileged po-sition.

The processes by which this position is maintained and legitimated are complex and contradictory and open to resistance and challenge by teachers and pupils. Part of that challenge needs to take place over particular categories within the official discourse that are routinely used to define pupils. The indi-vidual is enveloped by a label such as 'special needs pupil' or 'disruptive pu-pil'. Thus, pupils take up specific social spaces informed by the labels attached to them.

From this perspective, the historical significance of segregated special schooling set within distinct physical spaces can be viewed as representing the disabling barriers within a society. Such provisions and practices have le-gitimated reciprocal ignorance between disabled and non-disabled peers, leading to various forms of stereotypes, suspicion and fear (Morris, 1990).

Empowerment and the social context

An inclusive society is concerned with the issue of empowering individuals, and engaging in constructive ways with the question of power. Critical theorists such as Giroux and McLaren in the United States have provided a range of ideas relating to the question of the nature of empowerment and the pedagogical task. To 'empower' can be understood in terms of something being given, conferred and even taken away. In a discussion of the empowering impact of critical pedagogy, McLaren (1995) contends that

> it is a praxis that seeks to engage history with the intent of helping the powerless locate themselves in it…In other words, we need to resituate the challenge of teaching as a task of empowering the powerless from states of dependency and passivity as both an informed movement for revolutionary social and economic transformation and as areas of achieving what Brian Fay (1987) calls a 'state of reflective clarity'. (p 23)

Such a perspective has been criticized, for attributing extraordinary abilities to the teacher, for its failure adequately to address the work context of teachers, and for its over-reliance on the assumed power of critical discourse. In a critique of such ideas, and through an exploration of the position of Foucault with regard to the notion of power, Gore (1992) raises some further important issues. Refuting the idea that power can be *given*, she maintains that, 'When the agent of empowerment assumes to be already empowered, and so apart from those who are to be empowered, arrogance can underlie claims of "what we can do for you"'. (p 61)

Gore argues that power needs to be conceived as being *exercised* in an attempt to help others exercise power. This requires attention being given to the micro aspects of interactions and the importance of context. This, she contends, should involve a greater reflexivity and degree of humility with regard to 'what we can do for others'.

The discourse of empowerment tends to be presented in a romantic and context-free manner. For those concerned with the desire for an inclusive society, and with the position of excluded people and our relationship to them, Gore's analysis is a timely reminder of the need for greater self-criticism and humility.

Conclusion

Essential to a democratic participatory process of social interaction is the encouragement and opportunity to debate issues relating to the well-being both of the individual and the society as a whole. This form of engagement requires the development of sensitive listening skills, openness, humility and a willingness of all involved to acknowledge mistakes and/or the limitation of their own position. Part of overcoming dogmatism and exclusiveness will involve a recognition that all of us are *learners* and thus 'do not possess all the answers, are aware of the complexities of social reality and are confused or uncertain about many significant issues' (Lawn and Barton, 1981, p. 248).

The task involved in the struggle for an inclusive society is a difficult and urgent one. We cannot afford to be complacent and part of the process of change will involve risk-taking. Several important questions arising from this brief overview are examples of the issues that need to be debated. They include (in no particular order of priority) the following.

- Is there a difference between 'integration' and 'inclusion'?
- To what extent is inclusive education a human rights issue?
- How should we educate teachers and what rights and entitlements should they enjoy?
- What do we mean by 'teaching to diversity' and is this a requirement of all teachers?
- How useful is it to conceive of education in terms of a 'market'?
- Does a market-led policy of provision and practice encourage exclusionary values and demands?
- In what ways and why is the issue of difference central to an inclusive perspective?

Many voices have been excluded from participating in discussions and decisions over issues affecting the quality of their lives. Historically, disabled people have been part of an oppressed group who have experienced the indignity, frustration and dehumanization of being treated as an inferior, less-than-human species. The pursuit of an inclusive society is concerned with issues of equity and non-discrimination, in which the good of *all* citizens is a central commitment. By setting the issue of disability and all forms of oppression within a human rights perspective, the possibilities for the realization of a society based on community, solidarity and in which difference can be viewed in dignified ways, becomes much stronger.

Acknowledgement

I am grateful to Felicity Armstrong for her comments on an earlier draft of this paper.

References

Armstrong, F. (1998) 'Inclusion, Curriculum and the Struggle for Cultural Space', *International Journal of Inclusive Education*, 3 (3)

Atkinson, R. and Savage, S. (1994) 'The Conservatives and public policy', in S. Savage, R.

Atkinson and L. Robins, (eds) *Public Policy in Britain*, Macmillan, Basingstoke

Ball, S. J. (1994) *Education Reform: A Critical and Post-Structural Approach*, Open University Press, Buckingham

Barnes, C. (1991) *Disabled People in Britain and Discrimination: A Case for Anti-Discrimination Legislations*, Hurst and Company, London

Brown, P. and Lauder, H. (1992) 'Education, economy and security: an introduction to a new agenda', in P. Brown and H. Lauder (eds) *Education for Economic Survival: From Fordism to Post-Fordism?*, Routledge, London

David, M. (1990) 'Looking after the cubs: Women and 'work' in the decade of Thatcherism', in I. Taylor (ed.) *The Social Effects of Free Market Policies: An International Text*, Harvester Wheatsheaf, London

Fay, B. (1987) *Critical Social Science: Liberation and its Limits*, Polity Press, Cambridge

Gamble, A. (1994) *The Free Economy and the Strong State* (2nd edn), Macmillan, Basingstoke

Gore, J. (1992) 'What we can do for you! What can 'we' do for 'you'? Struggling over empowerment in critical and feminist pedagogy', in C. Luke and J. Gore (eds) *Feminisms and Critical Pedagogy*, Routledge, New York

Hall, S. (1980) 'Popular democratic versus authoritarian populism', in A. Hunt (ed.) *Marxism and Democracy*, Lawrence and Wishart, London

Henig, J. R. (1994) *Rethinking School Choice: Limits of the Market Metaphor*, Princeton University Press, Princeton

HMSO (1994) *Competitiveness Helping Business to Win* (CM 2563), HMSO, London

Jonathan, R. (1998) 'When there are urgent concerns about education, why worry about metaphysics', in W. Bauer, W. Lippitz, W. Marotzki, J. Ruhoff, A. Schäfer and C. Wulf (eds) *Fragen nach dem Menschen in der umstrittenen Moderne*, Schneider Verlag Hohengehren GmbH

Ladwig, J. (1996) *Academic Distinctions: Theory and Methodology in the Sociology of School Knowledge*, Falmer Press, London

Lawn, M. and Barton, L. (1981) 'Curriculum politics and emancipation', in M. Lawn, and L. Barton (eds) *Rethinking Curriculum Studies*, Croom Helm, London

McLaren, P. (1995) *Critical Pedagogy and Predatory Culture: Oppositional Politics in a Post-Modern Era*, Routledge, London

Morris, J. (1990) 'Progress with humanity: The experience of a disabled lecturer', in R. Rieser and M. Mason (eds) *Disability Equality in the Classroom: A Human Rights Issue*, ILEA, London

Mortimore, P. and Whitty, G. (1997) *Can School Improvement Overcome the Effects of Disadvantage?*, Institute of Education, University of London, London

Neave, G. (1998) 'On the cultivation of quality, efficiency and enterprise: an overview of recent trends in Higher Education in Western Europe', *European Journal of Education*, 23, (1/2), pp 7–23

Oliver, M. (1995) *Understanding Disability: From Theory To Practice*, Kingsley Press, London

Sultana, R. (1997) 'Towards a Critical Sociology of Education', in R. Sultana (ed.) *Inside/Outside Schools: Towards a Critical Sociology of Education in Malta*, Publishers Enterprises Group (PEG) Ltd, Malta

Taylor, I. (1990) 'Introduction: The concept of "social cost" in free market theory and the social effects of free market policies', in I. Taylor (ed.) *The Social Effects of Free Market Policies: An International Text*, Harvester Wheatsheaf, London

Walker, A. (1997) 'Introduction: The Strategy of Inequality', in A. Walker and C. Walker (eds) *Britain Divided: The Growth of Social Exclusion in the 1980s and 1990s*, CPAG Ltd, London

Walker, A. and Walker, C. (eds) (1997) *Britain Divided: The Growth of Social Exclusion in the 1980s and 1990s*, CPAG Ltd London

Section II
Dilemmas for inclusive education

Systems in reformulation

5. England and Wales: competition and control – or stakeholding and inclusion

Gary Thomas and John Dwyfor Davies

The new inclusivity in England and Wales: what is it?

The last few years in England and Wales have seen a dramatic change in political outlook. In less than a decade, competition and aggressive meritocracy have given way to co-operation and stakeholding. Inclusivity was one of the central planks on which the Labour government, newly elected in 1997, based its election campaign, and its most recent discussion paper on the future of special education (DfEE, 1997) promotes inclusion and encourages creative thinking about inclusive education.

This new notion of inclusivity is in contrast to the predominant political ethic of the 1980s, which was given academic credence by the economic doctrines of Hayek, Friedman and others. Hargreaves (1982) saw those as a manifestation of *egoism*, which has deep roots in northern European thought. The meritocratic, individualistic and competitive thought associated with that tradition provided ample justification for segregation. By contrast, in the new philosophy, which sees all members of society as stakeholders, it is natural to see schools as places where all are welcomed, and where duty is felt to all.

It can be argued that current ideas about inclusion have their roots in the ideas of the early twentieth-century English socialists of Fabianism. Fabianism placed an emphasis on the eclectic rather than on the synthetic, concentrating on practical detailed reforms and the rejection of grandiose theoretical speculations; indeed, their ideas had much in common with those of the 'New Left'. The purpose of education, according to Sidney Webb, was to develop 'the most civilized body of citizens, in the interests of the community as a whole, developing each to the "margin of cultivation"' (cited in McBriar, 1966, p 208).

The theme of community and collective belonging is echoed by Tawney, another of the forebears of the 'New Left'. Tawney (1964) linked the notion of belonging with the question of inequality in a civilized society and his reasoning is also relevant when thinking about the organization of education. He did not deny that people are born with different abilities. However, he asserted that a civilized society strives to reduce the inequalities that arise, both from these inherited 'givens', and from the society's own organization. The organization of institutions such as schools should lighten and reduce the inequalities that arise from birth or circumstance, rather than exaggerate them: 'While [people's] natural endowments differ profoundly, it is the mark of a civilized society to aim at eliminating such inequalities as have their source, not in individual differences, but in its own organization' (Tawney, 1964, p 57).

Does this view support inclusion? Some might say not. Those who favour an education system incorporating and employing special schools might argue that special schools do succeed in reducing circumstantial differences. However, existing inequalities between children cannot be compensated for simply by the physical and teaching resources they are given at school. Those inequalities lie more importantly in the opportunity, or lack of it, to do the same as other children: to share the same spaces as other children, and to 'speak the same language' as other children. Reducing inequality is thus about more than providing money and better resources; it is, rather, about providing the chance to share in the culture of the school.

Rizvi and Lingard (1996) make the point that redistribution by itself is not sufficient to achieve social justice. Their thesis is that redistribution on its own obscures, and thereby perpetuates, injustices in existing institutional organization. Emphasizing redistribution could mean merely shifting resources into special education, and this would not achieve the changes required if social justice is to be achieved. Roaf and Bines (1989) make a similar point: an emphasis on *needs* in special education detracts from a proper consideration of the *rights* of those who are being educated.

Social justice cannot therefore be achieved simply by the redistribution of resources, based on an assessment of need. Achievement of social justice does not come about simply through the removal of inequality.

Inclusion is driven by values. The values currently shaping political thought in England and Wales have emerged in different circumstances at different times in other parts of the world – a communist local government system in Italy; the social democracy of north-west Europe, and particularly Scandinavia; the civil rights agenda in North America; and, more recently, social justice as a theme across the world. In England and Wales, new thought about social justice is expressed in the ideas of stakeholding and inclusion.

Inclusion as an ethic of organizations

Most discussion on inclusion in education concentrates on curriculum, pastoral systems, attitudes and teaching methods, but there is a further dimension to the idea, which goes beyond these school-based considerations. This is the wider notion of inclusion in British society; the notion of inclusion is not unique to education. Indeed, the recent popularity of inclusion as an idea in education probably depends at least in part on its harmony with the popular notion of an inclusive society, in which each member has a stake. Commentators (including Hutton, 1995; Kay, 1996; Plender, 1997) have begun to discuss the meaning of this new inclusiveness. There is a notion of reciprocity in their discussion – a recognition of *mutual* obligations and expectations between the community and institutions such as schools, in such a way that these institutions are reminded of their responsibilities and public duties. The duty is to the community that, as a whole, finances them, not merely to the academically inclined students.

There is an unwritten mandate in the inclusive, stakeholding ethic, says Plender (1997), to take account of social costs and benefits that are never priced in the market. In this process, the role of state and individual is downplayed, while the role of intermediate institutions (like schools) is reinforced.

These commentators have proposed some mechanisms for making stakeholding and inclusion real in a commercial environment. At the heart of these mechanisms is the requirement that managers take financial account of their actions. Behind inclusion and stakeholding is the recognition that everyone shares in both the fruits and the damage produced by society's intermediate institutions (such as businesses and schools). These institutions must be obliged therefore to pay the price – literally – for adhering to practices that are anti-social. Commercial businesses will have to take account of the hidden costs of their less acceptable practices, such as restricted opportunity for employees, pollution of the environment, or whatever. At the moment, they may create damage through these practices, without having to pay for it.

This logic applies with equal force to schools. The social costs of segregation, many disabled people would argue, are high. The cost of exclusion and segregation is the stigmatization and alienation of a section of people who would otherwise be able and willing to take a fuller part in their society. Yet, neither schools nor those who administer the education system locally have had to bear the costs of such educational exclusion. In a society in which a stakeholding ethic takes hold, there should be increasing pressure for an obligation on schools, for whom these costs have in the past been invisible, to appreciate them and pay for them.

Therefore, to the curricular and social principles that educationists may wish to see embodied in the policy and practice of a school claiming to be inclusive, a broader set of principles might be added. These principles might be imposed not only by the direct stakeholders in the school (teachers, parents and students), but also by those in the local community, and in society at large, and recognized by politicians and the legislature. They relate to what Mason (1995) calls the 'intentional building of community'.

Inclusion and assumptions about difference and 'special need'

A central difference between inclusion and integration lies in assumptions about *difference*. 'Integration' has usually been used to describe the process of the assimilation of children with learning difficulties, sensory impairments or physical disabilities into mainstream schools. In fact, following the 1981 Education Act, the use of the term 'special educational needs' has usually specifically excluded other children – for example, children whose first language is not English. The key aspect of inclusion, however, is that children who are at a disadvantage for any reason are not excluded from mainstream education. This represents a modernizing of the term 'special needs' that is surely more consistent with the spirit of the Warnock Report (DES, 1978). The Warnock Committee recommended a fluid definition of 'special need', whereby categories would be abolished, and a child's needs would be defined as and when they arose.

Children's difficulties at school may arise from a wide range of factors related to disability, language, family income, cultural origin, ethnic origin or gender, and inclusive logic implies that it is inappropriate to differentiate among these. As Young (1990) makes clear, the existence of supposed groups forces us to categorize, and the categories encourage a particular mindset about a group; in reality, the groups in question are 'cross-cutting, fluid and shifting' (p 45). Assumptions about disadvantage and oppression rest on these categorizations where, in fact, they may not be warranted.

Meekosha and Jacubowicz (1996) make the similar point that there is no discrete class of people who are disabled, and that people with disabilities are as heterogeneous as people in general. The agglomeration of all disabilities alienates disabled people from other minorities. And the stressing of a minority status emphasizes the presumed vulnerability of the group in question, rather than the inadequacies of the system, which is supposed to be supporting.

'Inclusion' does not therefore set parameters around particular kinds of supposed disability. Rather, there is a fundamental principle of acceptance behind inclusion; this principle is about providing a framework within which all children – regardless of ability, gender, language, ethnic or cultural origin – can be valued equally, treated with respect, and provided with equal opportunities at school. Accepting inclusion means moving from what Roaf (1988) has called an 'obsession with individual learning difficulties' (p 7) to an agenda of rights.

Inclusion and the comprehensive ideal in England and Wales

The comprehensive ideal has a long tradition in England and Wales. As Booth (1995) has noted, one cannot separate the struggles of those who were at the forefront in promoting integration from this comprehensive tradition. Many campaigns for integration have been about individual children – to integrate a child with Down's Syndrome in one school, or a child with cerebral palsy in another, for example – and such struggles continue to this day. The Special Educational Needs Tribunal, recently set up for England and Wales, was established partly to resolve the tensions that emerged between LEAs and parents over the placement of children.

These struggles of individual children and their parents are mostly *ad hoc* and uncoordinated challenges to the system in England and Wales, which still defends the need for substantial segregation, even of children with only 'moderate' learning difficulties or physical disabilities. However, the broader aim of helping schools to become more inclusive demands that there be responses from schools and local authorities on a more significant scale. For real inclusion, the change has to be in the system and not just in the individual school.

The difficulties with which inclusive schools currently contend are of a similar nature to those facing schools in the 1960s, as they prepared to move from selective to comprehensive schooling. At that time, the systems and curricula of the schools had to be re-thought, in order to cater for children of a broader range of ability.

In the 1960s, LEAs and schools responded to the comprehensive challenge with varying degrees of success. The changes relating to inclusion are similarly inconsistent in their degree of success, since a whole new mindset is required to make those changes. Some local authorities are, in effect, implementing only re-placement policies, where a child is moved from a special school to the mainstream, perhaps with the support of a learning support assistant. The term 'maindumping' has been used to describe the worst examples of this process – where children are moved from special schools to mainstream schools without adequate preparation or resources. Many schools, in fact, have accepted disabled children only on the basis of 'assimilation' – that is, children are welcome only if they can benefit from what is already on offer.

Some local authorities have more sophisticated schemes, in which 'outreach' support is provided by specialist teachers who visit the mainstream. Sometimes, under the guidance of a forward-thinking headteacher, a special school has moved from its special location and re-formed on the premises of its local neighbourhood school. There are some published accounts of such developments – Wilson (1990), the head of a school for children with severe learning difficulties, describes just such a development; 'Bishopswood' (CSIE, 1992) contains an account of a school for children with severe learning difficulties that moved in its entirety to a mainstream institution; and Hrekow and Barrow (1993) recount another example.

One local authority, Newham, has planned the closure of all its special schools. This has involved moving all children from special schools to mainstream schools, with varying degrees of support (Jordan and Goodey, 1996). A controversial aspect of the closure programme has been the placement of the transferred children to 'resourced schools' – that is, schools that are especially resourced to take a group of former special-school pupils. The consequence of this policy is that children do not necessarily attend their neighbourhood school.

One of the most sophisticated and creative examples of inclusion planning comes with the planned dismantling of the special school in such a way that the school is reconstructed as a service, as in the Somerset Inclusion Project (see Thomas, Walker and Webb, 1998). In this example, the school was closed, children moved to local schools, and the personnel who taught them also moved to work in those schools. This carries significant advantages over the mass provision of a support service, not least the retention of a group of committed staff who know the students involved in the programme, and who have solidarity and direction as a team.

Table 5.1 demonstrates some of these recent changes.

Table 5.1 Moving to inclusion: forms of organization and reorganization

re-placement	moving individual children to the mainstream with varying degrees of support
moving the school	moving the special school – with its students and staff – into the mainstream
providing resourced schools	that is, schools which are especially resourced to take a group of former special school pupils
providing a support service	comprising support teachers and learning support assistants, usually from the former special schools
providing an inclusion service	that is, converting a special school to a service, whereby ex-special school staff re-structure and work in neighbourhood schools

(Adapted from Thomas, Walker and Webb, 1998)

Current arrangements for integration (rather than inclusion) in England and Wales are still dominated by the movement of individuals, or re-placement. However, there is now an increased awareness of the need for structural change, in order to free up the resources that will enable real inclusion. The result has been the introduction of a range of innovative schemes in which the skills and resources of the original special school are provided in the mainstream. Money follows children, and there is no dilution of resource provision as children move from special school to mainstream school.

Financing and implementing inclusion

One of the major stumbling blocks to inclusion lies in the financial arrangements currently in place. Funding arrangements do not encourage inclusion, and the problem is not unique to England and Wales. The situation is similar in the USA, where Hehir (in conversation with Miller, 1996) points out that, despite legislative commitment to inclusion in many states, money does not follow children as they move to inclusive placements.

In the 1980s, integration concentrated on moving individual children to special schools, and simultaneously arranging whatever support could be afforded in the mainstream. This movement of individuals presented serious difficulties in the funding of the integrated placements, since in the absence of funding from central Government to fund integration, the fixed costs of special schools did not diminish enough to free up the necessary resources to make those integration arrangements satisfactory. This problem is well documented in England and Wales by the Audit Commission (1992).

At the moment in England and Wales nearly five times as much is spent on each special-school pupil as on each mainstream pupil (OECD, 1994; Audit Commission/HMI, 1992), and when children transfer from special to mainstream that advantageous funding does not usually accompany them. In fact, significant amounts of schools' existing funding may have to be used in adapting teaching or resources for the new children. The moneys provided in no way adequately compensate for the costs of accommodating the new children, and placements therefore often ultimately break down, especially when the child's difficulties are multi-faceted, and may require support from personnel in a number of services. For example, a mainstream placement of a child with Down's Syndrome will often break down (see O'Hanlon, 1996), not because that child cannot benefit from mainstream placement, but because financial mechanisms do not allow the substantial resources associated with provision for such children to follow him or her.

At the moment, funding for special schools is usually 'place-led' – the schools receive funds on the basis of the number of their places, not the number of actual pupils. This is in stark contrast to the funding for mainstream schools, where funding is pupil-led – money is only available for the children in front of the teacher. Money is therefore locked up in the special schools. This seems to be continuing to happen after the Touche-Ross (1990) recommendation that specialist provision in special schools should be protected. Not only is the current financial system protecting that provision, it is also inhibiting the successful accommodation of children with special needs into ordinary schools. It does so by depriving those schools of the funds they need to educate *all* their children successfully.

The Audit Commission found that local authorities were reluctant to delegate more money to schools to enable inclusion, because, according to them, they could not be confident that the delegated money would be used wisely or correctly. However, at that time, they had no way of monitoring how well schools were performing with special pupils, and did not, therefore, know whether this assertion was true. Another problem identified by the Commission was that an authority – knowing that an inclusive placement would be expensive – would have 'an incentive…not to specify what is to be provided because they thereby avoid a long-term financial commitment' (Audit Commission/HMI, 1992, p 25).

There are, therefore, political and professional hurdles to be overcome in effecting transfers of resources. There are formidable interests in maintaining special education, and some genuinely held professional beliefs about the benefits of maintaining segregation. Many parents are cautious about inclusion and prefer a special-school place for their child, and there are advocacy groups – for example, for children with hearing impairment or specific learning difficulties – who argue for separate provision. In these circumstances, local authorities, aside from any financial considerations, have pressures imposed upon them to maintain an establishment of special schools. The solution, the OECD (1994) suggests, is to confront the issue, to take difficult decisions about the 'desired moves' to inclusion (instead of avoiding such decisions), and to press ahead with organizational changes that will effect the principled decision. It gives the example of Somerset's reduction in the percentage of the school population in special schools, from 2.3 to 1.6, in four years in the 1980s; this was made possible by 'pushing ahead with a firm policy in the face of opposition (for example, that of the association representing dyslexics, who wanted special classes)' (p 43).

Conclusion

The new move to inclusion has its origins in several strands of recent thought in England and Wales. There are, first, new assumptions about difference. 'Integration' has usually been used to describe the assimilation by the mainstream of what were assumed to be *particular kinds* of children – those with learning difficulties, challenging behaviour, sensory impairments or physical disabilities. In fact, the use of the term 'special educational needs' has usually specifically excluded other children – for example, children whose first language is not English.

The key aspect of inclusion, however, is that children who are at a disadvantage *for any reason* are not excluded from mainstream education. Children's difficulties at school may arise from a multiplicity of factors related to disability, language, family income, cultural background, gender or ethnic origin, and it is inappropriate to differentiate among these. The notion of inclusion used here will therefore rest on a far more fluid definition of need than has hitherto existed.

Presenting this side of the coin – non-exclusion – is perhaps a negative way of putting it. The obverse, or positive side is that inclusion is about acceptance of all. The new notions of inclusion – having their provenance in diverse strands of thought about social justice – do not set parameters (as the notion of integration did) around particular kinds of putative disability. Rather, inclusion is about a philosophy of acceptance; it is about providing a framework within which all children – regardless of the causes of their difficulty – can be valued equally, treated with respect and provided with equal opportunities at school.

References

Audit Commission/HMI (1992) *Getting in on the Act: Provision for Pupils with Special Educational Needs, the National Picture*, HMSO, London

Booth, T. (1995) 'Mapping inclusion and exclusion: concepts for all', in C. Clark, A. Dyson and A. Millward (eds) *Towards Inclusive Schools?*, David Fulton, London

CSIE (1992) *Bishopswood: Good Practice Transferred*, Centre for Studies on Inclusive Education, Bristol

DES (1978) *Special Educational Needs, Report of the Committee of Enquiry into the Education of Handicapped Children and Young People*, Cmnd 7212, HMSO, London

DfEE (1997) *Excellence for all Children: Meeting Special Educational Needs*, DfEE, London

Hargreaves, D. H. (1982) *The Challenge for the Comprehensive School*, Routledge and Kegan Paul, London

Hrekow, P. and Barrow, G. (1993) 'Developing a system of inclusive education for pupils with behavioural difficulties', *Pastoral Care*, June, pp 6–13

Hutton, W. (1995) *The State We're In*, Jonathan Cape, London

Jordan, L. and Goodey, C. (1996) *Human Rights and School Change: the Newham Story*, CSIE, Bristol

Kay, J. (1996) *The Business of Economics*, OUP, Oxford

Mason, M. (1995) *Invisible Children: Report of the Joint Conference on Children, Images and Disability*, Save the Children and the Integration Alliance, London

McBriar, A. M. (1966) *Fabian Socialism and English Politics 1884–1918*, Cambridge University Press, Cambridge

Meekosha, H. and Jacubowicz, A. (1996) 'Disability, participation, representation and social justice', in C. Christensen and F. Rizvi (eds) *Disability and the Dilemmas of Education and Justice*, Open University Press, Buckingham

Miller, E. (1996) 'Changing the way we think about kids with disabilities: a conversation with Tom Hehir', in E. Miller and R. Tovey *Inclusion and Special Education*, HEL Focus Series No. 1, Harvard Educational Publishing, Cambridge, MA

O'Hanlon, C. (1996) 'The integration of children with Down's Syndrome', Paper presented to the BERA, University of Lancaster, September

OECD (1994) *The Integration of Disabled Children into Mainstream Education: Ambitions, Theories and Practices*, Organization for Economic Co-operation and Development, Paris

Plender, J. (1997) *A Stake in the Future: The Stakeholding Solution*, Nicholas Brealey Publishing, London

Rizvi, F. and Lingard, B. (1996) 'Disability, education and the discourses of justice', in C. Christensen and F. Rizvi (eds) *Disability and the Dilemmas of Education and Justice*, Open University Press, Buckingham

Roaf, C. (1988) 'The concept of a whole school approach to special needs', in O. Robinson and G. Thomas (eds) *Tackling Learning Difficulties*, Hodder and Stoughton, London

Roaf, C. and Bines, H. (1989) *Needs, Rights and Opportunities*, Falmer, London

Tawney, R. H. (1964) *Equality*, George Allen and Unwin, London

Thomas, G., Walker, D. and Webb. J. (1998) *The Making of the Inclusive School*, Routledge, London

Touche-Ross (1990) *Extending Local Management to Special Schools*, Touche-Ross for DES, London

Wilson, D. (1990) 'Integration at John Watson School', in D. Baker and K. Bovair (eds) *Making the Special Schools Ordinary*: Volume 2, Falmer, London

Young, I. M. (1990) *Justice and the Politics of Difference*, Princeton University Press, Princeton, NJ

6. Deficit ideology and educational reform in the United States

Christopher Blake

Introduction

Despite robust self-confidence in its economy and a naive optimism in its New World Order hegemony, the United States is currently experiencing a cycle of distrust and self-doubt regarding its public education system (Bloom, 1987; National Commission, 1996). Such scepticism is not new, nor singularly dependent on wider political, economic or societal trends. What is novel about the present wave of dissatisfaction, however, is both its ubiquitous appeal and its call for specific kinds of remedies to the perceived inadequacies of the system through a series of structural interventions. These are primarily state bureaucratic but also economically libertarian in nature and, while viewing public schools as the vital arenas of change, neither position prizes professional vision and leadership as the driving force of that agenda (McLaren, 1994; Apple, 1996).

In this chapter I shall sketch the historical context to this late twentieth-century educational angst and shall suggest that the themes that underpin the reform agenda are part of a broader struggle of cultural identity and political dominance; in that struggle, competing categories of inclusivity and equity versus excellence and exclusivity are the defining qualities of a contemporary identity crisis in American public education.

Reform cycles in American education

The current reform mentality in education shares several themes, notably performance indicators and accountability, standards and their assessment, and the consideration of market-force capitalism in the planning of the funding and delivery of the educational service. This structural perspective on public-school reform also crosses the political spectrum, so that little policy shift is necessary, or discernible, between the Reagan–Bush educational agenda and that of the two Clinton administrations. Indeed, a seamless continuity can be drawn between the Bush and Clinton educational policies, with only superficial contrasts visible. Thus Bush's 'American 2000' Act, which set out a stall of simple national standards and objectives (such as, American students will be first in science and mathematics), and endorsed the principle of privatization, provided the ideological context for Clinton's Goals 2000 Act of 1993. In both cases, the marrying of market forces, particularly in the idea of school choice, to a bureaucratic control of curriculum standards was an essential standpoint.

The first Clinton administration certainly played down Bush's emphasis on privatization but, by his second term, Clinton had no further need to assuage Democratic sensibilities. Whilst reaffirming the need for national standards in mathematics, reading and science in his 1997 State of the Union address, Clinton's public announcements and policies in his second term have increasingly included basic neo-conservative ideas – school choice, enrichment programmes for 'talented students', charter schools with business backing, and so forth. In putting forward these policies, successive admininstrations have been confident of the appeal of their rhetoric to a receptive public (Johnson and Immerwahr, 1994).

Much of this policy rhetoric distills into a deficit view of education, whereby the assumption and conclusion is that American education is failing and is in relative decline (Wynne and Ryan, 1997). Failing whom, and at what, and in decline against which context, is not often seriously considered. Instead, it serves a peculiar function of societal consciousness to perceive a weakness, if not crisis, in the public education service, and to deduce from that assumption that structural reform is required. In this respect, Republican and Democratic administrations alike owe much of their policy positioning to a landmark report of the early 1980s, known as *A Nation at Risk* (National Commission, 1983). This struck a chord with various organizations and pressure groups, both inside and outside education, and rapidly gained credibility, especially in its claim that a 'rising tide of mediocrity' in public education threatened the very future of the nation. Critically, schools were seen to shoulder the blame for an increased threat to American hegemony in the global economy, and were effectively made responsible as the guardians of economic success. As Ornstein and Levine (1997) note, 'Stressing the challenge of international economic competition, the report emphasized the need to prepare a skilled workforce for the information age' (p 514).

This seminal moment in the public's perception of education was, however, not entirely new. Indeed, it fitted into a broader picture of social change and awareness that had triggered earlier reform epochs in education, which had made the public consciousness ripe for *A Nation at Risk*'s message of gloom. These reform epochs essentially fall into four phases, denoted by the space-race crisis of the mid-century, the civil rights era of emancipation, the retrenchment mentality of the 1970s, and the market-force technicism of the last decade. Collectively, these phases help us to understand the siege mentality facing education and the oscillating themes of equity and excellence that push and pull the educational fabric. Furthermore, that push and pull can be seen as part of a dialectical process of societal struggle within education, underpinned by deeper currents of tension within late capitalist democracy. This is apparent when the reforms of the 1950s and 1960s are viewed together. The Soviet launch of Sputnik in 1957 brought to a close a decade of educational progressivism, and inaugurated a period of stringent basic-skills and subject-centred programmes in schools that were based on the premise that, in Rickover's (1959) words, 'The educational process must be one of collecting factual knowledge to the limit of the pupil's capacity...Nothing can really make it fun' (p 61). The most advanced educational thinking of the time was also utilized to justify this perception of the need for improved academic standards. Thus, Jerome Bruner's (1960) ground-breaking ideas on the 'structure of a discipline' were used to legitimize the drive for higher academic standards through subject-centred school reform, since, as Hlebowitsch and Tellez (1998) note, 'The "structure of a discipline" put a great premium on discipline-specific skills and reconstructed the nature of the learner in the image of the scholar-specialist. The learner could now be treated as a miniature scholar' (p 256).

Of course, these approaches to learning were not motivated by pedagogical need or concern, but, rather, by the socio-political context of the Cold War. Put simply, education was to be a key element of national defence against the threat of Soviet communism, now heightened by the technological advances exhibited in the space race. This explains the passage through Congress of the National Defense Education Act in 1958, which ensured the prioritized resourcing of mathematics and science in schools and a heightened interest in ability grouping in schools. In short, by the start of the 1960s, the nature of school reform was driven by the socio-political mentality of the Cold War. The need for science and mathematics rigour was advanced for purposes of technological superiority, and stringent academic standards were established in order to equip the nation economically and militarily for world competition.

The era that followed this 'back-to-basics' trend can be seen as a direct and dialectical response. The upheaval of the 1960s and its explosive awareness of civil and political needs left a legacy in schools that could not have been more different. By the late 1960s, the subject-centred, academic training approach within schools was viewed as deficient in terms of human needs, and the interests and aptitudes of learners in schools were increasingly seen as being overlooked by the post-Sputnik reform initiatives. With the emergence of the civil rights movement and vehement divisions over the Vietnam War, the political climate moved toward an awareness of the problems inherent in American society, rather than of perceived external threats to the nation's existence. Conditions of poverty, racism, urban blight, and economic inequality demanded a new response from schools, just as they heralded a new political dynamism in Lyndon Johnson's famous 'War on Poverty'.

The result was a mixture of ideas and thinking, deriving much from the Plowden Report (1967) in Britain, as well as from radical social theorists who exposed the differentiating function of schooling in capitalist economies (Bowles and Gintis, 1976), and manifested itself in the States as an interest in 'open education'. This generic term meant different things, but collectively denoted a child-centredness, in which the learner, rather than the curriculum, became a focal point of school activity.

The period of the 1960s represents that last real moment in modern history, aside from current initiatives in multiculturalism, when progressivist and reconstructionist views of education were forces of significance within the public school system. The rapidly changing and unpredictable economic climate of the 1970s yielded a less trusting mindset regarding education, which harked back to the insecurities of the mid-century. Indeed, one direct pendulum swing against the learner-centredness of the 1960s was the emergence of a new accountability culture, in which student performance and assessment were the new focal points. Alongside this came the use of new 'teacher-proof' instructional materials, which effectively reduced the professionalism of the teacher to that of a curriculum deliverer. Teachers and students were no longer architects of learning, but had become servants. Such a move was not a direct precursor of the Bush-Clinton agenda, since in the 1970s it was driven as much by a cost-cutting attitude of economic stringency as by overt manipulation of the political power-bases in education. Nevertheless, whilst the motives may have been somewhat different, the effect was similar to the rhetoric of *A Nation at Risk* and its descendants – a return to simple discipline-based teaching, closely monitored and financially constrained.

The momentum of the last generation has been constant and one-directional. Whilst new and powerful themes, such as the mass availability of information technology and the rapidly changing demographic nature of American society, have had an impact on educational provision and opportunity, the essential agenda has remained in place, holding in tension two central themes. A combination of neo-liberalism in the economic planning of education, and neo-conservatism in its structure and function, has ensured that progressivist thinking has been marginalized, and that schools find themselves faced with a dualistic cultural context of market forces and performance accountability (Apple, 1996). An analysis of the way in which these factors are currently being played out within the school system is now needed.

The reform agenda today: a policy angle

The continuity in the view of education from the Reagan–Bush administrations to those of Clinton, combined with the pervasive influence of the accountability culture, has produced an overwhelming and consistent reform rhetoric in American public education. The over-arching value within this rhetoric is that of excellence – its necessity, demonstrability and accountability. The theme recurs throughout local, state and national policy initiatives, and takes its impetus most recently from Clinton's Goals 2000 agenda. That agenda highlighted eight goals for achievement by the year 2000, three concerned with curriculum excellence and standards (in literacy, science, mathematics, and overall achievement), and one concerned with improving the teaching profession. Only one goal focused on social problems in schools.

To illustrate the legacy of Goals 2000, two examples can be cited. The first and the most influential is that of the National Commission (1996) report, *What Matters Most*, which has been received across the nation with respect, enthusiasm and attention, but with little questioning of its premise and likely consequences. The Commission's report recognizes centrally the importance of the teaching profession, but does so from a starting point of its assumed under-performance and inadequacy for the current task.

The six recommendations that follow from this systemic reform position manifest a total endorsement of a performance and accountability dynamic in education: standards, quality controls, performance pay, abolition of tenure, reinvention of teacher training and new school cultures based on success. The value of excellence is central and the teaching profession is the means by which it is to be infused systemically throughout public education.

The contention here is that the issue is not excellence, which any reasoning citizen would endorse, but the assumption that excellence is only identifiable or can only be appropriated through these particular cultural ciphers, which happen to be taken from the conceptual framework of late corporate capitalism. As a consequence, educational excellence is perceived as a systemic, corporate entity in which the teacher is a pivotal, but subservient and accountable medium, through which the value of excellence is delineated, established and measured. This invasion of public education with the tenets of corporate capitalism is perhaps most visible in the rush towards the embracing of the concept of Total Quality Management in school reform in the past decade. Even the use of the term 'quality', rather than 'excellence', emphasizes the reliance on the industrial metaphor. For many commentators and administrators, such as Bonsting (1992), the reform imperative, driven by a deficit ideology regarding education, is to 'transform our Nation at Risk into a Nation of Quality, beginning with the creation of Schools of Quality' (p 9). According to this position, such schools are to be constructed on principles of customer-driven consumerism, continuous personal and corporate improvement, systemic views of organizational change, and top management control of the system.

The second example illustrates how such principles have been translated into public education policy. My home state, Maryland, is esteemed by the federal government as one of the most proactive in terms of educational policy and practice. It has, in US Secretary of Education Riley's words, 'clearly earned its reputation as a leader in school reform. Maryland's significant, sustained progress illustrates what is possible when you set higher standards' (Press release, 11/12/97). Not surprisingly, Maryland has overtly embraced the values and concepts of recent federal government policy. What is especially noteworthy is the state's reliance upon a bureaucratic control and standardization of education, in a way that promotes the culture of accountability in schools through the monitoring of performance via standardized tests. In particular, the Maryland School Performance Assessment Program (MSPAP) tests, administered to third-, fifth- and eighth-graders statewide, measure student proficiency in basic skills, although significantly the results are not reported for individual students, but collectively, for schools themselves, in the style of league tables. In other words, student achievement is the mechanism for whole-school performance and accountability. These tests have been coupled with the introduction of high school assessments, to be fully implemented by 2004. These will require stringent performance by students against state-mandated learning outcomes in core subject areas, in order for them to obtain a graduation certificate from their high school.

The underlying ideology to this control is clear and unambiguous. As State Superintendent Grasmick (1996) notes, in reviewing Maryland's reform history, 'The need to improve schools is urgent. The schools have not changed as rapidly as have the economy and society...Our common vision is shaped by the emerging information age. Every day we see new evidence of this transformation, and new reason to prepare students to become knowledge workers' (p 1). Aside from seeing here education's purpose primarily in economic and industrial terms, Maryland's educational leadership clearly embraces a broad national political trend that buys into the deficit ideology of public education. However, the state's preferred strategy for addressing that deficit is through bureaucratic control and standardization, rather than free-market consumerism. The latter option does remain on the table, however, with Baltimore City recently resorting to the use of private management firms to run the school board, and the Democratic mayor calling for school choice as a remedy to failing public schools.

The reform agenda today: wider concerns

This survey has shown that the theme of excellence drives policy initiatives in the United States today, and that this value is based on a view of the inadequacy of public education. For the present, owing much to the long tradition of the public funding of education, the answer to the deficit has been sought mainly in increased control, standardization and accountability of schools, rather than in market-force competition and the use of neo-liberal economics. Where late capitalism has provided a model for school reformers, it has been mostly in the values of quality management and systemic organization, rather than in *laissez-faire* free-market competition.

In this final section I wish to suggest that, within this picture, the traditional and unique role of American education – establishing educational equity and

providing opportunity for diverse populations – has been sidelined by the reform agenda, and that, hiding behind some assumed myths of failure, the real
problems facing schools, students and teachers, which require urgent remedy, have been neglected. The deficit ideology has, paradoxically, drawn attention to the problems of schools, but it has done so in a way that highlights
the wrong problems and the wrong solutions. Indeed, the abundance of
thought, time and resources that have been expended in the last decade ana-
lyzing how reform might be achieved has been at the expense of identifying
which reforms are necessary and desirable. This is not in itself surprising. The
American socio-political culture embraces both liberal capitalism and social
democracy at its core, and the two stand in uneasy tension. The tradition of
public education lies in the midst of that tension.

In recent years, the reform agenda in schools has drawn from both those
traditions: from the social democratic tradition it has taken the idea of control
and standardization; and from the liberal capitalist tradition, it has adopted
the emphasis on improvement and performance, and on free-market consumerism. In the process, other traditional educational values, such as equity,
diversity and opportunity, have been squeezed.

Despite the rhetorical commitment to education for diverse populations,
the political tendency, as shown here, has been in one direction, towards excellence through state control first, and market forces second. What is not being prized sufficiently is equity and opportunity in education, at a time when
the increasing diversities and inequalities of American society are posing increasing strains on the public school system. In this sense, an historical cycle is
called for – a rediscovery of the spirit of those humanizing reforms typified by
the trends of the 1960s, and now necessary as a corrective to today's rational
technicism (Cummins, 1998). This should not be confused with a romanti-
cized, retrospective hope, or a falsification of previous mistakes in the 1960s,
but should entail a recognition that the role of the teacher and student has today been reduced – and reified – in the customer-oriented and corporate
world of education.

Rather than being driven by the cultural norms and socio-political agenda
of current vogue, American education instead needs to rediscover Dewey's
reconstructionist insights by creating schools that, in McLaren's (1994) words,
'truly endanger the obviousness of culture…as a collection of unalterable
truths and unchangeable social relations' (p 241). For this to happen, reforms
need to be community-enriching and professionally driven, so that teachers
can be leaders and architects, accountable for their vision as well as their results. Without this, McLaren's (1994) description of the 'decline of moral passion and the socially induced depletion of the human spirit' (p 242) is likely to
become a commonplace truth in America's schools.

There is some indication that this radically different view of reform may
start to prevail, promising new hope for a new century. The exposure of the
'manufactured crisis' in education is an example of an awakened interest in

the real societal problems facing schools, may be hinting at the start of a coun-ter-reform trend. Such an approach would set different demands on schools, requiring 'equal opportunities for all, and true improvements in public educa-tion [that] will not come about unless they are based on compassion' (p 348). Compassion and equality of opportunity are not anathema to the American dream, but central to it. Certainly, current norms in public life have relegated such values to private or idealized ethics, but somewhere within the cultural fabric of American history lies the notion of community within diversity: *E pluribus unum* – 'from many one'. As the century draws to a close, it is towards this cultural tradition that the educational agenda needs urgently to direct it-self, so that schools may fulfil their potential as real change agents, for the ben-efit of a pluralist society as a whole.

References

Apple, M. (1996) *Cultural Politics and Education*, Teachers College Press, New York

Bloom, A. (1987) *The Closing of the American Mind*, Simon and Schuster, New York

Bonsting, J. (1992) 'The quality revolution in education', *Educational Leadership*, 50 (3), pp 4–9

Bowles, S. and Gintis, H. (1976) *Schooling in Capitalist America*, Basic Books, New York

Bruner, J. (1960) *The Process of Education*, Harvard University Press, Cambridge

Cummins, P. (1998) *For Mortal Stakes: Solutions for Schools and Society*, Peter Lang Publishing, New York

Grasmick, N. (1996) *Improving Learning for All Children – Education Reform in Maryland: 1977–1996*, Maryland State Department of Education, Baltimore

Hlebowitsh, P. and Tellez, K. (1998) *American Education: Purpose and Promise*, Wadsworth Publishing Company, Belmont

Johnson, J. and Immerwahr, J. (1994) *First Things First: What Americans Expect from the Public Schools*, Public Agenda, New York

Maryland State Department of Education (December 11, 1997) Press Release, *Maryland School 'Report Car' Shows Solid Gains*, MSDE, Baltimore

McLaren, P. (1994) *Life in Schools*, Longman, White Plains, New York

National Commission on Excellence in Education (April 1983) *A Nation At Risk: The Impera-tive for Educational Reform*, US Government Printing Office, Washington, DC

National Commission on Teaching and America's Future (1996) *What Matters Most: Teaching for America's Future*, US Government Printing Office, Washington, DC

Ornstein, A. and Levine, D. (1997) *Foundations of Education*, Houghton Mifflin, Boston

Plowden Committee (1967) *Children and Their Primary Schools*, Central Advisory Council for Education, London

Rickover, H. (1959) *Education and Freedom*, EP Dutton and Co., Inc., New York

Wynne, E. and Ryan, K. (1997) *Reclaiming Our Schools: Teaching Character, Academics and Dis-cipline*, Merrill/Prentice Hall, New Jersey

7. The Netherlands: supporting integration by re-directing cash-flows

Sip Jan Pijl and Cor J.W. Meijer

Analyses of problems

Dutch special education can be characterized as a wide-ranging, segregated system for pupils who cannot keep up in regular schools. In 1997, 4.3 per cent of pupils between 4 and 11 (Dutch primary-school age) were referred to one of the special education school types (Pijl, 1997). In 1972, this percentage was just 2.2 (Meijer, Pijl and Kramer, 1989). The growth of segregated special education is currently the subject of much debate, with an increasing number of policy-makers, educators and parents believing that segregated education has gone too far.

In the past few years, several studies of the factors contributing to the growth of segregated special education have been made (Doornbos and Stevens, 1987, 1988; Ministerie van OC&W, 1990, 1991; Meijer and Peschar, 1997). Generally, these factors fall into three categories: legislation and regulation, limitations within regular education, and the self-maintaining effects of a segregated system.

Until recently, Dutch education legislation supported the development of a segregated system. Additional teacher or student support is only available for those pupils who are labelled as eligible for special education, and then placed in a segregated setting. Regular school teams are by no means restricted in referring pupils to special schools and special schools gain by accepting referred pupils. The few regulations governing special-needs provision in regular schools are often difficult to implement, since they are limited to certain pupil categories, have a time span, and require extensive paperwork.

Van Rijswijk (1991) pointed to this so-called 'paradox of legislation'. He argued that government policy promoted integration on the one hand, but rewarded an ongoing increase in special education on the other. In short, the government actually stimulated something that it disliked. Indeed, educational funding was not linked to pupils, but depended on the type of school in which those pupils were placed. In effect, this means that the funding system rewarded special schools for every pupil they placed and undermined the maintaining in regular education of pupils with special needs. Thus, legislation supported segregation and, at the same time, inhibited integration.

A number of limitations in regular education have been identified (Doornbos and Stevens, 1987, 1988). Teachers in both regular and special education state that a growing number of pupils are in need of special services. Regular schools find it increasingly difficult to adapt to wider differences among pupils; they do not have the facilities to respond adequately, and often see referral as the only possible solution. This teacher response is enforced by parents' demands for 'other' and 'better' qualifications for their children, and by their reluctance to accept what is seen as the failure of their child. Thus, in the absence of special services in regular schools, parents and teachers also support special education referral.

A regular teacher rarely refers a pupil to special education. Each year, about 1 per cent of regular school pupils are referred, and regular teachers average one referral every four years (Pijl, 1997). For individual teachers, referral occurs incidentally and the placing in a special school of one of their pupils is taken as support for their own views on the pupil concerned; placement confirms their concern about the pupil's progress, behaviour, and so on. The assessment procedure generally backs up the opinion of teachers and parents that there is 'something wrong' with the pupil (Doornbos, 1991).

It is hardly surprising, therefore, that a large number of both regular and special education teachers, as well as most of the parents of pupils now in special education, object to integration. Although these teachers and parents do not reject integration on principle, they believe that special needs pupils are better off segregated, because the highly differentiated teaching and counselling provide by special education is more effective for them. They consider these pupils to have profound problems, which make regular schooling inappropriate, and the 'specialness' of special education necessary. They regard these pupils as 'different': after all, why would they have been referred in the first place?

The virtual segregation between regular and special education results in a one-way flow of pupils. Primary pupils referred to special schools tend to stay there until they are 12 years old, and then move on to secondary special education. Only a small minority (less than 1 per cent) of special needs pupils in schools for learning disabled and mild mentally disabled pupils are annually re-placed into regular primary schools (Centraal Bureau voor de Statistiek, 1996). In general, neither the special nor the regular school has much to gain by re-placing a special needs pupil. The special school loses out on funding, and the regular school needs to provide special facilities without receiving any additional funding. As with all organizations, the separate special school sector tends to support itself, which results in an increase in the sector rather than a reduction.

Certain policy papers – now obsolete – outlining the future development of special schools including plans for them to be transformed into quality education institutes offering intensive, highly specialized education for special needs pupils. However, this would have widened the gap between the two school systems even more (Doornbos, 1991). Regular teachers and parents are convinced that special education offers intensive, individualized education while regular schools are incapable of providing appropriate education for these pupils. Therefore maintaining special needs pupils in regular education is the last thing to do.

It is clear that special education referral offers material and immaterial incentives for almost all involved. It is difficult, however, to determine its effects on pupils. The majority of parents claim that their children benefit from such an education and that the negative effects can be discounted. However, there are no indications to show that low-performing pupils in regular schools in low referral areas in the Netherlands are being deprived in any way.

The current funding system

The system for funding special education provision has been fairly straightforward. The number of teachers, including the headteacher, is based on the number of pupils that the school has on a particular date. Currently there are 12 different types of special schools, ranging from those for learning difficulties to those for the multiply disabled. Each type of school is allotted a certain number of teacher minutes per pupil. Thus, in special primary schools, each pupil with learning difficulties equals 167 teacher minutes a week, while each hearing impaired pupil is allotted 426 teacher minutes. The number of teacher minutes differs for secondary special education, and for different subjects. Additional funding is available for schools having minorities who have Dutch as a second language, and for specific categories of pupils re-placed in regular education.

Similar regulations exist for assessing the numbers of non-teaching staff. For example, the psychologist of a school for learning difficulties is appointed on the basis of six minutes per pupil per week, while hearing impaired pupils merit 11 minutes per week. The numbers of administrative staff, physiotherapists, social workers and so on, are calculated on a similar basis.

This manner of funding special education is known as the 'waltz of the minutes', after a well-known Dutch cabaret song. Clearly, a greater number of pupils leads to an increase in staff. By providing a 'bonus' for admitting pupils with special needs to special education, the government stimulates the segregation of those pupils.

There are also regulations relating to the funding of peripatetic teaching – special services for pupils returning from special schools to regular ones. Again, the amount of funding depends on the disability, and whether the child is a primary or secondary-school pupil. The staff of the special school supports the teacher in the regular school in educating the returning pupil.

This regulation has a number of restrictions, relating to the time span of these services, the eligibility of the pupil for special education, and the school record of the re-placed pupil. For instance, support for pupils with learning difficulties or for educable mentally disabled pupils is only possible if the pupil has been in special education for at least one year, and even then the pupil only generates part of the funding. For most other categories, however, the pupil does not need to have been in a special school.

While these regulations offer an incentive to reintegrate children from special schools into regular ones (or not to refer them to special schools), it is relatively small and restricted by several conditions. The gain for the regular school is small, while the effort involved in teaching a child with special educational needs is relatively great, yet the number of pupils in peripatetic teaching has grown from a few hundred at the start in 1985 to about 8,000 in 1995 (Kool and Derriks, 1995).

For children with sensory and/or physical disabilities, or for children with Down's Syndrome, there are certain financial possibilities in the case of regular school placement. However, these are neither permanent nor structural. A school has to apply annually for funding, and the amount it receives depends on the number of applications and the available macro budget.

To sum up: the incentive for special school placement is relatively high, while the reward for referring pupils from special to regular schools is relatively low, especially in the case of children with mild mental disabilities, or learning disabilities. The incentives work, therefore, in favour of special school placement and are not in keeping with proclaimed integration policy. This partly explains the increase in special school placement rates over the last decades.

The calculating school

'Strategic behaviour' refers to all the activities of an organization aimed at protecting that organization from external threatening factors. Integration policy might result in strategic behaviour that is contradictory to integration. It is clear that a forceful integration policy is a danger for special schools. It directly threatens their existence. There are several indications that policy focused on reducing the number of referrals to special education in the Netherlands stimulates schools for special education to defend themselves (Meijer, Peschar and Scheerens, 1995). In fact, the dramatic increase in special school placements over the last decades demonstrates this (Meijer, 1995).

At the same time, the government tried to stop the ongoing growth by taking several initiatives – for example, massive teacher-training projects and support for experimental school clusters on different issues. However, this did not change the incentive structure. The Dutch experience is that an integration policy will fail, and may even contribute to segregation, if it is not properly financially regulated. The threat to special schools posed by integration seems to be an important factor in the growth of the special education sector. This is especially the case when assessment procedures fall under the responsibility of special schools.

Dutch policy on special needs funding

The Dutch government now regards a new funding structure as a key to integration. Currently, two separate systems are being developed: first, a system for educating pupils with learning difficulties (so-called LOM pupils) and mildly mentally disabled pupils (so-called MLK pupils) based on providing a lump sum to regional clusters of collaborating schools; and second, a demand-oriented system, known as the pupil-bound budget, for pupils with sensory, physical, mental disabilities and/or behavioral problems.

Lump sums to clusters

In the new system, most of the additional costs for special education (the former LOM and MLK schools) will be allocated to clusters of collaborating regular and special schools. School clusters may now decide to transfer parts of that provision to regular schools without losing funds. One important aspect of this new system is the fact that regular schools participate in the decision-making process concerning special needs provision.

Two main tools are therefore now available as a result of recent government integration policy: school clusters and a revamped funding system. The clusters comprise one or more special schools working co-operatively with a larger group of primary schools. In the last few years, the clusters have been implemented. This has resulted in a nationwide network, in which every special school (for the learning disabled and the mild mentally disabled) and regular school is part of a cluster. While schools were given a certain degree of freedom in the way they grouped, the aim was to have 15 regular schools working co-operatively with one special education institute. Recent findings, however, show considerable deviation from this ideal (Meijer and Peschar, 1997). Most affiliations comprise 30 schools on average, including two special schools. The numbers of pupils involved also vary enormously, from over 10 000 per cluster to less than 2 000.

Extra funding was made available for the setting up of these clusters. The resources that each cluster received depended on the number of 'ordinary' pupils and the number of special education schools, and was based on a figure of Dfl 28 per pupil and Dfl 5 000 per special school. Thus, an 'ideal' cluster (3 000 primary school pupils and one special school) received an additional amount of Dfl 90 000, which was earmarked for improving the provision of all schools for children with special needs.

The second instrument to encourage integration is a new funding structure. The idea of this new system is that (parts of) the additional costs for special education will be allocated jointly to the school clusters. This allows for variation in the way integration is carried out. School clusters may decide to maintain special needs provision in special schools. They could also decide to transfer parts of that provision to regular schools, in one form or another. The key factor is that regular schools participate in the decision-making process concerning the structure of special provision. Through this funding system the threat to special schools is less serious than before. Teachers at special school keep their jobs, but they now work in a different context, giving special support in a regular school.

Parliament has decided that each of the 300 school clusters will be funded equally, based on the total enrolment in primary education. About 50 per cent of this amount will be transferred directly to existing special provisions and the other half will be allocated to the school cluster. This will be implemented from 1998 onwards, and the new funding structure should be fully operational in 2003. By that time, regions will need to have adapted their special education provision to the new funding structure. Some regions may have to close special schools, where there was a high degree of segregated provisions compared to other regions, while other areas may receive additional funds as a reward for a effective regional integration policy.

The question is whether these two main resources will foster the government objective of integrating special and regular education. The setting up of school clusters will not directly result in a less segregated system, and much more attention is needed. However, it must be said that, without the necessary facilities (in terms of extra specialist help/time/attention), integration has little chance of succeeding. In this sense, introducing a new funding structure is one of the necessary pre-conditions for integration.

The pupil-bound budget

For centuries, Dutch special schools have played – and still play – an important role in educating pupils with sensory, physical, mental disabilities and/or behavioural problems. These pupils are only able to receive the services they need after admittance to a full-time special school. In principle, the necessary additional budgets are only available for these schools, so that financing special education can be described as supply-oriented.

It is assumed that supply-oriented financing hinders the integration of special needs pupils in regular education. There is growing pressure to change the way special education is financed. Recent government reports (Commissie leerlinggebonden financiering in het speciaal onderwijs, 1995; Ministerie van OC&W, 1996) propose that the financing of places in special schools for pupils with sensory, physical, mental disabilities and/or behavioral problems should be stopped, in favour of linking the financing of special services to the pupil involved, regardless of the type of their schooling. The pupil does not follow the funding, the funding follows the pupil. The idea is to change from supply-oriented financing to a system in which the means are forwarded to the person requiring special services, and this is known as demand-oriented financing. Under this system, means are made available only after a positive decision by a body of experts. If a pupil meets the criteria for a pupil-bound budget, parents and pupil can choose a school and take part in deciding how to use the funding.

The basic idea behind demand-oriented financing is that parents are given an important voice in choosing a school for their child. In the government report, it is proposed that their freedom of choice would be established by law. In principle, the parents themselves would choose between regular and special education. In fact, placement at a special school would only be necessary in situations where it is not possible to find a regular school capable of providing adequate education. An important contributing factor in reinforcing the parents' position is the ruling that regular schools would not be allowed, in principle, to refuse pupils. Placement would only be denied in cases where a school could clearly demonstrate that it is incapable of providing suitable schooling for a special needs pupil.

A set of objective and well-defined criteria is important in deciding the allocation of a pupil-bound budget. Currently, a decision on placement is made after both subjective information (impressions during the test, opinions of the teacher) and objective information (test results, medical data, school achievements) is obtained on the pupil, and the nature and gravity of the problem, plus the need for additional help, has been assessed. Research has shown that the practice in other countries of using a system of pupil-bound budgets, or a comparable system, has much in common with the Dutch one (Pijl and de Kam, 1996). Due to the absence of strict criteria, the decision about the allocation of the budget is reasonably easy to challenge (via an appeal, for example).

Partly as a result of experiences in other countries (Pijl and de Kam, 1996), there are some worries that the implementation of pupil-bound budgets will lead to an increase in the numbers of pupils acquiring a budget. The growth will be due not only to the increasing number of pupils being awarded a budget, but also to the longer period covered by the budget. An important factor here can be the actions of parents, who try to achieve optimal circumstances for their child. In education, this is expressed in their endeavour to obtain a statement on their child's needs, to secure ample resources combined with that statement, and to guard against such a statement being terminated.

The implementation of a pupil-bound budget will undoubtedly affect regular education. It will be difficult for schools to place special needs pupils in a location where they will face disabilities with which they are unfamiliar. Solving this will certainly require much effort in the initial stages, in terms of training, supervision, materials, and adjustments to the building. If this is successful, however, experiences in other countries show that it results in the education of other pupils with problems at that school, which will attract new pupils with similar, or even different, needs. Accordingly, certain regular schools may well develop into facilities for pupils with certain specific educational needs. There are a number of arguments for supporting this development – it can lead to better education by experienced and trained teaching staff; the school team will have the opportunity to build up expertise in a specific area; materials and adjustments to the buildings will be used more cost-effectively; and teaching personnel can be deployed more efficiently. The disadvantage is that, if there are too many facilities, the school will become a 'special' regular school.

Regarding special education, the development towards integration is expected to result in an increased workload. The special schools will be responsible for much of the support that is provided to regular schools. These schools will develop as centres of expertise, in which various resources are made available to regular education. There is a small chance that the introduction of pupil-bound financing in the Netherlands will greatly reduce the influx into special education within a few years. The group of pupils eligible for a pupil-bound budget comprises roughly 1.2 per cent of the 6–16 years old age group (Pijl, 1997), and that percentage could only be reduced to 1 per cent with considerable effort (Pijl and Meijer, 1991). In fact, it is probable that, in the coming years, the size of this section of special education will not reduce by more than a few tenths of one per cent. Since new tasks will arise for some of the special schools, there is no reason to fear a serious loss of expertise.

It remains to seen if the current implementation of two new funding systems for two different groups of pupils with special needs – groups that are sometimes difficult to distinguish – does not invite new kinds of strategic behaviour.

Conclusion

Debate about the education of pupils with special needs, and discussions on funding make poor bedfellows. Children who already have difficulty in moving, hearing or seeing, or in keeping up in education with their peers for any other reason, should not be hindered further by limited resources. Resources simply have to be made available and, to this end, integration should depend on the right attitudes, good organization, professionalization of teachers, inclusive curricula and school reform (Meijer, Pijl and Hegarty, 1997) more than on cash flow.

However, studies in the Netherlands show that the funding structure does influence the achievement of a more inclusive school system. The current funding regulations strongly support segregation in education and are, in fact, a significant barrier to any attempt to educate special needs pupils in regular schools. The Dutch government has, however, discovered funding as a policy instrument to bring about changes in the relation between regular and special education. The two newly developed funding systems are clearly directed towards reducing the out-flow from regular education, and to remove the financial restrictions to placing special needs pupils in regular schools.

It is more than likely that schools will react to the new regulations with all kinds of strategic behaviour. School boards will optimally use existing regulations, in order to profit from them fully. Parents, too, will attempt to realize the most optimal circumstances for their child. Schools and parents often prove to be more inventive than any policy-maker could imagine and all kinds of unintended use of the newly developed regulations will undoubtedly occur. This will lead to new, more restricted regulations, and to fresh forms of strategic behaviour. This is unavoidable, but what ultimately counts is that the new regulations, despite their shortcomings, will bring Dutch education one step closer to integration.

References

Centraal Bureau voor de Statistiek (1996) *Statistiek van het basisonderwijs, het speciaal onderwijs en het voortgezet speciaal onderwijs 1995/96*, Scholen en leerlingen, Voorburg/Heerlen: SDU

Commissie leerlinggebonden financiering in het speciaal onderwijs (1995) *Een steun in de rug*, Den Haag: SDU

Doornbos, K. (1991) 'School- en leermoeilijkheden: epidemie of systeemeffect?', in K. Doornbos *et al.* (eds) *Samen naar school. Aangepast onderwijs in gewone scholen*, Nijkerk: Intro. pp 11–30

Doornbos, K. and Stevens, L. M. (eds) (1987) *De groei van het speciaal onderwijs: Analyse van historie en onderzoek*, 's-Gravenhage: Staatsuitgeverij

Doornbos, K. and Stevens, L. M. (eds) (1988) *De groei van het speciaal onderwijs: Beeldvorming over beleid en praktijk*, 's-Gravenhage: Staatsuitgeverij

Kool, E. and Derriks, M. (1995) *Ambulante begeleiding: werkwijzen en effecten*, Gemeentelijk Pedologisch Instituut: Amsterdam; SCO Kohnstamm Instituut Faculteit der Pedagogische en Onderwijskundige Wetenschappen: Amsterdam

Meijer, C. J. W. (1995) *Halverwege*, De Lier: ABC

Meijer, C. J. W. and Peschar, J. L. (1997) *WSNS op weg*, Groningen, Wolters-Noordhoff

Meijer, C. J. W., Peschar, J. L. and Scheerens, J. (1995) *Prikkels*, De Lier, ABC

Meijer, C. J. W., Pijl, S. J. and Hegarty, S. (1997) 'Inclusion: Implementation and approaches', in S. J. Pijl, C. J. W. Meijer and S. Hegarty (eds) *Inclusive Education: a global agenda*, Routledge, London

Meijer, C. J. W., Pijl, S. J. and Kramer, L. J. L. M. (1989) 'Rekenen met groei', *Tijdschrift voor Orthopedagogiek*, 28, pp 71–82

Ministerie van Onderwijs and Wetenschappen (1990) *Weer samen naar school*, Perspectief om leerlingen ook in reguliere scholen onderwijs op maat te bieden, Hoofdlijnennotitie, 's-Gravenhage: SDU

Ministerie van Onderwijs and Wetenschappen (1991) *3x Akkoord*, 's-Gravenhage: SDU

Ministerie van Onderwijs and Wetenschappen (1996) *De rugzak. Beleidsplan voor het onderwijs aan leerlingen met een handicap*, 's-Gravenhage: SDU

Pijl, S. J. and Kam, C. A. de (1996) 'Een rugzak met guldens', in: R. De Groot, W. Ruijssenaers and H. Kapinga (eds) *Inclusief onderwijs*, Groningen, Wolters-Noordhoff

Pijl, S. J. and Meijer, C. J. W. (1991) 'Does integration count for much?', *European Journal of Special Needs Education*, 2, pp 100–111
Pijl, Y. J. (1997) *Twintig jaar groei van het speciaal onderwijs*, De Lier, ABC
Rijswijk, C.M. van (1991) 'Bestuur en beheer van geintegreerd primair onderwijs', in K. Doornbos *et al.* (eds) *Samen naar school*, Aangepast onderwijs in gewone scholen, Nijkerk

8. Integration in the changing Scandinavian welfare states

Anders Gustavsson

The context of the welfare state

This chapter will discuss Scandinavian experiences of integration, with a specific focus on people in Sweden with learning difficulties. It will be argued that the experiences of integration and inclusion[1] in this context should be understood in relation to the tradition of the Scandinavian welfare state.

The basic ideas of the Scandinavian welfare state were formulated early in its first phase – in Sweden called the 'Folkhemmet' (the 'people's home') – in the late 1920s. In a well-known speech, the leader of the Social-Democratic party, Per-Albin Hansson, described the principles of equality and support as follows: 'The good home knows no privileged or neglected people, no favourites and no stepchildren...The strong do not suppress and plunder the weak. In the good home, there is equality, care, collaboration, support' (Hansson, 1928, p 11).

The key actors in the 'people's home' project were the 'social engineers', who were expected to guide the work towards better living conditions, and equality. During the second, 'golden' phase of the Scandinavian welfare state (Pierson, 1991),[2] 1945–75, the idea of welfare programmes was extended through the expansion of the public sector and the increasing number of civil servants, who became the major instruments of what was then called 'the strong society'.

It was during the expansion of this 'strong society', in the late 1960s, that the ideas of integration were first spread. Two main discourses seem to have accompanied and facilitated the introduction of the new ideas of integration (Tøssebro, 1997). The first was a concern for the best programmes for people with disabilities. Large institutions and boarding schools were beginning to be criticized for not providing their residents with the best conditions for personal development. The second discourse was a critique of the existing welfare state for not having included certain forgotten groups in the welfare project. Despite the fact that P A Hansson had addressed the issue support for the weak, people with disabilities tended to be forgotten in the welfare project up to the late 1960s. At that time, the term 'the handicapped' began to be used in Sweden, and its use as a generic term for people with different types of disabilities was closely linked to the idea of a disadvantaged group's right to special support (Söder, 1990).

Similar patterns of experiences

Research on integration policies and practices in Scandinavia in general indicates some similar patterns of experience[3] (Söder, 1997; Tøssebro, 1996). In terms of implementing new ways of organizing services, integration has been quite successful. At the beginning of the decade, almost all pre-school children with learning disabilities who were receiving pre-school training in Sweden went to special pre-schools. At the end of the 1970s, almost all of them were integrated into regular, municipal day care. A considerable reduction in the numbers of pupils in special schools also began to take place during this period. Integrated living for adults with special needs developed more slowly, but during the 1970s and 1980s there was a great expansion of new group-homes, and many people moved into apartments of their own as institutions were gradually closed. A similar development took place in Denmark, and, a little later, in Norway.

Despite this development, expectations of social integration have not been fulfilled to the same extent. Proximity with non-disabled people has not led to the establishment of social relationships and community (Söder, 1979; Hill and Rabe, 1987; Wehn and Sommerschild, 1991; Holm *et al.*, 1997). Life in an 'integrated society' for people with disabilities has been associated with loneliness and isolation (Sætersdal, 1997). How might these patterns be understood against the background of current Scandinavian research?

From ideals to realities

From a social-science perspective, the disappointing experiences of social integration are in many ways trivial. More often than not, reforms fail to carry out the ideals that originally guided them. Furthermore, the programmes of integration long neglected the important issue of the kind of context in which integration was to take place, as well as how the existing social life in these contexts was likely to affect opportunities for participation and social relationships. Christie (1991) and Gustavsson (1992) have pointed out that modern, urban societies are characterized by relationships based on mutual choice. 'Different people' tend not to become chosen by non-disabled people and, therefore, tend to establish few such relationships.

Söder (1997) also argues that the Scandinavian discourse of integration is of a paradoxical nature, in that it pre-supposes the existence of a state of segregation from which integration is supposed to become initiated. Furthermore, the discourse of integration may be said to be counter-productive, in the sense that it pre-supposes a 'we', who will integrate 'them', thus maintaining that social distance between disabled and non-disabled people that it officially opposes (Sandvin, 1992). Another side of the paradox is that integration programmes tend to introduce labels that can promote exclusion. To a significant extent, the 'integrated person' is defined as special and, therefore, entitled to support. From a labelling perspective (Söder, 1997), this means that one label (such as 'retarded' or 'idiot') is replaced by another (such as 'integrated'). A Swedish study of low-achieving pupils in regular schools (IQ less than 70) – pupils indentified as such only within the contexts of the research project, not in the schools – has indicated that pupils not identified as integrated may be included to a greater extent than pupils who have been in special education. The studied, non-identified pupils represent, of course, the low achievers in the classes. However, they shared their shortcomings with many peers who had average test scores, and the studied pupils did not differ, for example, in terms of self-concepts and transition into the labour market, from peers (IQ more than 70) with no higher education experience (Sonnander, Emanuelsson and Kebbon, 1993; Emanuelsson, 1997).

The integration perspective revisited

The growing experience of the effects of integration practice has also led to a re-thinking of some of the original, utopian ideas of integration. An issue raised by several researchers is that 'integrated' people have been described as socially isolated, even when they are part of quite extensive social networks. The assumption seems to have been that many of their relationships are not regarded as 'real', as they are not spontaneously chosen relationships with non-disabled friends. The utopia of integration seems to have suffered from a very narrow ideal of social relationships, in other words, the norm of the middle-class, Western, urban citizen (Wærness, 1988; Tøssebro, 1992). Atkinson (1988), Day (1989), Bogdan and Taylor (1989) and Gustavsson (1998) have all pointed out that, for 'integrated' people, relationships with relatives and professionals, and especially with others with similar disabilities, can be quite significant.

Another way of re-thinking the perspective of integration has been presented by Holm *et al.* (1997), who point to the fact that people with learning difficulties also have difficulties establishing spontaneous relationships and, therefore, can be in need of support from professionals. They have introduced the idea of what they call 'created communities' – communities initiated by professionals for people with disabilities. The first independent association of people with learning disabilities (ULF) in Denmark, for instance, grew out of a series of cultural festivals arranged by social pedagogues. In 1997, ULF organized the first strikes of people with learning disabilities.

Re-thinking some of the ideas of integration has lead to a re-evaluation of some of the seemingly disappointing experiences of the practice of integration. The conclusion is not that things did not work out as planned, but, rather, that the experiences are much more complex than they at first seemed. It is also interesting to note that there seems to be a growing recognition of the value of good professional support in new welfare programmes. This raises the issue (which will be addressed) of whether the Scandinavian welfare state, primarily, is undergoing a transition towards a new model.

Three crises of the old welfare state

The post-war model of the Scandinavian welfare states has suffered three severe crises. One has been a series of budget cuts that have affected all three Scandinavian countries to varying degrees, and at various times. The second crisis may be characterized as ideological. Ekensteen (1996), himself severely disabled, has, for instance, criticized the strong-society approach, for its objectification of service consumers and for its demand that they accept services considered as suitable for all disabled persons. Third, a more general ideological re-orientation of the entire welfare state has also contributed to a development away from central government and social engineering, and towards decentralization and market control. These crises have seriously reduced faith in the 'strong society' model. In a review of integration research, Söder (1997) writes that

belief in the centrally directed political welfare project is, if not destroyed, at least greatly modified. Decentralization and individualization have altered the basic conditions. Opportunities for integration of people with disabilities have changed as well. Integration in practice is to a greater extent created through local units – schools and municipalities, working with less direct steering from the central authorities – in what may be called 'the civil society'. Many people see a threat in this development. (Söder, 1997, p 50, my translation)

It has been argued that the Scandinavian welfare states were replaced by the 'welfare municipalities' during the 1980s and 1990s (Tøssebro, Aalto and Brusén 1996). Decisions concerning services to people with disabilities are now decentralized, and made in each municipality. When general regulations and service structures are abandoned, people fear that those groups that are considered weak will not have the strength to defend their right to a good life. This is the threat to which Söder refers.

A welfare municipality of included individuals?

The changes in the organization of services to people with disabilities might, perhaps, also mean the creation of new opportunities for inclusion. Söder (1997) concluded the following:

> These societal changes may at the same time provide opportunities for transcending the implicit paradoxes of the integration discourse, which I have described above: the opportunity for a community beyond labelling categorizations and a dependence on formal organizations and professions, a community based on 'accepting relations' growing out of spontaneous efforts of people to organize along other lines and categories than those offered by the public services. In the intersection between the post-modern talk of multiple identities (Fawcett, 1996) and the strong belief in local communities of the communitarian ideology (Turnbull, 1991), such an opportunity can, in my view, be anticipated. (Söder, 1997, p 51, my translation)

A recent follow-up study of 10 people with learning difficulties who grew up during the 1970s and 1980s (Gustavsson, 1998) seems to provide some support for Söder's conclusion, but the results also raise questions concerning the threats of dismantling the traditional welfare states. The studied persons showed, for example, a surprising faith in their own ability to fulfil ordinary life roles, such as living on their own, maintaining a job, starting a family, and so on. To a significant extent, their faith seemed to be founded in locally established communities that encompassed others with similar disabilities, professionals, and relatives, who all shared similar perspectives on what it means to live with a disability. However, the particular perspectives maintained by these locally organized communities also drew extensively on the recognized rights of people with disabilities to services. Thus, the supportive communities to some degree seemed to depend on the type of special rights legislations and identification of persons with special needs that previously characterized the welfare model of the 'strong society'.

Kristin was one of the young women who took part in the study, and her case seemed to illustrate this when her boss at work reproached her for being too slow. Kristin turned to her supportive social network, in this case, the professionals in a service apartment that she often visited. In this case, Kristin referred to her learning difficulties as justification for special support and consideration.

The question is whether, and to what extent, the studied persons' experiences of the traditional welfare state model have been a necessary condition for the development of the supportive communities, or whether these communities are primarily the product of an inclusive municipality. This question is still an open one.

Endnotes

1. I use the term 'integration' when referring to the reforms that have been carried out and often spoken of in these terms. The main characteristics of integration seem to have been re-placement and entry into such ordinary settings. 'Inclusion' on the other hand, has to do with restructuring the ordinary social settings in a way that creates opportunities for true participation, belonging and social interaction.
2. Pierson originally coined this expression in an international description of the welfare state, but it may be said to hold true for the Scandinavian countries as well.
3. It should be pointed out that there are also important differences between Sweden, Norway and Denmark. Sweden and Denmark could be regarded as more 'developed' during the early welfare state, in terms of a more developed institutional system. In Norway, large institutions were not built until after the Second World War. During the 1980s and 90s, partly due to the economic recession, which affected Sweden and Denmark to a greater extent, Norway converged with the other two countries through a development now characterized by deinstitutionalization and integration.

References

Atkinson, D. (1988) 'Moving from hospitals to the community: factors influencing the life style of people with mental handicaps', *Mental Handicap*, 16 (8), pp 8–10

Bogdan, R. and Taylor, S. (1989) 'Relationships with severely disabled people: The social construction of humanness', *Social Problems*, 36 (2), pp 131–44

Christie, N. (1991) *Bort från anstalt och ensamhet till ett meningsfullt liv* ('From institutions and isolation to a meaningful life'), Rabén and Sjögren, Stockholm

Day, P. E. (1989) 'Uncertain future: Experiences and expectations of people with mental handicaps of life beyond the hospital and hostel', *Mental Handicap Research*, 2 (2), pp 166–85

Emanuelsson, I. (1997) 'Integration and segregation – inclusion and exclusion', paper presented at the Annual AERA Meeting, Chicago, Illinois, March 24–28, 1997

Fawcett, B. (1996) 'Post-modernism, feminism and disability', *Scandinavian Journal of Social Welfare* 5 (4), pp 259–67

Goffman, E. (1963) *Stigma: Notes on the Management of Spoiled Identity*, Prentice Hall, Englewood Cliffs

Gustavsson, A. (1992) 'Livet in "Integrasjonssamfunnet" – en analyse av naerhetens social betydning ('Living in "Integrated Society" – an analysis of the social meaning of proximity'), in J. Sandvin (ed.) *Mot normalt* ('Towards normality'), Kommuneforlaget, Oslo

Gustavsson A. (1998) *Inifrån utanförskapet* ('An insider's perspective on being an outsider'), Johansson and Skyttmo, Stockholm

Hanssen, J-I., Sandvin, J. and Söder, M. (1996) 'The Nordic welfare states in transition', in J. Tøssebro, A. Gustavsson and G. Dyrendahl (eds.) *Intellectual Disability in the Nordic Welfare States – Policies and Everyday Life*, Norwegian Academic press, Kristiansand

Hansson, P.A. (1928) *AK*, no. 3, p 11

Hill, A. and Rabe, T. (1987) 'Psykiskt utvecklingsstörda i kommunal förskola. Integrering belyst ur ett socialpsykologiskt perspektiv' ('The learning-disabled in the municipal pre-school. Integration analysed from a social-psychological perspective), *Studies in Educational Science*, Göteborg, Acta Universitas Gutenburgensis

Holm, P., Holst, J., Bach Olsen, S. and Pertl, B. (1997) 'Efter normaliseringen' (After normalization), in J. Tøssebro (ed.) *Den vanskelige integreringen* ('The difficult integration'), Universitetsforlaget, Oslo

Pierson, C. (1991) *Beyond the Welfare State*, Polity Press, Cambridge

Sandvin, J. (1992) 'Fra normalisering till social integrasjon', in J. Sandvin (ed.) *Mot normalt* ('Towards normality'), Kommuneforlaget, Oslo

Saetersdal, B. (1997) 'Integrering och mentalitetshistorie. Familieperspektiv på skiftende ideologier' ('Integration and the history of mentalities. Family perspectives on changing ideologies'), in J. Tøssebro (ed.) *Den vanskelige integreringen* ('The difficult integration'), Universitetsforlaget, Oslo.

Sonnander, K., Emanuelsson, I. and Kebbon, L. (1993) 'Pupils with mild mental retardation in regular Swedish schools: prevalence, objective characteristics, and subjective evaluations', *American Journal of Mental Retardation*, 97 (6), pp 692–701

Söder, M. (1979) *Skolmiljö och integrering. En empirisk studie av särskolans integrering i olika skolmiljöer* ('School environment and integration, an empirical study of integration in different school environments), Department of Sociology, Uppsala

Söder, M. (1988) The function of culture in the development of social policy', paper presented at the New Sweden seminars in Chicago

Söder, M. (1990) Föreställningar om handikapp i vardagsliv och politik. Ingår i Forskning om välfärd utgiven av DSF, s. 79–87

Söder, M. (1997) 'Integrering: Utopi, forskning, praktik', ('Integration: Utopia, research and practice'), in J. Tøssebro (ed.) *Den vanskelige integreringen* ('The difficult integration'), Universitetsforlaget, Oslo

Turnbull, H. R. III (1991) *The Communitarian Perspective. Thoughts on the Future for Persons with Developmental Disabilities*, Beach Centre on Families and Disability, University of Kansas

Tøssebro, J. (1992) *Institusjonsliv i velferdsstaten. Levekår under HVPU* ('Living in institutions in the welfare state. Living conditions during the HVPU'), Ad Notam Gyldendal, Oslo

Tøssebro, J. (1996) *En bedre hverdag?* ('A better everyday life?'), Kommuneforlaget, Oslo

Tøssebro, J. (1997) 'The discourses on intellectual disabilities during the emergence of the current policy: 1960–1975', paper presented at the 9th Nordic Social Policy Research Seminar, Køge

Tøssebro, J., Aalto, M. and Brusén, P. (1996) 'Changing ideologies and patterns of services', in J. Tøssebro, A. Gustavsson and G. Dyrendahl, (eds) *Intellectual Disability in the Nordic Welfare states – Policies and Everyday Life*, Norwegian Academic Press, Kristiansand

Wehn, I. and Sommerschild, H. (1991) *Når funksjonshemmed barn blir ungdommer* ('When disabled children become disabled youth'), Tano, Oslo

Waerness, K. (1988) 'Comment to Mike Oliver's "Social policy and disability": the creation of dependence', paper presented at the OECD seminar on adult status for youth with disabilities, Sigtuna

9. The inclusion movement in Canada: philosophies, promises and practice

Margret A. Winzer

Introduction

For both normally developing students and for special populations, the current atmosphere in Canadian education is one of change. Thrusts of reform and restructure, often re-invented and re-animated, are key, all intimately associated with and influenced by wider political and cultural trends in Canadian society.

Of the waves of reform that have surged across the Canadian educational system in the past decade, one of the strongest and most basic revolves around ensuring educational equality and opportunity for all students. This applies most especially to those who are disadvantaged, minority children, students from diverse cultural and linguistic backgrounds, and students with disabilities.

Within the discrete field of special education specifically, efforts to bring about basic structural changes in the fundamental operating mode, and to improve educational practice, are encompassed under a concept and practice variously termed 'inclusion', 'inclusive schooling', or 'inclusive education'. The over-arching objective of the movement towards reforming and restructuring special education is the creation of socially just and democratic communities. The aim is to achieve this by creating changes within schools that co-ordinate and bridge programmes and services, so that they are transformed into places where *all* students belong and learn together.

Discussions of the inclusionary movement in Canada must consider factors such as the pervasive influence of developments in the United States, the lack of a centralized school system, provincial legislation, and recent litigation. Nor can the widely varied theoretical positions and the fluidity of the ideas that characterize Canadian endeavours be discounted. While many professionals, parents and advocacy groups promote full inclusion, in which every child is integrated into the general education classroom, the ideal of full inclusion is not universally shared, and is not endorsed by all of those concerned with the education of children with exceptionalities. While the philosophical goals of inclusion are almost universally applauded among educators and allied professionals, the present form of its implementation has not found universal support.

A political will is manifest, but the integration of all students who are exceptional into regular milieus remains controversial and relatively precarious. Ideology has not enjoyed an easy transition to educational practice; the movement is balanced over an abyss of tight resources, changing demographics, teacher attitudes, parent expectations and other social and political variables.

Educational reform

In the complex 1980s and 1990s, the whole of Canadian public education came under attack from the media, governments, ad hoc commissions, parent and other interest groups, educational critics and academics. This unrelenting assault upon the content, processes and results of schooling in Canada has elevated school reform to a major movement for all levels and for all populations.

The outcomes of education became a key concern of educational reform during the 1980s. Contributing factors included dissatisfaction with the current educational system, public concern over the costs and outcomes of education, changing lifestyles and family structures, new and diverse needs in the marketplace, changing demographics in North American society, and an increasingly more culturally and linguistically diverse student population, which made concerns about equity 'desperately more pressing' (Li, 1994, p 132).

Reformers, calling for reconstruction of the entire education system as the solution to preparing at-risk and other children for the next century, advocate inclusive schools that eliminate segregation and tracking, and that emphasize the building of classroom cultures according to the multiple identities of school users.

The broad inclusive reform movement, focused variously on school management, governance, pedagogy, curriculum, and so on, embraces diversity, and sets out to deal with new social demands on education. Inclusion in special education flowered in this climate of criticism of educational services in general as both a part of and an extension of the effective schools movement towards including more groups in general education.

The Canadian system

Any discussion of special education in Canada must be referenced to the lack of a federal office of education, and to the autonomy of the ten provinces and two territories in matters of education. Although the federal government transfers monies to the provinces in areas such as justice, health, and higher education, it does not fund education. Without a central or federal department of education, each provincial government holds direct control over education through its departments or ministries of education. Each province develops its own separate school laws, acts, policies, regulations, procedures and legislation.

The lack of a federal office of education, combined with the huge geographical distances of Canada, the cultural diversity of the country, and the high urbanization of the population, makes it almost impossible to achieve or maintain policy coherence across the nation, and places in jeopardy any but the broadest statements about education. Different systems operate across the country. Most provinces have tax-supported separate public Catholic and Francophone systems. New Brunswick, a bilingual province, has Anglophone and Francophone schools; Quebec has a Catholic and a Protestant system (although legislation is pending to change to a language-based system). It was not until September 1997, that a referendum in Newfoundland changed the structure of schools operated traditionally by six religious denominations.

For special populations – those with special needs, the culturally diverse, and the linguistically different – the variability seen in the general education area is only compounded. The terrain in special education is remarkably diverse: differences in prevalence figures, in aetiology, in definitions of exceptionality and labelling, in identification and placement procedures, in eligibility for special education services, in funding formulas, in early intervention programmes, and in legislation are readily observed across the country.

Enabling legislation

In the absence of constitutional provisions, education in Canada is not a single uniform system that is available to every child in the same way, and it cannot be said that the law clearly and unequivocally obliges the publicly supported school system to provide appropriate forms of education for *all* students, exceptionality notwithstanding. Only two provincial human rights codes (those of Saskatchewan and Quebec) list education as a right (Mackay, 1987).

Studies dating from the late 1960s have drawn attention to the shortcomings of Canadian legislation and the provision of special education services (Csapo, 1981; Hall and Dennis, 1968; Poirier and Goguen, 1986; Poirier, Goguen and Leslie, 1988; Roberts and Lazure, 1970). Authors repeatedly contrast the progress made in special education in the United States, particularly with reference to PL 94-142, with the lack of progress in Canada (Carter and Rogers, 1989).

The infinity of detail and strict prescriptions for special education planning and implementation seen in the United States are absent in Canada. Canadian provinces have recognized the right to an education for all children in different ways, and not all of them provide equal access to schooling for students with disabilities. Seven of the ten provinces (Newfoundland, Nova Scotia,

New Brunswick, Quebec, Ontario, Manitoba and Saskatchewan) have mandatory legislation, while British Columbia, Alberta and Prince Edward Island have permissive legislation.

In Canada, there is no legal mandate on, or consistent definition of, 'inclusion'. Only the Ministry of Education policies in Saskatchewan and the Northwest Territories explicitly refer to inclusion. However, most Canadian legislation speaks to the idea of inclusion if not to the practice. All provincial and territorial education ministries and departments, based on a philosophy of integration, offer a continuum of services, and all promote the integration of students with special needs into the most appropriate and least restrictive learning environment.

Recent Canadian litigation in special education has been addressed under the elusive concept of equality enshrined in the Canadian Charter of Rights and Freedoms, the supreme law of Canada. Particularly telling is the Eaton case in Ontario, Canada's most populous province. While an Ontario Court of Appeals ruled that Emily Eaton, a child with severe multiple disabilities, had a constitutional right to attend school with fully able children, the Supreme Court of Canada decided that an individual child's needs are to be considered to determine the most appropriate placement from a range of options. Parents cannot decide on placement, and excluding some children from mainstream classes is an acceptable form of discrimination, provided that it is done in the best interests of the child. Decisions should be made on a one-to-one basis, using the yardstick of the best interests of an individual child (Bogie, 1997; Makin, 1997; Smith, 1996).

Contemporary definitions

About 15.5 per cent of all Canadians have a disability. Of the 390 000 children in this number, 89 per cent are mildly disabled, 8 per cent have a moderate disability, and 3 per cent, or about 11 500, have a severe disability ('Prevalence...', 1995). According to Statistics Canada and the Canadian Council for Exceptional Children, 23 to 26 per cent of these students are educated in separate settings; the remainder within the general school system (see Winzer, 1997).

> Essentially, inclusion in Canada means that students with disabilities will attend the school or classroom that they would attend if they were not disabled. Services are brought to the child rather than the child being removed in order to access services. Nevertheless, there remains considerable controversy over the nature and extent of reform as it relates to inclusion, which translates into various views of inclusion and a lack of easy interpretation of both concept and practice.
>
> Across Canada there is not one single model of inclusion. In general, there is cautious advancement of the inclusive point of view, which equates with retention of a full continuum of educational services. In Canada, for ex-

ample, the Council of Administrators of Special Education (CASE), in concert with most ministry policies and the recent Supreme Court ruling, supports the philosophy of inclusion, but adheres to the notion of individual decisions for each child

CASE does *not* support any policy/practice in which *all* students with disabilities, *regardless* of the severity of their disabilities and needs for related services, receive their total education within the regular classroom setting in the school where they would attend if not disabled. A continuum of service delivery options must always be available ('Council...', 1997, p 3; original italics).

Current status

The present reformist climate is making significant differences to special education in the areas of school responsibility, programme delivery, and programme implementation. Spurred by changing public attitudes, court cases, the work of advocates, and parent pressures, many school district personnel are re-analysing service delivery options, and debating the merits of whether to serve students with special needs in general or special education settings. The past decade has seen an increasing number of school districts make a commitment to the inclusion of all students with disabilities and, as the paradigm shift from segregation to integration becomes increasingly manifest, parents, ministries of education, and school boards express the desire to follow an inclusive philosophy whereby a child is effectively welcomed into the general classroom (Carney, 1996).

However, even as inclusion into regular classrooms is becoming more common, the manner in which more extensive integration can be achieved remains elusive and the argument, debate and counter-debate that surround the issue remain strikingly prevalent.

A recent national study of 1 492 Canadian teachers found that more than two-thirds believe that inclusion is academically beneficial to children with special needs and their peers in regular classrooms, and 90 per cent of teachers cite social benefits (Galt, 1997; 'Resistance...', 1997). Nevertheless, while a majority of teachers support the philosophical underpinnings of inclusion, many express a deep concern that in too many cases the inclusive process is not working and is, in fact, creating educationally unsound situations (for example, Alberta Teachers' Association, 1993; Buski, 1997; 'Report...', 1997).

A pervasive lack of support is a critical issue. Currently, the best intentions are being dragged down by large class sizes, inadequate teacher training, lack of outside support for classroom teachers, and concern about the inclusion of certain groups of students (Galt, 1997).

The implementation of inclusionary practices varies widely from province to province and even among neighbouring school boards (Chisholm, 1993), perhaps a reflection of the persistent uneasiness about the practice among educators. Change has occurred, but only in selected school districts and in a few provinces (Porter, 1994), and full inclusion is not the norm in the majority of schools across Canada.

Some systems support inclusive schooling and have made fundamental changes. New Brunswick and Nova Scotia, for example, have adopted integration. Other districts say that they support inclusive education, but have not made policy changes to ensure that integrated settings actually occur. In fact, many jurisdictions have adopted the language of inclusion but continue to rationalize the exceptions to the rule and to treat inclusion programmes as simply one more choice on the special education menu (Porter, 1994). Some schools and districts follow traditional eligibility criteria and a categorically based delivery system with autonomous special education and regular education.

Probably the most common model seen across Canada occurs in school districts that maintain a continuum of services that include segregated options and, typically, approach inclusion on a one-to-one basis. When determining whether to place a student in an inclusive classroom or alternative setting, educators base their decision on student outcomes – in which setting will the child succeed and be prepared to become a productive and active citizen? It is held that case-by-case decisions are consistent with the essence of special education. Rather than following a blanket policy, the special needs of each pupil must be carefully assessed, and the most appropriate educational placement for that child judged.

The critical issue is not where children sit; rather, the major placement objective is to determine where students can receive the most effective education. Whether this means receiving educational services in the general classroom, moving out of the classroom for remedial help for short periods of time, or working in a resource room, self-contained class, or even a separate setting, must be determined individually.

Conclusion

The current movement to educate all children in general education is variously termed 'inclusion', 'inclusive schooling', and 'inclusive education'. For many Canadian educators, advocacy groups and parents, inclusion is the clarion call of educational orthodoxy, an emerging educational paradigm with broad implications for the services provided to all students. For others, it is a radical reform to be approached cautiously, best viewed as yet another placement option that can be added to the continuum of services traditionally found in special education.

In the past two years, the emancipatory powers of inclusion have come under heavy attack and the goal of inclusion for all students has become inconsistent with the views expressed by many, both within and outside the special education community. Many parent and advocacy groups, as well as professional groups, primarily representing students with mild disabilities, speak against the elimination of a continuum of special education services.

Thus, many educators support inclusionary philosophies, but dispute inclusion as a universal template that assumes that only one solution exists to the various challenges faced by children with special needs. They hold that what is needed is not need a retreat from the principles that support a continuum, but a thoughtful deployment of the ideas. Inclusion in many areas is now regarded as an organizational rather than an educational intervention: it is not a place where students with disabilities receive services, but a way to deliver services effectively. Hence, the opportunities made available by the setting, not the setting itself, become important.

References

Alberta Teachers' Association (1993) *Trying to Teach*, Author, Edmonton

Bogie H. (1997) 'Eaton versus Brant County Board of Education: The Supreme Court of Canada Decision', released Feb. 6, 1997. *Keeping in Touch*, p 6

Buski, J. (1997) 'Education reform – What you've told us', Part 2, *ATA Magazine*, pp 34–5

Carney, P. (1996) 'Practitioners views of challenges and issues for school psychologists in the 21st century', *Canadian Journal of School Psychology*, 12, pp 98–102

Carter, D. and Rogers, W. (1989) 'Diagnostic and placement practice for mildly educable mentally handicapped students', *Canadian Journal of Special Education*, 5, p 15–23

Chisholm, P. (1993, March 27) 'Schooling the disabled', *MacLean's*, pp 2–54

Council of Administrators of Special Education (CASE) Inc. (1997) 'Position paper on delivery of services to students with disabilities', *Keeping in Touch*, p 3

Csapo, M. (1981) 'Teachers' federations in the mainstream', *BC Journal of Special Education*, 5, pp 197–218

Galt, V. (1997) 'Teachers support disabled in classes: Fiscal, social realities prevent student integration', *Globe and Mail*, 28 August, pp Al, A6

Hall, M. and Dennis, L. (1968) *Living and Learning: The Report of the Provincial Committee on Aims and Objectives of Education in the Schools of Ontario*, Newton Publishing, Toronto

Li, A. (1994) 'Equity in assessment: From the perspective of new immigrant students', *Canadian Journal of School Psychology*, 10, pp 131–7

Mackay, A. (1987) 'The Charter of Rights and special education: Blessing or curse?', *Canadian Journal of Exceptional Children*, 3, pp 118–27

Makin, K. (1997) 'Classroom exclusion acceptable, court says', *Globe and Mail*, p A 7

Poirier, D. and Goguen, L. (1986) 'The Canadian Charter of Rights and the right to education for exceptional children', *Canadian Journal of Education*, 11, pp 231–44

Poirier, D., Goguen, L. and Leslie, P. (1988) *Educational Rights of Exceptional Children in Canada: A National Study of Multi-Level Commitments*, Carswell, Toronto

Porter, G. (1994) 'Equity and excellence in education: An update', *Abilities*, pp 33–5

'Prevalence of disability in Canada rises', (1995) *Disability Today*, Winter, p 7

Report of the Blue Ribbon Panel on Special Education (1997) Alberta Teachers Association, Edmonton

'Resistance and acceptance: Educator attitudes to inclusion of students with disabilities',

(1997) *Keeping in Touch*, Fall, pp 1, 4

Roberts, C. and Lazure, M. (1970) *One Million Children: A National Study of Canadian Children with Emotional and Learning Disorders*, Crainford, Toronto

Smith, B. (1996) 'Implications of the Eaton case', *Keeping in Touch*, Summer p P9

Winzer, M. (1997) *Children with Exceptionalities: A Canadian Perspective*, Allyn and Bacon, Toronto

10. Spain: responses to inclusion in autonomous regions

Angeles Parrilla

Introduction

This chapter will discuss how integration and inclusion are currently developing in Spain. It is my aim to analyse briefly how ideas, practices and trends related to integration and inclusion have been formulated, developed, and discussed during the twelve years since their implementation.

The first section will illustrate the socio-political situation initiated in the mid-1970s after the death of General Franco, when Spain became engaged in a process characterized by democratization and decentralization. In-depth changes in territorial distribution, economy, society, cultural values, education and politics were substantial, and are briefly considered in an attempt to understand the specific characteristics and concerns behind the integration process in Spain.

The second section examines, from different points of view (policy and policy into practice), the contemporary problems associated with integration and education in diversity within Spanish schools and classrooms. Weaknesses, contradictions and challenges surrounding the current situation are described and analysed.

The last section presents some reflections to be kept in mind when thinking about and planning next steps in promoting inclusion. Three questions serve as a structural skeleton for the content of this section.

Social and political context – Spain as a state of autonomous communities

An understanding of the integration process in Spain is necessarily based on the Spanish Constitution of 1978, which created a democratic state with a form of decentralization somewhere between the federal and regional models. In fact, in the difficult years between 1976 and 1979, during the so-called 'democratic transition' (after the Franco dictatorship), Spain was simultaneously transformed into a democratic and decentralized state. As a result,

Spain became a parliamentary democracy, constructed around a central government and 17 self-governing Autonomous Communities.

Decentralization has not been total. According to the Organization for Economic Cooperation and Development (OECD, 1993), Spain can be defined as
a state where educational decision-making is not left to the central administration alone, but is delegated to intermediate structures such as the regional or
federal administration (the Autonomous Communities). Although the creation of Autonomous Communities resulted in a big step forward, decentralization is still far from placing decision-making power in the hands of local
educational authorities or schools.

In the Spanish case, the central government, through the Ministry of Education, has, above all, a nationwide legislative character. Among its responsibilities are general and common curriculum planning and the design of the
educational system, whereas Autonomous Communities are responsible for
legislative development and educational administration. Autonomies adapt
and apply national laws, control school institutions, select teachers, and establish and monitor educational inspection, support services and financial distribution.

A first look beyond the shared common legal framework sustained by national structures shows that differences between Autonomies are bigger than
one might expect. Divergences at any given level are not solely a question of
differences in the pace of application of national regulations, but are influenced as well by the political party in power in the respective Autonomous
Community. There are also variations grounded in the history, culture and
spoken language of each Autonomy, and these assume new importance in the
light of the current trend of increasing nationalism within Autonomies.

In trying to formulate a picture of inclusion in Spain it is clear that the integration process is one that takes multiple forms and is influenced by a wide
range of social and political forces. Hence, I will refer to the integration process
in general, trying to map and analyse, when needed, divergences or existing
contradictions. The reader should keep in mind that differences in elemental
issues are crucial to understanding inclusion in Spain.

Integration: policies and practices

Integration and inclusion in national policy

There is no doubt that integration in Spain was first promoted by administrators and politicians. In fact, a Ministry of Education decree (Real Decreto de
Ordenacion de la Educación Especial de 1985) questioned the state of education on the national level and proposed a new way of thinking about student
differences and schools, leading to a shift from educational segregation towards school integration. The decree, better known as the Integration

Programme, triggered vigorous, marked and prolonged changes in the educational setting. Key characteristics of the Integration Programme included:

1. Establishment of voluntary school-wide involvement and gradual incorporation into the Integration Programme during an experimental period of 8 years. After this period, in 1994, schools nationwide became integrative by law.
2. The rejection of deficit thinking, clearly outlined in the programme's policy documents. New language and concepts grounded in the British Warnock Report (1978), adopted to name and refer to the change from deficit to interactive and relative thinking about student needs. In this way, the notion of Special Educational Needs (SENs) was adopted at a legislative level.
3. The provision of resources to promote the transformation of schools – the incrementation of internal and external support teams for schools, and regular class-teacher training based in Teacher Centres.

In this way, the Integration Programme set regulations and made recommendations for the gradual introduction of integration in all schools. In addition, there was a strong concern for the encouragement of school transformation. However, the programme was not without its critics. The most important criticism was that integration was limited to the school. That is, the legislation was neither accompanied nor followed by mandates to ensure the continuity of integration in the social context.

An important legislative landmark occurred during the implementation of the ongoing programme, when integration became a general educational principle (Educational Reform of 1990) rather than a specialized programme in school. Educational Reform (MEC, 1990) was the first law promoting nationwide education for all that firmly supported inclusion and comprehensive education. It provided for a national curriculum and extended compulsory education. In so doing, Educational Reform provided the structural conditions necessary for increased democratization and participation in schools – the creation of school boards; democratic school head election; participation in curriculum adaptation; school fund distribution; creation of Teacher Centres.

However, full inclusion has never been achieved in the legislation. The power to exclude from schooling (based on individual characteristics attributed to pupils) remains legitimated by the administration. The Educational Reform states: 'Unlike neighbouring countries integration is not generalized, but depends on the characteristics and possibilities of the pupil.' (MEC, 1990, p 71.) A later regulation clarifying school responsibilities added that every school must integrate students in accordance with resources and limits determined by educational administrations (MEC, 1995). While statistical data shows an enormous and very welcome national decrease in students attending special education schools and classrooms, from 98 971 in 1984 to 29 369 in

1995, exclusion has never be eliminated by law (MEC, 1997).

At this point, a final legislative landmark can be identified revolving around changes made by the central conservative party (Partido Popular), which came to power in 1996. Some analysts point out that the new government may be interested in retarding the general process of integration and re-focusing education in harmony with economic priorities. Although no specific policies related to inclusion have come about, other changes being faced by schools indicate this new phase in integrative policy: The introduction of an unprecedented system of school evaluation (initiating a struggle between competing principles – academic excellence versus equity), recommendations enhancing parent rights to school choice, the emerging use of student achievement statistics in the assessment of school quality, and a rigorous dismantling of Teacher Centres all warn of possible dangers to the field of school integration, and denote a new stage in educational policy.

Policy into practice: integration in schools

A well-documented criticism of the integration process focuses on the way in which integration policy ideology was translated into schools. There is a general consensus among studies from different Autonomous Communities (Fortes, 1992; Alberte, 1995; Arnaiz, 1997a) that policy ideology contained in the Integration Programme has not been followed up by systematic dissemination measures and implementation in school. In other words, policy values, principles and aims were clearly articulated in the legal framework. Nevertheless, structures, conditions and processes provided by authorities at national and Autonomous Community level, in order to develop integration practices, were not appropriate nor adequate. As a result, integration was received with scepticism by many schools and teachers.

The extent of the gap between policy and practice is especially evident in the various interpretations of the new ideology and related concepts in schools. As early studies show, the legislative (written) definition of integration is interpreted, in school practice, in various ways (Parrilla, 1987; Illan, 1989). The most extensive of these is the idea of integration as a process aimed at relocating only those students identified as having SEN in regular classes and schools. This idea has been criticized on the basis that it limits integration to one type of student (those identified as having SEN), and in so doing redefines integration in selective and reduced terms, excluding race, religion and other considerations. Yet another misinterpretation defines integration as a process aimed at adapting the individual child to the school. This implies that institutions have little or nothing to do with the process, as integration appears to be up to the child.

In such a contradictory and confusing arena, many authors call for a new term to describe the concept of integration. Rather than adopting the expression 'inclusive education', as many countries have done, Spanish educators increasingly prefer the use of 'education in diversity'. This term highlights school responsibility to provide an educational answer for the unlimited diversity of students, and places the school at the heart of the process. In this way, answering to diversity requires that schools develop inclusive answers for all students (López Melero, 1995). Thus, with the exception of some academic reports, terms such as 'inclusive schools' or 'inclusion' are not common in Spain.

How did this happen? Can such changes be described and explained within schools? In answering these questions I will discuss the curriculum debate that emerged in Spain after the Educational Reform as there is no doubt that the central integration controversy in the 1990s has developed in the pedagogical and curricular arena. This debate is founded on the different positions taken in schools with the implementation of a curriculum for all that must be adapted to the needs of diversity. The single most important question is: 'How should a curriculum be adapted?' At least three strong practical positions can be identified, as follows:

1. Some schools, teachers and local educational authorities have not truly accepted the idea of a curriculum for all. Despite the compulsory nature of such a curriculum, the supposed need for an individual-based curriculum for SEN students is defended. A small yet significant proportion of schools continues to implement traditional individual educational plans based on child-centred assessment and resulting in a special individual curriculum. The predominant argument for such a curriculum perspective is rooted in the aforementioned legislative acceptance of exclusion. While statistics do not reflect school practices so much as policy trends (the best practices can be developed under the worst circumstances), it could be illustrative to mention that the Autonomous Community of the Basque Country allows 25 special schools whereas the Autonomous Community of Catalonia permits 114 (MEC, 1997).

2. A second and majority position within the curriculum debate comes from those schools, authorities and researchers vigorously engaged in the challenge of adapting the common curriculum to individual student needs. The underlying idea is that, taking the common curriculum as a basis, it is possible to differentiate and adapt it to individual students. Teacher training, support teachers, resources and classrooms are key in this process, which is conceived as highly specialized and technical by supporters (Molina, 1987; Gonzalez Manjón, 1995).

An Individual Curriculum Adaptation is a document where the special and general education that a student needs during a period of time, is described and justified, in which efforts developed to promote the student towards a less restrictive environment must appear, as well as those attempts to reduce the provision of special services, if this is possible and convenient (Ruiz, 1988, p 96).

This model has shown many weaknesses and contradictions in its implementation. In adapting the common curriculum to individual students, schools engage in a process defined by law as a collaborative task between teachers and specialists. However, in doing this, schools are both facing and creating important problems, exposing themselves to the risk of establishing a new form of segregation. The assessment of SEN (a compulsory step in developing an Individual Curricular Adaptation) is a process dependent on external support services, where the power to select SEN students resides. Also, the Individual Curriculum Adaptation process is almost wholly determined by educational inspectors, who must approve the document and provide for additional special resources as deemed needed. Such control from educational inspectors, and dependence on external support services, results in a dynamic of school control and domination in contradiction with written policy about integration and school autonomy. Finally, a process aimed at adapting the school to individual needs tends to segregate the student, who is clearly labelled as 'special'. School autonomy restrictions are also frustrating for schools, which are considered to be little more than puppet organizations dependent on experts and authorities. Despite the benevolent intentions of advocates of such curriculum policy, it has resulted in a dangerous turn towards a process that involves schools and teachers in student labelling and segregation.

A growing (yet still small) number of schools and educators opposing this position centre their work around whether integration should be achieved through individual curriculum adaptations (as legislation mandates), or whether it is classroom curriculum that must be reconstructed to respond to diversity needs. For those – Parrilla, 1992; López Melero, 1996; Arnaiz, 1997a – who argue in favour of this trend, curriculum adaptation is a school process, not an individual matter. It involves an examination of curriculum from a school-wide point of view, guided by the idea of curriculum development and adaptation to the collective diversity of students and groups, rather than to individual differences. Arnaiz's (1997b) case studies of classrooms working with this approach in the Autonomous Community of Murcia, as well as case studies by López Melero (1996) in the Community of Andalucía, confirms the need to move towards structural and conceptual changes in curriculum instead of individual proposals for differentiated children. Four main effects are linked to the diversification of learning experiences at the classroom level: decreased labelling, increased school autonomy, the legitimation of a discourse aimed to empower schools staff over specialists, and the creation of a learning environment adapted for all. While it would be nice to think that this perspective is well rooted in practice, recent analysis of the discourse of various support teachers in Andalucía (Parrilla, Hernandez and Murillo, 1997) points out the presence of a number of forces operating in schools that hinder healthy progress. Education in diversity, as this study proposes, should not be seen as a question of teamwork between specialized educational agents, but, rather, as a co-operative effort between school professionals. It is in such a context that the curriculum may be seen as a powerful force in the process of creating a school that is responsive and open to the diversity of needs.

Three questions for the future

Three crucial questions reflect some of the most important and outstanding problems for integration in Spain.

How can democratic education be enhanced?

The strong legal commitment to integration in Spain, as well as subsequent steps towards decentralization and school autonomy, are not free from contradictions and critiques. Questions raised in relation to exclusion, external control and new labelling must not be neglected. Democracy within schools, outlined in legislation *and* practised, which recognizes participation, equal rights and common destiny among members, is inevitable. Otherwise, there will always be those who are ready to make decisions for, and to exclude, others (considering them as not belonging to the group). Unless schooling can develop teaching and educational practices for all, based on autonomy and equity in participation and decision-making, exclusion will continue to exist.

Can the school become a learning community through integration?

The issue of democracy addresses schools as learning communities that grow, evolve and learn. If this is assumed, it is necessary to create a unified school identity, with a whole school looking for and building answers and resources inside its own community. The role of resources in the implementation of integration must be reconsidered, connecting resources to the school. Thinking of schools and staff as resources implies a trust in their ability to improve themselves and to use their own creativity, potential and knowledge to solve their problems. Because integration, in general terms, has been a contradictory experience, faced by schools in a culture that accepts dependence on experts, external support and resources, it is essential that schools consider themselves as communities that do not aim to perpetuate this system, but desire to alter it.

Can a school-based integration policy transform a social system?

Although this chapter is limited to inclusive education, a few words about the relation between school and social inclusion are needed. Current Spanish educational legislation seems to be very optimistic in expecting that social integration will be the end result of school integration. Today, it can be asserted that an integrative ideology is being assumed by schools, but its effects are far from penetrating general society and its institutions; at a national level, only

0.8 per cent of the active population are people with disabilities. Integration in schools can be seen as a mere token gesture as long as exclusion in general society continues. A coherent policy should recognize practices of exclusion and extend inclusive policy across social institutions. Government legislation needs to show evidence of a serious attempt both to create and to maintain inclusion.

References

Alberte, J. R. (1995) *Avaliación do proceso de integración en Galicia*, ACK Editores, Santiago

Arnaiz, P. (1997a) 'Innovación y Diversidad: Hacia nuevas propuestas didácticas', in J. Torres, M. Román and E. Rueda (eds) *La Innovación de la Educación Especial*, Universidad de Jaén, Jaén, pp 745–53

Arnaiz, P. (1997b) 'Adapting curriculum in inclusive classrooms', paper presented at European Conference on Educational Research, Frankfurt, September, 1997

Fortes, J. (1992) 'Una evaluación externa e independiente del impacto de las políticas públicas sobre necesidades educativas especiales en una comunidad educativa', Tesis Doctoral, Málaga

Gonzalez Manjón, D. (1995) *Adaptaciones curriculares: guía para su elaboración*, Aljibe, Málaga

Illan, N. (1989) *La integración escolar y los profesores*, Nau Llibres, Valencia

López Melero, M. (1995) 'Diversidad y cultura: una escuela sin exclusiones', *Kikiriki*, 38, pp 26–88

López Melero, M. (1996) 'Informe de estudios de caso de la integración escolar en la Comunidad Andaluza', Junta de Andalucía

Ministerio de Educación y Cultura (MEC) (1985) Real Decreto de Ordenación de la Educación Especial de 1985, MEC, Madrid

Ministerio de Educación y Cultura (MEC) (1990) *Libro Blanco para la Reforma del Sistema Educativo*, MEC, Madrid

Ministerio de Educación y Cultura (MEC) (1995) Ley Orgánica de la participación, la evaluación y el gobierno de los centros docentes, MEC, Madrid

Ministerio de Educación y Cultura (MEC) (1997) *Informe sobre el estado y situación del sistema educativo*. MEC, Consejo Escolar del Estado, Madrid

Molina, S. (1987) *La integración en el aula: programas de desarrollo individual*, Graó, Barcelona

OECD (1993) *Education at a glance. OECD indicators*, Centre for Educational Research and Innovation, Paris

Ruiz i Bel, R. (1988)*Técnicas de individualización didáctica*, Cincel, Madrid

Parrilla, A. (1987) 'La figura y la formación del profesor ante la integración', in C. García (ed.) *La formación de los profesionales de la educación especial*, Servicio de Publicaciones de la Universidad, Sevilla, pp 45–67

Parrilla, A. (1992) *El profesor ante la integración: investigación y formación*, Ediciones Pedagógicas, Madrid

Parrilla, A., Hernandez, E. and Murillo, P. (1997) 'Developing a shared approach to support: a support group case study', *European Journal of Special Needs Education*, 12 (3), pp 209–24

Warnock, M. (1978) *Special Educational Needs. Report of the committee of enquiry into the education of handicapped children and young people*, HMSO, London

Systems in change

11. Towards a healing society: perspectives from Japanese special education

Gerald K. LeTendre and Hidetada Shimizu

Introduction

Over the last few decades, a wealth of data on Japanese education in general has been amassed in the English language. Starting with Passin's (1967) summary, scholars have branched out to study various levels and aspects of Japanese schooling: Peak, 1991; Hendry, 1986; Lewis, 1995; Rohlen and LeTendre, 1996. However, little attention has been paid to the topic of 'special education' (*tokushu kyôiku*) in Japan, nor has much been written with regard to how differently abled students are (or are not) integrated into Japanese classrooms (see Demoulin and Kendall, 1993, or Masawa *et al.*, 1993, for some of the few published works in the area).

This lack of research into special education is startling, considering the wealth of general information and the amount of work carried out by researchers on general topics. Perhaps this area has been 'forgotten' partly because it raises uneasy questions for Western researchers, in terms of their views of Japan, and in terms of the difficulties of providing inclusive education in their own countries. Research into provision for differently abled children and adolescents often dramatically shows up the limitations of education systems, and increases awareness of the assumptions and values that we, as researchers, bring to this field of study. We wish, therefore, to make it clear that we intend no 'Japan bashing', or 'America bashing'; we are dealing with an area in which many national systems of education have remaining inadequacies, and where researchers themselves may well not have explored the degree to which cultural values (which are taken for granted) have an impact upon their research. We use a reflexive approach to highlight how different researchers (ourselves) reacted to doing research in special education classrooms.

Our argument is that the study of special education in Japan, and especially the associated concept of inclusivity, provides evidence that we need to move beyond a simple comparative strategy using 'de-centered translation' to one that integrates ethnographic studies with analytic quantitative studies. In this way, it should be possible accurately to describe the experience of education for individuals, the social values at play in any given educational system, and the wider social impacts that educational policies have upon individual chances for academic achievement and social mobility.

This chapter begins by briefly outlining the formal divisions within the Japanese public system related to the education of differently abled children and adolescents. A visual and numerical study of the number of students in various schools and classrooms is provided, and we then discuss how these systems (schools and classrooms) are integrated into the larger education system. In the next two sections, we will present our perspectives on special education classrooms in public elementary and middle schools. Both authors have worked extensively in the field of Japanese education. Gerald LeTendre presents the perspective of an American researcher sent to investigate the subject of adolescent lives, while Hidetada Shimizu presents the perspective of a Japanese researcher investigating the topic of individual differences.

In conclusion, we discuss pertinent research that might further expand knowledge of special education in Japan as well as 'trouble' current constructions of inclusivity, individual differences and ability. We also consider how the education of students who are differently abled reflects on the concept of a 'closed' society – a society that has closed off certain members of itself from participation in the full range of life of the community. For both Japan and the US, the issue of a 'closed' society is one that goes against the formal legal foundations, as well as, we think, against the beliefs of the majority of the population. Using Kenzaburo Oe's ideas (1995) we argue that future research in this area is crucial not only for better schooling, but also for 'healing society'. The issue of special education is thus an opportunity not to learn how to treat others 'differently', but to see how well society can, essentially, care for itself.

Special education in Japan

Most people familiar with Japanese education will remember that there are a whole set of 'special education schools' that are distinct from the public system of early, elementary, junior high and senior high schools (see Ministry of Education, Science and Culture, 1989, p 14 for a graphic summary). These 'schools for the blind, the deaf and the otherwise handicapped' constitute a separate system from the general public schools (Statistics Bureau, 1996, p 696). It should be kept in mind that enrolment in these schools constitutes less that one per cent of total overall enrolments at any given level.

These special schools constitute a separate track within the Japanese system. Progression through the levels occurs within the special education system and students do not take the same kind of high school entrance exam that other students do. At the college level, students can and sometimes do compete in university entrance exams in the same way as graduates of the 'mainstream' public and private schools. In general, students in these schools have the most severe forms of impairment in terms of vision or hearing, and in the 'otherwise handicapped' schools (*yôgo gakkô*) they often have multiple impairments (both developmental and mobility disability). For many of the students in this latter category, full-time care is required.

However, many differently abled children and adolescents are not educated in these separate schools, but in 'special education' classrooms (*tokushu gakkyû*) within the public schools. Of these kind of students, 110 568 are educated in 21 605 classrooms in the public elementary and junior high schools in Japan (Monbusho, 1987, p 14). Students in special education classes will often take part in non-academic classes and will participate as a class in the school's yearly events and festivals. As compulsory education only last for nine years in Japan, high schools are not required to provide these special education classrooms. Within any given elementary or middle school, the numbers of students in special education classes varies, but the size of these classes is considerably smaller than regular classrooms. In most Japanese elementary schools, enrolments of 30 and more per class are common. However, enrolments in special education classrooms range between five and 15 students.

With regard to differences between students in the separate special education schools versus students in special education classes in public schools, one Japanese public school teacher interviewed by Shimizu stated,

> First, children in a separate 'handicapped' school are much more severely handicapped than students [in public schools]. Also, they are very isolated, so it's hard for them to have contact with regular children. I moved out of a 'handicapped school' because it was so isolated from the rest of the world, and was a far cry from a 'society which lives alongside with disabled children' – which is my ideal. I felt I was in a very special world, and I did not want to lose touch with being with other kind of children.

The special education classes are open to students with less severe disabilities, and allow students to maintain close contact with students in the regular classes. However, students in special education classrooms often have very different learning needs. According to official statistics, the largest number of students are categorized as having 'mental weakness' (*seishin hakujaku*, 85 613) with 'emotional disability' (*jôcho shôgai*, 9 346) making up the next largest category (Monbusho, 1987, p 14). Only 316 students with visual disabilities were listed as being enrolled in these classes (Monbusho, 1987, p 14). In an interview with teachers in a large city in Japan, Shimizu found that students with autism, Down's Syndrome and epilepsy were all taught in the special education classrooms. In the rural areas, where LeTendre worked, small school size and long distances appeared to acerbate this tendency towards putting differently abled students together in one room, regardless of their specific learning needs.

Special education teachers receive training distinct from that of regular education teachers and have special certification procedures. The most radically different aspect of this teaching is a focus on individual differences, and creating individualized learning plans for each student. This practice appears analogous to the individualized educational plans that are used in the US. Also, there is some form of 'mainstreaming' in many schools. Like school counsellors, special education teachers tend to use a 'softer' pedagogical approach, which usually characterizes the earliest levels of public education (see Peak, 1991; Lewis, 1995).

Selection into special education

How are children identified and streamed into special education in Japan? In interviewing teachers for the Third International Math–Science Project, Shimizu recorded one teacher's explanation:

Shimizu: How is a child usually referred to the special education class? What's the process?

Teacher: Normally, most disabled children get identified before entering pre-school. You get the notice from your local city hall to give your child a check-up at six months, one and a half years and three years. In the case of rather severely handicapped children, they can be picked up easily by the six-month normal check-up because their heads do not sit stable on the neck. Normal children's necks become "stabilized" after about three months.

Shimizu: How serious [is this condition]?

Teacher: It could be very serious, so a child with this condition is referred to a doctor immediately. Now in the case of the one-and-a-half-year check-up, most children are able to walk by then, so if a child is unable to walk at this time, he/she is referred to a doctor. Most autistic children, by the way, pass both the six-month and one-and-a-half-year check-up. At the three-year-old check-up, children are asked questions verbally. If a child does not respond at all, or tries to avoid the examiner all together, autism is suspected and he/she is referred to a doctor. After seeing a doctor, if parents still think that their child may be slower than others, they have to make a decision to put the child in a regular pre-school or in a special school for disabled children. Children who go to such special schools usually advance either to a regular school with a class for disabled children or to a school that is primarily for disabled children. When parents have a hard time deciding, they sometimes go to the Educational Center [for information].

The process of identifying children with special needs, then, exemplifies a highly developed system of early detection and referral. In general, previous studies of early childcare in Japan suggest that Japan has developed a system of childcare and referral that is among the most advanced in the world (see Peak, 1991; Hendry, 1986). Long before a child enters school, most parents will have had the opportunity to receive professional guidance and counselling on these matters. Japan's highly socialized system of medical care allows relatively high-quality diagnosis and referral to be available even for the poorest families.

This process of early detection and assessment of the individual's needs, as well as the power given to parents in terms of placement decisions, sharply contrasts with many Western impressions of Japanese society as 'group-centred' and 'homogeneous.' It is in keeping, however, with a substantial body of scholarly work (see Sato, 1996 in addition to authors already cited), which shows a high emphasis on prevention and individual attention in early childcare in Japan. This focus on the individual, in a culture that explicitly manifests ideals of group participation, provides a challenge to the understanding of how groups or individuals are segregated from or incorporated into society.

Our own research on Japan suggests that there is a tension in Japanese culture between cultural ideals that emphasize group-belonging and harmony and ideals of democratic participation, and sensitivity to individual needs and a value on individual accomplishment. The study of Japanese education by Western observers has often been seriously influenced by implicit cultural values about what an 'individual' is and how 'individuals' are to be treated (see LeTendre, forthcoming). The next two sections present excerpts from the authors' field notes, taken in special education classrooms during the TIMSS study, which highlight the impact these implicit values have on education research.

An American perspective

The following excerpts are from LeTendre's field notes from a visit to a special education classroom in a medium-sized Japanese city.

> Today was the first time that I was allowed to see a special education class [on the TIMSS study]. It was virtually identical to the classes that I observed during my dissertation research. Students are off in a classroom by themselves which has a special name – usually a fine-sounding combination of characters. Like the rest of the students they wear uniforms and have the complete set of mottoes and the like.
>
> One of the children appeared to have Down's Syndrome. One girl appeared to have epilepsy and another to be extremely nervous and shy. Several of the children showed developmental disabilities as evinced in their command of Japanese and the work I saw them studying.
>
> It appeared that, like the other classes I have seen, no distinction was

made between various handicaps. Students with developmental disabilities, emotional disabilities, and epilepsy were all in one class and studied together as a unit. There appeared to be ample staffing, for the eight children there were at times three adults in the room.

The one teacher I talked with had majored in special education in college and there appears to be national standards for the training of teachers who work in these 'tokushu' classes.

The nagging question remains – are students allowed to fully develop their potential, or are they limited to a second-class status in the education of the school? Clearly the classes they are offered are inferior. They are taught all subjects by the special education teachers, not by regular teachers who have subject-specialty training. In my experience they do not receive lessons from the visiting English teachers (foreign). The two 3rd year students I interviewed – the girl who appeared to have epilepsy and a boy who had no apparent handicap – were going on to 'handicapped high schools' (yôgo kôkô). The boy hoped to be a carpenter.

While little of substantive value could be gained from this short visit, it is clear that all over Japan students are isolated at elementary and middle schools in 'special education' classes, which appear to track them into 'handicapped' schools. How many of these students could have made their way in regular classes – in other words, how many do not have developmental disabilities, which would hinder them from exam-prep study – is difficult to say.

As an American, my first reaction to seeing a special classroom for students with various special needs was profoundly disturbing. My cultural associations were with the 'warehousing' of special needs students in segregated schools and classrooms, as was common in the past in US education. Most disturbing to me was the possibility that some of the students might not be challenged to their full intellectual potential. Severe mobility or emotional disabilities might mean these students had to learn in very distinct ways, but did not mean that they could not succeed in the same kind of studies that other students took.

Socially, I was also shocked that these students were not integrated into the mainstream classrooms. How did these students feel, shut away from other students in their own room? Whenever I visited students in these classrooms during my original fieldwork, they seemed very shy and unaccustomed to visitors. What kind of discrimination as individuals must they feel?

After a cursory reading of the struggles that differently abled individuals have waged in Japan for recognition of individual rights, I remain convinced that this area of Japanese education is one that requires profound reconceptualization and reform. However, I am less willing overtly to castigate the teachers and schools, for I am coming to an understanding that my interpretations were based on both a lack of knowledge, and on cultural values that are distinct from those of many Japanese. I have also now been made aware of cases where young adolescents with fairly severe mobility impairments have been accommodated in mainstream classrooms. My increased knowledge has made me more aware of how my own implicit values at first affected my depiction of Japanese classrooms.

A Japanese perspective

Shimizu's account provides a marked contrast.

Imagine being told to visit a Japanese elementary school in a lower-class or working-class neighbourhood of one of the largest metropolitan areas. Imagine also that you are scheduled to visit the 'special education' classroom there. What might be your gut-level imagination of what your visit may be like? Having attended a Japanese elementary school nearly 30 years ago, I had little memory of my own elementary school, which did have a 'special education class' like that one I was visiting on this sunny March morning. Several things defied my expectations. The following is a description of my visit to this classroom.

This school no longer used the term my generation grew up with, 'special education class' (*gakkyû*). In the visiting schedule prepared for me by the school vice-principal, the class was referred to as a 'class for students with disabilities' (*shôaiji gakkyû*). Upon visiting the school, I told the principal who escorted me to the class about my surprise. Nodding with a sign of understanding, he said,

> That's right. I know what you are talking about. We used to use that term 'special education class', but we no longer do. The reason we do not is to avoid suggesting that these students are 'special' by any means. Our current approach is to call them 'students with disabilities'. The rationale behind the change is that they are no different from all the other children, except that there are areas in which they are disabled.

As soon as we arrived at the class, I noticed immediately a sign that said *hikari gakkyû*, or 'Class of Light'. The principal had explained earlier, 'The name comes from the concept of being "stirred by" the [light of] hope.'

Inside the class, I saw four students. After my class observation, the teacher, Ms Ishida, told me they were Miho-chan, a 4th grade girl with autism, Kayo-chan, a 6th grade girl with epilepsy, Hiro-kun, a 5th grade boy with Down's Syndrome, and Fumi-kun, a 4th grade boy with autism. (-chan and -kun are familiar, diminutive suffixes attached to girl's and boy's names, respectively, in the way that -san is attached to adult names.)

The class had a different arrangement from a regular class. Instead of over 30, it had only four desk-chair set at the middle of the room. It had two carpeted stages, about 6 inches tall, six by four feet, placed at both the front and back areas of the class. There is a home-sized trampoline placed at the back of the room. The room is bright with the morning sun, illuminating the fish tank placed next to the teachers' desk.

The class gave me a different impression from a regular class, mostly because of its informal 'homey' atmosphere, coupled with the lack of conformity. When I arrived at the class at 9.45 a.m., for example, some students were watching a popular TV programme made for children called *Okaasan to Issho* ('Being with Mummy'). Ms Ishida let children watch the programme for about 15 minutes. She did not care much to give a good impression to me or to the principal. Instead, she was casually conversing with, or having monologue to, Miho, who looked glued to one of the two stages: 'Oh yes, Miho-chan. That's your place, isn't it? Miyo-chan is playing her own station.' Next, Ms Ishida made sure if anyone wanted to go to the bathroom before the class started. Miho-chan, again, said 'yes'. The whole class waited for Miho-chan and Ms Ishida to come back.

When the two came back, the teacher finally said to the class, 'Let's start [the lesson]. I wonder what neat things we are buying today.' The class had been 'practising' the errand game. The teacher is the salesperson, and her students are her 'customers'. Each student is given a chance to make her or his purchase. The focus of the lesson is two fold: to pay the amount asked by the 'sales person,' as well as to be part of the set 'script' that the sale's clear and customer goes through in a Japanese store:

> Teacher/salesperson: "Welcome to the store" (*irasshai mase*). What can I offer you (*nani ni itashi mashôka*)?
> Mihochan points to the bag of potato chips.
> Teacher/salesperson: "Thank you! 500 yen please!"
> She points to the tray of toy coins, and urges Miho to pick five 100-yen coins. Miho takes a few seconds and picks five. Ms Ishida says, "Very nice. Thank you very much. Come again!"

Although the level of maths taught here was low, the emotional bonding among the students and the students' fondness for the class looked strong. It was where *amae* (sweet permissiveness) was permitted, as the Japanese would say – a place where one can expect others to treat you gently and benevolently regardless of your performance level. On the outside (*soto*), however, *amae* must be tamed, so that one may attune oneself to the collective activities and norms of the group. That is the area in which students with disabilities have slimmer chances of finding acceptance.

In my later interview with her, Ms Ishida indicated such ambivalence about the 'place' of these students in Japanese schools. In her own perception, her students are 'no different from other kids. They are just unable to do certain things that other kids can.' She said the problems are not in her students, but inside her own value system and the larger socio-cultural context, in which individuals are expected to assimilate themselves with norms and common values of a group; and this is in fact what the majority of them want to do.

In the school's annual 'Sports Day' (*undo-kai*), for example, Ms Ishida tried to let one of her students compete in the short-distance race. This was not an unusual experience for her student, because her class regularly participated in regular classrooms during non-academic subject hours such as art, music, and physical education. The only difference was that it was the once-a-year official event in which the eyes of every parent, student, and teacher were fixed on the competitors. But, even before the race started, it became apparent that Ms Ishida's student could not line up at the start. He refused to stay still before the pistol was shot. Her response shows a very deep level of reflection about the tensions that exist within Japanese society, between ideals of group harmony and solidarity, and individual accomplishment. Ms Ishida noted,

> My intention was to help this student to be on the same stage with other students. But in Japanese schools, when students are told to be set [on the line], it is really meant. And if someone fails to do it, it really becomes noticeable. I think most people did not know how to react when they saw this. And I found myself wanting my student to do it. Just to show the world that he can do that, too. Then I realized, 'Well, does he really have to?' I said to myself, 'Am I really thinking for my student's benefit, or is it just to satisfy my ego that I want my student [to] be at the same ballpark with other students?'

Ms Ishida is not alone in wishing for a disabled student to at least be given a chance to try to make it in the 'real' (non-disabled) world. Many parents, at least in the past, wanted to place their children in a regular class in a regular school, 'just so that *seken* (the watchful community) will not know' that their children were 'special' (ie sub-normal). Kenta-kun, an autistic 6th grade boy, who was attending home-economics class with his non-disabled peers at the time of my class observation, is a good example. In pre-school, he was diagnosed as autistic. His parents 'did everything they could', including sending him to autism specialists at university clinics. 'Somewhere they got the idea that it helps an autistic child to mingle with non-autistic children,' so they decided to place Kenta-kun in a regular classroom at Ms Ishida's school.

Since teachers in regular classes had no training in special education, Kenta was treated no differently from other students, and given no special attention. As a result, he became bored and walked out of the class on many occasions. At one time, he could not be found anywhere for hours, and mainstreaming him became a school-wide issue. However, on his mother's insistence that she would attend the class with him, he remained in this class. Later it became clear, even to her, that he was not being benefited from being in this class, so she decided to put him in Ms Ishida's special education class, on a 'part-time basis, without an official membership'. Kenta, however, liked the instruction, which was adjusted to his level and, every time he was sent to a regular class, he would mutter the name of Ms Ishida's class. Finally, his parents agreed to put him in her class full time.

I could not help but empathize with the hopes and frustrations of special education teachers, students and their parents. They were critical of the 'groupism' that their culture demands of them: they felt that it was unreasonable to expect everyone to act alike in a group situation. At the same time, they knew that everyone, not just disabled students, needed a place to belong, for this was the cultural mandate of wider Japanese society. In order to belong to a group, however, each person has to be able to perform the basic tasks expected of every group member (such as remaining seated for an entire class period). Disabled students lack such basic abilities. As a result, most of those with severe emotional and psychological problems go to a special education school after graduating from junior high schools. Many stay and find employment within these institutions after graduation.

Analysis

These two ethnographic reflections bring to light two inter-related issues. The first is the tension expressed within current Japanese society over how individuals who are differently abled are to be integrated into schools. The second is how Western researchers, whose basic assumptions about individuals, individualism and 'inclusion' are conditioned in a Western cultural context, make sense of this area of Japanese education. Let us address the methodological question first.

Far from arguing that only Japanese people can understand Japanese culture, we argue that multiple research perspectives are essential to identify and 'bring to light' the values and conflicts that shape Japanese perceptions as well as American perceptions about education for differently abled students. Our awareness of the complexity of describing these phenomena grew substantially in the course of writing this chapter. While there are clear limitations in trying to analyse Japanese culture in purely 'Western categories', it is equally limiting to ignore the degree to which Western theories and models have an impact on Japanese schools and teachers (and on the schools and teachers of other national systems). As Miron and Katoda (1991) note, the movement for inclusion of differently abled students affects Japanese attitudes, and Japanese teachers appear to be struggling with questions that would not be unfamiliar to American special education teachers.

In terms of understanding Japanese educational processes, the study of special education in Japan highlights the existence of different pedagogical approaches and the tension between Japanese ideals for group identity and individual achievement. Simply to label the system of special education in Japan as 'segregation' sheds no light on the psychological motives and ambivalence underlying the system. Special education teachers know that some of their students would rather be more completely integrated into the wider school. As Ms Ishida noted, 'Children take notice when I give each of them different play materials. So I have to give them the same things. Kenta-kun, for example, becomes quite unhappy when he is not being part of what everyone is doing.'

Teachers themselves wish to 'integrate' (*tôgô*) their students with the mainstream education. One problem, Ms Ishida noted, is that most students and teachers in regular classrooms tend to give too much help for disabled students, assuming that they are 'helpless'. Disabled students, who are generally capable of handling more things than the regular students and teachers assume (such as putting on clothes, eating and so on), are often unable to communicate to others in what areas they can use their help. She notes,

> It is not that everyone doesn't want to include disabled students in their lives. They just don't know what to do once they come to face to face contact with disabled children. Everyone wants *tôgô kyôiku* ('integrative education'), but they don't know how to invite them to be part of their life. Many teachers say, 'Please bring your students to my class, but tell me what to do because I don't have the slightest idea.' So I tell them to watch me work with them. I help them to help themselves. I teach my students to let their wishes and ideas be known to others. That's the first and most important thing they can learn. Without it, they simply won't be able to make it out there.

The regular classroom students and teachers who want differently abled students to come to their classes are expressing deeply held Japanese beliefs about the importance of including everyone. In pre-schools and early elementary grades, Japanese teachers strive very hard to construct activities where students learn how to work in groups and develop a sensitivity (*omoiyari*) to the needs of others. This training is continued in elementary and middle schools, often through the use of reflective activities (*hansei*) during social studies or moral education classes.

However, Japanese teachers and parents are also keenly aware that Japanese society is hierarchically segmented, and that education is a key element in attaining social mobility. Students who wish to achieve must achieve in exams, and also in a society organized around levels of seniority. Indeed, part of the emphasis on order, and what (to American eyes) appears to be rather rigid adherence to certain rules, can alternatively be read as respect for others in a social situation that often demands the precise co-ordination of group movement. The strict adherence to rules in the sports festival that Shimizu noted is readily acknowledged by Japanese teachers as important 'training' for life in the adult world.

As Lewis notes, the Japanese borrow the English term 'wet' (*uetto*) to distinguish this emotionally sensitive education from what they perceive to be more logical or 'dry' (*durai*) Western forms of schooling. However, within Japanese education itself, two distinct pedagogical streams can be identified. Over time, Japanese students move from the warmth of the home to the loving atmosphere (*amae*) of the pre-school and early elementary grades. However, this atmosphere shifts in the upper elementary grades and middle school to one that emphasizes order and strictness and ordered behaviour (*majime/kibishii*).

It is striking to note that, when confronted with students that do not tend to be able to adapt easily to Japanese norms for adult behaviour in a hierarchical society, many Japanese educators access the wet, or 'soft', form of education. The climate depicted by Shimizu in his field notes is strikingly similar to that observed by LeTendre in his visit to a middle school that educated significant numbers of Vietnamese refugee children. In both schools, the emphasis on or-dered behaviour and rules is relaxed in favour of an atmosphere that focuses on the emotional needs of the child or adolescent. The emphasis shifts from a rather narrow focus on academic achievement to one that focuses on what the individual can achieve.

Perhaps the most dramatic depiction of this style of pedagogy in Japanese education can be found in Kuroyanagi's enchanting story *Totto-chan* (1986). In describing her experiences at a private school designed to educate students who did not fit into the highly militarized atmosphere of pre-war Japanese schools, Kuroyanagi describes a school that strove to include all children. In relating her experiences, Kuroyanagi describes the educational philosophy of Kobayashi Sosaku, the founder of the school, thus:

> [Mr. Kobayashi] believed all children are born with an innate good nature, which can be easily damaged by their environment and the wrong adult in-fluences. His aim was to uncover their 'good nature' and develop it, so that the children would grow into people with individuality. (Kuroyanagi, 1988, pp 228–9)

At Kobayashi's school, a range of differently abled students were welcomed be-cause of his strong belief in the goodness in *all* children. Moreover, the explicit belief in the value of developing individuality drove him to create curricula that developed the strengths of individual children. The fact that this school was es-tablished in 1937 – at the height of Japan's Emperor-worship cult and militarism – demonstrates, we argue, how deep-seated is the Japanese value of developing the goodness in each individual child. The conflict – in the 1930s in a school sys-tem tightly linked to the war effort, and currently in a school system linked to exam success – is not lost on most Japanese people. It is a pervasive tension that permeates Japanese society as well as Japanese schools.

Conclusion

One of Japan's foremost writers has also been one of the country's foremost advocators of inclusive education. Kenzaburo Oe's son, born with a develop-mental disability, has been his inspiration for numerous works, which appear to have had a profound impact on modern Japanese consciousness of the lives of differently abled children and adolescents. As Shimizu noted, there have been social movements in Japan to move from a stigmatizing view of students as 'special' – and therefore inferior or damaged – to one that focuses on individual abilities. This consciousness would seem to be linked to a more worldwide awareness of the limit of inclusivity found in most industrial nations.

However, Oe pushes his understanding of the issues even deeper to form a critique not only of special education, but society as a whole. Oe wrote,

> I can only speak on the basis of my experience of the one model I've seen of a community that does not shut out the handicapped, namely, that of the University of California at Berkeley where I once spent some time. The campus is built on the side of a mountain, and the difference in elevation from one end to the other is so extreme that one could almost imagine they had to import vegetation from various altitudes to ensure that it would grow in the various microclimates...One can't help thinking it would prove a major obstacle for those with physical disabilities. Nevertheless, at Berkeley it isn't at all uncommon to see people crisscrossing the campus in motorized wheelchairs at remarkable speeds. Where, I wondered to myself, would these handicapped students (and among them were some with mental disabilities as well) have gone if Berkeley had shut them out? Some of them, no doubt, would have gone home to live in seclusion; others would have been institutionalized. Now I am the first to recognize that institutions are sometimes necessary and, if properly run, can even serve as staging grounds for the integration of the disabled into society at large...But, it is equally true that there have been and in all probability still are places that have as their express purpose – or their effective result – the isolation of the handicapped, functioning thus as the necessary complements to a closed society. (Oe, 1995, pp 93–4)

Oe's reputation as one of today's foremost writers is largely due to his unflagging dedication to writing about the way in which society is 'closed'. Oe's definition of 'closed' is one that speaks not just to Japan, but to all societies that claim to be 'open' and 'inclusive'. A society that is 'closed' to the participation of certain members is one that has limited itself. Rather than defining inclusiveness as a benign gesture on the part of 'society' – something society does for the 'disabled' or the 'less advantaged' members – Oe suggests that inclusiveness is something that society must achieve if it is to grow, survive and heal itself. Rather than 'doing something for' others, society itself needs those 'others' – those persons who have been closed off, shut out, hidden away – if it is to flourish and live.

The exaggerated image of US 'inclusivity' is, we argue, linked to the implicit belief in the value of the individual and its central role in Western culture and thought. While it is clear that the Japanese have struggled with issues of inclusivity for some time, and have faced significant cultural and social contradictions, the issues in Japan draw both on Western ideas of individuality and on more 'indigenous' Japanese values. The tensions expressed by teachers highlight alternative ways of considering the meaning of inclusivity and the importance of individuals.

The quote above should not be taken as Oe's recognition of inclusivity in the USA (this is the kind of mistake that LeTendre made in his first assessment of special education in Japan). Oe is suggesting that neither Japan nor the US can beguile itself with delusions of its 'inclusivity' in terms of its overall school system – each society has much 'healing' to do, in terms of moving from a closed society to an inclusive one, and this is confirmed by continued research into our awareness (or lack of awareness) of the values that frame special education in Japan. The first step, we suggest, must be one of compassion rather than invidious comparison. However, it should not be the misplaced 'compassion' for the 'disabled', but, rather, compassion for societies that have shut off parts of themselves. Such societies have closed doors on their own citizens.

From this position, Japan and the US can be perceived as sharing many similar concerns and problems. We can move away from trying to 'de-centre' our translations of 'handicapped' or 'ability' – exercises that tend to lead to comparing one society against the other – to an analysis of how cultural values make certain choices available, and others difficult to obtain. Seen from this perspective, the Japanese ability to involve special education classes to such a high degree in school life challenges the US construction of special education. While educators in the US pride themselves on maximizing individual ability, how much of this is accomplished by creating special 'categories' of persons? Can the US learn from Japan how to be better at including groups?

Conversely, the effort made by many US teachers to include all students in the mainstream classroom suggests a sincere desire to move towards a society in which every individual is included *as an individual*. This is a provocative idea in Japan, perhaps echoing one teacher's desires to have a society that 'lives alongside disabled children'. As Japan faces the question of how to adapt and grow in the twenty-first century, the inclusion of *all* Japan's individuals is crucial for the health of its society.

It is something of a cliché to suggest that, because Japan is a *semai shimaguni*, a narrow island land, the recognition that a closed society is an ill society may be more pressing. At least in terms of Japanese consciousness, if not in terms of economic reality, survival of the society is something that is questioned. Americans, with a cultural history of 'Utopia around the corner' may, oddly, be less likely to face the consequences of a 'closed' society. If either society can move the place of 'special education' nearer to its core definition of school as a model of inclusion, rather than as a separate stream or separate programmes, then both societies can move toward healing.

References

Demoulin, D. and Kendall, R. (1993) 'Education of students with disabilities: a joint research study between the United States and Japan', *Education*, 114, p 206

Goodman, R. (1990) *Japan's 'International Youth'*, Clarendon Press, Oxford

Hendry, J. (1986) *Becoming Japanese: The World of the Pre-School Child*, Manchester University Press, Manchester, UK

Kuroyanagi, T. (1986) *Totto-chan*, Kodansha, Tokyo

LeTendre, G. (1994) 'Willpower and willfulness: adolescence in the US and Japan', in School of Education, Stanford University, Stanford, CA

LeTendre, G. (1996) 'Constructed aspirations: decision-making processes in Japanese educational selection', *Sociology of Education*, 69, pp 193–216

LeTendre, G. (ed.) (forthcoming), Comparison or competition: the abuses of Japanese education in American policy debates, Garland, New York

Lewis, C. (1995) *Educating Hearts and Minds*, Cambridge University Press, New York

Masawa, G. *et al.* (1993) 'Teacher education to enhance the quality of special education in Japan', *Peabody Journal of Education*, 68, pp 47–59

Miron, G. and Katoda, H. (1991) 'Education for persons with handicaps in Japan, the USA and Sweden', *Scandinavian Journal of Educational Research*, 35, pp 163–78

Monbusho (1987) *Tokushu Gakkyû no Kyôiku no Jissai*, Ookurasho, Tokyo

Oe, K. (1989) *An Echo of Heaven*, Kodansha International, Tokyo

Oe, K. (1995) *A Healing Family*, Kodansha, Tokyo

Passin, H. (1967) *Society and Education in Japan*, Teachers College Press, New York

Peak, L. (1991) *Learning to go to School in Japan*, University of California Press, Berkeley

Rohlen, T. and LeTendre, G. (1996) *Teaching and Learning in Japan*, Cambridge University Press, New York

Sato, N. (1996) 'Honoring the individual', in T. Rohlen and G. LeTendre (eds) *Teaching and Learning in Japan*, Cambridge University Press, New York, pp 119–53

Shimizu, H. (1993) 'Adolescents in a Japanese school: ethnographic approaches to achievement, morality, and behavioral inhibition', paper given in Graduate School of Education, Harvard University, Cambridge, MA

Statistics Bureau (1996) *Japan Statistical Yearbook*, Government Printing Office, Tokyo

12. Issues of inclusive education in the Czech Republic – a system in change

Marie Cerná

Introduction: historical backgrounds

The process of democratization and humanization of Czech society in which we are participating at present is highly dynamic, taking many varied shapes and forms. In spite of numerous obstacles and emerging problems, it proceeds with considerable success. This process incorporates, as one of its elements, attempts to address the difficulties faced by people with disabilities. One of the crucial arenas for action in this respect is education.

The Czech Republic has a long and revered history of providing for and educating children with disabilities. The first educational institutions were established as early as 1786 for the deaf, 1807 for the blind, 1871 for the 'feeble-minded', and the first auxiliary school was set up in 1896. In the same period, the Empire Law (at that time the country belonged to the Austro-Hungarian Empire) ensured care for the handicapped, and a 1929 enactment stipulated that compulsory education for handicapped children should last eight years.

According to Pánek (1991), the tradition goes even further back into Czech history. As long ago as the seventeenth century, Jan Amos Komensky-Comenius (1592-1670), brilliant thinker, philosopher, messenger of peace and priest of the Community of Czech Brethren, advocated that 'backward' children were entitled to education.

Throughout Czech history, there have been many excellent thinkers, scientists and politicians. In many historical periods, the Czech nation was one of the most important in Europe. This was true especially in the 1920s and 1930s, for example, when this country set an example for many other countries in various spheres of life. World War II brought an end to the existence of such humanistic achievements and ideas. When Czechoslovakia (1918–1993) was restored in 1945, it returned to a democratic state system, and parliamentary democracy based on the previous philosophical background was re-established. Political freedom, human rights, independence and democracy, however, did not last long. From 1948, after the Communist *putsch*, until 1989, Czechoslovakia was part of the Soviet block and governed in this 40-year period as a totalitarian regime.

During this time, so-called 'socialist' principles of education were adopted. Schools were owned, maintained and supervised by the state. Education was based on Marxist-Leninist ideology and was considered mainly as a means of economic development and ideological stability. In spite of the fact that no exact evaluations of the results of teaching and learning are available, it is possible to estimate the level of education as diminishing, especially in foreign languages, methods of scientific work, research, educational technologies, computer science and humanities.

During the totalitarian regime, both positive and negative policies and experiences existed in the field of services for people with disabilities. Proclamations and generally acceptable legislation on the one hand strongly contrasted with the practical segregation of people with disabilities, and the isolation of special services including severely isolated education, on the other. It is also true that the standard of living for disabled people was not dramatically different from that of the rest of the population. Unemployment was unknown by those individuals with disabilities who were capable of work. Education for children with disabilities, although segregated, was a part of the general education system, and was provided free of charge.

Principles into practice

Almost 40 years of Marxist-Leninist ideology left the country with a residue of concepts that focused on 'defects' and 'defectology' in special education theory and in the social service system. Ideology changed after the 'Velvet Revolution' of 1989 and newly adopted ideas of humanism and democracy brought major changes in the concept of disability. (The influence of external factors on the physical, mental and social development of the personality of every person with disabilities has now gained greater emphasis.)

There has been a shift from the concept of the 'impairment of mind and body' to the concept of the 'satisfaction of basic and special needs'. The idea that satisfaction of these needs is specific for every group of disabled persons, and is entirely individualized with regard to the personality of every individual, is becoming the main principle of theory for social support and assistance as well. The recent opening to Western ideas exposed special services, all at once, to the fruits of decades of research and innovative thinking. It will, presumably, take some time for Czech educators and service providers to filter and absorb the wealth of ideas, and then to see changes reflected in the special education theory, social system and services.

The Czech Republic today still faces many problems, connected mainly with political and economic questions. The basic changes – from a communist/socialist society to a democratic/capitalist structure, and from a bureaucratic/hierarchical system to a collaborative one – require enormous reversals in beliefs about personal empowerment, and public attitudes towards life in general.

In the spiritual sphere, pluralism of views and ideas, and implementation of humanitarian and democratic values are being reinforced, but it is certain now that it will take a long time before the situation is fully rectified. People are not used to realizing that life includes more important concerns than their own immediate and particular personal needs. It is evident that the main problems of society can be solved only if and when human spirituality and real human qualities are re-born. This is mainly reflected in the field of citizens with disabilities. The principle that handicapped persons have the same basic rights as other citizens is widely agreed. Many people recognize and respect the fact that all people have the same rights. However, we do not always think about our disabled fellow citizens in this respect. Even less frequently do we admit the fact that society needs every individual, including those with specific personality features and needs. Having the same rights, and recognizing everyone's natural justified claim of respecting and exercizing these rights, also implies a recognition of the right to differ. It means, even more, a recognition and understanding that the specific, unique and different features of these individuals enrich human society. The recognition of the right to differ, and the recognition of the value of every human being, gives moral strength to society. General consensus is that democratic society accepts its disabled citizens and creates the best possible prerequisites for the support of and assistance to every one of them. Unfortunately, the current Czech society is still far from translating these principles into practice.

Individual rights: legislation

The disability policy is expressed by law, by guidelines adopted by the government and by policy adopted by non-governmental organizations. The policy of normalization has not yet been fully adopted as a general social policy, nor has it been reflected in the legislation pertaining to equal education, inclusion, employment possibilities, community living, social activities, self-advocacy, and so on. The guidelines adopted by Parliament in September 1993 – the so-called 'National Plan of Measures to Reduce the Negative Impact of Disability' – determines the main tasks for the respective ministries and other governmental bodies aimed at improving quality of life for people with disabilities. The Plan is a visionary document, which addresses various fields, as follows:

1. classification of disabilities;
2. prevention and therapy;
3. counselling and social rehabilitation;
4. technical aids;
5. education and vocational training;
6. vocational rehabilitation, employment, sheltered jobs;

7. elimination of barriers;
8. independent living;
9. institutional care;
10. financing and quality guarantees of services afforded to disabled persons;
11. organizations of people with disabilities;
12. preparation of specialists for work with people with disabilities;
13. public education;
14. leisure time, culture, sports; and
15. legislation.

Five years after the document's adoption, it is necessary to update its content according to the general positive progresses in society. In December 1997, the Governmental Board for People with Disabilities (a national co-ordinating committee reporting to the Prime Minister's office) submitted the modified version to the Parliament, but it has not yet been approved. This updated policy conveys the message of full participation. Based on the Standard Rules, it addresses some of the various features of the principle of normalization.

The basic rationale underlying the changes is that people with disabilities should reside in their local community. There are plans, therefore, to provide trained personal assistants for people with disabilities so that they might live independently rather than in an institution. Deinstitutionalization will also be carried out via the establishment of small community care units. These facilities are mostly privatized. It has been suggested that people with disabilities receive a voucher allowing them (or their guardian) to choose the care unit where they will spend their subsidy. The individual also has the option of living with his/her family. It is anticipated that this strategy will result in competition among the care facilities, which, in turn, will lead to improved quality of care.

The rights of persons with disabilities are protected by a combination of special and general legislation. The judicial mechanisms available for the protection of their rights is due process. (Permanent Mission to the UN, 1996). In Czech society there is a common understanding that the role of legislation in the implementation of generally applicable world trends in the field of human rights for persons with disabilities is essential. These trends lead to improvement in the life of people with disabilities, and include normalization, personalization, participation, partnership, decentralization, deinstitutionalization, and so on. The laws and legal measures guarantee the protection of the rights and interests of people with disabilities and make available to them the support, assistance and services they need. The general legislation applies to persons with different disabilities with respect to education, employment, political rights, access to court-of-law, right to privacy and property rights. The following benefits are guaranteed by law: medical/health care, training, rehabilitation and counselling, financial security, employment and participation in decisions that affect an individual with a disability.

Since the adoption of the National Plan, the legislation of the Czech Republic has been changed to a great extent. Every law and regulation concerning disability contains special article(s) applying to the persons involved.

Integration

The right to equal educational opportunities for all is widely accepted. It is agreed that democratic progress can be made only through an insistence on basic rights for all, including the right of pupils/students with special needs to inclusive education. Not to ensure this would be to accept second-class citizenship for people with disabilities, for the families with a child with a disability and for the professionals who work with them.

The first priority for school-age children is to ensure that they have access to schools. Although it is a matter of rights that they be educated, proper legislation is needed if this is to be achieved. In the current provisions, made by Ministry of Education in 1996, children with profound disabilities can no longer be excluded from obligatory school education; this is a big step towards avoiding discrimination.

Inclusion is considered as a moral phenomenon in society. It is an issue of morality rather than an issue of law. We agree with Villa *et al.* (1992), that

> inclusive education represents a concrete step that can be taken in a school system to ensure that all students begin to learn that belonging is a right, not a privileged status that is earned. If we are to create schools in which students feel welcomed and part of a community, then we must begin by creating schools that welcome the diversity of all children. (p 38)

The Czech school is still, unfortunately, far from the idea of the 'School for All'.

The educational reform, however, implemented the idea of school integration into its proposals. The Ministry of Education, Youth and Physical Training of the Czech Republic defined the task of 'implementing the right of handicapped children and young people to education as a qualified preparation for future professional as well as family and civic life'. The Ministry's Program Declaration of August 1992 had already stated its intention

> to make the necessary changes in the structure of special schools, to create the prerequisites for the work of alternative special schools, and to innovate adequately the program, methods, and content of education and training in these schools and facilities, and also to support integration of handicapped children in standard school environments.

School integration is often defined as an admittance of children with disabilities to mainstream schools. Jesensky (1993) states that it is the

> most discussed and most profoundly elaborated part of an extensive phenomenon and movement for the integration of the handicapped people. Its

definition and characteristics are far from being unified, although in a number of countries the pedagogical integration is codified, sometimes even a preferred component of the school system.

Integration tendencies are not entirely new, but their assertion is difficult in a society that is still struggling with its democratization and humanization. The Czech integration policy is based on an explicit acceptance of the fact that individuals with disabilities can learn and be educated and that their education is equally as important as the education of all others. There is no doubt that every child has the right to adequate education while of school age, however, the right to lifelong education cannot be denied to persons with disabilities either.

Pedagogical integration does not mean the simple incorporation of a child with disability in a group of his/her mates in a standard school, although this way is generally considered the most suitable. The purpose or aim of education is substantially the same for all children, although the methods and forms of education and training of individual children may differ. Because inclusion is a part of the Czech educational policy, special programmes have been developed, and special facilities run for those individuals who require highly intensive educational assistance.

Since 1991, numerous educational regulations and decrees have created the legal foundations for the implementation of integration. In the field of pre-school education, mentally, sensually and physically handicapped children, and children with speech disorders (these are the official terms), may be admitted to nursery schools or special nursery schools. Documents allow the admission of children with disabilities to standard nursery schools and define the conditions of work in an integrated class. The same 'possibility' (not yet 'duty') is granted to the headmaster of the elementary school, who may admit the child with disability to the appropriate class of his or her school. This decision is formed on the basis of an application of the child's parents, statement of the appropriate medical specialist, the Pedagogical and Psychological Advisory Centre or Special Education Centre. The study programme of such students may be subjected to special modification, and preferably an individual educational programme will be drawn up for them.

The headmaster of the elementary school may also establish a special class for students with disabilities in his or her school. This will form part of the system of special schools and will, therefore, be taught by a teacher with a special education qualification.

Possibilities for the integration of students with disabilities in medium-grade schools are also provided by the Decree of the Ministry of Education. The director of the school may establish special classes for sensorily or physically handicapped students (not mentally handicapped), and he or she may also enable a student with a disability, or impaired by long-term illness, to prepare for and sit examinations in extraordinary circumstances. The integration of students with disabilities and the implementation of their right to education and training are contributed to by private schools and facilities, the establishment of which has been enabled by the Decree of the Ministry of Education since 1991.

Czech integration involves many problems. Many teachers and even some parents are not committed to it. They are worried about dismantling hundreds of special schools and institutions, and dispersing the children and the staff into standard schools. Resistance to change is understandable, since a tried system for the provision of services is being replaced by the unknown. For these, and other similar reasons, integration is progressing step by step, starting with nursery schools. Integration is more and more the central issue of special education, as indeed, it is of education in general.

The policy of educational integration has generated a diverse response from parents, teachers and administrators. While some people receive it as progressive and possessing substantive benefits for the children concerned, other express the opposite point of view. Although teachers in general agree with the concept of integration, in principle they do not support it personally. The 'NIMBY' ('not in my back yard') attitude became common among teachers in standard school, while many special-school teachers are afraid of losing their jobs and argue against integration, claiming that it will not provide handicapped students with the proper educational services and environment. There are, however, many professionals and parents who believe that, whatever popular opinion is, a new democratic school system will change into an inclusive system – 'school for all' – and will offer special children learning experiences enabling them to enjoy life to the fullest.

There is no doubt that inclusion influences the whole of society, especially its moral profile. The Czech population today does not have any experience of communicating with people with disabilities. During the communist regime, non-disabled children, by and large, did not interact with their peers with disabilities, and a majority of healthy adults had very little contact with fellow citizens with disabilities. This heritage has provided a basis for the negative attitudes towards people with disabilities that are still being faced.

Final remarks

As the Czech Republic moves towards the world community, the importance of inclusion of people with disabilities is clear. Despite the changes, the positive legislative provisions and the first investment in services for these people, many still remain socially isolated. There are many reasons for this situation. The attitudes of society need to be changed, and myths, false perceptions and stereotypes about humankind with disability must be destroyed. Everyone needs to learn how to work together, how to develop partnerships among professionals at national and international levels, and partnerships between professionals and parents, as well as collaboration and linkages between policy-makers and service providers. It is important to accept the idea that, through working together, the quality of life for people with disabilities in the Czech Republic can be much improved.

References

Cerná, M. (1994) 'Czechoslovakia', in Mazurek, K. and Winzer, M. (eds) *Comparative Studies in Special Education* (pp 274–85) Gallaudet University Press, Washington, DC.

Gargiulo, R. and Cerná, M. 'Special education in Czechoslovakia: Characteristics and issues', *International Journal of Special Education*, 7, (1), pp 60–70

Jesensky, J. (1993) *Prostor pro integraci* ('Room for integration'), Comenia Consult, Prague

Ministry of Education, Youth and Physical Training (1992) *Programme Declaration*, Ministry of Education, Youth and Physical Training, Prague

National Plan of Measures to Reduce the Negative Impact of Disability (1993) Resolution of the Government of the Czech Republic, No. 493, Board of Representatives from the Organizations of Disabled People, Prague

Pánek, J. (1991) *Joan Amos Comenius*, Orbis, Kosice, Prague

Philpot, T. (1990) 'Out of sight, out of mind', *Community Care*, November 22, pp 16–19

Villa, R., Thousand, J., Stainback, W. and Stainback, S. (1992) *Restructuring for Caring and Effective Education*, Paul H. Brookes Publishing Co., Baltimore

13. Bulgaria: gypsy children and changing social concepts of special education

Diana Tzokova and Zlatko Dobrev

Introduction

The importance of determining the social and educational status of gypsy children in Bulgaria is being highlighted in the reform agenda immediately following the political changes of 1989. This is partly because of an increasing interest among educationists and researchers in particular, and in society in general. An important part of this process is to provide insights relating to the experiences of ethnic minorities in Bulgaria, their rights, and the extent to which these rights have been enhanced or guaranteed by a process of social inclusion. The over-arching political aim of the reform agenda is to transform the traditional hegemonic state order into a democratic one; during this period of transition, a closer look at issues concerning culture and ethnicity has been required, and will be required in the future.

This interest has grown even more during the last five years and there are now attempts to explore different aspects of gypsy culture, language and education. An increasing number of publications in this area have contributed to a raising of the awareness of the social, economic and educational problems gypsy children have to face at present, whilst arguing for justified solutions that are in keeping with an emergent democracy.

In this chapter, we will try to outline some of the legal, social and educational dimensions of the 'problem' related to the situation of gypsy children. We shall subsequently draw attention to the reasons behind the existence of the axiomatic relationship between gypsy children and special needs education, and the underlying philosophies and practices that have reinforced this relationship.

The context

Bulgaria is a small, former communist-block country currently undergoing major political and economic changes in order to establish the foundations of a democratic society. These changes have quickly reached every aspect and level of social and political life, from the creation of a new order of law, to the day-to-day experiences and actions of individual people.

There are about 8 340 000 inhabitants in Bulgaria and two major ethnic minorities: Turkish and Gypsy. The Turkish people comprise 11 per cent of the total population, whilst there is diverse data about the number of gypsy people. This is due both to the methodological approaches used in data collection and the problems of ethnic identity and 'belonging'. The latest figures (Marushiakova and Popov, 1993 and Kuchukov, 1997) show that there are around 800 000 gypsies in Bulgaria. This comprises over 10 per cent of the total population and makes Bulgaria the country with the largest proportion of gypsy inhabitants.

During the communist regime, gypsies were subjected to political measures aimed at their total and forceful assimilation within the dominant idiom. In the 1980s, the official position within the country was that 'there are no gypsies', this view being manifest in overt and covert discrimination, exclusion and ultimate isolation of this large group of people.

The official policy in respect of ethnic minorities prior to 1989 has had a harmful effect on societal attitudes towards ethnic minorities in general. Marushiakova and Popov (1993) point out that the dominant attitudinal model in Bulgarian society at that time (and currently) is the nationalistic one, allegiance to which has been destructive to inclusive practices. Its main characteristic is that the gypsy's status is seen as different from that of the Bulgarian nationals, and is regarded as inferior. We would argue that this model is represented both at the state-political level (in the legislature and official procedures of the country) and in the everyday life experiences of the country's inhabitants. Recent shifts towards more inclusive, democratic attitudes, whilst important, have nevertheless been relatively weak in impact, although there are certain positive steps in this direction. Unfortunately, the shift in attitude is evident mainly at a legislative level whilst little is being done to ensure that the democratic rights and freedoms of minority groups are truly being protected in practice.

Legislation

The New Bulgarian Constitution, published in the *State Newspaper* Nr. 56/1991 sets the basic principles of equality by stating, in Article No. 6, that all people are born free and equal in dignity and rights. All citizens are equal in law. No limitations to the rights or privileges, based on race, nationality, ethnic belonging, origins, religion, education, beliefs, political affiliations, personal and social status or economic (wealth) status, are allowed.

This statement is also reaffirmed clearly within parts of that educational legislation developed in the period after 1989, namely The General Education Law (1991), The Regulations for Implementation (1992) and, most recently,

The Law for Amendment and Addition to the General Education Law (1998). There are clauses in each of them that relate directly to the education of children from ethnic minorities.

For example, new legislation allows for linguistic diversity. The Bulgarian language is affirmed as the official language in all educational institutions. Nevertheless, those students for whom it is not a mother language are allowed to study their mother language on a voluntary basis outside the state schools (which, in 1998, became 'municipality schools'), as long as the number of students requesting this provision is sufficient to form a group. Under this scheme, children's language preparation is organized in 'preparation groups' at kindergartens or 'preparation classes' at schools, such classes being designated for children who are not fluent in the Bulgarian language (Article 20, (1) and (2) (1991), amended in 1998).

Both the General Education Law and the Regulations for Implementation address special education matters. There is, though, a confusion in the use of terminology within them. The General Education Law mentions children with chronic illnesses and children with specific educational needs and states that they should be educated in residential schools.

Section five of the Regulations for Implementation of the General Education Law is devoted entirely to the special education system. It differentiates between children with chronic illnesses, permanent impairments and specific educational needs. Children in the second group are those with intellectual disabilities, speech disorders, visual impairment and additional impairments. They are supposed to be educated in special schools according to their respective category of impairment. The enrolment for such schools is based on the decisions made by a medical-pedagogical commission, appointed by the Ministry of Health and the Ministry of Education and Science. The latter commission is empowered to decide whether children's learning difficulties have been met and compensated for to a sufficient degree so that they can be re-directed to an ordinary school, in which they may be able to follow an amended or adapted curriculum.

Children with specific educational needs are regarded to be those children who do not have families or whose parents are refused parental rights. And, finally, educational residential schools are for children and juveniles with anti-social behaviour.

Apparently, the educational legislation continues to preserve a segregated system of special education. It still tends to support the 'within child' explanation of learning difficulty and, furthermore, is not sophisticated in its differentiation of the resultant categories. This situation does little to contribute to a positive self-image for children with special educational needs, or to improve the perception of others and, in consequence, limits those children's right to access and fully participate in and benefit from the education system.

Attitudes in Bulgarian society towards people with disabilities are no different from the official view and support clearly what in special education is called a 'medicalized model' of disability. In this respect, it is possible to draw a parallel between current attitudes and residual attitudes towards ethnic minorities, particularly gypsy people.

In terms of integration and inclusion of children who are 'different', the Bulgarian legal and education system has failed to provide any advance. Unfortunately – but understandably, if heritage and tradition are taken into account – integration and inclusion are largely viewed in terms of changing the children and their characteristics, rather than reforming the system itself to achieve greater flexibility and inclusivity.

Gypsy children in the education system

In general education

The education of gypsy children is a fundamental social factor for the realization of the rights and freedoms of all, and particularly those belonging to ethnic and/or cultural minorities, in the context of the developing civic society. One of the basic human rights – to be promoted by education – is the opportunity to learn and develop one's maternal language. Although Bulgaria has begun moves to make this opportunity more widely available, options relating to language within the Bulgarian state education system remain relatively limited.

Kuchukov (1994) notes that, over the last 40 years, many initiatives and experiments to educate gypsy children in the ordinary school have been attempted. The results of these have been very modest. Only 10–15 per cent of the school-age gypsy population reach the average level of educational attainment. Kuchukov sees this failure as lying in the fact that almost all Bulgarian schools do not recognize Bulgarian as a second language for these children, and they are, therefore, unable to experience the full curriculum taught in their mother tongue.

In addition, Kuchukov points out that the mainstream curriculum itself is not inclusive and is mainly directed to meet the needs of an average and above-average learner. There is a lack of methodology and pedagogical awareness for work with children for whom Bulgarian is their second language. Even where there are specific efforts in the area of language, its success with gypsy children is limited because of a disregard for their own culture and personality.

Few teachers in mainstream schools have knowledge and information about gypsy culture and language. In general, they are not prepared or trained to work with those children who are from different ethnic and cultural backgrounds, and for whom Bulgarian is a second language.

The proposed solution in Kuchukov's work is to start early with the socialization of gypsy children, to explore the world-wide experience in bilingual education, as well as introducing new approaches to teaching and assessment. It seems that the chances for an early language education for gypsy children are diminished by the latest legislation, in which preparation groups at kindergartens are no longer mentioned as an option.

Kuchukov (1997) has also researched the level to which gypsy children are able to use both their own and the Bulgarian language before they enter school. The data clearly shows difficulties in language development, but the difference between their mastery of their mother tongue and of the Bulgarian language is only insignificantly in favour of the former. The concluding interpretation is that the delayed language development is due both to social and educational disadvantage.

Marushiakova and Popov (1993) stress that there is not a comprehensive state strategy to deal with the variety of problems encountered by the gypsy population in Bulgaria. They also emphasize that the so-called 'gypsy problem' is not likely to disappear, even after an eventual solution to the recent and currently ongoing social and economic crisis in Bulgaria; and the possible integration of Bulgaria into the formal European economic, social and political structures is too distant a prospect at the present time to be considered as a viable influence for positive change. The core question that these authors raise is whether the Bulgarian politicians, intellectuals and others will be able to realize and promote in practice (as opposed to their rhetorical manifestation in legislation) the democratic principles of the civic society in respect of gypsy people.

The situation applies in the same way to the Bulgarian education system as a whole as it does to the position of gypsy children within it. The failure to ensure equal educational opportunities for this minority group within mainstream education has led to the continuation and prevalence of the exclusionary practice of placing them in segregated special education schools or other institutions. A consideration of this is the focus of the next section of this chapter.

In special education

The concept of special educational needs in Bulgaria, as indicated earlier, is based entirely on the so-called psycho-medical paradigm, defined by Clark, Dyson and Millward (1998). SEN or disability is understood in terms of characteristics of the disabled individual. As Dyson and Millward (1997) stress, these characteristics are seen to account for the inability of certain children to flourish within the provision made for them in mainstream education.

On this basis, the alternative provision for children with SEN is characterized by the following:

1. special/separated and segregated schools;
2. special, adapted or modified curricula;
3. specialized teacher training, expertise and qualifications;

4. actions directed to care, protect and secure the individuals concerned;
5. children still excluded from the education system.

Radulov (1996) argues that the categorical approach and the labelling of children within the medical model hinders the development of positive attitudes, and the acceptance of children with disabilities within society as a whole. He also draws attention to the almost total and traditional dominance and influence of this model in Bulgarian special education; arguably, the clumsy translation to 'defectology' has been in this respect more revealing of attitudes and approaches than of shortcomings in the English–Russian dictionary or in word usage.

The educational model of disability and the respective terminology – 'special educational needs', 'learning difficulties', and so on – were continuously utilized, and assumed the position of professional jargon, during the educational debates of the last decade in Bulgaria. None the less, there has been an identifiable shift in conceptual understanding of special needs education, the interpretation of which has broadened considerably during the last decade.

Contributing to this debate, Cholakova (1995) writes about the concepts of special educational needs and special needs, and about the differences between them. The suggestion is that gypsy children could be regarded as children with special needs, in that the latter category is meant to include children from ethnic minorities, travellers' children and those children from disadvantaged social and economic backgrounds.

The learning difficulties that gypsy children experience are considered to originate in the following:

1. decreased social, emotional and intellectual maturity;
2. problems in language development and language education;
3. non-attendance at pre-school establishments and schools;
4. insufficient motivation and stimulation for learning;
5. indirectly, the low social and economic status;
6. decreased level of intellectual functioning, which places them often in the (Bulgarian) category of mild intellectual disability.

Some of the reasons for the learning difficulties in gypsy children are perceived to lie in their social and economic disadvantage, others in their specific ethnic and cultural traditions, the nature and importance of which is largely unacknowledged by the education system. A further group of reasons, often underestimated, is associated with the quality and efficiency of the educational system itself. Referring to the intellectual functioning and the intellectual disability issue, gypsy children are often wrongly identified as intellectually disabled and, subsequently, placed in schools providing for children with mild intellectual disability. This situation recalls that which exists in England and Wales, where there is frequently tension between the issues that might lie behind educational under-performance of (some) minority groups.

There are further problems in respect of the organization of provision, which frequently does little to encourage educational inclusion of minority groups. Thus, the medical-pedagogical commission responsible for the multi-professional assessment of children, and the recommendation of a type of school, could be criticized for a number of reasons. Weaknesses in the work of the assessment teams have been noted in Dobrev (1992, 1995) and Tzokova (1993, 1997). The problems originate in the lack of professionalism and professional ethics amongst the team members, as well as in the use of inappropriate procedures and methodology.

Failure of this kind of practice is not ameliorated by the social and economic disadvantage of gypsy families. The majority live below the poverty threshold, and any social security that might be available is insufficient to support anything other than subsistence living. Almost perversely, as special schools in Bulgaria are funded directly by the state, from an economic perspective, they become a convenient option for the families of gypsy children. In such circumstances, there is little to encourage educational inclusion.

In addition, the curriculum in special schools for students with so-called intellectual disability includes a restricted set of academic requirements, whilst the teaching is more differentiated and individualized. This creates more chances for success for gypsy children, who have to adapt to a less marginalizing environment. Special schools, in this sense, offer an environment where disability becomes the over-arching notion, and race, culture, and so on, are slightly pushed into the background. Success is invariably limited, and, although it does mark something rather more positive than what is available in the mainstream, again, there is little incentive to change.

According to our own unofficial enquiry, approximately 40 to 45 per cent of the children in Bulgarian special schools are of gypsy origin. This summarizes an unacceptable and discriminatory situation, calling for official attention, action and, ultimately, some solutions.

These tendencies continue at present mainly because of the following issues:

1. The social and economic crisis. Gypsy people are among the most severely affected groups in society. Bulgaria is currently in an economic hiatus, as the full impact of capitalism and the breakdown of traditional economic networks continues to be felt. In recent years, after the initial surge of optimism following 1989, the country has witnessed the closing-down of businesses, industrial establishments, factories, and so on, and a marked increase of unemployment. Gypsy people are especially vulnerable to these events, because of both their generally low educational or professional qualification, and their marginalized position within the labour force. The latter is being maintained by the traditionally negative stereotypical attitudes within society towards gypsies, who are perceived to lack the necessary professional qualities and discipline to sustain regular

employment. The exclusion of adults from employment and from social life has, undoubtedly, a major effect, directly and indirectly, on the education of gypsy children.

2. The decrease in the status of education. This is reflected particularly in gypsy people's attitudes towards an education system that has never been inclusive for them. It is a system that they perceive as providing them with no means of access.

3. The civic society is in its infant phase of development. There is still a long way to go in order to create a society that is more tolerant to human differences.

Balkanski and Zachariev (1998) note that the period of economic and political transition to societal order that is fundamentally oppositional tests the whole system of values in human relations. They stress that one can observe a spiritual crisis in Bulgaria that is due to the shift in values. The ethical vacuum is filled in uncontrollably with the most retrograde forms of social and economic life, to the detriment of inclusionary initiatives.

These authors write about the foundations of civic education from a theoretical point of view and as a part of the school curriculum. In civic education, delivered as a formal component of the curriculum, they argue that there should be elements focused on multiculturalism, respect and protection of the ethnic minorities from discrimination, knowledge of and tolerance to different religious beliefs, and so on. It is important that all mainstream Bulgarian schools should be active and enthusiastic in promoting these principles in practice.

Conclusion

Efforts towards an enhancement of the quality of life of gypsy people in Bulgaria will no doubt continue in the future, irrespective of the difficulties currently being encountered. Motivation to develop opportunities that might ultimately result in more widespread inclusion will be dictated, on the one hand, by a growing awareness of the countless problems that minority groups face in many of the newly established democracies of Eastern Europe. Perhaps more pragmatically, however, they may be prompted by the ambition of Bulgaria and other ex-Soviet bloc nations to integrate the machineries and processes of the European Union. Therefore, it appears essential for a state priority to be affirmed, with supporting strategies, so that more effective forms of ethnic and cultural minority inclusion in society, and specifically within its educational processes, might ensue.

This places an imperative upon increased flexibility in educational politics and inclusiveness of the education system. Curricular and extra-curricular activities must be established with an emphasis on, for example, a range of ethnic cultures and national celebrations of relevant historic events. Moreover, civic education needs to become accessible for all children, as an important component of the curriculum, in which the notions of rights and inclusion are seen as central.

From a special educational perspective there is a need for a greater shift towards an educational and social, rather than medicalized paradigm. This would mark a major conceptual shift and signal an accelerating movement towards the inclusion of certain groups of children in mainstream education. This means nothing less than developing, refining and implementing a national concept for inclusive education.

There has been some advance in this respect during the last few years. This has been evident mainly in literature theorizing special needs education and in teacher education for special needs (notably the teacher training curricula). Unfortunately, these developments tend to remain isolated from practice. In consequence, most attempts to influence the national special needs policy, or the agenda underpinning it, have not been altogether fruitful. An illustration of this situation is the fact that official pronouncements from government continue to remain at the level of inference, rather than being presented as direct statements of intent on the part of administrators. In the mean time, statutory assessment for special needs has to consider the use of those methodologies that give freedom from cultural influences, and are respectful to language and ethnic differences.

References

Balkanski, P. and Zachariev, Z. (1998) *Introduction into the Civic Education*, Laska, Sofia

Clark, M., Dyson, A. and Millward, A. (1998) *Theorizing Special Education*, Routledge, London

Cholakova, M. (1995) 'Gypsy children and the category Special Needs', *Bulgarian Journal of Special Education*, 1 (1), pp 38–43

Dobrev, Z. (1992) *Foundations of Defectology*, University Publications, St Kliment Ochridsky, Sofia

Dobrev, Z. (1995) *Children with Intellectual Disability*, University Publications, St Kliment Ochridsky, Sofia

Dyson, A. and Millward, A. (1997) 'The reform of special education or the transformation of mainstream schools', in S. Pijl, C. Meijer and S. Hegarty (eds) *Inclusive Education*, Routledge, London

General Education Law (1991) *State Newspaper*, No. 86, Sofia

Kuchukov, C. (1994) *Preparation for Literacy in Bilinguism (in Turkish and Gypsy Children of a Pre-school Age)*, University Publications, St Kliment Ochridsky, Sofia

Kuchukov, C. (1997) *Psycholinguistics and Sociolinguistics: Phycholinguistic and Sociolinguistic Aspects of the Early Bilinguism*, sponsored by the Balkan Foundation for Intercultural Education and Understanding, Sofia

Law for the Amendment and Addition to the General Education Law (1998) *State Newspaper* No. 36, Sofia

Marushiakova, E. and Popov, V. (1993) *Gypsies in Bulgaria*, Club 90, Sofia

Ministry of Education and Science (1992) Regulations for the Implementation of the General

Education Law, *State Newspaper* No. 31, Sofia

Radoulov, V. (1996) *Children with Special Educational Needs in School and Society*, DARS, Bourgas

Tzokova, D. (1993) *Education Opportunities for Children with Considerable Learning Difficulties*, Agency Data Ltd, Sofia

Tzokova, D. (1997) 'Young people with severe learning difficulties: enhancing practice through professional development', paper presented at ECER, Frankfurt am Main, 24–27 September 1997

Tzokova, D. (1993) 'Diagnostics of Developmental Cognitive Delay in Children', unpublished doctoral dissertation, Sofia University, 'St. Kliment Ochridsky', Sofia

14. Developing inclusive education in Chile: private versus public systems

Maria Baez

Introduction

The development of inclusive education, from the perspective of social justice and human rights, has been given a special relevance in Chile in the last eight years (La Comisión Nacional, 1995). Responses have aimed to address un-solved social issues generated from the violent events of previous decades in the country (Aedo-Richmond and Richmond, 1996).

An inclusive education system should be envisaged as being part of an in-clusive society, and to accept otherwise is to see inclusion as an empty rhetoric (Barton, 1995). An overview of international experiences of inclusion reveals that there is no magic formula for success and countries have a long way to go before the rhetoric becomes a reality. The inclusive discourse in Chile has been examined within the wider issues of social justice. From this perspective, the Chilean government is attempting to provide quality education and equity distribution for all. However, whilst responses are being given, questions arise as to whether the way in which the Chilean government is attempting to ad-dress social issues is really favouring the development of an inclusive educa-tional system. This chapter aims to examine these dilemmas.

Social justice and an inclusive society

When democracy was reinstalled in Chile, in 1990, and the first democratically elected government took office, the fundamental aim was the promotion of national reconciliation (Cox, 1996). The first democratic government found the country divided by the profound social inequalities produced during the administration of the military government. Issues of human rights and social inclusion were a priority on the political agenda, as a way of addressing national reconciliation in a country deeply affected by a long period of authoritarianism (Gajardo, 1994). The transition to a truly democratic society – one in which the rights of all citizens would be accepted and respected – demanded the successful implementation of a number of changes (Urzúa, 1994).

This conviction led the government of president Patricio Aylwyn (1990–94) to take up the challenge of national reconciliation and social justice. One of its main concerns was the education sector, which reflected the deep social inequalities generally observed in the country. Priority was given to education, and this has been continued by the present government of president Eduardo Frei (1994–2000), who initiated its mandate with the slogan that the country should 'grow with equity' (Helgo, 1996).

Consequently, one of the main social tasks undertaken by the present government has been the transformation of the educational system. The aim is to develop a quality educational system according to the demands of modern times. The issue of quality education has been highly valued for its effect on the economic development of countries in the region (Carnoy and De Moura, 1997). A social investment in education has the purpose of eradicating poverty, by creating a population that has been educated in a high-quality system. This, of course, is seen by the government as a long-term social investment, and a number of additional initiatives have been set in place to produce the desired short-term effects (Lagos, 1994). More recently, these initiatives have been reflected in the promotion and implementation of the 1997 educational reform (see later).

From a social perspective, these initiatives aim to tackle the traditionally reductionist approach to social policy-making in Chile, and to go beyond the educational system by emphasizing the prominent role of education in a democracy. The initiatives attempt to address the fundamental principles of living in a democracy through an effective promotion of human rights, to seek social justice and the total inclusion of all citizens in a democratic society. The promotion of appropriate channels of participation are to be encouraged, with the aim of empowering citizens and promoting civic duties. In this context, education is regarded as having a pivotal role, not only as a direct contributor for the maintainance of democracy, but also in sustaining the economic growth of the country (Avalos, 1996).

The Chilean education system of the 1990s

Chile was completing a cycle of educational policy in 1990 (Cox, 1996). This included the completion of programmes of greater expansion of education provision and the process of administrative decentralization of the system, which was the focal point of the educational agenda of the 1980s. These two processes, expansion and decentralization, cannot be discussed separately. The present government has also undertaken the challenge of solving the dilemma generated from the greater expansion of provision over the quality of Chilean education and the effects of decentralization, especially on disadvantaged sectors of Chilean society (CIDE, 1994).

The effects of decentralization, though, are contradictory. On one side, the success of the expansion of provision is reflected in the high rates of school enrolment – 100 per cent for primary and 75 per cent for secondary education (Lagos, 1994). However, a great iniquity is observed in terms of the existing inequality of results in sectors of the population (García-Huidobro and Jara, 1994). This low quality of education is especially observed in the public sector schools. It has been reported that these schools have suffered from the negative effects of the process of administrative decentralization (Espínola, 1994).

The legacy of the past

In the past, the Chilean educational system developed a tradition of centralization, which was the result of an entrenched view of the role of the state in education (*estado docente*). Within this framework, the role of the state was to provide financial resources and to manage the entire education system, including staff appointments in schools and all matters concerning the schools' curricula.

The educational reform introduced in 1981 changed the traditional (centralized) role of the state to a subsidiary (decentralized) role, by transferring the administration of education to municipalities (Aedo-Richmond and Richmond, 1996). Following a neo-liberal model, economic competition was introduced to increase the quality of education (Schiefelbein, 1991). The assumption contained in this reform was that schools in the public and subsidized sector should compete on equal terms in order to enrol and retain students. The number of students on the school roll constituted the basis for obtaining funds from the state. The logic was that schools with higher results would attract a larger number of students, and, consequently, more financial resources from the state, as a reward for its efforts (Cahmi, 1994). This was to be monitored by a system of national assessment tests to measure the quality of education (SIMCE).

The 1981 education reform also gave access to private bodies and organizations to create new tuition-free schools funded by the state, but administered by private owners. In theory, decentralization and the introduction of economic competition between schools should have had the effect of increasing the quality of service provided to pupils and parents (Matte and Sancho 1991). However, soon after the implementation of the reform, the quality of education in schools in the public sector was affected, especially in those that were located in poor urban and rural areas. Guttman (1993) noticed the detrimental effects of these policies on low-income sectors of the population. They can be seen, for example, in the high rates of failure in the first years of primary for this sector of the Chilean population (Benito and Filp, 1996).

Responses from the democratic governments

The issue of the low quality of education in municipal schools, and particularly its negative social distribution, being concentrated in the poorest sectors, generated some immediate action on the part of the Chilean government in 1990. Its response was to deal with the problem by implementing two main programmes – the Programme of the 900 schools (P-900) and the Programme for Improving the Quality of Education (MECE programme).

P-900

The 'Programme of the 900 Schools' (P-900, 1990) was created as an emergency response to improve the quality of education by introducing a policy of positive discrimination (García-Huidobro and Jara, 1994). It aimed to raise levels of achievements in those primary schools in poor urban and rural areas with the lowest achievement records. The records of achievement in this programme were reported in the annual scores of the National System for Measuring Quality in Education, SIMCE (*Sistema Nacional de Medición de la Calidad de la Educación*, 1988). This assessment, which comprises written tests to evaluate the level of attainment targets reached by individual pupils, by schools and by regions, revealed that the national average of learning targets reached in year 4 was only 54.2 per cent in Spanish and 51.8 per cent in mathematics (Guttman, 1993). The negative social distribution of these school results is described as follows:

> Experts estimated the scores of public schools trailed those of private ones by at least 25 points. In Spanish, the highest scores were registered in the private paid primary schools located in the high-income neighbourhoods of Santiago, while the lowest scores were recorded in rural municipal schools. This gap widened in the 1982 to 1989 period. (Guttman, 1993, p 8)

Table 14.1   School attainments in Spanish and mathematics by social stratification in year 8 of primary education in 1993

Social group	School attainment %		Annual income*
	Spanish	Mathematics	
Low	53.92	51.69	818
Medium	64.23	60.89	1747
High	76.33	74.16	n/a

Source: Benito and Filp (1996) *International Journal of Educational Research*, 25 (1), p 57.
* in US dollars in 1992

Table 14.1 illustrates the differences in school attainments by Chilean social groups. The percentages are evidence of the markedly low attainments of pupils of low-income families in their final year of primary schooling. The major aims of P-900, therefore, were to improve the attainment targets of pupils in the basic core subjects of the school curricula in the first four years of primary education. Guttman (1993) points out that

> poor achievement [in SIMCE] coincided with low socio-economic status, reinforcing the idea that positive discrimination could achieve a fairer distribution of education and to ensure the most underprivileged not only had access to education, but could acquire reading, writing and mathematical skills, the roots of all further learning. (Guttman, 1993, p 8)

The idea of addressing social issues through innovatory programmes was to target a cohort of disadvantaged school populations and to make the most effective use of resources. The programme constituted a core element of the educational policy of the Aylwyn government through 1990.

The P-900 comprised actions to improve schools' teaching resources: infrastructure, learning resources, textbooks, libraries, teaching and learning materials, and resource centres. Materials were also made available to support the teaching of literacy and numeracy. Learning workshops for children were set up to help those who were falling behind in learning those core subjects that caused pupils greater difficulty in understanding. This aimed to raise their self-confidence and social skills. The ultimate aim of these workshops was to prevent academic failure and, eventually, school drop-out (García-Huidobro and Jara, 1994). In-service training workshops were set up to improve teaching strategies and to develop an understanding of pupils' cultural environment, and the relationships between school and community (Edwards, Assael and Egaña, 1991). Between 1990 and 1996, the programme was implemented in 2 099 primary schools (Cox, 1996).

The effects of the P-900 programme on improving the quality of educational attainment in the poorest schools of the country has been evaluated in contradictory terms (Helgo, 1996). The immediate positive effect produced in the morale of teachers, pupils and parents of those schools participating in this programme must be acknowledged. This was also reflected in the statistics of school performance. However, it must be mentioned that, while the performance of pupils in schools participating in P-900 was improving in comparison with initial scores, pupils in the subsidized and private schools also showed a commensurate improvement (Aedo-Richmond and Richmond, 1996).

The major difficulty for the success of P-900 was the severely unequal circumstances prevailing in the municipal, subsidized and private schools. Municipal and subsidized schools are both subject to the same source of funding, but schools in the public system are intrinsically different, in terms of infrastructure, pupils, social stratification, management, and these differences are even greater in comparison with the private sector. Aedo-Richmond and Richmond (1996) note that 'even the best planned and enthusiastic implementations do not guarantee unequivocally positive results'.

In this respect, the lesson to be learned is that policy implementation is a social process, encompassing more than the simple allocation of additional resources and good intentions. In the case of the Chilean education system, the gap between social groups represented in the schooling system is so significant that it has been impossible to reduce it simply by using positive discrimination and additional resources (as in P-900) (Helgo, 1996; Aedo-Richmond and Richmond, 1996).

However, it is fair to say that the programme has produced some positive results. Schools indicated as disadvantaged and, therefore, included in P-900, will be able to improve only up to a point. Municipal schools will never be able to reach a state similar to that of those schools of the subsidized and private systems, as long as the educational system in Chile remains divided into two types of free education, and is governed by the laws of an open market (CIDE, 1994). Disadvantaged groups will benefit from this type of programme, but the programme does not change the conditions in society itself. Overall, the impact of P-900 was restricted to short-term results by improving learning outcomes of disadvantaged pupils in primary schools.

MECE programme

Another initiative undertaken by the Aylwyn government was launched through the MECE programme in 1992. It has cost US$243 million, of which two-thirds has been provided by a loan from the World Bank (CIDE, 1994). The MECE programme proposes several objectives, apart from the aim of improving the quality and equity of education in primary and secondary schools. It is intended to increase access to pre-school education, to strengthen and improve the organizational capacity of the Ministry of Education, and to assess and review secondary education with a view to improving its relevance (Avalos, 1996).

At primary level, the MECE programme comprises two courses of action, which are very similar to those of P-900:

1. to improve the quality of education by providing teaching resources and in-service training for teachers in core subjects of the curriculum;
2. to promote incentives for curricular innovations.

Traditionally, teachers' instructional practices have been directed by the central level of the Ministry of Education by a 'national curriculum'. This has allowed for very little flexibility in curriculum delivery. However, the aim of this initiative is to promote a more participatory pedagogy, based on encouraging teachers to be autonomous and, thereby, create conditions for innovation (Políticas Educacionales, Temas de Gestión, MINEDUC, 1993). Both initiatives

have been channelled through the Projects of Educational Improvement, or
PMEs (*Proyectos de Mejoramiento Educativo*).

In contrast to the P-900 programme, which applies a targeting concept by
using positive discrimination, the MECE programme applies a universal principle. This means that all subsidized schools at all phases can apply for the formulation of projects. These projects operate on the basis that any school of the
municipal or subsidized sector can bid for funds in order to implement one.
Table 14.2 shows the distribution of these projects by primary schools.

Table 14.2   Distribution of PMEs by type of school and by year at primary
level

Type of school	1992	1993	1994	Total
Municipal schools	385	668	658	1711
Subventioned schools	90	138	134	362
Total of schools	475	806	792	2073

Source: MECE/Basica, MINEDUC, 1994

Each project should contain, as a prerequisite for funding, an innovative curricular project for the improvement of a given school and its immediate community. The project should be designed by teachers in schools (CIDE, 1994).
This process has prompted a two-fold way forward for quality improvement.
First, it empowers teachers to write self-planned curricula, and second, by doing so, it reinforces teachers' autonomy and reduces the central control of the
curriculum exercised by the Ministry of Education. In other words, it gives
them the chance to include local cultural themes, and to reduce the uniformity
of themes and the lack of pertinence produced by the application of a national
curriculum.

There are, however, some issues that might interfere with the flow of these
initiatives. One of them is that, traditionally, Chilean teachers have never had
access to curriculum flexibility in order to plan their own curriculum
(Aedo-Richmond and Richmond, 1996). In order to facilitate the design and
implementation of PMEs, the Ministry of Education has created a special team
of supervisors to assist teachers with their projects, although the effectiveness
of these teams in producing the empowering effects on teachers is arguable.
Helgo (1996) highlights the fact that social policy implementation in Chile has
to deal with a number of typical problems. One of them is the lack of organization and involvement of individuals to whom these programmes are directed.
Therefore, to maximize and sustain the expected result of the programme, the
Ministry of Education has addressed the significant differences between
schools that were shown in the results of P-900. A process of positive resource
discrimination has been set up, giving more opportunities for bids from
schools classified as 'high risk', than from 'medium-risk' or 'low-risk schools

(Aedo-Richmond and Richmond, 1996). The criteria underpinning this formula are similar to those used in the P-900 programme.

Undoubtedly, the MECE programme and the PMEs represent an opportunity for teachers to break up the centralized control of the curriculum in Chile, and to go beyond the fixed administrative decentralization of the education system (Espínola, 1995). The fundamental question arises as to whether all schools will be able to take the opportunity and to bid successfully for projects.

Concerns have been voiced about the importance of safeguarding the principle of equal opportunity, and collaboration, to improve access to the programme for rural and special schools (La Comisión Nacional, 1995). These two groups have been reported as having a minimum representation in the bidding for funds, in comparison with regular primary schools.

The low quality of education in the primary sector was one issue addressed by the MECE programme, but the case of secondary schools was considered even more important; the financial investment for the secondary-level programme is double that made at the primary level. At the secondary level, the MECE programme (MECE-Media, 1995) aims to modernize the sector and to introduce a significant change in practices (CIDE, 1994). The courses of action of the secondary programme are similar to those of the primary programme, in the sense that both are targeting the improvement of learning processes in classrooms, and the improvement in quality and quantity of instructional materials and inter-agency co-ordination, especially with the Ministry of Health and the agency for school buildings improvement (CIDE, 1994).

The programme MECE-Media aims to improve practices and to empower schools so that they may propose a relevant curricular design. The idea is to produce better student outcomes by raising levels of performance, on the understanding that a relevant curriculum will have positive effects on the learning process and on pupils' attitudes to learning (Avalos, 1996).

The programme to modernize secondary education started as a pilot experience with 120 secondary schools, and extended to 300 in 1995. It is scheduled for completion in the year 2000, and is expected to cover the total number of secondary schools by that time (MINEDUC, 1994).

Up to the present time, there has been no official evaluation of these programmes. However, their success is likely, in the opinion of foreign observers and funding agencies (*TES*, 1996).

In 1997, the Chilean government officially launched its reform of the education sector. The government used a particular strategy in the implementation of the reform. Change was introduced incrementally into the system. Thus, the implementation was actually made by turning the innovation programmes, described above, into a reform. The operative framework was provided by a systematic extension of programmes already in place. The viability of these programmes was enhanced by the passing of legislation to support the financial and administrative aspects. Thus, programmes could be supported by the community, by the private sector, or through partnership with institutions and organizations.

It is relevant to highlight the change in the customary approach to the processes of reform previously used in Chile. Traditionally, a reform was a normative process implemented from the Ministry of Education to schools. The 1997 reform keeps the intrinsic concept – a process of change and transformation – however, it differs in the incremental style of introducing changes in the system. The educational reform of 1997 aims to produce a transformation in the Chilean culture of schooling. It encourages flexibility in the curriculum management of schools, which could produce a positive change and, subsequently, a readiness to adapt to the demands of modern times. More relevant to this chapter are the reforms that aim to consolidate a new concept of equity. Equity is seen as the way in which all pupils can access equal opportunities and, subsequently, produce results of equal quality. The Chilean government is fully aware of the existing inequalitites in the schooling system and is ready to acknowledge that under this 'new meaning', the education system will 'grow with equity' (Cox, 1996).

The dilemmas for inclusive education

The development of inclusive education in Chile, from the point of view of social justice, raises a number of issues for discussion. First, how far is the view of providing equity and quality education through targeting programmes a realistic approach to social justice? In spite of the initiatives undertaken by the democratic governments, there is still a big gap between the public, the subsidized and the private system of schools. There is no doubt that the innovatory programmes have favoured the most needy pupils in the country and those involved – recipients and providers – regard the experience as positive for both parties. In addition, the introduction of curriculum flexibility and in-service training for teachers has been praised (Undurraga, 1994).

However, from the point of view of developing an inclusive schooling – within the government's current thinking – some issues need to be addressed further. Helgo (1996) points out that 'from a financial point of view, it is unlikely that the poorest municipal schools will ever be able to match the resources of private fee-paying schools'. From an administrative perspective, it is also unlikely that the public-sector schools will be given the necessary administrative freedom to manage their finances as well as the private subsidized and fee-paying schools. This issue becomes even more relevant when a curriculum flexibility has been granted and schools need to bid for projects. Subject to the law of supply and demand, the subsidized and the private schools will always attract better human resources – 'well-behaved pupils' and responsive parents – and, hence, highly qualified teachers.

The second issue is whether inclusive education can be developed in this market-oriented educational system. Barton (1995) notices that 'within a market-driven system of provision there will be winners and losers'. In the case of Chile, the aim of the present government – to link education to a wider strategy for economic competitiveness within the region – will undoubtedly contribute to an accentuation of the differences between groups in society. There are few chances that socially disadvantaged groups will spot and take advantage of the opportunities provided in a market-oriented schooling system.

Lagos (1994) has pointed out that, in Chile, there was still a need to re-define educational policy, especially that of secondary education. Presently, the transformation of secondary education promises to address this issue, but there is a long way to go before socially disadvantaged groups in Chile will be able to enter into the competitive market through education.

The final issue for discussion is whether a change in the orientation of policies should be implemented. Undoubtedly, the implementation of an inclusive society that seeks social justice should envisage a structural change of society. In Chile, there is little doubt that this transformation needs to take place, however contradictory it seems, insofar as no consensus has been achieved on how this redistributive transformation should be implemented (Urzúa, 1994).

There is an apparent contradiction between the general agreement on the necessity of seeking social justice and the little progress made towards an inclusive education system. Currently, changes are being introduced in education to support a model of society oriented towards economic growth, social development, and social justice. This model of society is based upon the competence of all citizens to be actively involved in participating and supporting the democratic process (Garretón, 1994). However, whilst the structure of the educational system remains largely untouched, differences will remain, to the detriment of the 'losers' in the system.

Conclusion

In spite of the many efforts of the Chilean government to address issues of social justice, the question arises as to whether these efforts are geared in the right direction. From the point of view of achieving inclusive schools, this requires a careful response. Policies oriented towards social redistribution appear to be incompatible with a 'market-driven' educational system (Helgo, 1996). A final question is whether the present reform makes it any easier for 'exclusive schools' to become 'inclusive', or for excluded pupils to become included? An optimistic response might say that it does – programmes with 'built-in incentives for teachers, parents and pupils will make a difference for the groups which acquire initial information about the programmes, spot the opportunities and have the time and the financial resources to take part' (Helgo, 1996). From a more sceptical – or perhaps realistic – point of view, one can only wait and hope that the promised social justice and the development of inclusive education in Chile will happen in the not too distant future.

References

Aedo-Richmond, R. and Richmond, M. (1996) 'Recent curriculum change in post-Pinochet Chile', *Compare*, 26 (2), pp 197–215

Avalos, B. (1996) 'Education for global/regional competitiveness: Chilean policies and reforms in secondary education', *Compare*, 26 (2), pp 217–32

Barton, L. (1995) 'The politics of education for all', *Support for Learning* 10, (4), pp 156–60

Benito, M. and Filp, J. (1996) 'The transition from home to school: a socio-economic analysis of benefits of an educational intervention with families and school', *International Journal of Educational Research*, 25, (1), pp 53–65

Cahmi, R. (1994) 'Provision privada de servicios sociales: dos ejemplos', in L. Tomassini (ed.), *Qué Espera la Sociedad del Gobierno*, Centro de Análisis de Políticas Públicas, Universidad de Chile, Santiago de Chile

Carnoy, M. and De Moura, C. (1997) *Que Rumbo Debe Tomar la Educación en America Latina*, Banco Interamericano de Desarrollo, Washington DC

CIDE (1994) *La Decentralización de la Educación en Chile: Continuidad y Cambio de un Proceso de Modernización*, CIDE, Santiago de Chile

Comisíon National para la Modernizacion de la Educacion (1995) 'Los desafios de la Educacion Chilena frente al siglo XXI', Editonal Universitaria, Santiago de Chile

Cox, C. (1996) *La Reforma de la Educación Chilena: Contexto, Contenidos, Implementación* Programa de Promoción de la Reforma Educativa en América Latina, No 8 CIDE, Santiago de Chile

Edwards, V., Assael, J. and Egaña, L. (1991) *Capacitación de Supervisores y Perfeccionamiento Docente*, PIIE, Santiago de Chile

Espínola, V. (1994) *La Decentralización de la Educación en Chile: Continuidad y Cambio de un Proceso de Modernización*, Centro de Investigación y Desarrollo de la Educación, CIDE, Santiago de Chile

Espínola, V. (1995) 'El impacto de la decentralización sobre la educación gratuita en Chile', paper presented at Seminario Internacional: La Construcción de Políticas Educativas Locales, Buenos Aires, Argentina 10–11 April 1995

Gajardo, M. (1994) (ed) *Cooperación Internacional y Desarrollo de la Educación*, Agencia de Cooperación Internacional, Santiago de Chile

García-Huidobro, J. E. and Jara, C. (1994) 'El Programa de las 900 Escuelas' in M. Gajardo (ed), *Cooperación Internacional y Desarrollo de la Educación*, Agencia de Cooperación Internacional, Santiago de Chile

Garretón, E. (1994) 'Redefinición de Gobernabilidad y Cambio Político', in L. Tomassini (ed), *Qué Espera la Sociedad del Gobierno*, Centro de Análisis de Políticas Públicas, Universidad de Chile, Santiago

Guttman, C. (1993) *All Children Can Learn*, UNESCO, Paris

Helgo, C. (1996) 'Chilean social policy reforms in a social mobility perspective', M.Phil Dissertation, Centre of Latin American Studies, University of Cambridge, UK

Lagos, R. (1994) 'Educación y Pobreza: La Experiencia Reciente en Chile', in L. Tomassini (ed), *Qué Espera la Sociedad del Gobierno*, Centro de Anlisis de Políticas Publicas, Universidad de Chile, Santiago

Matte, P. and Sancho, A. (1991) 'Sector de Educación Básica y Media' in C. Larroulet (ed), *Soluciones Privadas a Problemas Públicos* Instituto Libertad y Desarrollo, Santiago de Chile

Ministerio de Educación, *Resultados del SIMCE 1988*, Ministerio de Educación, Santiago de Chile

Ministerio de Educación (1990) *Normas Legalles Sobre Educación Especial*, Santiago de Chile

Ministerio de Educación (1994) Programa de Modernizacieon de la EnseÒanza Media (1995–2000), Santiago de Chile

Políticas Educationales: Temas de Gestión (1993) Ministerio de Educación, Santiago de Chile

Schiefelbein, E. (1991) 'Restructuring Education through Economic Competition: The Case of Chile', *Journal of Educational Administration* 29 (4), pp 17–29

Times Educational Supplement (1996) 31 May 1996, London

Tomassini, L (1994) (ed) *Qué Espera la Sociedad del Gobierno*, Centro de Análisis de Políticas Públicas, Universidad de Chile, Santiago

Undurraga, C. (1994) 'Pedagogía y Gestión. Informe de Evaluación del Programa de las 900 Escuelas' in M. Gajardo (ed), '*Cooperación Internacional y Desarrollo de la Educación*', Agencia de Cooperación Internacional, Santiago de Chile

Urzúa, R. (1994) 'Desarrollo Social y Reforma del Estado: Algunos Temas de Reflexión', in L. Tomassini (ed), *Qué Espera la Sociedad del Gobierno*, Centro de Análisis de Políticas Públicas, Universidad de Chile, Santiago

15. Inclusive education in South Africa: achieving equity and majority rights

Pam Christie

Introduction

The demise of apartheid in South Africa in 1994, heralded around the world as a victory for democracy and human rights, came shortly after the crumbling of the eastern bloc states in the late 1980s and early 1990s. The synchronicity of the victory of South Africa's national liberation struggle with the ascendancy of neo-liberalism globally has profoundly influenced the social and economic policies of post-apartheid South Africa. Nowhere is this more evident than in education, where new policies are being simultaneously shaped by two imperatives: a modernist project of extending equal citizenship rights to all, following on from national liberation; and a macro-economic project oriented towards participation in the neo-liberal framework of globalization.

This chapter will argue that education policies for equity, redress and social development are being sharply constrained by demands for efficiency, fiscal restraint and curbs on social spending. Ironically, the nature of new policies, as well as the policy-making process in education, have not promoted redress, as the national government has concentrated on formulating ideal-type, framework policies, which provincial departments have struggled to implement. The cumulative result seems to have been that, while formal equity is enshrined in policy, the gross inequalities of apartheid schooling have hardly shifted in the first four years of the post-apartheid government.

The modernist project: a framework of rights

When the African National Congress (ANC) came to government, it brought with it an alliance of the Congress of South African Trade Unions (COSATU), and the unbarred and relaunched South African Communist Party. Because the transfer of power was brought about through negotiated settlements and compromises between major social and political actors, the alliance joined with the erstwhile apartheid formulators, the National Party, as well as a number of smaller political groupings, in a Government of National Unity. The political compromises of this form of government, with its emphasis on negotiation and consensus, fundamentally curbed the agenda for change from the broad visions of the alliance partners before 1994, and brought added complexities to the struggle for social transformation.

One of the first tasks of the ANC-led alliance, begun before it assumed government, was to develop and adopt a new Constitution and Bill of Rights; its aim was to 'heal the divisions of the past and establish a society based on democratic values, social justice and fundamental human rights' (Constitution of the Republic of South Africa Bill, 1996, p 3).

The Constitution enshrined liberal rights such as equality, human dignity, and freedom, and outlawed discrimination on the basis of race, gender, sex, ethnic origin, sexual orientation, age, disability, culture, language, and so on. This framework of rights was taken up in the first White Paper on Education and Training (1995), which affirmed the right to basic education for all, as well as the right of equal access to educational institutions, protection from unfair discrimination on the basis of disability, and rights to language, culture and religion.

Such universalist statements of equal citizenship stand in welcome contrast to the fragmented racial and ethnic identities of apartheid, and they bring South Africa into line with other modern states. Yet, as Bryan Turner (1986) points out, ideologies of equality have been accompanied by profound social and economic inequalities in modern states. In his words, inequality in the modern state is 'ubiquitous, endemic and resistant to social policies aimed at bringing about a substantial measure of equality in practice' (1986, pp 24–5). Certainly, in South Africa, the profound, cumulative inequalities of apartheid capitalism of class, race, gender, region are proving hard to shift.

Apartheid was notorious for its unequal distribution of education according to racial classification. By 1994, the apartheid government was spending four times as much on the education of a white child than a black child, and, at the height of apartheid, this was as much as twelve times. White children were given more years of schooling, had smaller classes in better provisioned schools, were taught by better-qualified teachers, and had lower failure and repetition rates. In contrast, the Schools Register of Needs, completed by the new government in 1996, starkly shows the deprivation of the majority of schools: 24 per cent have no water within walking distance, 13 per cent have no toilet facilities at all, 57 per cent have no electricity, 69 per cent have no learning materials, 83 per cent have no library facilities, 6 per cent are in such poor condition that they are not suitable for education at all, and a further 11 per cent are in serious need of repair. The greatest deprivation is in rural schools, and, consequently, in that are largely rural. In the Northern Province, for example, 49 per cent of schools have no water within walking distance, 79 per cent have no toilets, 95 per cent have no library facilities and 41 per cent need serious repairs (see Bot, 1997; Motala, 1997).

Social theorists such as Iris Young (1990) and Bob Connell (1992) usefully warn that notions of distributive justice have limited value in education, since rights are relationships not things, and educational inequalities go beyond issues of access. None the less, when inequalities are so profound, redistribution to redress material disadvantage has a compelling logic. However, the question facing the new government has been how to finance such redress. A prevailing assumption has been that South Africa's budgetary allocation for education should not be increased, and that increased education spending should be based on economic growth proposals consonant with World Bank recommendations on education spending (see Fateaar, 1997; Chisholm, 1997). In the short term, at least, it has proved almost impossible to rectify the material distribution of education within existing education budget allocations.

Given that teachers' salaries absorb a large part of the education budget, and that discrepancies in teacher qualifications have resulted in racially differentiated earnings, the new government has turned to teacher policies in order to achieve equity within the system. One of its most dismal failures was its attempt to bring greater equity by establishing uniform student:teacher ratios for all schools (these had ranged from an average of 43:1 in historically African schools, to an average of 23:1 in historically white schools). Government policy decided that, over a five-year period, class sizes should be adjusted to 40 in all state primary schools and to 35 in secondary schools. The goal was to re-deploy teachers to those schools with the greatest need, and to offer voluntary severance packages to surplus teachers or to those unwilling to be transferred. This poorly planned endeavour at 'right sizing' cost more than R1 billion in voluntary severance packages, instead of the anticipated R6 million; it led to a drain in skills and experience, as numbers of well-qualified white teachers took the opportunity to leave teaching; it brought conflict with teachers' unions; and it profoundly unsettled many teachers and schools.

Clearly, attempting to change a key dimension of the education system conditions of teachers' work means engagement with complex institutional forms in bureaucracies and schools, as well as engagement with social forces beyond these. It requires more careful planning, strategic management and political negotiation than the government had anticipated.

Within two years, the government acknowledged its failure and moved away from attempts to set national standards on class sizes. It was not a constructive step, but this is not to imply that the new government has made *no* progress in reducing unequal access to schooling. Between 1991 and 1996, school enrolment increased by 18 per cent, while the numbers of out-of-school children reduced considerably. Additional schools and classrooms are slowly being provided, and historically white, Indian and coloured schools are becoming increasingly integrated. However, conditions in the poorest and most marginalized communities and their schools have not improved.

The macro-economic project: a neo-liberal framework for globalization

Prior to the 1994 elections, the alliance partners had formulated the Reconstruction and Development Plan (RDP) as a strategy for radical economic and social transformation. Based on the central principle of 'growth through redistribution', the strategy of the RDP was to stimulate economic growth through a coherent and integrated development strategy. However, by the end of 1996, the RDP had faded into insignificance as a set of policies for transformation. In its place, the government introduced its Growth, Employment and Redistribution (GEAR) strategy, an unabashedly neo-liberal macro-economic programme of deregulation, privatization and fiscal restraint.

Although supporters of GEAR have argued that these strategies are necessary for participation in the framework imposed by globalization (see Chisholm, 1997), it is important to recognize that GEAR was not an imposition but a political choice. A key issue it raises is the fate of social spending, including spending on education, within what amounts to a self-imposed structural adjustment framework.

As a result of GEAR, the government's attitude towards education spending has hardened. The 1997/8 education budget allocation amounted to nearly 20 per cent of the overall budget, and, although this was an increased percentage, it represented a cut in real terms. Within this, the government has developed no special funding allocations for redress spending, to reduce the stark inequalities outlined in the School Register of Needs. Provinces with large numbers of rural African schools are particularly disadvantaged. In Greenstein's view:

> In the absence of specific funds targeting backlogs, high repetition, drop-out and failure rates caused by poorly qualified teachers, disrupted schooling environment, lack of learning materials, and poor physical infrastructure, the possibilities for redistribution…remain limited. The existing situation, in which differently endowed communities enjoy widely varying levels of provision, and are able to supplement state resources from their own pockets, has not changed. (1997, p 4)

Within the framework of GEAR, all of the provinces have battled to keep education spending within budget limits, and have experienced budgetary crises. Given that teachers' salaries absorb nearly 85 per cent of provincial budgets, there has been little left over at provincial level for redress or for funding changes. Provinces have struggled to continue school building programmes, to purchase textbooks and stationery, and to meet salary bills. The government's view is that the crisis is not a straightforward financial one, but rather a result of the provinces' lack of capacity, and of mismanagement of resources. In GEAR terms, solutions lie in improving internal efficiencies in the system, building technical capacity and developing management competence.

This chapter has so far illustrated that South Africa's modernist project of extending equal rights has proved difficult to achieve within a macro-economic project that includes curbs in social spending. It is now appropriate to consider the education policies developed in this context, as well as the policymaking process. Here, the main argument is that there is a massive disjuncture between formal policies and their implementation', with the unintended consequence that the gap between historically advantaged and disadvantaged schools may be widened even further.

Post-apartheid policies and policy-making processes

In the lead-up to the 1994 elections, significant policy actors, including the ANC, COSATU, private sector groups and even the National Party, began to explore educational alternatives. As Nzimande points out,

> there was unprecedented co-operation between the national liberation movement and mass democratic movement on the one hand, and progressive left-wing academics on the other…around the development of policies for the democratic movement in preparation for the ascendancy of the movement into state and governmental power. (1997, pp iii-iv)

This process envisaged the following: the integration of education and training in a system of lifelong learning that would articulate adult basic education and training, formal schooling, and learning programmes for out-of-school children and youth. Structures representing stakeholder interests would ensure accountability and participation at all levels of the integrated system. A national qualification framework (NQF) would plot equivalences between qualifications to maximize horizontal and vertical mobility. New policies would articulate changes across the whole of the existing education and training system.

As it happened, there were considerable shifts after the 1994 elections. In the new government, education and training were kept in separate ministries, and policies for the two were developed separately. The government's moderate politics of compromise tempered the alliance's more radical pre-election ideals. Crucially, the new Constitution protected the employment of senior civil servants of the old order, whose influence continued into the new era, with mixed benefits. New appointees – many of them people with political and activist backgrounds – generally lacked experience in government. The macro-economic climate provided further constraints. As de Clercq points out, the challenge facing ANC-led ministries under these conditions was to 'create a terrain favourable to a shift of power relations in favour of the traditionally excluded, despite various structural constraints' (1997, p 135). Present indications are that this shift has not been taking place in education. One of the reasons for this is the nature of the policy-making process in education.

Under the new Constitution, the national Department of Education has responsibility for developing norms and standards, frameworks and national policies for the system as a whole, while provincial departments are responsible for implementation and service delivery within these frameworks. The national department has concentrated on developing a series of ideal-type, blueprint policy frameworks, and putting in place the legal and regulatory conditions for these. The first White Paper on Education and Training (1995) provides an impressive overview of the developmental initiatives considered by the government to be priorities. Subsequently, the national department has been working to put frameworks in place for each. In 1998, these initiatives included the following:

1. the NQF has been given effect in the South African Qualifications Authority, established in 1996. A set of seven 'essential outcomes' has been developed for all qualifications, and twelve areas of learning, linked to the labour market, have been identified;
2. the South Africa Schools Act (1996) has set out frameworks, norms and standards for the finance and governance of schools. It stipulates that all schools should have democratically elected governing bodies on which parents are the majority, with powers to determine admissions policy, language policy and school fees;
3. a National Commission on Higher Education has provided the basis for the Higher Education Act of 1997;
4. Curriculum 2005, an outcomes-based curriculum is being phased into schools from 1998, starting with Grade 1;
5. a National Committee on Further Education and Training (post-compulsory education) presented its report in 1997, as the basis for legislation on Further Education and Training;
6. a National Commission on Special Needs in Education and Training presented its report in 1998.

In many ways, these are state-of-the-art policy documents, culling from those international practices that are judged to be the best. However, although they may be admirable in their sentiments and elegant in their formulation, the proposals generally lack detail and specificity, and suggest no strategies for transforming actual conditions on the ground. In spite of the superficial sophistication of the policy documents, they fall into a basic policy trap of separating formulation from implementation. As Greenstein observes, provincial departments, which play a minimal role in policy formulation, 'have to follow imperatives not of their own making and bear the budgetary brunt of these' (1997, p 2). In his view, this structural disjuncture between power and accountability promises to be an ongoing source of tension in education.

In defence of the documents, it may be argued that paradigm-switching policy visions have a role to play in displacing the social engineering of apartheid, and that they provide an enticing picture of an alternative system.

However, as they stand, the national department's policy documents are ideal-istic texts in an essentially top-down policy process that is not rooted in the realities of schools, or responsive to conditions on the ground. They have no equity or redress provisions; nor do they, in de Clercq's terms, attempt to address mobilization or capacity-building in disadvantaged communities, or their schools. Moreover, the sophistication of the policies brings the unin-tended effect that they are of most benefit to those communities and schools that have the resources to take advantage of the opportunities they offer. For under-resourced communities and schools, these policies may produce the opposite effect, acting as an extra burden rather than an opportunity for im-provement. To illustrate this, Curriculum 2005 provides a good case study.

2005

The idea of an outcomes-based curriculum was developed in the pre-1994 pol-icy period, as part of a set of policy proposals drawing heavily on international experience, particularly that of the UK, Australia and New Zealand. During this period, it was argued that a competence- or outcomes-based curriculum could satisfy the dual goals of equity and human-resource development (see Christie, 1997).

Under the new government, as one of the compromise procedures in the newly arranged bureaucracy, the ANC's pre-election curriculum proposals were merged with existing curriculum development work undertaken by the previous government. After a short-term exercise in 'cleansing' the curricu-lum of its most obvious errors for the start of the 1995-year, frameworks for the outcomes-based Curriculum 2005 were put out in 1997.

This curriculum is an important step away from the content-laden, often ideologically distorted, examinations-oriented apartheid curricula. It empha-sizes 'learning by doing', problem-solving, skills development and continu-ous assessment. Through a complex matrix of 'essential' and 'specific' outcomes, 'range statements', assessment criteria' and 'performance indica-tors', teachers are able to construct 'learning programmes' and prepare les-sons based on outcomes. In many ways, Curriculum 2005 and the NQF represent specific South African forms of global, late-modern curriculum pat-terns (see Cowen, 1996; Christie, 1997; Young, 1990). Common features in-clude the incorporation of work-related competencies into curricula, modular credit accumulation with more frequent assessment, and a network of path-ways in a lifelong learning system.

However, the implementation of Curriculum 2005 has proved to be prob-lematic. Because of poor planning, short notice and lack of capacity and funds at the provincial level, the national department was forced to scale down the introduction of the new curriculum, from three grades to two, and then to one. Very little in-service work has been carried out, with the result that teachers have not been adequately prepared for the changes in pedagogy and assessment. In some cases, under financial pressures from GEAR, provinces have been unable to supply textbooks and learning materials to schools. By the end of the first quarter of 1998, up to half of the primary schools in some provinces, including those with the most rural schools, have ignored the launch of Curriculum 2005 ('Curriculum 2005 falls further behind', *Weekly Mail*, 3-8 April 1998).

Apart from poor implementation, a major failing of Curriculum 2005 is that it is context-blind. It does not address teaching and learning conditions in the majority of South African schools, where resources are short and more than 40 per cent of African teachers are unqualified or under-qualified. Nor does it address the persistent problems of dysfunctional township schools – absenteeism among students and staff, violence, sexual abuse, substance abuse – that have proved to be an enduring legacy of apartheid. Being decontextualized and content-free, it also does not address crucial issues such as racism, sexism, and Africanization (Jansen, 1997; Greenstein, 1997), and thus provides no basis for dealing with the complexities of identity and difference, which are key issues in South Africa.

Conclusion

This chapter has argued that education policies in the early years of post-apartheid South Africa have been the product of complex contradictory forces. The curbs on social spending that are attendant on neo-liberal macro-economic policies have cut into the modernist project of equal rights. The government's politics of consensus and negotiation have tempered the vision of social change provided by the ANC and its allies in the struggle against apartheid. And the tensions of the policy-making process in education have brought contradictory consequences, strengthening the position of historically privileged schools and communities, and doing little to shift the balance of power in favour of the historically disadvantaged and marginalized. The net result is that, in the first term of office of the ANC-led government, the profound inequalities of apartheid schooling have hardly been addressed, let alone shifted. Inclusive education, equality and majority rights have proved hard to achieve.

It is important, however, to recognize that a transformation of the deeply entrenched inequalities of apartheid capitalism is unlikely to be smoothly or speedily achieved. This chapter has shown that shifting the balance of forces needs continuous engagement between vision and conditions on the ground. Social and educational transformation is not delivered by democratic elections and policy visions alone. It needs to be won in complex and concerted engagement with social, political and economic forces, in which the development of new policies is simply one step.

References

Bot, M. (1997) 'School Register of Needs: a provincial comparison of school facilities, 1996', *Edusource Data News*, 17 August, Education Foundation, Johannesburg

Chisholm, L. (1997) 'The restructuring of South African education and training in comparative context', in P. Kallaway, G. Truss, A. Fataar and G. Donn (eds), *Education After Apartheid: South African Education in Transition*, University of Capetown Press, Capetown

Christie, P. (1997) 'Global trends in local contexts: a South African perspective on competence debates', *Discourse: Studies in the Cultural Politics of Education*, 18 (1), pp 55–69

Connell, R. (1992) 'Citizenship, Social Justice and the Curriculum', paper presented to International Conference on Sociology of Education, Westhill College, Birmingham

Cowen, R. (1996) 'Last past the post: comparative education, modernity and perhaps post-modernity', *Comparative Education*, 32 (2), pp 151–70

De Clerq, F. (1997) 'Policy intervention and power shifts: an evaluation of South Africa's education restructuring policies', *Journal of Education Policy*, 12 (3), pp 127–46

Fateaar, A. (1997) 'Access to schooling in post-apartheid South Africa: linking concepts to Ccontext', in P. Kallaway, G. Truss, A. Fataar and G. Donn (eds), *Education After Apartheid: South African Education in Transition*, University of Capetown Press, Capetown

Greenstein, R. (1997) 'New policies and the challenges of budgetary constraints', *Wits EPU Quarterly Review of Education and Training*, 4 (4), 15 June, University of the Witwatersrand Education Policy Unit, Johannesburg

Jansen, J. (1997) 'Why OBE will fail: perspectives on Outcomes-Based Education (OBE), proceedings of a National Conference held at the University of Durban-Westville

Motala, S. (1997) 'From policy to implementation: ongoing challenges and constraints' *Wits EPU Quarterly Review of Education and Training*, 5 (1), 15 22 September, University of the Witwatersrand Education Policy Unit, Johannesburg

Nzimande, B. (1997) 'Foreword', in P. Kallaway, G. Truss, A. Fataar and G. Donn (eds), *Education After Apartheid: South African Education in Transition*, University of Capetown Press, Capetown

Turner, B. (1986) *Equality*, Tavistock Publications, London

Young, I. (1990) *Justice and the Politics of Difference*, Princeton University Press, New Jersey

16. Pedagogic discourse and academic failure in southern Brazil

Magda Damiani

Scenario

The objective of this chapter is to establish the importance of studying the characteristics of the pedagogic discourse that predominates in educational institutions. It is argued that this provides a means of understanding the phenomenon of academic failure (defined as grade retention and school drop-out), a major problem affecting the Brazilian educational system.

Educational inequalities are very serious in Brazil. High levels of educational failure in primary school children have been reported in this country since the 1930s, and the situation has not changed recently (Brandão et al., 1983). Brazil occupies the seventeenth position among Latin American and Caribbean countries in terms of the efficiency of its educational system (UNICEF, 1995). The excluding character of the Brazilian system is evidenced by the fact that only 56 per cent of children reach Year 5 of primary school in the country. According to UNICEF, for the Brazilian level of per capita gross national product, this figure should be 85 per cent (UNICEF, 1995). The excluding nature of the system is also illustrated by 1996 data provided by the Ministry of Education (MEC, 1998) – 67 per cent of the children and youths (aged between nine and 14) out of school were drop-outs. The number of children who do not initially have access to the educational system is comparatively small.

The educational system requires that pupils are retained in a grade when they do not achieve a certain performance level. The rates of grade retention can be as high as 50 per cent in Year 1 of primary school in certain regions of the country (Mello, 1993, Ribeiro, 1990). Grade retention leads to school drop-out (Verhine and Melo, 1988; Patrinos and Psacharopoulos, 1996). In the long run, children out of school also become socially excluded (EURYDICE, 1994, OECD, 1995). Therefore, granting children the possibility to reach higher levels of formal education is an essential task in a democracy. The appropriation of knowledge and the development of cognitive skills are considered essential if individuals are to participate more fully in their society.

Academic failure tends to be considered as independent from the schooling process and its organization by Brazilian primary school teachers (Mello,

1985; Verhine and Melo, 1988; Davico, 1990; Gama *et al.*, 1991; Penin, 1994; Arroyo, 1997). Teachers blame the victims for their failure and leave the role of the educational institutions under-explored. A large proportion of the research on failure that was (and is) produced in Brazil, and in other South American countries, has been directed at studying the relationships between children's attainment and their personal and family background characteristics (Brandão *et al.*, 1983; Hasenbalg and Silva, 1990; Psacharopoulos and Yang, 1991; Wolff, Schiefelbein and Valenzuela, 1994; Patrinos and Psacharopoulos, 1996). Neglecting the role of schools in academic failure, a practice that is also observed in countries such as Britain and the USA, has been attributed to governmental interest in explaining failure in terms of home-based factors. In some ways, this may be seen as less threatening to the state (Reynolds, 1985).

The influence of intra-institutional processes on children's educational outcomes has also been investigated, both in Brazil and internationally by a number of researchers (Penin, 1989, 1994, Neves, 1991, Daniels, 1995, 1996, Morais *et al.*, 1995). Their findings provide important information, which may be used to guide educational policies. Such findings, however, have not been as widely shared and valued as the findings from correlation studies that have been focused on extra-school variables.

The study reported in this chapter investigated the process of inclusion/exclusion of children from Brazilian primary schools, relating children's educational outcomes to specific characteristics of the educational institutions they attended. The study was focused on the influence of context on children's academic behaviour and followed the theoretical guidance of different authors, who studied the process of social formation of the human mind. Before reporting on the study's findings, a summary of the theoretical background that illuminated the research will be useful.

Theoretical background of the research

The research model was developed from the ideas, put forward by Vygotsky, Leontiev and Bakhtin, about the social formation of the mind, and the relationship between cognition and context. These were integrated with the model of cultural transmission developed by Basil Bernstein.

Vygotsky (1978) believed that the human mind is formed in dialectical transactions between the individual and the social milieu. He attributed a great deal of importance to formal instruction for the development of children's mental functions and learning. Bakhtin also asserted that consciousness takes shape by being in the material world of signs created by an organized group through social intercourse (Volosinov, 1973). The activity theory, developed by Leontiev (1981, 1986), further claimed that the organization of systems of activity[1] at the societal level establishes important parameters. These parameters influence the manner in which an individual or group of individuals carries out and masters a particular type of goal-oriented action (Wertsch, Minick and Arns, 1984).

This theoretical position contrasts with the individualistic perspective that explains behaviour in terms of cognitive, affective and values differences, and would explain the differences in pupils' academic performance through such factors. It stresses the importance of social factors on the development of thinking and behaviour. The authors, however, failed to theorize these social factors and to explore the specific ways through which institutions or cultures exert their influence over the individual. Such an endeavour was carried out by Bernstein (1977, 1981, 1990, 1996), who developed a general model to understand the process within educational institutions.

For Bernstein (1996), a school cannot be considered to be a neutral institution that serves the sole purpose of teaching skills of various kinds to new members of societies. The school is a carrier of ideological messages that produce and reproduce the consciousness of people. The school translates the power relations that exist in society into pedagogic discourses, and these discourses regulate the forms of consciousness and identities of their pupils. By distributing people of different groups (social class, gender, race, religion and region) to different levels of education, for instance, schools preserve the structural relations existing in society.

Furthermore, schools create what Bernstein called a 'mythological discourse' to deal with the issues of social justice, and the possible conflicts engendered by the social function of schooling. Such a discourse disconnects the hierarchy of success internal to the school from the hierarchies external to it, resulting in schooling being generally considered neutral, in terms of producing different levels of success in its pupils. The deficit position, which claims that certain groups of children fail in schools because they lack certain attributes (cognitive, linguistic and cultural), for instance, transfers the responsibility for failure from the school to the family or the community.

Bernstein (1996) further claimed that it is through the structure of pedagogic discourse that the external power relations are realized. He considered that pedagogic discourse is a rule for the embedding of two discourses: the discourse of skills and their interrelations (instructional), and the discourse of social order, relation and identity (regulative). He also claimed that the two are often regarded as distinct and kept apart, as if there is a conspiracy to disguise the fact that there is only one embedded discourse, producing one embedded inseparable text. Further, he considered that the regulative discourse is the dominant discourse and produces order in the instructional discourse.

The theoretical model summarized above allows for the investigation of intra-school processes associated with academic failure. It does so by providing elements for the understanding of the manner through which the social environment influences the development of children's minds, and their academic behaviour.

The research

To study the role of the educational institutions in the production of academic failure, two primary schools from the city of Pelotas (Southern Brazil) were selected. They were administered by the municipality and located in the same borough. Such schools were attended by working-class children,[2] the group that is most affected by academic failure in Brazil. The pupils in both schools presented a high degree of similarity in terms of the risk factors for academic failure identified in a previous correlation study – gender, maternal age, family income, occupation of the head of the family, size of family, type of dwelling and nutritional status (Damiani, 1998). The schools differed in terms of the rate of academic failure among their pupils – in 1995, 43 per cent of the pupils attending Years 1 to 5 in the first school (the high-failure, or HF, school) had repeated or dropped out of school at least once in their schooling history. In the second school (the low-failure, or LF, school) this percentage was 10 per cent. Contrary to expectations, the educational level of both mothers and fathers of the children attending HF was higher than that of children attending LF.

Data on the schools was gathered through interviews with parents, teachers, headteachers and deputy headteachers, classroom observation, informal observation of all school activities, and children's essays describing the schools. The fieldwork lasted two months.

The findings from the case studies are complex and cannot be presented in complete detail in this chapter. The analyses of the findings, however, are significant, suggesting as they do that the differences in the rates of academic failure were due to differences related to the type of discourse that predominated in each school.

Differences in pedagogic practice were small, and could not explain the large discrepancies in the performance of the schools. In HF, for instance, a higher number of the observed lessons included drilling exercises than in LF. Teachers in LF spent more time imparting new information to pupils. These teachers probably believed in the importance of equipping children with the knowledge they did not possess. The emphasis on the decontextualized repetition of exercises, observed in HF, could be an indication that teachers in this school believed that their pupils had difficulties in learning. Therefore, pupils should only be taught a limited amount of content, which had to be rehearsed through endless exercises in order to be learned.

The privileging discourse in HF had a predominately regulative character, that is, it emphasized matters of social order, and placed less importance on the instructional aspects of schooling. In fact, the description of HF provided by one of its pupils was a perfect summary of the culture developed in this school. The boy said, 'It feels like home there', and this impression was shared by some of the teachers working in HF, by a group of student-teachers who were carrying out their practice in the school at the time of the fieldwork, and by the researcher. Pupils' essays describing the school also illustrated the predominance of the regulative discourse in HF. The essays did not refer to instructional aspects and were centred around issues of relationships among pupils and between pupils and staff in the school. In LF, pupils' essays included positive comments that made reference to educational aspects, such as the academic quality of the teaching or the school (instructional aspects). Essays from LF's pupils were longer and more formal in appearance, suggesting a tendency to taking essay-writing as a more serious and demanding activity, and placing a greater emphasis on the formal instructional discourse in this school.

The following matters were predominant in the discourse of HF's staff – relationships among staff, issues related to pupils' life history, concerns with pastoral care, providing pupils with models of behaviour, and keeping children protected in school. Regulative aspects were also present in the discourse of LF's teachers. However, teachers in LF did not show the same degree of emphasis on matters of social order as teachers in HF. The majority of teachers in both schools considered that academic failure is caused by extra-school factors – mainly related to pupils' family characteristics.

This position reflects the general tendency observed among Brazilian primary school teachers, as described above. Nevertheless, when the content of teachers' answers was analysed according to a regulative/instructional continuum, the opinions of LF's teachers were closer to the instructional end of the continuum than those of HF's teachers. LF's teachers highlighted the lack of academic support from the families of working-class children as the main cause of failure. A small number of teachers in this school also mentioned instructional causes for failure. They referred to the poor academic behaviour of teachers, or to the incapacity of the educational system to deal with working-class children. The majority of teachers in HF emphasized the lack of emotional stability in the home of working-class children as the main cause of failure, thus positioning themselves nearer the regulative end of the continuum.

The communities served by the two schools were fairly similar in most respects, except for the fact that, on average, families in HF had a higher educational level and probably a higher socio-economic level as a consequence. Staff from this school, however, reported that the majority of their pupils and families were very poor and needy; in making this assertion, they were perhaps influenced by the existence of a small group of families, at a very low socio-economic level, whose children attended this school (approximately 10 per cent of the total). Staff in LF, on the other hand, did not evaluate their pupils and families as poor and needy, and reported that they belonged to middle socio-economic level.

Since poverty, and the emotional imbalance it causes in families, was seen as the main factor in academic failure in HF, it is possible to suppose that staff in this school expected their pupils to be academically unsuccessful. Staff, therefore, transmitted such a message to the pupils through their predominant discourse – the regulative. Pupils' identities – as people who would not participate in the academic system – were thus constructed. The objectives that prevailed in this school were to teach pupils the most basic skills and content, to socialize pupils into the behaviours and value norms of the society, and to protect them from the hazards of being left on the streets. Having access to large amounts of the systematic knowledge accumulated by society, or to the more abstract principles that organize such knowledge, and routine progress through the educational system, were not important motives for schooling in HF. The meaning of schooling in HF was related to the reproduction of class relations, a common pattern observed in the schooling of working-class children in a class-divided society such as Brazil.

In LF, staff expected their pupils to succeed academically, as pupils were not considered to belong to the lower socio-economic level of the population, which was seen as bound to fail. The expectations of pupil success created a culture geared to instruction, rather than to the simple socialization and care of pupils. Such a culture allowed pupils to reach a level of achievement that resulted in grade promotion, and permanence in the educational system.

Conclusion

This study provided a strong indication that the structure and content of pedagogic discourse is a significant factor in the determination of academic failure. However, more research is necessary to provide a fuller understanding of the way in which different motives are generated and expressed in different educational contexts. It is also far from clear how to influence the culture of a school. The findings, nevertheless, imply that encouraging the development of institutional cultures, which privilege the instructional aspects of schooling, might have an impact on children's educational performance and, therefore, promote the development of a more inclusive system.

The case studies suggest that one way to influence the culture of a school could be to invest in the way teachers are trained for their jobs. This training is currently based on technical aspects. However, teachers' training (both pre-service and in-service) should also include critical and political matters, according to several Brazilian researchers, such as Mello (1985), Penin (1994), and Frigotto (1996). In addition, future and current teachers need to be aware of research findings that indicate the importance of intra-school factors in the production of educational failure. Attributing failure to extra-school factors is convenient for teachers; it does not require them to be critical about their practices, or to try to organize a schooling process that can make a difference to the poorer layers of the Brazilian population.

There is a need for teachers to be able to understand all the potential determinants of academic failure, in order to be able to devise their solutions to the problem. This process, however, requires delicate and locally tailored actions and cannot be accomplished by top-down, standardized, mechanistic policy proposals.

An understanding of the different motives present in different types of schooling might lead teachers to recognize the importance of creating an instructional culture in their schools. Such a culture would have the potential to develop pupils' skills' and to enable pupils to share the knowledge produced by the society. Such a culture would allow for work on the Zone of Proximal Development of the school, as defined by Engestràm (1987), that is, the area where co-operative action for social change is possible. If teachers were more aware of the ways in which children are positioned in different forms of pedagogic practices, they would be able to produce a different educational narrative for the working-class children. They would be in a position to create a local pedagogic discourse that challenged the official pedagogic discourse, which continues to position school failure as a function of individual deficit or family pathology.

Endnotes

1. Russel (1997, p 4) defined an activity system as any ongoing object-directed, historically conditioned, dialectically structured, tool-mediated human interaction: a family, a religious organization, an advocacy group, a political movement, a course of study, a school, a discipline, a research laboratory, a profession, and so on.
2. Measuring social class in Brazil involves a high degree of complexity. The term 'working class' is used in this chapter to refer to families whose heads belong to the following occupational groups: manual qualified, manual semi-qualified and manual non-qualified.

References

Arroyo, M. (1997) 'Fracasso-sucesso: o peso da cultura escolar e do ordenamento da educação básica' ('Failure-success: the weight of the school culture and the ordering of basic education), in A. Abramowicz and J. Moll (eds) *Para Além do Fracasso Escolar (Beyond School Failure)*, Papirus, São Paulo

Bakhtin, M. M. (1981) *The Dialogical Imagination: Four Essays by M. M. Bakhtin*, ed. M. Holquist, University of Texas Press, Austin

Bakhtin, M. M. (1986) *Speech Genres and Other Late Essays*, edited by C. Emerson and M. Holquist, University of Texas Press, Austin

Bernstein, B. (1977) *Class Codes and Control Volume 3: Towards a Theory of Educational Transmissions*, Routledge and Kegan Paul, London

Bernstein, B. (1981) 'Codes, Modalities and the Process of Cultural Reproduction: a Model', *Language in Society* 10, pp 327–63

Bernstein, B. (1990) *The Structuring of Pedagogic Discourse*, Routledge, London

Bernstein, B. (1996) *Pedagogy, Symbolic Control and Identity: Theory, Research, Critique*, Taylor and Francis, London

Brandão, Z., Baeta, A. M. B., Rocha, A. D. C. (1983) *Evasão e Repetíncia no Brasil: A Escola em*

Questão (Drop-Out and Repetition in Brazil: The School in Question), Achiamé, Rio de Janeiro

Damiani, M. F. (1998) Academic failure among Primeiro Grau children in Southern Brazil: from extra-school risk factors to intra-school processes, unpublished Ph.D. thesis, University of London

Daniels, H. (1995) 'Pedagogic practices, tacit knowledge and discursive discrimination: Bernstein and post-Vygotskian research', *British Journal of Sociology of Education*, 14, pp 517–32

Daniels, H. (1996) (ed) *An Introduction to Vygotsky*, Routledge, London

Davico, M. I. (1990) 'The repeat and drop-out problem: a study in Brazil on the role of the teacher', *Prospects*, 20, pp 107–13

Engestràm, Y. (1987) *Learning by Expanding: An Activity-Theoretical Approach to Developmental Research*, Orienta-Konsultit Oy, Helsinki

EURYDICE: European Unit (1994) *Measures to Combat Failure at School: A Challenge for the Construction of Europe*, Office for Official Publications on the European Communities, Luxemburg

Ferraro, A. (1995) 'Subsídios dos Censos e das PNADs para Diagnóstico da Alfabetização e Escolarização das Crianças e Adolescentes de 5 a 17 Anos de Idade no Estado do Rio Grande do Sul' ('The Censuses and the PNADs as sources to diagnose literacy and schooling in children and adolescents aged 5 to 17 in the State of Rio Grande do Sul'), 'Caderno de Textos do Seminário Estadual do Projeto O Direito de Aprender' ('Papers from the State Seminar of the Right to Learn Project'), AJURIS/AMPRGS/FAMURS/UNICEF, Porto Alegre

Frigotto, G. (1996) 'A formação e a profissionalização do educador: novos desafios' ('The formation and professionalization of the educator: new challenges'), in T. T. da Silva and P Gentili (eds) *Escola S.A.: Quem Ganha e Quem Perde no Mercado Educacional do Neoliberalismo* ('School plc: Who Wins and Who Loses in the Neoliberal Educational Market'), CNTE: Brasília.

Gama, E. M. P., Lucas, L. O., Salviato, M. de L., de Jesus, D. M., Carvalho, J. M. and Doxsey, J. R. (1991) 'As percepçoes sobre a causalidade do fracassso escolar no discurso descontente do magistério' ('Perceptions about the causes of academic failure in the unhappy discourse of teachers'), *Revista Brasileira de Estudos Pedagógicos*, 72, pp 356–84

Hasenbalg, C. A. and Silva, N. V. (1990) 'Raça e oportunidades educacionais no Brasil' ('Race and educational opportunities in Brazil'), *Cadernos de Pesquisa*, 73, pp 5–12

Leontiev, A. N. (1981) *Problems of Development of the Mind*, Progress Publishers, Moscow

Leontiev, A. N. (1986) 'The problem of activity in the history of Soviet psychology', *Voprosy Psikhologii*, 4, pp 109–20

MEC (Ministry of Education and Sports) (1998) 'O Brasil Quer Toda Criança na Escola' ('Brazil wants all children in school], '), http://www.mec.gov.br

Mello, G. N. de (1985) *Magistério de 1o. Grau: da Competíncia Técnica ao Compromisso Político (First-grade teachers: from technical competence to political commitment)*, Cortez, São Paulo

Mello, G. N. de (1993) *Cidadania e Competitividade: Desafios Educacionais do Terceiro Milenio (Citizenship and competitiveness: educational challenges for the third millennium)*, Cortez, São Paulo

Morais, A. M., Neves, I. P., Medeiros, A., Peneda, D., Fontinhas, F. and Antunes, H. (1995) *Socialização Primária e Prática Pedagógica, Vol. II: Análise de Aprendizagens na Família e na Escola* [Primary Socialization and Pedagogic Practice, vol. 2: Analysis of Learning in the Family and in School], Fundação Calouste Gulbenkian, Lisboa

Neves, I. P. (1991) 'Práticas Pedagógicas Diferenciais na Família e suas Implicaioes no (In)Sucesso em Ciíncias: Fontes de Continuidade e de Descontinuidade entre os Códigos da Família e da Escola' ('Differential pedagogic practices in the family and its implications for (non) success in science: sources of discontinuity between family and school codes), unpublished Ph.D. thesis, University of Lisbon

OECD/Organization for Economic Co-operation and Development (1995) *Our Children at Risk*, Centre for Educational Research and Innovation (CERI), Paris

Patrinos, A. A. and Psacharopoulos, G. (1996) 'Socio-economic and ethnic determinants of age-grade distortion in Bolivian and Guatemalan primary schools', *International Journal of Educational Development*, 16, pp 3–14

Penin, S. (1989) *Cotidiano e Escola: a Obra em Construção (Everyday Life and School: The Building under Construction)*, Cortez, São Paulo

Penin, S. (1994) *A Aula: Espação de Conhecimento, Lugar de Cultura (The Classroom: Space of Knowledge, Place of Culture)*, Papirus, Campinas

Psacharopoulos, G. and Yang, H. (1991) 'Educational attainment among Venezuelan youth: an analysis of its determinants', *International Journal of Educational Development*, 11, pp 289–94

Reynolds, D. (1985) (ed) *Studying School Effectiveness*, Falmer, London

Ribeiro, S. C. (1990) 'A pedagogia da repetíncia' ('The pedagogy of repetition'), *Tecnologia Educacional*, 19, pp 13–20

Russel, D. R. (1997) 'Rethinking genre in school and society: an activity theory analysis', http://www.iastate.edu/ drussel/at%26genre.html

UNICEF/United Nations Childrens Fund (1995) *The Progress of Nations*, UNICEF, Paris

Verhine, R. E. and Melo, A. M. P. de (1988) 'Causes of school failure: the case of the state of Bahia in Brazil', *Prospects*, 18, pp 557–68

Volosinov, V. N. (1973) *Marxism and the Philosophy of Language*, Seminar Press, London

Vygotsky, L. S, (1978) *Mind in Society*, Harvard University Press, Cambridge

Wertsch, J. V., Minick, N. and Arns, F. J. (1984) 'The creation of context in joint problem-solving', in B. Rogoff and J. Lave (eds) *Everyday Cognition: Its Development in Social Context*, Harvard University Press, Cambridge

Wolff, L., Schiefelbein, E. and Valenzuela, J. (1994) *Improving the Quality of Primary Education in Latin America and the Caribbean*, The World Bank, Washington DC

World Bank (1986) *Brazil: Finance of Public Education*, The World Bank, Washington DC

This chapter is based on the work carried out for the researcher's PhD thesis submitted to the University of London's Institute of Education. During the course, the researcher received financial support from the Brazilian government through CNPq – Conselho de Desenvolvimento Científico e Tecnológico.

Section III
Dialogues on inclusive education

17. The welfare state and individual freedom

Jesper Holst

In the course of the last decade, new insights and attitudes have gained ground in terms of social pedagogy and policies relating to the disabled, both in Danish schools and in Danish society in general. Central concepts such as normalization, integration and training have been replaced by, or further developed through such ideas and concepts as quality of life, own culture, communication and the formation of a public sphere.

This chapter will attempt to examine the development of policies relating to the disabled in the light of recent developments in governmental control and management strategies – in other words, the development of the relationship between individual and state.

Criticism of normalization, integration and training

In 1959, the Danish Parliament passed the Mentally Retarded Act, later known as the 'Normalization Act'. This act laid down the principles and guidelines that have governed Danish policies relating to the disabled to the present day, including such familiar principles as the following:

1. Normalization: the mentally disabled should be able to live a life as close to the normal as possible. The point of the normalization principle was, and is, to ensure that the disabled had equal rights and duties compared with other citizens. (Bank-Mikkelsen, 1971)
2. Integration: if normalization was the goal, the integration of the mentally disabled into the life situations of normal people became the means to reject an 'abnormal', segregated life in centralized institutions and special schools. (Halse, 1981)
3. Development: the 1959 Act mentioned for the first time the rights of the mentally disabled, especially the right to teaching and training. This formed the basis for replacing a static, medicinal view of care by an educational, developmental approach. (Bank-Mikkelsen, 1971)

These principles, building on values such as equality, the values of the individual, solidarity and the right to personal development, initiated a process. Up to the present day, this has radically altered the life and living conditions of the mentally disabled, both in schools and in society in general.

However, despite broad agreement on these values – on which the principles of normalization are based – there is criticism today of the whole ideology of normalization, and of its consequences for the social and learning opportunities of the mentally disabled.

This criticism has various axes, which can be outlined as follows: the normalization principle – the idea that disabled people should be able to live a life as close as possible to the normal – has often meant that the 'generality' has been the norm used by schools and society to provide a framework for the life and education of the disabled. However, making 'generality' the norm for the everyday life of a socially defined group of people carries with it certain problems and pitfalls.

In the first place, it is questionable whether 'a normal life' is to be found other than in statistics and the Utopian picture presented by the media. Recent social research indicates that people in Denmark live in a variety of ways – we each have our own way of organizing daily life, both work and leisure. We live in a pluralist society, each with our own norms, values and concepts of 'the good life' (Holm et al., 1994).

In the second place, it may be asked whether these attempts at normalization have not led to what has been called 'the tyranny of the normal' (Goode, 1994). When the right to 'an ordinary life' means that 'an ordinary life' becomes the prescriptive norm for the way in which life conditions should be organized for the mentally disabled, the naturalistic fallacy is just round the corner. The implication is that ordinary people live in a certain way, therefore the disabled should do the same.

Even if there is some truth in the assertion that ordinary people in high-powered industrial societies live pretty stressful, alienated, rootless and divided lives, is it at all meaningful (anything visionary is out of the question) to use the concept of a normal life as the yardstick for the management of the framework for the daily lives of disabled people?

In connection with this, some (Victor, 1994) have maintained that normalization has made the mentally disabled truly unhappy. Before these attempts at normalization, the mentally disabled were unhappy in their large institutions. After normalization they have become 'really' unhappy, that is, unhappy in the 'real' way in which everyone else in modern society is unhappy.

In the period up to the middle of the 1980s, the principle of integration meant that many disabled children were integrated into ordinary schools. At the same time, mentally disabled people were moved out of the eleven large centralized institutions to new forms of accommodation and living, as a rule in their own local authority. Criticism of this policy of integration has been directed at the following factors: integration has taken place on the basis of the 'normal society' concept, and has been characterized by administrative decisions and established practice, rather than by respect for the needs and wishes of the disabled themselves. There are good grounds for maintaining that many mentally disabled people were simply moved around like packages in the post (Lihme, 1984). The mentally disabled came home to their own local authority, and this put them totally under the control of this authority, which was responsible for arranging suitable living and working conditions for them, as well as for looking after them in other ways.

Not infrequently, integration led to problems of isolation and loneliness. Being formally integrated into a school or the local environment did not necessarily mean that the individual was part of a social fellowship that went beyond those with similar disabilities (Gustavsson, 1997). Moreover, the drawbacks associated with life in the large centralized institutions had a tendency to reappear in the new types of integrated accommodation (Sletved and Haubro, 1985). The following daily programme from a new mini-community provides a hair-raising example:

07.30 Wake residents, bathe, get dressed
08.15 Breakfast with all the residents
09.00 Out for a walk, in all weathers
10.00 Morning coffee in the activity groups
10.15 Sing, play instruments in the activity groups
11.30 Lunch, medicine
12.15 Siesta
14.00 Go to the toilet
14.30 Afternoon tea/coffee
16.00 Footbath
16.45 Free
17.30 Evening meal, medicine
18.00 Toilet training
18.30 Change into pyjamas or tracksuits
20.30 Evening coffee, medicine
21.15 Go to the toilet, personal hygiene
21.30 Bedtime

In addition, 'The above applies in general to all residents. The schedule can also be seen on the activity plan on the notice board. In addition, charts for bowel movement, weight and menstruation are to be found in the card index.' (Holst et al., 1991.)

The developmental principle used involved the application of professionally guided systematic training of functions. ADL (a Danish abbreviation for 'ordinary daily living') programmes, and development and teaching programmes, stressed that mentally disabled people should be helped to become as independent as possible.

The question is, of course, whether these professionally controlled attempts at training were not, in fact, in opposition to independence, and the kind of support needed to help people manage their own lives (Holm et al., 1994).

People with severe disabilities have been accustomed for years to living

closely supported by people who always know what is best for their development, and who in many respects define their needs and the aims of their development. It is not surprising, therefore, that such people are alienated from
the idea of making their own choices and managing their own lives.

The meta-learning here – the hidden curriculum in many forms of educational programmes, in ADL training and the modification of behaviour – will
often be: 'The staff, the professionals, know what is best for me, they know my
needs better than I do, so why should I choose. Why should I try to communicate what I want to do?'

Another result has been a tendency to deprive the mentally disabled of
their own time. Their days are filled with work and other occupations, with
teaching and training, often planned and managed by others. It is considered
important for the mentally disabled to be able to look after themselves, but
sometimes, so much time is spent on ordinary daily activities, such as cooking,
washing, and so on, that very little is left over for activities chosen and managed by the people themselves.

New approaches to a policy for the disabled

In the last few years, new approaches to a policy for the disabled have
emerged in connection with the increasing criticism of the consequences of
the normalization concept. New ideas are gradually being accepted, connected with such concepts as quality of life (Holm *et al.*, 1994), sub-culture
(Jessen, 1991), inclusion, communication (Kirkebaek and Clausen, 1985) and
the formation of a public sphere (Bylov, 1995). The reasons for this new direction in policies relating to the disabled can be explained, and are discussed, in
many different ways.

It has been maintained that we are experiencing the second phase of normalization (Bylov, 1990, 1995). The first phase consisted of normalizing the
formal life conditions of mentally disabled people, by freeing them from
segregative and oppressive legislation, structures and frameworks. The central point was the struggle for equality. The second phase, on the other hand,
is concerned with ensuring that the mentally disabled are able to create a good
life for themselves within this normalized framework. The new challenge is
the struggle for the individual's freedom to form his or her own life through
communication, the making of choices, and access to social groupings of his or
her own choice that create identity and meaning. This calls for radical alter-
ations to the relationship between the professional support personnel provided by public authorities and the mentally disabled themselves.

Others are of the opinion that the ideology of normalization is on its last
legs, and can no longer offer an answer to the problems at present facing policies relating to the disabled. Söder (1992) points out that decisive changes to
the prevailing discourse and ideology concerning these policies arise when, in

the course of time, a discrepancy appears between this ideology and the problems being faced in practice, in the sense that the prevailing discourse and ideology represent an attempt to solve past problems. Finally, a new approach can be understood in connection with the development of the whole general pattern of social control. In tune with an increasing demand for legitimation on the part of the state and other sources of power, there is an increasing refinement and lack of visibility of the techniques of social control.

This is not only true of the field of handicap provision. With regard to education, youth services, psychiatry, and the prison service, we have witnessed a development characterized by decentralization, de-institutionalization, individualization, more humane sanctions, less visible presence, a call for the minimalization of state control, the removal of categories and deprofessionalization. (Cohen 1985; Holst 1988)

The outward forms of social control are changing, as a certain de-institutionalization is taking the place of the earlier, totalitarian institutions, which were characterized by isolation, surveillance and training. A new type of state-controlled provision is now emerging, consisting of a less visible, flexible, decentralized network of support and control measures (Poulantzas, 1981). This development, which means that the carefully planned process of normalization is moving towards new structures, is also decisive for any understanding of the new approaches to policies.

In what follows, without questioning the validity, or rejecting the understanding of the background for these new approaches, emphasis will be placed on a distinction between the ideology as such and the ideology as applied, ie, between the principle of normality and the management of this principle. This distinction emphasizes the fact that actual measures aimed at normalization are not simply a result of the normalization principle alone. They are just as much an outcome of the way in which this principle is implemented within the framework of a particular logic of control, management and professionalism pursued by the state, in other words, within a predetermined structure for the relationship between the individual and the state.

Criticism of the measures and actions aimed at normalization at any particular time is not, therefore, necessarily a criticism of the principles of equality, solidarity and the value of the individual, on which normalization is based. In fact, this has rarely been the case. As has often been the case in the ongoing debate about policies relating to the disabled, it is more likely to be a criticism of the way in which the ideology of normalization is translated into practical action within the dominant management logic of the time.

Criticism of the traditional management logic of the welfare state

The development of public administration in Denmark is a clear example of the gradual formation of a welfare state stabilized over a period of time. This development has taken place in a number of phases, all characterized by the fact that the state gradually expanded its spheres of control and management towards what has been called the 'happy phase' of the welfare state in the 1960s. At this time, the ideology of the welfare state had become a common ideology, above and beyond political differences (Dahlberg-Larsen, 1984).

The traditional management logic of the welfare state was based on the idea that it was possible to plan, control and regulate the economy, and the life of society, centrally, down to the smallest details. Any type of problem could be referred to the institutions of the welfare state, which are staffed by a horde of highly qualified professionals. This management logic has the following characteristics: central planning and regulation; professionally correct decisions; the production of uniform and efficient services, financed by taxes; case orientation, reflecting a specialist–client relationship, between the professional worker and the public (Bergsøe and Brydensholt, 1986).

With the development of the welfare state, the state became the great bearer of gifts, the great provider of security for its citizens, who were regarded as those clients to whom the state's professional specialists could supply the good life.

In the course of the 1970s, the traditional welfare state ran into a crisis. In the wake of an economic crisis that revealed the vulnerability of a state-regulated economy, and of increasing criticism of the social consequences of the traditional welfare state, cracks began to appear in the surface of the reigning political consensus regarding the welfare state. Criticism of these social consequences, expressed both on the right and the left of the political spectrum, was directed at state pampering and the increasing professionalization of human caring and solidarity. Put rather strongly, this criticism has run along the following lines: with the development of the welfare state, the state extends its domain and powers, blocking the ability of ordinary people to manage and organize their own lives. This development marks a shift in power – and, thereby, the ability to solve life's problems, including those of human need – from the relatively independent structures of civil society to the institutions of the state.

The results of this move towards formal structures and state centralism are clear: state institutions, such as the social and health services, education, and the legal and tax systems, expand, both in extent and in terms of power. These institutions run people's lives. They determine the framework of how and where people live. They manage the culture. They regulate the extent to which one may love one's neighbour, without this activity being regarded as salaried work, subject to taxes and dues. The institutions look after people who become social cases, fall ill or simply give up. The institutions manage; people are managed. The institutions of the state help; the citizens receive help.

This growth of the centralized state and its institutions affects the lives and spheres of action of individuals. People gradually get used to the idea that they are professional specialists attached to a state institution, which can and must solve problems. People seek the help of specialists in the health service and lose the ability to interpret for themselves with any confidence the signals sent by their own bodies. They approach the social services if they need help in solving social problems, and lose the ability to tackle life's problems with the help of neighbours, family and friends. Because human caring, nursing and help have been moved out of daily life – out of the close and immediate social network – people become alienated from their own humanity. Thus, the ring is closed, for this alienation and sense of powerlessness creates in itself new social problems such as isolation and loneliness. The solution of these problems calls for further state-employed counsellors, kindergarten teachers, psychologists, school teachers and social workers (Thyssen, 1985).

The development of the welfare state has seen the parallel development of a whole range of new professions within the educational, health and social sectors. Professions have arisen to deal with every conceivable form of human problem. We now have experts in sexuality, in marriage, in healthy living, in social life and learning, in movement and in the upbringing of children. To become a practitioner of these professions requires training in the special problems tackled by the profession, and in the methods used to solve them. This increases the numbers (and areas of competence) of those professional problem-solvers whose formal qualifications give them access to solving the problems people have with their health, their social and emotional life, and the upbringing of their children. Those who have not gained access to the professions are regarded as quacks, amateurs, clients or ignorant parents, who ought to keep their hands off the professionals' areas of work.

The consequence of professionalization has been that human solidarity has become a question of paying a certain amount of money in taxes in order to allow professionals to carry out their tasks. In this way, love of one's neighbour becomes more instrumental. People are together, help each other, and show caring, perhaps indeed because they find it important and meaningful to do so, but also because they get paid for it. Charity is on the payroll.

A more serious consequence is that the growth of the professions – the fact that there are expert solutions to any kind of human problem – means that ordinary people no longer feel qualified or responsible enough to tackle these problems. People lose the ability to solve their own problems, no longer trusting to their own experience or their own solutions. Instead, they wait for help and guidance from those who are deemed to have knowledge, who can solve their problems.

Finally, not only do the professions help to render ordinary citizens helpless in the face of the problems life creates, but there is also the ever-present danger that the experts who know how the good life should be lived, and how the good society should be organized, will gradually and insidiously replace a popular debate by a professional one.

There is a thin line between aid and control; between helping people who have problems, and authoritatively defining their problems and needs. All forms of supportive work tread a narrow, dangerous path. On the one side, there is the danger that nothing is done about the conditions that create want and suffering, and on the other side there is the danger that the professionals, who have a knowledge of the causes of suffering and want, may, in their efforts to act in solidarity with the population, feel that they alone can act in the interests of those people. When this happens, the public democratic debate is replaced by the professional debate between experts.

This tendency can be clearly seen, for example, in a text from 1984 entitled *The Public Sector – Solidarity or Guardianship*, which concludes as follows:

> But at the same time this modern version of solidarity will involve an organization of the public service sector in accordance with the interests of the vulnerable and underprivileged. As a result, the public sector will not simply be thrown about between Social Democratic ideals of equality on the one hand or the Conservative ideology of freedom on the other, but can be developed through the application of the knowledge and expertise of the professional groups, and in accordance with their responsibility for the weakest members of society. (Jensen, 1984)

These tendencies towards a crisis in the welfare state are closely related to the fact that belief in the detailed, centralized management of the economy and of social life is weakening, and to the authoritarian and bureaucratic relationship between the welfare state and individuals in society. This involves three interconnected symptoms of crisis (Hegland, 1995):

1. a crisis of resources, because increasing demand for social benefits leads to spiralling public costs, and the social welfare budget begins to burst at the seams;
2. a functional crisis, because public systems and institutions become so entrenched that they can no longer adapt to new or altered requirements in the population;
3. a crisis of legitimations, because that sense of social solidarity with people in need, which has been part of our historical ballast for generations, is now mostly exercised by paying taxes. This means that people lose touch with the idea of thinking and acting on the basis of common responsibility.

In this context, the criticism of the principle of normalization outlined here is not so much a rejection of the ideas of equality, solidarity and the value of the individual that lie behind the principle, as an attack on the way the principle is implemented within the framework of the welfare state. That framework looks for standard solutions, bureaucratic control and professional decisions regarding the problems faced by citizens, and their lives in general.

This was revealed by an investigation carried out in Sweden as part of the work leading up to a reform of provision for the disabled. The investigation (Söder, Barron and Nilsson, 1991) identified four obstacles to people with

severe disabilities being able to have an influence on their own lives. The conclusions of the investigation are quoted here from Sandvin and Söder (1996).

The first obstacle was professionalism. The meeting between professional
experts and a person with severe disabilities sometimes becomes a clash between different types of knowledge, where the disabled person is at a disadvantage. The expert is normally in power, and this is most clearly
demonstrated in situations where he or she controls scarce resources which
the disabled person wants and could benefit from.

A second obstacle identified by the researchers was stiff and bureaucratic
rule systems. Many areas of importance for persons with severe disabilities
have been governed by rules that have been politically sanctioned and
aimed at controlling the allocation of resources for support and service. But
no matter how much influence the organizations of persons with disabilities
might have had on the design of those rule systems – when applied in the
concrete cases the problem of fitting one unique individual into the frames
of the rule system arises.

A third obstacle is the procedural and bureaucratic ways of organizing
services. Many persons with severe disabilities depend on daily assistance,
some of them 24 hours a day. Especially those living in 'service-homes' –
own apartments with round-the-clock access to help and assistance – tell
stories about how difficult it is to make service personel work on their own
terms. Often, norms and rules are set by the needs of the organization to
function smoothly rather than by the needs of the clients.

The fourth obstacle to influence is the attitude to and image of disabled
persons among people in general, and professionals in particular. One dimension of the image non-disabled persons seem to have of persons with
disabilities is what has been referred to as 'the myth of eternal childhood'
(Kirkebaek, 1993). They assume that people with disabilities cannot make
judgements, or even speak for themselves, and, consequently, tend to 'take
over' and make decisions for them.

The reconstruction of the welfare state

During the last decade, the symptoms of a crisis within the welfare state have
seen the advent of a number of efforts to re-define the relationship between
the state and the individual, by an alteration of the logic governing patterns of
state control, management and professional care.

To this end, a number of programmes have been launched that are concerned with change, development and modernization, with the aim of giving
citizens a greater degree of influence, and of reducing the corpus of state control. Self-management has become one of the key concepts in this development, and one with which everyone apparently could agree, although, in all
honesty, there are many different ways of interpreting the concept.

For the forces of liberalism, self-management means, first and foremost, modernization through the liberalization and privatization of state institutions; in this respect, a battle is being waged against the social democratic welfare state (Rasmussen, 1993).

For the forces of socialism, self-management does not imply a rejection of the welfare state, but, rather, a development or reconstruction of the way in which the state functions, so that the individual citizen and civil society are strengthened in the face of market forces and the power of the state.

The crisis of the welfare state has launched a debate about the theory of the state, in which concepts such as 'the self-management state', or 'the responsive state' have introduced new ways of understanding the activities of the state.

The following table can be used to illustrate the differences between the traditional welfare state and the new understanding of the state that is developing (Bergsöe and Brydensholt, 1986).

Table 17.1

	The Welfare State	The Responsive State
Control	Emphasis on central planning and rules	Framework for decisions made by those affected
Types of decision	Correct, professional	What can be agreed on
Product	Public Authority produces uniform service provision	A variety of public and private services
Finance	Tax financed 'free services'	Block grant, private right of disposal
Organization	Case-oriented	Value-oriented
Roles	Specialist–client	Consultant–citizen

The revolt against the traditional logic of control and management characteristic of the welfare state also involves the development of new norms for contact between citizens and the public sector. The state must abandon the idea of controlling, and taking full responsibility for the individual citizen. Instead, it must be willing to negotiate with citizens who are regarded as responsible individuals.

In this way, the state would be accorded a number of new and very different functions, since society would no longer lay down general sets of regulations governing the situation of the individual citizen. Instead, there would be a regulative framework that would allow the individuals involved to negotiate for themselves the rules by which they wish to live. The function of this legal and administrative regulative framework would primarily be to ensure that individuals possess real authority as negotiators in these situations, whilst, of course, making sure that certain higher-order principles are respected and safeguarded (Bergsøe and Brydensholt, 1986).

Today, we are beginning to catch sight of the results of the attempts made in the last decade to modernize the public sector, as the outlines of a new administrative model gradually emerge. Whereas previously the ideal model for public administration involved the application of detailed regulations within a hierarchical administrative structure, there would now appear to be a development towards the provision of a regulative framework, offering a high degree of personal choice and decision with regard to a wide range of private and public services. It is now also clear, at least, as far as terminology goes, that the 'clients' of the welfare state have become 'users', 'residents' and 'customers'.

In the wake of criticism of the traditional welfare state, the ideal of equality has been replaced, or at least supplemented by the ideal of individual freedom. State administration must to a greater extent respect the needs of the individual and the right of individuals to choose the pattern of their own lives.

Alongside, and interacting with these changes in the relationship between individual and state, new frameworks of discourse have been created. These have led to a series of social and political developments. This is true of developments regarding policies relating to the disabled, and of the type of discourse employed.

Developments in policies relating to the disabled

Critics of the principle of normalization, or, rather, of the way in which the traditional welfare state administered this principle, have maintained that normalization is an aim without vision, and may easily lead to mere levelling, or to the tyranny of the normal. This criticism has led to new discussions about the aims of policies relating to the disabled; in these discussions, the aim of normalization tends to be replaced by, or supplemented by the idea of quality of life.

This concept opens the way to a readiness to listen to the individual's subjective understanding of the good life. The task of the professional supportive personnel appointed by the state is therefore no longer primarily to make the lives of the mentally disabled as close to the 'normal' as possible, but to enter into a dialogue with the disabled person, regarding his or her dreams, hopes or ideas about the organization of everyday life. The purpose of the state, and of those professional helpers employed by the state, is not to direct the lives of other people, but, through dialogue, to help people create a good life for themselves along the lines they themselves have chosen.

The criticism of the principle of normalization and the development of the concept of quality of life cannot be understood outside the context of criticism of the equality ideal of the welfare state, and the development of a responsive and responsible ideal of freedom. However, one obvious danger is that criticism of the welfare state, and the aim of normalization, may mean the replacement of earlier efforts to ensure equality and solidarity by the idea that individuals themselves are responsible for, and have the freedom to create, their own quality of life.

It would be a dubious advance if the concepts of equality, social solidarity and justice were to be replaced by the idea that each individual is responsible for his own conditions and quality of life. In this connection, it is important for the development of policies relating to the disabled for the values behind the normalization principle to be preserved. In this way, society will continue to ensure that individuals have the same opportunities and conditions, and, therefore, as much freedom to shape their own daily lives as they wish, and to do this according to their own concept of 'the good life' (Holm *et al.*, 1994).

It is important to preserve the basic values of the welfare state, pursuing at the same time the reform of administrative and professional structures, in the direction of a more responsive and flexible relationship between the individual and the state. Criticism of the traditional efforts at integration found in the welfare state also pave the way for new discourses and developments with regard to policies relating to the disabled.

Efforts at integration were criticized as being mostly for the benefit of society and the school, with the disabled being expected to adjust to normal schools and normal society. Integration is assimilative (Schousboe, 1989). This criticism opened up discussion about the idea of inclusion, and led to efforts governed by the idea that human differences constitute a resource. The aim must be to develop the institutions of society in a direction marked by an openness, and by a respect for the needs of the individual.

Efforts at integration are also criticized for being purely formal. They do not lead to real social integration in a society in which social relations are established and dissolved by conscious choice (Gustavsson, 1992). The mentally disabled would seem to a great extent to be expected to create social relationships with each other (Gustavsson, 1997). This criticism has led to a discussion about the culture pertaining to and created by the disabled. Efforts have been made in Denmark in recent years – in the form of cafés, journals, radio programmes and music festivals for the mentally disabled – to provide them with an opportunity to form relationships with each other (Jessen, 1991; Holm *et al.*, 1994).

There would seem to be a certain opposition to efforts at inclusion, aimed at creating more open institutions and living environments, and cultural policies that regard the mentally handicapped as a sub-culture in society. On the other hand, recent events in Denmark, such as the first recorded strike by the mentally handicapped at a protected workshop, and the creation of a special NGO for the mentally handicapped (ULF in Danish), have grown out of the fact that the mentally disabled had their own meeting-places, and had gathered together for common cultural events. A movement away from efforts to create a culture of the disabled, towards the beginnings of the creation of a public domain in which the mentally disabled define the political agenda and their own political demands, can now be discerned (Bylov, 1995).

Regarding differences as a resource, challenging social institutions to develop in such a way that they can meet the requirements of different individuals, and a cultural approach that celebrates diferences – all of these must be seen in relation to the altered relationship between individual and state that has arisen in connection with the recent reconstruction of the welfare state in crisis.

Finally, criticism of professionally defined programmes of training and development has helped to start a debate about the role of the state and professional experts in relation to the mentally disabled. At the moment, we are seeing a tendency to move away from the client concept, in which professionals see it as their task to do something for their clients, towards an interpersonal approach, in which dialogue and communication between the professionals and those who need help are of great importance in defining the aims and structure of the support offered.

Even though no direct causal link can be established, the reconstruction of the welfare state in the last few decades, in the course of which an attempt has been made to re-define the relationship between individual and state, has undoubtedly contributed to the new approaches now apparent in the debate about policies relating to the disabled.

References

Bank-Mikkelsen, N. E. (1971) 'Noget om åndssvage', in J. Jepsen (ed.), *Afvigerbehandling*, Thanning and Apple, Copenhagen

Bergsøe, T. and Brydensholt, H. H. (1986) 'Markedsføring af en samfundsomstilling', in *Fra nutud til nytid*, Dafolo, Frederikshavn

Bylov, F. (1990) *Fra enfoldighed til mangfoldighed*, Specialpaedagogik, no.3

Bylov, F. (1995) 'The cultural discourse of quality of life', unpublished paper

Cohen, S. (1985) *Visions of Social Control*, Polity Press, Oxford

Dahlberg-Larsen, J. (1984) *Retsstaten, velfoerdsstaten og hvad så?*, Akademisk Forlag, Copenhagen

Goode, D. A. (1994) *Quality of Life for Persons with Disabilities: International Perspectives and Issues*, Brookline Books, USA

Gustavsson, A. (1992) 'Livet i "integrasjonssamfundet"', in *Mot Normalt? Omsorgsideologier i forandring*, Kommuneforlaget, Oslo

Gustavsson, A. (1997) 'Inifrån utanfàrskapet', in J. Tössebro, (ed.) *Den vanskelige integrering*, Universitetsforlaget, Oslo

Halse, J. (ed.) (1981) *Integration i folkeskolen*, Gyldendals Paedagogiske Bibliotek, Copenhagen

Hegland, T. J. (1995) 'Den menneskelige orden', in E. Clausen (ed.) *Det gode samfund*, Socialministeriet, København

Holm, P. et al., (1994) *Liv og kvalitet i omsorg og paedagogik*, Systime, Århus

Holst, J. (1988) 'I sandhedens tjeneste -eller på sporet af klienten', in *Udviklinger*

-socialpaedagogik til tiden?, Aalborg Socialpaedagogiske Seminarium, Aalborg

Holst, J. et al. (1991) Samvoer, Kommunikation, Samarbejde, LEV's Forlag, Copenhagen

Jensen, U. J. (1984) Den offentlige sektor -solidaritet eller formynderi, Socialarbejdernes Faellesudvalg, Copenhagen

Jessen, C. (1991) Det kulturelle spring, Speciallaererforeningen af 1981, Copenhagen

Kirkebaek, B. (1993) Da de åndssvage blev farlige, Forlager SOCPOL, Copenhagen

Kirkebaek, B. and Clausen, H. (1985) Aktiv kommunikation hos multihandicappede, Specialpaedagogisk Forlag, Herning

Lihme, J. (1984) in K. E. Jessen, et al., (1985), Et integreret liv, Socialstyrelsen, Copenhagen

Poulantzas, N. (1981) Staten, magten og socialismen, Bibliotek Rhodos, Copenhagen

Rasmussen, A. F. (1993) Fra socialstat til minimal stat, Samleren, Copenhagen

Sandvin J. T. and Söder, M. (1996) 'Welfare state reconstruction – de-differentiation and individualism' in J. Tössebro, et al. (eds) Intellectual Disabilities in the Nordic Welfare States, Høyskole Forlaget, Kristianssand

Schousboe, I. (1989) Integrationsformer, Udkast, Dansk Tidsskrift for Kritisk Samfundsvidenskab, no. 1

Sletved, H. and Haubro, H. (1985) Hvad er der galt med institutionerne, Sydjysk Universitetsforlag, Esbjerg

Söder, M. (1992) 'Omsorgsideologier i et samfunn i endring', in Mot Normalt? Omsorgsideologier i forandring, Kommuneforlaget, Oslo

Söder, M., Barron, K. K. and Nilsson, I. (1991) Inflytande för människor med omfattende funktionshinder, SOU 1990.19, Bilagsrapport, Allmänna Förlaget, Stockholm

Thyssen, O. (1985) Teknokosmos – om teknik og menneskerettigheder, Gyldendal, Copenhagen

Victor, A. (1994) 'Livskvalitet og socialforsorgens tidehverv', in P. Holm, et al. (eds) Liv og kvalitet i omsorg og paedagogik, Systime, Århus

18. Policies and practices? Inclusive education and its effects on schooling

Roger Slee

Introduction

Attending the American Educational Research Association Annual Meeting in Chicago last year, I was having breakfast one morning at the 'Old Timer's Diner' across the street from my hotel. Half-way through my eggs 'over easy', I noticed the gentleman at the next table stand to greet a companion. Flustered, the latter apologized for his lateness, blaming it on a late night in front of the television watching the Academy Awards ceremony. They sat, and began to work through their respective lists of Oscars highlights and disappointments. The attention of the 'social researcher' (or eavesdropper) in me was caught when one of them exclaimed, 'What about the best actor – Geoffrey Rush? That film [Shine] was unbelievable.'

In the seconds that followed this statement, I went over my own reactions to this film, which had favourably impressed me. 'Unbelievable?' Did he mean piano virtuoso David Helfgott's disability was difficult to reconcile with his exceptional talent? Perhaps he found the very troubled relationship between Helfgott and his father incredible? I was snapped back from my search for an answer by the American gentleman's explanation:

'Unbelievable! I mean, who ever heard of an Australian concert pianist?'

This traveller's tale serves a purpose here. Had I left the 'Old Timer's Diner' prior to the explanation, I would have continued to puzzle over aspects of the film's screenplay, trying to account for the man's scepticism about Rush's award. Having heard that he found the notion of a musically gifted Australian a cultural absurdity, I know where I would begin any conversation with him. Rather than engage in discussion about the nuances of the script, I would challenge his assumptions about Australian culture and identity.

The same principles apply to discussions about inclusive education policy and its impact upon schooling. Dialogues on inclusive education require us to be stipulative about discourse and its application. Moreover, we need to be prepared to allow the dialogue to venture into 'new times' (Hall and Jacques, 1989) analysis that eschews the re-articulation of the 'ideology of expertism' (Young, 1990; Troyna and Vincent, 1996). Educators, bureaucrats and the community at large must continue to debate the politics of identity and difference before scripting 'inclusive educational settlements', which fail to acknowledge and make explicit their conceptual underpinnings.

This chapter will highlight the difficulties encountered when discussing and developing inclusive education policy, at a time when reductionist thinking underscores exclusionary educational policy-making (Ball, 1994; Whitty, Power and Halpin, 1998). Lamenting the co-modification of 'unmediated knowledgability', through the education management and school effectiveness industries, Stephen Ball (1998, p 78) suggests that 'we have too much knowledge and not enough understanding'. Pursuant to, though not pretending foreclosure on, a contribution to greater understanding of expert knowledge and its usage, I intend to do the following:

- subject special educational needs knowledge to critical scrutiny;
- consider the politics of distribution, identity and difference in educational policy-making;
- provide a summary of current education policy themes that are in tension with inclusive education; and
- foreshadow the discussion of the effects of different understandings of inclusive education on schooling.

At the outset, I want to make two observations. First, in the following discussion, 'inclusive education' refers to education for allcomers. It is a reaction against educational discourses that exclude on the basis of a range of student characteristics, including class, race, ethnicity, religion, gender, sexuality, perceived level of ability or disability, or age. Notwithstanding this broad church of social theory and educational policy interest, my focus will be narrowed to the intersection between inclusive education and disability.

Second, I do not subscribe to a false dichotomy between educational policy as an 'expression of intent' (Codd, 1994) and practice as implementational pragmatics. Following Foucault, Allan, Brown and Riddell take the view that

policies are viewed…as instruments of power/knowledge relations through which the identities and experiences of children with special educational needs are constructed. (Allan, Brown and Riddell, 1998, p 30)

Special educational needs, the 'ideology of expertism' and inclusive education

In her analysis of the 'welfare corporate society', Young (1990, p 80) identifies the ideology of expertism, which legitimizes the structures of domination, and circumscribes the 'life world'. Submitting to the authority of institutions such as hospitals, schools, universities, government offices, social service agencies, banks and countless others, consumers or clients have their behaviour prescribed by officials; those officials draw upon various disciplines or discourses in order to standardize, universalize and normalize the population (1990, p 79). Nikolas Rose (1989) depicts the pervasive power of knowledge/discourses as the population at large working from the scripts of experts, to become self-regulating and normalizing, developing their own 'governmentality'. In other words, powerful systems of knowledge impose order upon an unruly world. Expert knowledge is used to calibrate and normalize the population, in order to render it governable. Skrtic contends that the professions have risen to 'a position of prominence and authority' on the basis of a practical and a political claim:

> the practical claim was that the professions have exclusive access to the knowledge that society needs if it is to solve its problems. The political claim was that professionals will apply this knowledge to society's problems in a disinterested way, in the interest of their clients and the common good, rather than for personal gain. (Skrtic, 1995, p 3)

A number of researchers have described and analysed this operation of social governance, and exercise of professional interest, through special educational discourses (Tomlinson, 1982; Barton, 1987; Fulcher, 1989; Skrtic, 1991; Oliver, 1996). For Barton (1987), 'special educational needs' (SEN) remains a euphemism for the failure of schools (Barton and Slee, forthcoming). Tomlinson (1982) highlighted the disproportionate referral of Caribbean children to special education in the UK, and the professional interest manifest in the steady expansion of categories of special educational needs. Consistent with C. Wright Mills' (1959) observations about the political imperative of representing 'social issues' as 'personal troubles', the language of special education de-politicizes failure, and shifts responsibility to defective or disabled individuals (Oliver, 1996). The role of special educational professionals is to diagnose students' levels of disability, and then to provide, according to their special needs, individual programmes outside of the normal educational provision. Such practice has its origins in the medical forays into education by French physicians Itard and Seguin. The psycho-medical paradigm that dominates SEN research and practices extends from an essentialist view of individual defectiveness. According to Skidmore,

> this paradigm conceptualizes special needs as arising from deficits in the neurological or psychological make-up of the child, analogous to an illness or medical condition. Borrowing from the medical discipline, authors often speak of the 'aetiology' of a given 'syndrome'; in the US literature on learning disabilities, for example, this conceptualization becomes quite explicit, in the form of the 'minimal brain dysfunction' hypothesis, which ascribes difficulties in learning to otherwise undetected cortical lesions. (Skidmore, 1996, p 34)

Just as the medical origins of special education provided its epistemological foundations and contingent medical model of diagnosis and treatment, through individual educational programmes (IEPs), the technical apparatus for identifying defective students was elaborated by the discovery of measurable intelligence (IQ), courtesy of the expanding field of educational psychology (Ford *et al.*, 1982; Franklin, 1994). Bernstein (1996, p 11) refers to a 'spurious biology or set of biological metaphors', advanced to deflect from the social construction of failure and the project of democratic education.

In the face of international pressure for the integration of disabled students into regular classrooms, the special educational industry has proven remarkably resilient. Professional special educational discourse appropriates the lexicon of inclusive schooling and comfortably relocates itself to both regular and segregated educational settings (Slee, 1993). The growing and particular expression of equity in special education (Howe and Miramontes, 1992) reveals a flawed attempt to fuse contradictory discourses:

> Discourses on equity and social justice are grafted to the contradictory languages of special education based on a deficit-bound medical model of disability and corporate managerialism to produce a hybrid inclusive policy text...It is hardly surprising that the implementation of policy founders upon attempts at the reconciliation or delimitation of implacable conflicts. (Slee, 1996, p 22)

The quest for inclusive education becomes a technical problem to be solved through what remain assimilationist policies.

> The 'disabled', a marginalized group whose failures to satisfy the culturally specific, historically specific standards of behavioural 'normality', display 'handicaps', inabilities to deal 'effectively' as individuals, with life in Western capitalist society, their 'handicaps' demanding, in the eyes of those for whom they are an 'other', a 'policy', an objective, clearly formulated, bureaucratically realisable, logical, coherent approach to dealing with, or coping with, their 'handicaps'. (Branson and Miller, 1989, p 144)

Surveys of SEN policy texts in the UK (Heward and Lloyd-Smith, 1990; Clark, Dyson, Millward and Skidmore, 1997) and Australia (Fulcher, 1989; Slee, 1996; Jenkinson, 1997) reflects Branson and Miller's description of the construction, surveillance and regulation of special needs students through 'inclusive' policy. Let us consider how this process operates.

Some students present differences that are difficult for present institutional and cultural arrangements to accommodate. Equity suggests that these students be given equal opportunity to an 'appropriate' standard of education. The challenge is whether to consider how the cultural and institutional arrangements of a school may disable the child, and produce a culture of schooling that takes allcomers, or whether to hold the institutional line, and provide support for 'disabled children' to allow them to attend regular classes with minimal disruption to the institutional equilibrium? In other words, is the

policy problem an issue of cultural politics, or a technical issue, to be managed
through resources and professional practice?

Present policy approaches accept, within reason, a version of distributive
justice mediated through diagnostic or ascertainment schedules. In the US,
this is expressed through the requirements of Public Law 94-142, the Education of All Handicapped Children Act, itself derived from the *Brown v. Board of
Education* decision of 1954, which concerned the issue of separation on the basis of race. I have referred to this as 'special education for the modern bureaucracy'. Justice is delivered through a 'calculus of equity'.

The task is first to ascertain the level of disability within the individual.
Having decided how disabled a student is, the professional actuaries must decide the resources required for redressing the disability. Once the additional
resources are delivered to the school, inclusion will proceed. This discourse issues little challenge to the traditional special educational assumptions about
disability and difference. The bureaucratic language of the UK's code of practice, Australia's state education department's inclusive schooling guidelines,
and the US provisions of public law is conditional. Such expressions as 'least
restrictive environments', 'most appropriate settings', 'individual education
programmes' all provide latitude for professional prerogative and persuasion.
Classrooms are not a site for cultural transformation, they simply allow a seat
at, or by, the table for some 'other' visitors. After all, how often is the tenure of
the disabled child contingent upon the continuity of additional resources?

There is much to be learned in the arena of education disability politics
from disability movements, and from other struggles for inclusive education.
bell hooks (1994, p 31) reminds us that inclusive education is 'cultural work', a
political engagement and struggle, which eschews the liberal blancmange of
'everyone wearing the same have-a-nice-day smile'. She calls on Peter Mc-
Laren to lend further force to her argument:

> Diversity that somehow constitutes itself as a harmonious ensemble of be-
> nign cultural spheres is a conservative and liberal model of multiculturalism
> that, in my mind, deserves to be jettisoned because, when we try to make
> culture an undisturbed space of harmony and agreement where social rela-
> tions exist within cultural forms of uninterrupted accords we subscribe to a
> form of social amnesia in which we forget that all knowledge is forged in his-
> tories that are played out in the field of social antagonisms. (McLaren,
> quoted in bell hooks, 1994, p 31)

Considering the progress of anti-racist and anti-sexist education, those working in the area of disability and inclusive education policy must address central questions about the interplay of power, value, representation and identity
and curriculum, pedagogy and school organization. These questions might
include:

- Where are the voices of the disabled in the policy process?
- How do we regard different identities?

- How are they represented in and articulated through the culture of the school (curriculum, pedagogy, organization)?

I have yet to encounter these kinds of questions forming the conceptual foundation for inclusive educational policy-making. Tom Shakespeare, a disabled activist and researcher, issues a similar challenge to the disability research industry:

> There is quite an industry producing work around the issue of sexuality and disability, but it is an industry controlled by professionals from medical and psychological and sexological backgrounds. The voice and experience of disabled people is absent in almost every case. As in other areas, disabled people are displaced as subjects, and fetishized as objects. A medical tragedy model predominates, whereby disabled people are defined by deficit, and sexuality is either not a problem, because it is not an issue, or is an issue, because it is seen as a problem. (Shakespeare, 1996, p 191)

Other questions arise, as follows:

- Who sets the inclusive schooling research agenda?
- Who commissions the research projects?
- Who undertakes the research?

Inclusive education in an exclusive policy climate?

This section will not rehearse the education policy analyses that are already available (such as Ball, 1994; Taylor *et al.*, 1996; Marginson, 1997a, b; Whitty, Power and Halpin, 1998). Instead, I simply wish to raise two policy themes that undermine 'inclusive education' for disabled students, and, of course a host of 'others'. These themes are the following:

- education, competition and the marketplace; and
- effective schooling research and the school improvement movement.

Shoved out by invisible hands

At the heart of school exclusion and inclusion lie the curriculum and pedagogy. Engagement and the representation of student identities are critical to an inclusive education. Employing lively metaphor, Ball (1994, p 34) has dubbed the National Curriculum in England and Wales 'the curriculum as museum'. It is seen as an artefact of Conservative cultural restorationism that fails to engage with the experience, cultures and aspirations of a range of student groups in English schools. It is worth revisiting Ball's consideration of music 'education' in this 'curriculum of the dead':

> Music is defined solely in terms of product, in terms of what others, listed in the canon, do. For the restorationists, music is not a putting together of

sounds to create effect or shared activity, it is not a matter of creativity but rather a lonely appreciation, a fossilized tradition, a mental abstraction divorced from the here and now and from the possibility of engagement. Education and learning here are founded upon alienation, a negation of self; knowledge is valued precisely for its irrelevance, esotericism, detachment, elitism and intrinsic difficulty; learning is an act of abasement, of passivity, of deference. The learner comes to the knowledge naive and innocent and leaves that which is learned untouched and unchanged. (Ball, 1994, p 35)

Paulo Friere's banker treads the well-worn boards of these classrooms. The popular discourse on standards in education tends to be both backward-looking, and narrow in its cultural references. Increasing numbers of students are placed at educational risk, or disabled by the traditional academic curriculum. Current education policy discourse suggests that the intensification of student competition, together with the offer of additional support, will promote understanding. A more robust discussion of the complex relationships between curriculum, pedagogy and the preferred learning styles and requirements of individual students may move us closer to inclusive schooling than standards slogans can. Is the educational exchange teacher-centred or student-centred? Is it dialogic or transmissive? Does it celebrate behaviourism, where students follow the steps to be able to retrace them on command, or is understanding through enquiry-based learning encouraged?

Of course, the question of the site of learning is critical to inclusion. This is not a straightforward question of location. The question must probe the cultural and social architecture of the classroom and school, and has been put before, in *Apart or A Part?* (Cole, 1989). These questions travel beyond schooling in the UK. Moreover, there is a growing body of research to assist in this continuing enquiry into differentiaon and a pedagogy of recognition (Berres *et al.*, 1996; Hart, 1996, 1998; Mehan *et al.*, 1996; Nixon *et al.*, 1996; Fraser, 1997; Ainscow, 1998).

The paradox in UK education policy is that the highly regulated National Curriculum is delivered through a discourse of 'parental choice' to be conducted in the marketplace. Following Hayek, British education policy discourse, as in Australia (Marginson, 1997a, b) and the US (Apple, 1996), presents the market as a benign agent of efficiency, excellence and equity. Equity, accordingly, accepts inequality as the natural order, and advocates that individuals must demonstrate that they deserve to be rewarded. Writing in 1944, Hayek expounded upon this theme:

There will always exist inequalities which will appear unjust to those who suffer from them, disappointments which will appear unmerited, and strokes of misfortune which those hit have not deserved. But when these things appear in a society which is consciously directed, the way in which people will react will be very different from what it is when they are nobody's conscious choice. Inequality is undoubtedly more readily borne, and affects the dignity of the person much less, if it is determined by impersonal forces than when it is due to design. (Hayek, 1993, p 79)

Expunged from Hayek's social mosaic, and from many architects of contemporary education policy, is the notion of unequal points of commencement for its constituents (Rawls, 1972), or of the state as the puppeteer, the director of 'action from a distance' (Giddens, 1994, p 4).

Notwithstanding the deflective discourse, the 'free' market is operationalized and protected through the presence of the state. Gewirtz, Ball and Bowe (1995) tracked 'choice', as played out in a number of London schools. The highly differentiated groups of choosers demonstrated the failure of the market to achieve other than the 'revalorization of class selection' (Gewirtz *et al.*, 1995, p 23), disadvantage and the further exclusion of marginal groups. The publication of school performance league tables presses schools to become choosy about students. The 'special needs' student becomes a poor risk for the upwardly aspiring school community. It is little wonder that, in this policy climate, the rate of exclusions in the UK continues to climb (Parsons and Castle, 1998), and Pupil Referral Units become the *de facto* classroom for less than docile bodies.

Are highly reliable organizations inclusive schools?

School effectiveness research, and the school improvement movement, has something of a global grip on educational research and policy-making. This is not surprising, as it is difficult to argue against the desire for effective schools and an improvement in the quality and outcomes of schooling. Nevertheless, it seems to be worth it to swim against the policy tide; school effectiveness research seems to be incapable of addressing the complex requirements for inclusive schooling. Outcomes-obsessed school effectiveness may be seen as part of the growing performativity (Lyotard, 1984) of post-modern bureaucratic culture. It does not engage with the complexity of school life; instead, it is determined to distil a catalogue of discreet factors that coincide with improved student scores in reading, mathematics and non-verbal reasoning.

Tilts are made at the affective domain of schooling, with mixed results (Sammons, Hillman and Mortimore, 1995). Rather than repeat recent commentary on this problematic area of education research and policy, I will simply raise two fundamental tensions for those considering a cocktail of school effectiveness and inclusive schooling.

Reductionism

Adherents to this research and policy genre are given to quick analogies, which suggest a simplicity alien to the experience of life in schools. Flight control operations, nuclear power plants and surgical theatres are likened to schools, to press the case for standardized approaches to teaching and learning, school organization and the practice of educational administrators. Cultural specificity is dimmed by the gloss of astonishing international comparisons and projections. The pedagogical culture of different countries is forfeited to Cartesian logic. Reynolds and Farrell (1996) suggest links between student outcomes, teacher-centred instruction and economic performance. Implicit in this is a call for the transplantation of Eastern pedagogy into Western classrooms for similar academic and, therefore, economic results.

Flat-earth functionalism

School effectiveness is silent on questions of curriculum. The knowledge to be consumed and examined is generally uncontested. Relatively little is said about equity (Sammons, Hillman and Mortimore, 1995). Problems of identity and difference are shunned. The effectiveness researcher is impatient with ponderous questions about the complexities of cultural relations in the classroom. School effectiveness is confused with school effects. The long-term project of the reconstruction of education pursuant to inclusive schooling is ignored; preferred instead are lists of factors that can be adjusted or formatted as lock-step improvement packages.

School effectiveness has become a management technology, a language and set of procedures for school surveillance. The normalizing view of school effectiveness researchers is incompatible with the profound changes required for inclusive schooling. Yeatman captures this requirement for specificity:

> it is not just that a service needs to be adjusted so that it is culturally appropriate for its potential range of culturally different users, the service will become altogether more dialogical, more responsive to the expressed needs of all the individuals using it. In short, it will become a service oriented to the substantive particularity of individual and group needs. (Yeatman, 1994, p 86)

Continuing the dialogue

Much of this discussion has been dominated by the stipulation of what inclusive education is *not*. In order to become more explicit about terms of reference, there has been an emphasis on the deconstruction of 'expert special educational knowledge'. Deconstructing this knowledge provides space to interject with questions that do not share the prior assumptions of special educational discourse. Moreover, it allows questions to be asked about whose interests are served by particular conceptions of inclusion. Challenging 'established wisdom' is simultaneously disturbing and disruptive.

> Despite the contemporary focus on multiculturalism in society, particularly in education, there is not nearly enough practical discussion of ways classroom settings can be transformed so that the learning experience is inclu-

sive. If the effort to respect and honor the social reality and experiences of groups in this society who are non-white is to be reflected in a pedagogical process, then as teachers…we must acknowledge that our styles of teaching may need to change. Let's face it: most of us were taught in classrooms where styles of teaching reflected the notion of a single norm of thought and experience, which we were encouraged to believe was universal. This has been just as true for non-white teachers as for white teachers. Most of us learned to teach emulating this model. As a consequence, many teachers are disturbed by the political implications of a multicultural education because they fear losing control in a classroom where there is no one way to approach a subject – only multiple ways and multiple references. (bell hooks, 1994, pp 35 and 36)

The necessity for disturbing and fundamental changes, as opposed to a mild reform programme of school improvement, is evidenced by the high rate of exclusion from schooling. As Booth (1995) urges, understanding inclusion makes a much more careful analysis of exclusion necessary. We know that exclusions are increasing. In the Australian state of Queensland there was a reported 16 per cent increase in the volume of suspensions and exclusions, from 13 374 in 1996 to 15 485 in 1997 (Sunday Mail, 1998). According to Parsons and Castle (1998), the number of students permanently excluded from school in the UK between September 1995 and July 1996 had reached 13 581.

At one level, we should not be alarmed by the fact that so many young people are defecting from, or being ejected from, the regular classroom. Students have always left school prematurely. Previously it was not a problem, as they had somewhere to go – the farm, the factory, the shop. The unskilled youth labour market, along with segregated special education, concealed the fact that schools were never intended for all students (Slee, 1996). In the past, falling out from school or being ushered out, was not so problematic; it was still possible to get started, and to lead an autonomous adult working life. Now it is a problem, as there is no where else for young people to go. It is hardly surprising, then, that special educational provision has broadened in order to contain the growing population of 'problem students'. One might be forgiven for speculating about the likelihood for some of these people to submit to syndromes such as ADHD, which distract from the profound crisis in education.

Deconstruction is not the aim of this dialogue, it is a device for making clearer the terms of engagement for the ensuing conversation. A number of propositions need to be set down as themes for a continuing conversation about how to construct a more inclusive education. Inviting a range of constituents to the forum, this conversation may set the following proposition against David Skidmore's (1996) recent attempt to develop an integrated theoretical framework, each interrogating and challenging the other. The propositions – or prompts – are deliberately tentative and under-developed, as they are intended to remain suggestive.

Proposition One

The question of voice is central to the development of inclusive educational research, policy and schooling. The field of inclusive education cannot allow itself to be dominated by any one voice. Experts need to become listeners, and need to learn to be told about needs. An Aboriginal curriculum could not be drafted by knowledgeable white educators for Aboriginal children; women have demonstrated that their educational failure was a product of patriarchy, and not of individual pathological shortcomings; in the same way, disabled activists/educators/students need to be exercising leadership in this policy dialogue. We all need to listen to those who have been marginalized if we are to contribute to the development of a pedagogy of recognition.

Proposition Two

Reform needs to take the long view. This proposition proceeds from a sense of profound crisis. The crisis is uneven in its impacts. Its depth is seen in relation to specific areas of disadvantage and privilege. For many, the crisis of schooling is personalized and restricted to a private struggle. Is there any sense in including people in schools that are not working for many of the students already there? Perhaps the task is one of an educational reconstruction that transcends incremental reform? Political quick-fixes will not suffice if we are interested in reaching the substantive particularity that Yeatman talks about as a pre-condition for an inclusive model of service delivery.

Proposition Three

Teacher education is currently about acquiring fragmented knowledge. National frameworks for teacher training are not framed to produce the critically reflective practitioners or cultural workers who ought to teach in inclusive schools. There is, as noted earlier, a growing body of research into inclusive curriculum and pedagogy. This has not been central to the work of teacher education. We need to be reminded, through this continuing dialogue, of the need for extensive change in this arena.

Proposition Four

Researching inclusive education must respond to the first proposition and not submit to the dominance of particular disciplines as the custodians of inclusive educational research know-how. This proposition invites those in this conversation to challenge present funding models for research, and to assert a diversity of researchers and methods in the development of projects.

Proposition Five

This is linked to Proposition One, and states that inclusive education is an issue of cultural politics. It is not assimilation; it has an anti-racist, anti-sexist, anti-disablist agenda. Inclusive education does not avoid uncomfortable questions about oppression, rights and the value of difference.

Proposition Six

Progress towards inclusive education is obsessed with specificity and the locale. Policy needs to recognize the particularity of the range of sites to which it speaks. Policy is subject to interpretation, subversion, generalization and rejection. Making policy should recognize and respond to this dynamic.

References

Ainscow, M. (1998) 'Would it work in theory? Arguments for practitioner research and theorising in the special needs field', in Clark, C., Dyson, A. and Millward, A. (eds) *Theorising Special Education*, Routledge, London

Allan, J., Brown, S. and Riddell, S. (1998) 'Permission to speak? Theorising special education in the classroom', in C. Clark, A. Dyson and A. Millward (eds) *Theorising Special Education*, Routledge, London

Apple, M. (1996) *Cultural Politics and Education*, Open University Press, Buckingham

Ball, S. J. (1994) *Education Reform: A Critical and Post-Structural Approach*, Open University Press, Buckingham

Ball, S. J. (1998) 'Educational studies, policy entrepreneurship and social theory', in R. Slee, G. Weiner and S. Tomlinson (eds) *School Effectiveness for Whom?*, Falmer Press, London

Barton, L. (ed.) (1987) *The Politics of Special Educational Needs*, Falmer Press, Lewes

Barton, L. and Slee, R. (forthcoming) 'Competition, selection and inclusive education: some observations', *International Journal of Inclusive Education*, Vol. 3, No. 1

Bernstein, B. (1996) *Pedagogy, Symbolic Control and Identity: Theory, Research, Critique*, Taylor and Francis, London

Berres, M., Ferguson, D., Knoblock, P. and Woods, C. (eds) (1996) *Creating Tomorrow's Schools Today. Stories of Inclusion, Change and Renewal.*, Teachers College Press, New York

Booth, T. (1995) 'Mapping Inclusion and Exclusion: concepts for all', in Clark, C., Dyson A. and Millwald, A. (eds) *Towards Inclusive Schools?* (pp 96–108) David Fulton, London

Branson, J. and Miller, D. (1989) 'Beyond policy: the deconstruction of disability', in L. Barton (ed.) *Integration: Myth or Reality?*, Falmer Press, Lewes

Clark, C., Dyson, A., Millward, A. J. and Skidmore, D. (1997) *New Directions in Special Needs: Innovations in Mainstream Schools*, Cassell, London

Codd, J. (1994) 'Educational reform and the contradictory discourses of evaluation', *Evaluation and Research in Education*, Vol. 8, No. 1, pp 41–54

Cole, T. (1989) *Apart or a Part? Integration and the Growth of British Special Education*, Open University Press, Milton Keynes

Ford, J., Mongon, D. and Whelan, M. (1982) *Invisible Disasters: Special Education and Social Control*, Croom Helm, London

Franklin, B. (1994) *From 'Backwardness' to 'At-Risk'. Childhood Learning Difficulties and the Contradictions of School Reform*, State University of New York Press, New York

Fraser, J. (1997) *Reading, Writing, and Justice: School Reform as if Democracy Matters*, SUNY Press, New York

Fulcher, G. (1989) *Disabling Policies*, Falmer Press, Lewes

Gewirtz, S., Ball, S. and Bowe, R. (1995) *Markets, Choice and Equity in Education*, Open University Press, Buckingham

Giddens (1994) *Beyond Left and Right: the future of radical politics*, Polity Press, Cambridge

Hall, S. and Jacques, M. (eds) (1989) *New Times. The Changing Face of Politics in the 1990s*, Lawrence and Wishart, London

Hart, S. (1996) *Beyond Special Needs: Enhancing Children's Learning Through Innovative Thinking*, Paul Chapman, London

Heward, C. and Lloyd-Smith, M. (1990) 'Assessing the impact of legislation on special education policy: an historical analysis', *Journal of Education Policy*, Vol. 5, No. 1

hooks, bell (1994) *Teaching to Transgress*, Routledge, New York

Howe, K. R. and Miramontes, O. B. (1992) *The Ethics of Special Education*, Teachers College Press, New York

Jenkinson, J. (1997) *Mainstream or Special? Educating Students with Disabilities*, Routledge, London

Lyotard, J. (1984) *The Postmodern Condition: a report on knowledge*, Manchester University Press, Manchester

Marginson, S. (1997a) *Markets in Education*, Allen and Unwin, St. Leonards

Marginson, S. (1997b) *Educating Australia*, Cambridge University Press, Cambridge

Mehan, H., Villanueva, I., Hubbard, L. and Lintz, A. (1996) *Constructing School Success. The consequences of untracking low-achieving students*, Cambridge University Press, New York

Nixon, J., Martin, J., McKeown, P. and Ranson, S. (1996) *Encouraging Learning. Towards a Theory of the Learning School*, Open University Press, Buckingham

Oliver, M. (1996) *Understanding Disability: From Theory to Practice*, Macmillan, London

Rawls, J. (1972) *A Theory of Justice*, Clarendon Press, Oxford

Rose, N. (1989) *Governing the Soul*, Routledge, London

Sammons, P., Hillman J. and Mortimore P. (1995) 'Key Characteristics of Effective Schools: a review of school effectiveness research', *A Report by the Institute of Education for OFSTED*, Institute of Education and University of London, London

Shakespeare, T. (1996) 'Power and Prejudice: issues of gender, sexuality and disability', in L. Barton (ed.) *Disability and Society: Emerging Issues and Insights*, Addison Wesley Longman, Harlow

Skidmore, D. (1996) 'Towards an integrated theoretical framework for research into special educational needs', *European Journal of Special Needs Education*, Vol. 11, No. 1, pp 33–47

Skrtic, T. (1991) *Behind Special Education: A Critical Analysis of Professional Culture and School Organisation*, Love Publishing, Denver

Skrtic, T. (ed.) (1995) *Disability and Democracy. Reconstructing (Special) Education for Post-modernity*, Teachers College Press, New York

Slee, R. (1993) 'The Politics of Integration – New Sites for Old Practices?', *Disability, Handicap and Society*, Vol. 8, No. 4, pp 351–60

Slee, R. (1996) 'Inclusive Education in Australia? Not Yet!', *Cambridge Journal of Education*, Vol. 26, No.1, pp 19–32

Taylor, S., Rizvi, F., Lingard, B. and Henry, M. (1997) *Education Policy and the Politics of Change*, Routledge, London

Tomlinson, S. (1982) *A Sociology of Special Education*, Routledge and Kegan Paul, London

Troyna, B. and Vincent, C. (1996) 'The ideology of expertism: the framing of special education and racial policies in the local state', in C. Christensen and F. Rizvi (eds) *Disability and the Dilemmas of Education and Justice*, Open University Press, Buckingham

Whitty, G., Power, S. and Halpin, D. (1998) *Devolution and Choice in Education*, Open University Press, Buckingham

Young, I. M. (1990) *Justice and the Politics of Difference*, Princeton University Press, Princeton, NJ

19. Racism, ethnic identity and education of South Asian adolescents

Paul A. S. Ghuman

Introduction

This extended discussion of identity and ethnicity invites the reader to identify parallels between one marginalized group within a post-industrial West European setting, and other similarly challenged groupings in spatially diverse settings world-wide. My focus is on South Asian adolescents in the context of Britain, but the underlying issues are invariably echoed elsewhere, and with other populations. It has frequently been inferred that ethnicity is linked with educational under-performance; it is necessary to consider the extent to which the tapestry of excluding conditions might be structural in many countries, and which of those conditions retain currency across a spectrum of human characteristics.

According to Goodnow and Collins (1990), many parents expect adolescents to go through a period of storm and stress. Erickson and his school of thought (Erickson, 1968; Marcia, 1994) have attributed this turmoil to identity confusion. Sociologists and anthropologists, on the other hand, have underlined the social factors behind the predicament. It is argued that the 'different role expectations' demanded of young people can lead to inter-generational conflict, which, in turn, often becomes a source of anxiety and confusion. The media's reporting of young people's drug-taking, promiscuity, and aggressive behaviour (for example, at football matches) reinforces the stereotyping of the adolescent's life as full of turmoil.

Coleman and Hendry (1990) argue that adolescence has been viewed as a stressful period in human development. However, critical examination of empirical research to date suggests that the majority of adolescents pass through this phase without any major difficulties. They conclude their analysis, as follows:

> None the less, there is general agreement that during the teenage years major adaptation has to occur. The transition between childhood and adulthood cannot be achieved without substantial adjustment of both a psychological and social nature; and yet most young people appear to cope without undue stress. (Coleman and Hendry, 1990, p 205)

There is some empirical evidence to substantiate the claim that drug abuse, and psycho-social disorders, have increased since the 1950s. Smith and Rutter (1996) analysed the post World War II data on alcohol and drug use and other psycho-social disorders of young people in the UK. They concluded, 'Yet, after taking account of the problems and limitations [of data collection and methodology], it must still be concluded that there has been a real rise in psycho-social disorders of youth in the post-war period' (Smith and Rutter, 1996, p 781).

South Asian young people share with their white peers most of the problems and challenges of growing up in multicultural Britain. However, over and above the normal pains and joys of adolescence, they face two inter-related problems. They often receive conflicting messages from their families and wider society about what constitutes 'proper' behaviour, values and attitudes' (see Rosenthal, 1987). Additionally, most of them have to learn to cope with the racial prejudice of white society, which they encounter from their childhood through adolescence to adulthood. On leaving school and institutions of higher education, ethnic-minority youth often face further discrimination in the employment market (see Cheng and Heath, 1993; Modood et al., 1997). Asian girls, in addition, have to learn to cope with their parents' orthodox and traditional views, which favour boys in all walks of life.

Most of the South Asian migrants of the 1950s and early 1960s were initially sojourners who decided to seek permanent settlement in the UK as a result of the impending control of visa-free entry in 1963. Successive Immigration Acts (see Fryer, 1984) controlled, and eventually abolished, the right of Commonwealth citizens to visa-free entry into the UK. The vast majority of Asian migrants were from rural areas (although there was a minority of teachers, doctors and other professionals), with few skills and virtually no knowledge of the English language and culture, and of the British way of life. They found jobs on the lower rungs of the employment ladder, mostly as unskilled workers, and settled in inner-city (downtown) areas. They re-created institutions of religion, kinship (caste/*gotra*) and marriage, and the 'mini-economic' markets of their 'home' countries. One of these ethnic enclaves is Southhall, in London, which has become well known as the 'little Punjab'.

The first-generation migrants encountered racial prejudice in their places of work, in housing allocation and in access to welfare services. Their children attended inner-city schools where standards of achievement were below the national norm, and where the general morale of the teachers was low (see Rex and Tomlinson, 1979).

Ethnic awareness and racial prejudice

The new younger generation of migrants, born in the UK, face different kinds of problem. The unemployment rate among Asian young people is often higher than amongst their white peers, although there are within-group variations (Modood *et al.*, 1997; Jones, 1993). One of the major factors (as with their forefathers) explaining this situation is the prevalence of racial discrimination against Asians in the employment market (see Jones, 1993, Brown, 1985). In addition, they have to develop their personal and social identity in a bicultural and multicultural setting.

From an examination of literature on the development of racial awareness, it becomes clear that children as young as three years old (Katz, 1976) become aware of their ethnicity and, soon after, begin to attach feelings of 'likes' and 'dislikes' to their own group and to others. The research findings of both Milner (1983) and Davey (1983), with British-born South Asian, black and white children, have clearly demonstrated the 'in-group' preferences of children, irrespective of their ethnic origin. Smith and Tomlinson (1989), in their large-scale study of multicultural secondary schools, found that 'there is a fairly strong tendency for children to chose friends within their own group...this shows that no ethnic group tends to be generally popular or unpopular' (p 101). This finding is generally in accord with the results of other studies (see Verma *et al.*, 1994; Cohen and Manion, 1983).

Milner's (1983) studies on adolescence report relatively little change in the children's attitudes towards various ethnic and national groups as they approach their teenage years and late adolescence. Indeed, he argues that the racial attitudes tend towards greater consistency and stability as adolescents approach adulthood. The findings of recent reports (Roberts and Sachdev, 1996; Modood *et al.*, 1997) on young people clearly demonstrate the disturbingly high degree of racial prejudice of white youth towards Asians in the UK. One of the tasks facing teachers in schools in the UK, and elsewhere, is to deal with students' negative racial stereotypes.

Ethnic identity

Tajfel (1981) defines ethnic identity as 'that part of an individual's self-concept which derives from his knowledge of his membership of a social group (or groups), together with the value and emotional significance attached to that membership' (p 255). Other definitions and interpretations of ethnicity include self-identification, feelings of belongingness and commitment; and the sense of shared values and attitudes (Phinney, 1990).

The only quantitatively planned research strictly relevant to this topic in the UK was carried out with Indian adolescents by Huthnik (1991). In a series of investigations, she found that ethnicity is a salient factor only when an ethnic group has a distinctive presence – when it is politically and socially a significant force. She also found that the ethnic identity of the boys and girls was closely tied to their religion and being 'Indian' – the former being more central than the latter. In addition, Hutnik found that 'ethnicity is not a very salient component relative to other components of identity, such as Psychic style and Inter-personal style' (1991, p 108). However, she argues that ethnicity might become more salient in adulthood, when individuals have to make choices in the field of housing and employment, and when young people are likely to meet racial discrimination.

A qualitative study by Modood *et al.* (1994), using ethnographic procedures, studied the identity-related issues with South Asian young people. One of the salient findings was that religion still plays an important part in defining their ethnicity. The researchers discussed at some length the young peoples' responses to the notion of 'Britishness'. More than half of the respondents felt themselves to a large extent to be culturally British. This was strongly affirmed by their clothes, forms of socializing and choice of entertainment. Despite this cultural change, they felt strongly that they were still not accepted by white British. The rest of the group argued for some form of biculturalism, which they justified on the grounds that white British are reluctant to accept their distinctive ethnicity, and that they ought to retain the essential elements of their cultural traditions. The authors concluded that

> most of the second generation wanted to retain some core heritage, some amalgam of family cohesion, religion and language, probably in adapted form, but did not expect this to mean segregated social lives, for they lived and wanted to live in an ethnically mixed way. (Modood *et al.*, 1994, p 110)

This is small-scale research with many shortcomings, such as subjective interpretation of the data, and an omission of the important variables of gender and social class and/or education. Nevertheless, it adds another piece to the jigsaw of ethnic identity, which is multi-faceted and complex.

Researchers in the USA (Phinney, 1992) and Australia (Rosenthal, 1987) have empirically established the significance of ethnic identity. It has been found that young people of ethnic minorities, with few exceptions, regard the 'achievement' of their ethnic identity to be an important part of their ego identity (Erikson, 1968). Roberts *et al.* (1997) concluded the following from the comprehensive research that they conducted with twenty ethnic groups in America:

> It seems clear from this study that the concept of ethnic identity is meaningful for young adolescents, and that it is related in theoretically meaningful ways to other dimensions of the adolescents' experience'. (p 8)

Phinney (1996a) treats ethnic identity as 'a dynamic construct that changes over time and context and varies across individuals' (p 145). To re-phrase and interpret this, ethnic identity is context-dependent, and there are intra-individual differences in its development. Phinney argues that it is important for both white and non-white youths to explore their ethnicities. For the former, this should lead to better understanding of existing (white) racism and the privileged position of their own ethnic group. For the latter, it should allow the development of an understanding and acceptance of their cultural traditions, and the contribution they have made to wider society. Phinney suggests several exercises that are suitable for secondary school teachers to use in the classroom. In sum, the author argues that

> learning about ethnicity involves more than acquiring information; it requires the exploration of attitudes and feelings. The study of ethnic identity provides a way of exploring the meaning of ethnicity for oneself and others while avoiding the stereotypes and clichés that may result from attempts to describe particular groups. (Phinney, 1996a, p 151)

Despite her reservation about the significance of ethnic identity, Huthnik (1991), reviewing her own research and that of other scholars on the identity of South Asian young people, concludes that 'such speculations suggest that it would be beneficial for the psychological well-being of the ethnic minority individual to be aware of his/her ethnic origins in order that s/he may acquire adequate psychological strategies to cope with prejudice and discrimination' (p 167). She found that Indian teenagers most frequently choose an acculturation strategy (Berry, 1997), as opposed to assimilation or separation.

From this analysis, Huthnik argues that acculturation policies in Britain would not only provide minority groups with functional knowledge of the British way of life, but would also enable them to explore their own ethnicity. Ghuman's researches (1980a, 1980b, 1995a, 1996) have clearly demonstrated that the young people of South Asian origin prefer integration to other modes of adaptation, although there are within-group differences. The Hindu and Sikh girls in the studies opted for deeper levels of integration (almost assimilation), whereas Muslim boys tended to be at the other end of the spectrum, preferring to stay with their own cultural traditions (separation). A study of de Domanico et al. (1994) with Mexican American adolescents found that 'bicultural adolescents may be better adjusted, more flexible, and better able to mediate acculturative stress in culturally ambiguous circumstances' (p 197). Berry (1997) advocates integration as a more humane and functional strategy for multicultural societies to adopt and implement.

Rosenthal (1987) has provided a useful summary of Australian research on the development of ethnic identity and its effect on the well-being of ethnic-minority adolescents. She concluded, 'Happily, the evidence seems to suggest that the integration of two cultural worlds can be an enriching experience yielding flexible individuals with skills that enable them to function adaptaviely in a variety of contexts.' (p 179)

South Asian young people in the UK enjoy many other benefits of being bicultural. Brannen et al. (1994, p 128) found that, as a result of greater parental restrictiveness, South Asian young people emerge as less likely to smoke, drink alcohol and take drugs than their white peers. On 'going out', South Asian parents were found to be stricter with girls than with boys, but parents are equally strict with both sexes about drinking and smoking. Furthermore, the young people are exploiting the psychological tension and anxiety caused by the 'culture conflict' syndrome for creative purposes. Syal (1997), an artist of Punjabi origin, has written a novel *Anita and Me*, which draws heavily on her own bicultural (Punjabi and English) childhood experiences in the Midlands of England. She described her thinking on the subject of culture-conflict:

Syal describes her life as schizophrenic, acknowledging that much of the creative impetus for her writing and performing comes from the clash of two cultures she has grown up with...a lot of women of my generation see the qualities in both cultures and find them perplexing, but amusing not desperate. (*The Guardian*, 14 May 1991)

There are other writers of note in the UK (Kureishi, *The Buddha of Suburbia*; Naipaul, *Home Coming*; Rushdie, *The Moor's Last Sigh*), who have capitalized on their own inner turmoil of living in two distinctive cultural traditions. In the same way, intellectuals and writers of Jewish ancestry in Europe (including Berlin and Steiner) have creatively utilized the conflict that has arisen from living both in the traditional religious-led home culture, and in the secular and individualistic society of the West.

Alienation of South Asian youth

A significant number of young people in the inner-city areas of the UK are alienated both from their community and from the wider society. One of the reasons for this is that, in some parts of the UK, the rate of unemployment of South Asian and black youths is nearly twice that of whites (Jones, 1993; Brown, 1985). Long-term unemployment – partly due to racial discrimination – has bred cynicism and alienation in some youths. Consequently, to the shock of their parents, some have drifted into the sort of petty crime and drug-trafficking rarely found in South Asian communities hitherto. In Berry's model of acculturation, such a process of alienation is called marginalization (also see Huthnik, 1991, p 158).

Some young people appear to be rejecting both their parents' culture and the British way of life – the former, because it denies them personal freedom and autonomy, and the latter, because they face racial discrimination in employment, and harassment from the police. Parekh analysed the situation in the aftermath of rioting in Bradford, England, as follows:

Drug-taking has increased within the Asian community, and so has drug-related crime...All this has naturally worried the Muslim community. It undermines their traditional values, subverts their family life and heightens the inescapable inter-generational tensions within the Muslim community...As inner-city areas become cultural deserts and fall prey to commercial exploitation of drugs and sex, those condemned to live there feel beleaguered. (Parekh, 1995, p 15)

There have been running fights between gangs of Sikh and Muslim youths in Slough, near London, and in the Midlands in England, despite pleas for restraint from their elders. Most of the gang members seem to be disenchanted youths who are venting their anger on the property of one another's communities. There have been other such fights between gangs in the north of England (*The Guardian*, 24 July 1992). A social worker from Birmingham gave me (Ghuman, 1994) an account of these events:

> Asian communities are too busy with the old order of things...Koran says this and that. These kids are facing different sorts of problems: Threat of unemployment, rigid restrictions of family, particularly on girls, drugs, and so on. I find it quite frustrating...I say cultures change, these kids are bicultural and living in England not in Pakistan, and parents should wake up to this reality. (p 134)

The role of schools and other education institutions is pivotal in integrating South Asian young people – and, indeed, other ethnic minorities – into the mainstream British way of life, and in developing ethnic identities. Furthermore, they play an important part in preparing young people for adult roles, including entry into higher education and future employment. The rest of this review is, therefore, devoted to those educational matters (such as cognitive styles, achievement, access to higher education, bilingualism, inter-ethnic relationships, and gender relations), which are deemed to be important in understanding the predicament of young South Asian people in Britain.

Educational issues: basic cognitive processes

Bruner (1996) argues that 'you cannot understand mental activity unless you take into account the cultural setting and its resources, the very things that give mind its shape and scope' (p. [0]). Research on the cognitive processes of the thinking, reasoning and problem-solving abilities of Asian children and young people is sparse, and most of the extant research has been with children rather than with adolescents.

One of the earliest studies was carried out in Glasgow (Ashby *et al.*, 1970), to discover the effect of British schooling on the cognitive abilities of South Asian children. The researchers gave a comprehensive set of tests to 11-year-old children of Indian and Pakistani origin, and included a comparative sample of indigenous Scottish whites. The tests included Glasgow and Moray House verbal reasoning, Goodenough Draw-a-Man test and Raven Matrices. The findings of this research showed quite clearly that the Asian children who were either born in Britain, or of long stay (nine or more years), performed as well as their white Scottish peers. The authors reinforced previous studies in finding that test performance is related to environmental factors rather than to the genetic make-up of children.

Ghuman (1975) extended the conceptual framework of cross-cultural re-searches by including an indigenous sample from India. A battery of tests was given to British Punjabi boys (aged 10–11) in the English Midlands, to find out if there were any differences in their thinking processes, compared with their English counterparts. A comparable group of Punjabi boys from the Punjab was also included. In all the cognitive tests, the performance of the Punjabi boys was similar to that of their English counterparts, but both the groups were significantly superior in performance to the Punjabi group from the Punjab. The research showed the significant impact of the social milieu and schooling on the development of basic thinking processes.

A follow-up study (Ghuman, 1978), which also included girls, confirmed the saliency of environmental factors, even on the performance of generally accepted 'culture-free' tests such as the Raven Matrices and Draw-a-Man.

Vyas (1983) tested Gujrati children in Gujrat (India) and London on a vari-ety of tests, including Piagetian tests and Children's Embedded Figures Test (CEFT – a test of analytical ability). His findings showed quite clearly that Gujrati children in London were scoring higher compared with their counter-parts in Gujrat and were close to the European norms for the tests. A recent study by Ghuman (1994) of Indian adolescents in Delhi showed their compar-atively poor performance on a variety of Piagetian tests and tasks of logical reasoning. This was attributed to the poor quality of Indian schooling, with its emphasis on rote learning and memory work.

A comparative study by Ghuman (1980a) of cognitive styles using Witkin's field-dependence/independence test (and a maths and a spatial test) also showed the strong influence of schooling and the social milieu on reasoning abilities. The research was carrried out in the English Midlands with a sample of young adolescents (aged 13–14) of Indian and Pakistani origin. A sample of English adolescents was also tested, to provide a comparative perspective. There was no significant difference between the two groups on the field-dependent/independent and the spatial tests, although the Asian boys and girls performed better than the English did on the mathematical achieve-ment test.

It was argued that the effect of schooling may be more salient and pervasive than the effect of the child's early upbringing. Such a contention is supported by Wagner (1982), who came to a similar conclusion after his research with Mexican children in the USA.

The National Foundation for Educational Research team (Taylor and Hegarty, 1985) reviewed the research extant until 1984 on cognitive abilities, and came to the following conclusion:

This 20-year review of research on the assessment of ability of pupils of Asian origin has chartered methodological changes, from employing IQ tests to verbal, later non-verbal and more recently learning and cognitive ability tests…Indeed there is considerable cumulative evidence that the per-formance of pupils of Asian origin increases with length of schooling so that recent research shows that by the end of their primary years the intellectual abilities of those with full schooling, as measured by conventional tests approaches those of their British peers. (Taylor and Hegarty, 1985, pp 142–3)

Scholastic achievement and examination performance

Studies between 1960 and 1970 with 'immigrant' South Asian secondary school students found that their performance was generally lower than that of their indigenous white peers on English and mathematics attainment tests (Taylor and Hegarty, 1985, pp 284–8). However, most studies (Ashby *et al.*, 1970; Dickinson *et al.*, 1975; Ghuman, 1980a) found that 'long-term' attendance at British schools generally brought their achievement closer to that of their white counterparts. Tomlinson drew this conclusion from her review of the research extant:

> Asian pupils have tended to score lower than their white peers on tests of ability and attainment. Most of the studies undertaken in the 1960 and 1970 show Asians performing less well than their white peers, but Asian performance is improving with length of stay and length of schooling in Britain...Hindu and Sikh pupils seems to score higher than Pakistani pupils... Evidence on sex difference is equivocal. (Tomlinson, 1983, p 390)

Taylor and Hegarty (1985), in their survey of literature, cite over thirty studies and conclude the following: 'In spite of these methodological difficulties, some tentative conclusions can be drawn. It certainly can be stated that Asians do not in general perform worse at public examinations than indigenous peers from the same schools and neighbourhoods' (p. 308). However, the authors also draw attention to the fact that, although the performance of South Asians is as good as that of their white peers in the inner-city schools (which both groups attend), it does fall short of the national norms. The Swann Report (DES, 1985) puts it pithily:

> In general terms the findings of the two exercises, taken together, show Asian leavers to be achieving very much on a par with, and in some cases marginally better than, their school fellows from all other groups in the same LEAs [Local Education Authorities] in terms of various measures used. (p 64)

These measures included passes at GCE 'A' level (at the age of 18) and GCE 'O' level and CSE (at the age of 16). A relatively recent research on this topic, carried out by Smith and Tomlinson (1989, p 306), tells a similar story. They found that the performance of secondary school students of South Asian origin (except Chinese) in the public examination at 16 (GCSE) was similar to that of the white students although, at the point of entry into secondary school, the Asians scored below the whites. The researchers emphasized the importance of the quality of schooling and students' motivation in this 'catching up'.

A recently published research report (Gillborn and Gipps, 1996) on the achievement of ethnic-minority students in England and Wales is of great interest, because of its scope. It compares the performance of South Asians, mixed race (for example, Pakistani/white), Afro-Caribbean, Black and white secondary school students at age 11 and at the end of compulsory education (age 16). At age 11, the achievement of 2 500 children from 17 LEAs is considered on the Standard Assessment Tasks (SAT). It was found that the performance of children of Pakistani origin tended to be lower in English, maths and science tests than that of the Indian, Afro-Caribbean and white children. The determining factor in the achievement of South Asians was whether or not the pupils spoke English at home.

Relative performances in the school-leaving examination (GCSE) at 16 are also interesting. From a nationally derived sample, Drew and Gray (1990) analysed the results of 256 South Asians, 88 Afro-Caribbeans and 335 whites. The analysis took due account of the social class and gender of the students, and the authors concluded the following:

> For each one, there is a similar pattern. Young people from white backgrounds reported the highest results; the gap between them and the Asian group was mostly rather small. On the other hand, the gap between these two groups and the Afro-Caribbean group was rather large. (p 112)

No differences were found between the South Asian boys and girls, but girls performed better than boys in the white sample. The study claims to support the findings of previous large-scale researches in the field (DES, 1985; Kysel, 1988). Drew and Grey (1990) made no distinction between the students of Indian, Pakistani and Bangladeshi backgrounds. Gillborn and Gipps (1996), however, presented an analysis that took this distinction into consideration. They analysed the GCSE exams results (1992-4) of ethnic and white students from the various LEAs, including Birmingham, the largest authority outside London. They concluded:

> Indian pupils are achieving levels of success consistently in excess of their white counterparts in some (but not all) urban areas. Among South Asian pupils, those of Indian ethnic origin tend to achieve the highest average results…it appears that, in general, therefore, on average, Pakistani pupils are not achieving as highly as their white peers. (Gillborn and Gipps, 1996, p 26)

The young people of Bangladeshi origin, in general, tend to perform below those of Pakistani and Indian origin. This is attributed to a number of factors, including high unemployment of their parents, a high proportion of parents in manual occupations, and a less well-established position than other groups.

Post-compulsory education

On their entry to Britain, most first-generation Asian parents could only secure jobs that were generally far below their educational level. For example, thousands of university-trained teachers from the Indian sub-continent found employment as bus conductors, because their qualifications were not recognized by the Department of Education and Science (see Ghuman, 1995a). Likewise, many doctors and other professionals found it difficult to obtain positions compatible with their ability and experience. The majority of the less-educated migrants, who were from rural backgrounds and had mostly worked on small farms, invariably ended up in factories and foundries, filling the unskilled jobs available at the time.

However, the majority of the migrants (even those who lacked education) were from the middle strata of their respective 'home' countries, and therefore had high aspirations for their children. Researchers have found that people of Asian origin generally hold education in high regard, both for its 'potential wisdom' and its resultant occupational mobility (Bhachu, 1985a, 1985b). Consequently, their children are encouraged to stay on for post-compulsory education, and many parents would like them to go to university for higher education and/or professional training in order to gain some advantage in competition with their white peers.

The widespread racial discrimination in British society (see Jones, 1993) gives a further impetus to this motivation for higher qualification. The Swann Committee (DES, 1985) found statistical evidence to support this, as did Craft and Craft (1983). However, the large-scale research by Cheng and Heath (1993), with controlled variables, such as social class, gender and parental occupation, confirmed the earlier reports. Gillborn and Gipps (1996) draw the conclusion that a majority of Asian youth are still in full-time education (mostly studying 'A' levels) three years after the end of their compulsory schooling. They quote from the research of Drew et al. (1992):

> Other things being equal, the odds of Afro-Caribbeans staying on were three times higher than whites; for Asians they were ten times higher than for whites. (p 64)

Gender differences in staying on do exist, with more men tending to stay on than women. According to one source (Drew et al., 1994), the participation rate of Chinese-origin 16–19-year-olds in full-time education is the highest (over 80 per cent), while that of Bangladeshis is the lowest (just over 50 per cent) within the Asian groups. Modood et al. (1997, p 75) found that twice as many Pakistani and Bangladeshi young men (aged 16–24) as whites were without qualifications – thus supporting the findings of other researchers in the field.

Higher education

The rates of admission of Asians to university and the former polytechnics have varied widely (Modood and Shiner, 1994). Modood and Shiner present an analysis of the figures collected in 1992 from the UCCA and PCAS (respectively, the university and polytechnic admissions services in the UK). While the Chinese have been hugely over-represented (being twice as likely to be admitted compared with their percentage share in the 15–24 age group at large), Bangladeshis have been slightly under-represented in both sectors. Pakistanis are over-represented in the former polytechnics but under-represented in universities. Indians are slightly over-represented in universities, and did as well as the Chinese in the former polytechnics.

Modood's (1993) previous paper on the subject was based on the analysis of the admissions data for 1990 and 1991. The author summarizes his findings thus: 'in UCCA, notwithstanding variations between institutions, the acceptance rates show a hierarchy with whites at the top, closely followed by the Chinese, with the Indians and Bangladeshis 5–10 per cent below, Pakistani about 15 per cent' (p 181).

The somewhat lower level of acceptance of South Asians is attributed by Modood (1993) to the fact that their 'A' level scores are below those of their white peers. This is compounded by the fact that they tend to apply for courses (such as medicine and accountancy) that require a higher level of entry qualifications.

Vocational aspirations

The evidence presented here would lead to the belief that Asian young people have high vocational aspirations. In the early 1960s, it was considered almost a 'joke' among teachers, who were used to hearing from Asian parents that they wanted their son or daughter to be a doctor or an engineer, regardless of his or her ability. Accountancy and pharmacy have now been added to the list.

These aspirations are grounded partly in the unfulfilled ambitions of parents, especially women, who could only find jobs at the lower level of the employment market. It is also a well-established fact that migrants tend to have high motivation and drive to improve their social status, in order to gain respect, both from their own ethnic group and from the host society.

Verma and his co-workers (see Verma and Ashworth, 1986) carried out an extensive investigation in West Yorkshire, England, to throw light on achievement-related issues. It was found that South Asian young people had higher vocational aspirations than their white counterparts. The researchers argued that some teachers stereotyped South Asian children as 'over-aspiring'. However, this was a misinterpretation of the facts, as it was clear that their educational achievement and positive attitude towards school –

which was, incidentally, higher than that of whites – closely corresponded to their high aspirations. The South Asian students had a more positive attitude towards school and education compared with their white peers. The researchers put this down to the young people's perception of education as a means of social mobility.

The South Asian girls in the study gave unemployment as their major reason for staying on for the sixth form. Some Muslim girls in the study, however, did *not* stay on at school or apply for a particular type of job (such as nursing, in which they would have to wear a skirt) because of the traditional outlook of their families, which emphasizes the domestic role for women. The researchers also found that some South Asian young people had encountered racism from employers, which caused much frustration and lowered their motivation.

The self-esteem of Asians, while still at school, was significantly higher than that of whites. However, when it was tested a year later, it had become noticeably lower. In both groups, the unemployed youths had lower self-esteem than those in employment. The career advice that they received at school was inadequate; in many cases, the careers interview was devoted mainly to disabusing Asian pupils of their 'unreasonable' aspirations.

Teachers' attitudes to Asian students

The successful adjustment and development of ethnic-minority students (as, indeed, of all students) is dependent upon a teacher–student relationship that is based on mutual trust and respect. Traditionally, Asians hold teachers in very high esteem, considering them to be mentors and guardians (or gurus) of intellectual as well as moral and spiritual development. The research literature (Tomlinson, 1984; Bhachu, 1985a, 1985b) demonstrates quite clearly the respect and trust shown also by Asian parents towards their children's teachers.

However, it is a matter of concern that parents' attitudes are not always reciprocated by white teachers. The Swann Report (DES, 1985) commissioned a research investigation into this topic. The team visited some 26 schools and, after intensive observations and in-depth interviews with a selected number of teachers, concluded the following:

> The whole gamut of racial misunderstandings and folk mythology was revealed, racial stereotypes were common and attitudes range from the unveiled hostility of a few, thorough the apathy of many and the condescension of others, to total acceptance and respect by a minority. (DES, 1985, p 236)

Verma and Ashworth (1986) conducted research in West Yorkshire, where they found evidence of discrimination and prejudice on the part of a signifi-

cant number of teachers. In their report, they quoted verbatim from interviews, in order to illustrate the pain and anxiety that the racism of teachers,
often unintentional, causes young people.

Ghuman (1995a) interviewed small groups of South Asian and white teachers on a range of professional issues. These included their perceptions of
South Asian students in terms of their achievement and social adjustment at
school. The white teachers in the research were of the opinion that South
Asian parents, especially Muslims, do not give girls equal opportunity on a par
with boys, and that this is a cause of resentment among the girls. The other
points made by South Asian and white teachers were that South Asian parents
do not attend parents' meetings, and that some of them tend to have unrealis-
tic aspirations, which are not quite in keeping with their young people's ability. On the positive side, the teachers praised the good behaviour, hardwork
and tenacity of the students. They also showed some sympathy for the predicament of the young people, especially the girls, in having to reconcile the differing expectations of parents and school.

Home and school

It is a truism that the healthy intellectual and social development of young
people requires a good link and a continuous dialogue between school and
home. Research findings (Ghuman, 1980a, 1994, 1997; Tomlinson, 1984;
Bhachu, 1985a, 1985b) illustrate misunderstandings on several social and educational matters, such as the wearing of school uniform, separate classes for
boys and girls, and the teaching of religion and community languages. This
cultural continuity between home and school can be achieved in a 'planned
system' of schooling. In Britain, an example of this is to be found in the denominational schools (Roman Catholic, Anglican, Methodist), which were allowed
within the state system under the 1944 Education Act. However, successive
British governments cannot be said to have applied the provisions of the Act
in a fair way.

One of the recommendations of the Swann Report (DES, 1985) is that separate denominational schools for the ethnic minorities should be discouraged, in
the interest of the wider pluralistic objective of education. Consequently, Asian
parents are obliged to send their children to LEA-run multicultural schools. The
ethos of such schools is naturally based on, and sustained by, British traditions
and values, and the vast majority of the teachers in these schools are white. Although there are many common objectives between the school and home (including high academic achievement and good discipline), there is a divergence
of attitudes and values between the two on many social and religious matters.
This divergence is chiefly in three areas: an emphasis on individuality as opposed to collectivity and interdependece; gender equality, as opposed to bias
towards boys; and a secular outlook, as opposed to a religious orientation (see

Ghuman, 1997, 1994). Development of the former is the major concern of the school, whereas the latter are the preferred aims of the Asian home.

The most contentious area for the South Asians is that of religion, because parents would like to see some support for the spiritual dimension and practice of their religion in schools. However, apart from the agreed syllabuses on religious education (which tend to be in comparative religions) and the morning assembly, the school ethos tends to be secular. Teachers encourage an inquiring and questioning attitude in their students, and this may sometimes conflict with the deeply cherished religious traditions of the South Asian family. Apart from religious matters, there is also a deeply held tradition of respect for the views and opinions of elders, and this is now being questioned by the younger generation.

For these reasons, many Muslim parents believe in separate schools (religious and single-sex) within the state system, where they can inculcate Islamic values in their children and young people (Modood *et al.*, 1997). However, according to one observer (Khanum, 1996), when it has come to voting on the issue, parents have tended to support the LEA-run school. Halstead sums up the dilemma of the Muslim parent in Britain:

> The problem for British Muslims…is that these two goals [maintenance of home culture and the benefits of modern scientific and technological culture] cannot currently be achieved in the same educational institution. The second goal can only be achieved through attendance at a common (state-maintained) school, but such a school exposes Muslim children to what may be perceived as secular, non-Islamic cultural influences which the combined influence of the home and the mosque may not always be sufficient to counteract. (Halstead, 1994, p 320)

The worries and anxieties of Muslim parents concerning their young people have been well documented by many academics (Ashraf, 1988), as well as by Muslim organizations such as the UK Committee on Islamic Affairs (UKACIA, 1993). However, it must be stressed that the other religious groups in the South Asian communities (Sikhs, Hindus, Buddhists) are far less apprehensive of British schools. The middle classes are increasingly inclined to send their children to private fee-paying schools, in order to acquire many 'advantages' (of accent, mannerism and confidence; see Dosanjh and Ghuman, 1996) for their children, so that those children can compete successfully with their white peers in the employment market, where they anticipate racial discrimination (see, Cheng and Heath, 1993).

Inter-ethnic relationships in schools

Schools are the only places where ethnic minority young people are obliged to meet their white counterparts in an atmosphere of British traditions and ways of thinking. Although many inner-city schools have become monocultural (for example, mostly Asian or Black) or 'bi-ethnic' rather than multicultural, even in these schools the majority of teachers are white, and the school curriculum is British in substance and style. The Swann Report felt that the British schools

> should...seek to develop in all pupils, both ethnic majority and minority, a flexibility of mind and an ability to analyse critically and rationally the nature of British society today within a global context...The aim of education should be to ensure that from their earliest years children learn to accept the normality and justice of a variety of points of view without feeling threatened...' (DES, 1985, p 324)

The extent to which the aims and objectives of the Swann Report have been realized is difficult to evaluate, as there has been little research in this area. The situation, moreover, is further complicated by the change in policy brought about by the Conservative government in the period 1985–9. During this time, and subsequently, the priority of the government shifted to a 'raising of standards' of achievement in all schools, by introducing a compulsory National Curriculum and Assessment for all pupils aged 5–16. In the making of this policy, there was a marked neglect and marginalization of multicultural and equal opportunity issues.

With regard to the inclusion of multiculturalism/anti-racism perspectives in British schools, there is wide variation among the LEAs (see Taylor, 1992). Some authorities are pursuing and consolidating their aims and objectives on race-related issues, but a number of others have either diluted or totally given up on their initiatives.

A similar educational policy has been pursued by the Labour government since its election in May 1997.

Within this context, Smith and Tomlinson (1989), in their large-scale study of 16 comprehensive schools, found that teenagers' 'choice of a friend' was overwhelmingly based on gender: 97 per cent of the boys chose a boy and 98 per cent of the girls chose a girl. As far as ethnicity was concerned, the researchers concluded that there was a 'fairly strong tendency' for individuals to choose friends from within their own ethnic group. However, in the choice of friends, no particular ethnic group was popular, or unpopular. Although the effect of the 'ethnic mix' of a school on friendship could not be accurately assessed (because of the small numbers of South Asians, and other complicating variables), the authors concluded that it was likely that the policies and practices of schools had some bearing on the matter.

One substantial piece of research (Verma *et al.*, 1994) focuses on inter-ethnic relationships, and a detailed discussion of its findings is relevant. The research method used is mainly ethnographic. In addition, a questionnaire was given to a sample of students (aged 12–16) in nine schools in Greater Manchester and London, England.

Overall, the researchers found 'the quality of inter-ethnic relationship to be quite good' in all schools, but more so in multicultural than in 'bi-ethnic' (Bangladeshi and English) schools. In one of the bi-ethnic schools, relationships between the Bangladeshi and the majority white young people were not good, largely reflecting the poor and deteriorating communal tensions in the school neighbourhood. The best situation was to be found in a Church of England school, which took students from some eighty primary schools and reflected the very wide ethnic diversity of the London area, and also the diverse socio-economic backgrounds of its pupils. The head of this school provided a strong leadership and the staffing was quite stable. The school treated racist incidents seriously, in that the staff were asked to report them to a deputy head. On inter-ethnic 'mixing', the report found that, in bi-ethnic schools, there was little mixing of the two groups, but in multicultural schools 'social mixing' was more based on gender than on ethnicity. On the whole, teachers saw merits in inter-ethnic grouping in the classroom, but did not engineer it.

From this literature review, it seems that some teachers are still influenced by their negative stereotypes of Asian pupils as noted by the Swann Report (DES, 1985) over a decade ago. This is a cause of concern for those parents and others who believe in respect and tolerance for all who live and work in multicultural Britain.

To summarize, the importance of the school ethos and its leadership on inter-ethnic relationships and students' achievement should not be underestimated (Smith and Tomlinson, 1989). Schools that have clear anti-racist policies, and back them up with practical measures, have been shown to promote 'good' inter-ethnic relationships (Verma et al., 1994). Schools in which cultural diversity is respected, where teachers show sensitivity and understanding, and promote biculturalism and ethnic 'pride' in their students achieve similar results (Ghuman, 1995a). The employment of ethnic-minority teachers in multicultural schools, and indeed in majority-white schools, can be useful in many ways. They can provide useful role models and help build up home-school links and, thereby, gain the confidence of ethnic communities.

Mother-tongue teaching and bilingualism in schools

Language is universally regarded as the core element of a person's culture. It encapsulates 'world views', and is the chief instrument for the transmission of values, attitudes, sentiments and skills. Some scholars (Cummins, 1988) argue that it plays an important part in the development of personal identity, and also serves as a social identity marker. For South Asian migrants, their community languages (Punjabi, Urdu, Gujrati and Hindi) are important vehicles for the teaching of their religion.

In the first half of the twentieth century, bilingualism was by and large considered (see Baker, 1995) to be a liability, which, among other disadvantages, consumed much of the learner's time and effort and lowered his or her all-round mental functioning, thus resulting in poor performance on IQ tests. However, opinion began to change when systematic and controlled studies began to show that, not only do bilinguals score as well as their monolingual counterparts in IQ tests, but also that their bilingualism offers several benefits in the field of cognitive functioning, and personal and social development (Bellin, 1995). Bilinguals have performed better than monolinguals in the divergent ability test (use of objects), and have access to two systems for constructing meanings, and for self-expression.

Provision for the teaching of minority languages in British schools has been very paltry indeed, due to the half-hearted support of the LEAs and the Department of Education and Science (DES). Two influential DES reports (the Swann Report, 1985 and the Bullock Report, 1975) failed to see the importance of ethnic-minority languages in the maintenance of distinctive cultural identities, and did not recommend their inclusion in the formal curriculum of schools. However, in a survey of research literature on the South Asian minority languages, Taylor and Hegarty concluded that

> overall there is considerable consensus across the relatively few studies on language attitudes that the South Asian language speakers value both their first languages and English. Their mother tongues are seen to have considerable importance for communication at all levels, for cultural maintenance and for identity. (Taylor and Hegarty, 1985, p 188)

Although there are no exact statistics available on the number of Asian young people who were born in Britain, it is estimated that the vast majority (over 80 per cent; see Modood *et al.*, 1994 and Verma *et al.*, 1994) are the second- or third-generation offspring of immigrants (with the exception of Bangladeshis). In most cases (over three-quarters, see Smith and Tomlinson, 1989), the first language of young people born in the UK is English, but they also speak their community language. Smith and Tomlinson (1989, p 92) reported in their survey of 20 secondary comprehensive schools that 85 per cent of South Asian students were bilingual to some degree. Furthermore, they found that, in general, over one-third of South Asians (and 71 and 49 per cent of Bangladeshis and Pakistanis, respectively) attended supplementary schools in order to learn their mother tongue.

Smith and Tomlinson (1989) describe the predicament of minority languages as follows:

> Minority languages in Britain have long been regarded, along with their speakers, as being of low status. They seldom appear on the modern language curriculum for all pupils and are thereby implicitly devalued...One of the most important steps that schools can take towards a multicultural education policy is to develop the teaching of Asian languages and literatures within the framework of the National Curriculum. (Smith and Tomlinson, 1989)

As the provision for the teaching of community languages is likely to remain unsatisfactory in British schools, it is even more imperative that the ethnic minorities continue to provide facilities from their own resources.

Gender-related issues

This section deals with the difficulties of South Asian girls in coping with their unique predicament.

The literature on gender related-issues highlights the predicament of Asian girls, in particular those belonging to the Muslim (and, to some extent, Sikh) faith. Many of them are still encountering a dual handicap – one imposed by their parents, and the other by the wider society (racism). Asian parents tend to prefer boys in all walks of life and give them more freedom and opportunities. Girls, on the other hand, are expected to carry the *izzat* (honour) of the family, and are obliged to be chaste and virtuous and family-orientated. At school, some white teachers tend to hold negative stereotypes of Asian girls, and are prone to reinforce some of the traditional values of the Asian home.

As a consequence of these additional handicaps of social adjustment, some young girls seem to suffer from psychological tension and acute anxiety, which in turn has caused serious psychosomatic illnesses. A case study by Bhate and Bhate (1996) of an Asian teenager, Shamma, makes some relevant points:

> Shamma as an in-patient revealed two major areas of difficulty. [She] attributed her overdoses to her family's unwillingness to allow her the freedom that her 'English' friends enjoyed, and that her family suspected, but not yet openly acknowledged, the existence of an English boyfriend. (Bhate and Bhate, 1996, p 105)

Although there have been no large-scale studies, with controlled samples and conditions, which demonstrate conclusively that South Asian girls are more prone to suffer from eating disorders and other psychiatric illnesses than their white counterparts, nevertheless, the findings of the studies carried out (Ahmad, et al., 1994; Lacy and Dolan, 1988; Bryant-Waugh and Lask, 1991; Kingsbury, 1994; and Merril and Owens, 1986) reveal a trend that may be cause for concern. From the literature survey it becomes clear that some Asian girls, especially of Muslim and Sikh families, seem to need extra help in coping with the disadvantages imposed by their parents and by the wider society. In this context, it is interesting to note that, according to some researchers (including Groer et al., 1992), teenage girls report experiencing stressful events and being affected by stressful events more than boys do.

References

Ahmad, S., Waller, G. and Verduyn, C. (1994) 'Eating attitudes and body satisfaction among Asian and Caucasian adolescents', *Journal of Adolescence*, 17, pp 461–70

Ashby, B., Morrison, A. and Butcher, H. J. (1970) 'The abilities and attainments of immigrant children', *Research in Education*, 4, 73–80

Ashraf, A. S. (1988) 'A view of education – An Islamic perspective', in B. O'Keefe (ed.) *Schools for Tomorrow*, Farmer Press, London, pp 69–80

Baker, C. (1995) *Foundations of Bilingualism*, Multilingual Matters, Clevedon

Bellin, W. (1995) 'Psychology and bilingualism', in B. Jones and P. A. S. Ghuman (eds.) *Bilingualism, Education and Identity*, University of Wales Press, Cardiff

Berry, W. J. (1997) 'Immigration, Acculturation, and Adaptation', *Applied Psychology: An International Review*, 46, 1, pp 5–68

Bhachu, P. (1985a) *Twice Immigrants: East African Settlers in Britain*, Tavistock, London

Bhachu, P. (1985b) 'Multilingual education: Parental views', *New Community*, XII, 1, pp 9–21

Bhate, S. and Bhate, S. (1996) 'Psychiatric needs of ethnic minority children', in N. K. Dwivedi and P. V. Varma (eds.) *Meeting the Needs of Ethnic Minority Children: A Handbook for Professionals*, Jessica Kingsley Publishers, London and Bristol

Brannen, J., Dodd, K., Oakley A., and Storey, P. (1994) *Young People, Health and Family Life*, Open University Press, Buckingham

Brown, C. (1985) *Black and White Britain: The Third PSI Survey*, Bower, London

Bruner, S. J. (1996) *The Culture of Education*, Harvard University Press, London

Bryant-Waugh, R. and Lask, B. (1991) 'Anorexia nervosa in groups of Asian children living in Britain', *British Journal of Psychiatry*, 158, pp 229–33

Cheng, Y. and Heath, A. (1993) 'Ethnic and class destinations', *Oxford Review of Education*, 19 (2) pp. 151–165

Cohen, L. and Manion, L. (1983) *Multicultural Classrooms: Perspectives for Teachers*, Croom Helms, London

Craft, M. and Craft, A. (1983) 'The participation of ethnic minority pupils in further and higher education', *Educational Research*, 25 (1) pp 10–19

Cummins, J. (1988) 'From multicultural to anti-racist education: an analysis of programmes and policies in Ontario', in T. Skuttnabb-Kangas and J. Cummins (eds) *Minority Education*, Multilingual Matters, Clevedon. pp 127–60

Davey, A. (1983) *Learning to be Prejudiced: Growing up in Multi-Ethnic Britain*, Edward Arnold, London

de Domanico, B. Y., Crawford, I. and DeWolfe, S. A. (1994) 'Ethnic identity and self-concept in Mexican-American adolescents: Is bicultural identity related to stress or better adjustment?', *Child and Youth Care Forum*, 23 (3) pp 197–206

Dickinson, I. et al., (1975) *The Immigrant School Learner: A Study of Pakistani Pupils in Glasgow*, NFER-NELSON, Windsor

Dosanjh, J. S. and Ghuman, P. A. S. (1996) *Child-Rearing in Ethnic Minorities*, Multilingual Matters, Clevedon

Drew, D. and Gray, J. (1990) 'The fifth-year examination achievement of black young people in England and Wales', *Educational Research*, 32 (3) pp 107–17

Drew, D., Gray, J. and Sime, N. (1992) *Against the Odds: The Education and Labour Market Experiences of Black young People*, England and Wales Youth Cohort Study, Report R and D no. 68, Sheffield, Employment Department

Drew, D., Gray, J. and Sporton, D. (1994) 'Ethnic differences in the educational participation of 16–19 year olds', unpublished paper presented to the OPCS/ESCR Census Analysis Group conference, University of Leeds, September 1994

Erickson, H. E. (1968) *Identity: Youth and Crisis*, Faber and Faber, London

Fryer, P. (1984) *Staying Power: The History of Black People in Britain*, Pluto Press, London

Ghuman, P. A. S. (1975) *The Cultural Context of Thinking: A Comparative Study of Punjabi and English Boys*, National Foundation for Educational Research, Slough

Ghuman, P. A. S. (1978) 'Nature of intellectual development of Punjabi children', *International Journal of Psychology*, 13, pp 287–94

Ghuman, P. A. S. (1980a) 'A comparative study of cognitive styles in three ethnic groups', *International Review of Applied Psychology*, 29, pp 75–87

Ghuman, P. A. S. (1980b) 'Punjabi parents and English education', *Educational Research*, 22, pp 121–30

Ghuman, P. A. S. (1995a) *Asian Teachers in British Schools: A Study of Two Generations*, Multilingual Matters, Clevedon

Ghuman, P. A. S. (1995b) 'Cognition and culture: The nature of intellectual development of Indian adolescents', *Scientia Paedagogica Experimentalis*, XXXII (2) pp 275–90

Ghuman, P. A. S. (1996) 'A study of identities of Asian-origin primary school children', *Early Child Development and Care*, 132, pp 65–74

Ghuman, P. A. S. (1997) unpublished paper, University of Wales, Aberystwyth

Gillborn, D. and Gipps, C. (1996) *Recent Research on the Achievements of Ethnic Minority Pupils*, Her Majesty's Stationery Office, London

Goodnow, J. J. and Collins, S. (1990) 'Parental behaviour in diverse societies', *Contemporary Psychology*, 8, pp 789–95

Groer, M. W., Thomas, S. P. and Shoffner, D. (1992) 'Adolescent stress and coping: a longitudinal study', *Research in Nursing and Health*, 15, pp 209–17

Halstead, M. (1994) 'Between two cultures: Muslim children in Western liberal society', *Children and Society*, 8 (4), pp 312–26

Huthnik, N. (1991) *Ethnic Minority Identity in Britain: A Social Psychological Perspective*, Clarendon Press, Oxford

Jones, T. (1993) *Britain's Ethnic Minorities*, Policy Studies Institute, London

Katz, P. A. (1976) *Towards the Elimination of Racism*, Pergamon, New York

Khanum, S. (1996) 'Education and the Muslim girl', in Blair, M. *et al.* (eds) *Identity and Diversity: Gender and the Experience of Education*, Multilingual Matters in association with The Open university, Clevedon

Kingsbury, S. (1994) 'The psychological and social characteristics of Asian adolescent overdose', *Journal of Adolescence*, 17 (2), pp 131, 135

Kysel, F. (1988) 'Ethnic background and examination results', *Educational Research*, 3 (2), pp 83–9

Lacy, J. H. and Dolan, B. M. (1988) 'Bulimia in British Blacks and Asians: A catchment area study', *British Journal of Psychiatry*, 12, pp 73–9

Marcia, E. J. (1994) 'The empirical study of ego identity', in A. H. Bosma, *et al.* (eds) *Identity and Development: An Interdisciplinary Approach*, Sage Publications, London

Merrill, J. and Owens, J. (1986) 'Ethnic differences in self-poisoning: A comparison of Asian and white groups', *British Journal of Psychiatry*, 148, pp 708–12

Milner, D. (1983) *Children and Race: Ten Years On*, Ward Lock Educational, London

Modood, T. (1993) 'The number of ethnic minority students in British higher education: Some grounds for optimism', *Oxford Review of Education*, 19 (2) pp 167–82

Modood, T. and Shiner, M. (1994) *Ethnic Minorities and Higher Education: Why are there differential rates of entry?*, Policy Studies Institute, London

Modood, T., Beishon, S. and Virdee, S. (1994) *Changing Ethnic Identities*, Policy Studies Institute, London

Modood, T. *et al.*, (1997) *Ethnic Minorities in Britain: Diversity and Disadvantage*, Policy Studies Institute, London

Parekh, B. (1995) 'Bradford's culture clash', *The Observer*, 12 June 1995, p 15

Phinney, S. J. (1990) 'Ethnic identity in adolescents and adults: review of research', *Psycho-*

logical Bulletin, 108 (3) pp 499–514

Phinney, S. J. (1992) 'The multigroup ethnic identity measure: a new scale for use with diverse groups', *Journal of Adolescence*, 7 (2) pp 156–76

Phinney, S. J. (1996a) 'Understanding ethnic diversity: the role of ethnic identity', *American Behavioural Scientist*, 40 (2), pp 143–52

Phinney, S. J. (1996b) 'When we talk about American ethnic groups, what do we mean?', *American Psychologist*, 51 (9), pp 918–27

Rex, J. and Tomlinson, S. (1979) *Colonial Immigrants in a British City: A Class Analysis*, Routledge and Kegan Paul, London

Roberts, E. R., Phinney, S. J., Romero, A. and Chen, R.Y. (1997) *Structure of Ethnic Identity*, under review

Roberts, H. and Sachdev, D. (1996) *Young People's Social Attitudes: Having Their Say – The Views of 12–19 year olds*, Barnardos, Essex

Rosenthal, A. D. (1987) 'Ethnic identity development in adolescents', in S. J. Phinney and J. M. Rotherham (eds) *Children's Ethnic Socialzation: Pluralism and Development*, Sage Publications, London

Smith, D. and Tomlinson, S. (1989) *The School Effect: A Study of Multi-Racial Comprehensives*, Policy Studies Institute, London

Smith, J. D. and Rutter, M. (1996) 'Time Trends in Psychosocial Disorders of Youth', in M. Rutter and D. J. Smith (eds) *Psychosocial Disorders in Young people: Times, Trends and Their Causes*, John Wiley and Sons for the Academia Europea, Chichester

Swann Report, DES (1985) *Education for All*, HMSO, London

Syal, M. (1997) *Anita and Me*, Flamingo, London

Tajfel, H. (1981) *Human Groups and Social Categories*, Cambridge University Press, Cambridge

Taylor, J. M. (1992) *Multicultural Anti-Racist Education after ERA: Concerns, Constraints and Challenges*, National Foundation for Educational Research, Slough

Taylor, J. M. and Hegarty, S. (1985) *The Best of Both Worlds…?*, NFER-Nelson, Windsor

Tomlinson, S. (1983) 'The educational performance of Asian children', *New Community*, X (3), pp 381–92

Tomlinson, S. (1984) *Home and School in Multicultural Britain*, Batsford, London

UK Action Committee on Islamic Affairs (UKACIA, 1993) *Muslims and the Law in Multi-Faith Britain*, UKACIA, London

Verma, G. K., Zec, P. and Skinner, G. (1994) *The Ethnic Crucible: Harmony and Hostility in Multi-Ethnic Schools*, Falmer Press, London

Verma, V. (ed) (1986) *Ethnicity and Educational Achievement in British Schools*, Macmillan, London

Vyas, H. (1983) 'Education and cognitive styles: a case study of Gujarati children in Britain, Eastern United States of America and India', in C. Bagley and G. K. Verma (eds) *Multicultural Childhood: Education, Ethnicity and Cognitive Styles*, Gower, Aldershot (England)

Wagner, A. (1982) 'Ontogeny in the study of culture and cognition', in A. Wagner and H. W. Roberts (eds) *Cultural Perspectives on Child Development*, W. H. Freeman and Company, San Francisco

Wilson, A. (1978) *Finding a Voice: Asian Women in Britain*, Virago, London

20. Globalization and cultural transmission: the role of international agencies in developing inclusive practice

Peter Evans

Introduction

Despite considerable variation across the world in education systems, and the practices of schooling, there is widespread concern everywhere about the quality and, indeed, quantity of education that students receive. The high political profile of education in all countries makes reform a slow process that needs careful planning with broad consultation. Education currently has a higher position on the national agenda of most countries than ever before; it is seen as a key instrument in preventing social exclusion, and in providing citizens with the necessary skills and motivation for maintaining economies into the next millennium. This is not a new role for education, but it is now the subject of greater emphasis than before. There is much concern that the current organizational structure of education, and the associated support services for families, is mismatched with student needs.

The most direct impact on education systems and schooling are of necessity the result of local and national policy debates. However, these considerations have often been presaged by – and, indeed, may even have stimulated – a wider set of discussions. These debates have taken place in various international fora, and have served the purpose of allowing policy-makers to develop, test out and refine their ideas against the multi-coloured backdrop of the cultures of other education systems and their plans for reform. In reality, national cultures of education are very strong and rather resistant to change in the way they work. None the less, the significance of issues such as national curricula, the raising of standards, inclusion, and the importance of information and communications technology have a global realization and will have an impact on national systems. The internet is perhaps the most powerful media form yet developed for achieving a form of global homogeneity, and its threat to national cultures has not gone unremarked.

The fact that almost every country is undertaking reforms to its education system, and learning from the experiences of others, is an important part of the process of reflection and reconstruction, and this is certainly an important way through which ideas become globalized. However, there is another important element that feeds into the discussions, namely, the globalization of the world's economy. Information and communication technology is changing the ways in which economies and societies function, and education systems are a formative part of this. However, the advent of the knowledge economy is also pressing for changes in the content of the knowledge base itself, as well as in the educational levels that need to be obtained if all citizens are to be a contributing part of the social order of the coming years.

At the same time, there have been significant changes in our knowledge about the education process – the way schools function, teaching methods, the learning process, the concept of childhood, and an understanding of the human condition. The concept of inclusion is part of this development, which has been slowly gaining pace as part of the growing democratization of society. It has its roots in the response to Fascism before and during the Second World War, in human rights movements, and in the drive towards 'normalization', in which disabled persons have rights to the same treatment as non-disabled people.

More recently, the ideals behind these movements have been encapsulated in a number of statements from the United Nations (UN) about the rights of children. The UN works hard to support human rights in many fields, including education, by negotiating and agreeing with its member nations broad frames of reference; these, if signed up to, carry the broad force of international law.

The convention on the rights of the child, agreed in 1989, sets out the framework and has been signed up to by most nations. Article 28 refers to education, and clause 1(a) demands that primary education should be 'compulsory and available free to all'. The special rights of disabled children are covered in Article 23, which includes their right to education that is responsive to their individuality. While inclusive education in the sense of mainstreaming is not specifically covered, Article 23 (3 and 4) are not incompatible with such an interpretation.

These ideals have been reaffirmed by subsequent declarations, notably at the 1990 World Conference on Education for All, and through the 1993 UN Standard Rules on the Equalization of Opportunities for Persons with Disabilities. Further commitment to these principles was made in the UNESCO (United Nations Educational, Scientific and Cultural Organization) *Salamanca Statement*, and Framework for Action on special needs education. Specifically, that framework reaffirms the imperative for all children to receive education in the regular education system. It goes on to proclaim that 'those with special educational needs must have access to regular schools which should accommodate them within a child-centred pedagogy capable of meeting these needs' and that 'regular schools with this inclusive orientation are the most effective means of combating discriminatory attitudes, creating welcoming communities, building an inclusive society and achieving education for all'.

The *Salamanca Statement* goes on to urge governments to move to inclusive education through changes in law, and through the adoption of policy frameworks and demonstration projects, and participatory decentralized decision-making. The importance of early intervention and teacher training is also emphasized.

Who are the international community?

There can be no doubt that, in the area of inclusion, the various UN declarations and proclamations on human rights have had a powerful influence on nations. However, these agreements encapsulate the work in which nations have been involved, through international co-operation via organizations such as UNESCO and the OECD (Organization for Economic Co-operation and Development). There is an 'international community' that serves to mediate between nations and act as one of the main highways in the process of globalization. Of course, this 'community' is a rather undefined entity, comprising a number of different organizations and individuals, who interact with each other to a greater or lesser extent, using different networks in different fields of activity.

From the point of view of international organizations – remembering that these organizations work with individuals who are members of other national or international organizations, such as universities – a number of main players can be identified in the field of inclusive education. The following list, which is not exhaustive, uses examples to indicate the various types of agencies involved.

At the level of government, the players include international organizations, such as the OECD, and the various members of the United Nations family, such as UNESCO, UNICEF (United Nations Children's Fund) and the UN special rapporteur. In Europe, the European Union (EU) has the status of a supra-national organization. Over the past years, these organizations have been carrying out the majority of the comparative work in integration and inclusion, and providing goverments with arguments, practical examples, and (in the case of UNESCO technical aid) influencing decision-making and encouraging inclusion. The EU through its HELIOS programme has also stressed the importance of professionals, such as teachers, in the development of inclusive practices by providing opportunities for them to meet and share experiences and also carry out research.

Working independently of these organizations are other government-based aid agencies, such as the Swedish SIDA, the Danish DANIDA, and the US Department of Health and Human Services and the US Department of Education, which also support inclusive practices. More recently, the UK Commonwealth Secretariat and USAID have also taken an interest, along with loan agencies such as the World Bank and the Inter-American Development Bank.

In addition to these, there are non-governmental organizations (NGOs), Foundations and other charitable organizations, which support developments on the ground. Many of these organizations focus on developing countries and disability groups; among them, Rehabilitation International, the World Institute for the Blind and Inclusion International play an active role in promoting inclusive education world-wide.

The 'international community', comprising those who work for and with these agencies, is therefore a large group of individuals and different organizations, who have all developed their own role in analysing or promoting inclusive education.

What is inclusive education in the international context?

At an international level, the concept of inclusive education carries a wide variety of meanings. It is self-evident that the guiding philosophy is one of human rights and social justice, but the goals for each country will be different. One country may be aiming to provide education for all children of primary age, while another may want to educate all children in mainstream classes at both primary and secondary levels. A third may be trying to establish appropriate provision at tertiary level. In no country has all of this yet been achieved.

The rest of this chapter will give examples of how inclusive practices are being promoted internationally, mainly from the perspective of the OECD. The first part will briefly describe some aspects of the process of working in an international agency, and examples will then be given of collaboration across agencies.

The Organization for Economic Co-operation and Development (OECD)

Background

The Organization for Economic Co-operation and Development (OECD)[1] was established after World War II in order to administer funds supplied under the Marshall Plan for the reconstruction of Europe. The OECD has grown in membership and influence since those days, and is now essentially a policy think-tank. It brings together mainly politicians, civil servants and researchers, who share ideas and agree on mutually beneficial policies that will serve to improve the economies and societies not only of the member countries, but also of all countries all over the world. In the field of education, much of the orientation of the work is towards innovation and reform, particularly with respect to improving students opportunities in the labour market.

In the field of special needs, the work to date has focused on two issues – the education of disabled students in mainstream schools, and efforts to develop approaches to creating job opportunities. These are both key elements of the broad concept of inclusion. Outside the education field, substantial work takes place on social policy, especially concerning transfers and benefits, which are of great importance in tackling poverty and exclusion. Recently, OECD analyses have focused increasingly on efforts to bring different ministries together, to understand how their various policy programmes can be aligned, and how wasteful policy clashes can be avoided. The recently published work on co-ordinating services for children at risk is a relevant example.

Process of working

While organizations like the OECD and UNESCO function within the world of diplomacy and have a political component, they also provide a means for politicians and their civil servants to discuss issues in a research forum. Ministerial meetings are a regular part of this process. Unlike the EU, issues can be debated without the need for decisions to be taken, since the OECD has few instruments available for enforcing policy agreements. Economic and social reforms come about therefore through persuasion rather than fiat.

In this way, they also serve as a means of in-service training for country experts and civil servants, as real national political issues are debated in the context of comparative analysis and informed international academic work. If similar solutions are found in different contexts, this can help their generalizability and give them more intellectual force. Furthermore, countries can be given access to innovations, and have the opportunity to understand how these ideas are working and to appreciate their implications in a real context.

Providing relatively neutral territory can be very helpful in bringing many different perspectives to bear on complex social, political and economic issues. In the field of education, different countries are at very different stages in terms of their own research development and even capability, and the sharing of information gathered by other countries can be especially helpful. Also, research is an expensive process and the pooling of resources is an economically sensible way of studying topics and developing new policy initiatives. Research and development work at the OECD is often carried out many years before it enters into the public policy arena in some countries. Many countries use policy fora deliberately to help them formulate new policies and legal frameworks. For instance, during the course of the development of recent revisions to the inclusion laws in one country, representatives of that country joined in meetings at which such issues were actively being discussed, and were able to use these discussions to help them formulate their own strategies and policies.

Working across agencies

There are many international agencies working in the field of inclusion and, recently, they have made considerable efforts to link their experiences. Two examples follow.

Recent moves to accountability in all public services have stimulated the need in administrations for indicators of the state of the system. Recently, OECD has pioneered and published educational indicators. Growing interest in the field of special education and inclusion has led to co-operation between OECD, UNESCO and the EU and Eurostat to develop indicators in this field, working jointly within a framework. This framework will allow for meaningful international comparisons about what is happening about the education of excluded groups, such as the disadvantaged and the disabled. This work – complementing that of the World Health Organization (WHO) – represents the first time an attempt has been made to develop such comparisons in the context of education policy-making. It has proved possible because of the long-established co-operation between countries in this field.

It is hoped that the publication of comparative statistics will help to move along the inclusion debate, and that bringing together different ministerial departments in their elaboration will lead to a breaking down of the boundaries that exist between special education and mainstream education within the administration of many countries. Doing this brings together administrators from very different domains, and this can be of considerable help in rationalizing data-gathering and establishing new procedures, and in developing new insights.

Although this work on comparative special education is at a very early stage, the first publication is due to appear in 1998, and it will be developed subsequently with new data-gathering and data sets being established. This is more than the routine gathering of statistics; it represents a process in which countries are involved and has its own dynamic, which can respond to emerging policy questions through new data-gathering.

The second example is rather different. In an effort to respond more coherently to the needs of disabled people in developing nations, there have been meetings of a large number of different international agencies from the public and voluntary sectors and the development banks; these groups have shared their knowledge about how best to provide financial and technical aid to the education systems of developing nations, which will have inclusion as a particular goal. The fact that this has happened has been very much due to the efforts of agencies such as UNESCO and OECD, which have stimulated interest through numerous conferences up to the landmark Salamanca conference, and carried out research work over the years. It is a slow process, but there are tangible changes.

Recent work in the field of inclusive education

OECD works by speaking truth to power. More accurately, policy debates take place in the context of both OECD comparative research, and research completed by other agencies. Furthermore, the work carried out is completed because it is requested by the member countries; for this reason, it has direct policy relevance for the countries. The fact that inclusion has been on the agenda for so many years is indicative, therefore, of the interest taken by all countries in this topic, and in the way it is working and developing in other countries. Its durability is probably also testament to the difficulties involved in implementing the necessary reforms.

It is interesting to understand the process involved in a study on inclusion, and to have the details of some of the outcomes. A description of a recent study follows.

OECD work is almost always, if not always, a collaboration between the OECD secretariat, the member countries' administrations, and central, local and national researchers. Teams such as these work together to understand the complexities of an education system and to provide accurate descriptions. This method was used to look at inclusive practices in eight OECD member countries: Australia, Canada, Denmark, Germany, Iceland, Italy, the UK and the USA. Cases studies were completed and verified, providing descriptions of the inclusive practices studied, and conclusions were drawn. The next step in the process is for the work to be considered and discussed by all the 29 member countries of the OECD; in this way, it enters the policy arena.

Based on the case studies, it was possible to draw certain conclusions. From the policy perspective, reforms towards inclusion need to tackle three main areas.

First, consideration needs to be given to providing a unified legal framework to guide policy-making. Most countries have legislation that covers education and special education separately. In those countries which have moved furthest towards inclusion, the two legislative elements have been rolled into one. The advantage here is that decisions made in the context of the law should consider the implications for all students and not just part of school-age population, with the inevitable corollary that specific issues for those with special needs will need to be resolved at a later date. Accountability procedures, which are so often linked with funding arrangements, must also not inherently lend bias to provision decisions. The issue of school choice is particularly sensitive; if an education system is to be fully inclusive, individual schools cannot have the right to turn students away against parental wishes.

Second, funding arrangements have to create a level playing field. There has to be no financial advantage to segregated provision for students to be educated there. Because of the substantial additional finance provided for special education, and, often, its different source (for example, it may come through health insurance schemes), care must be taken that it is distributed equitably across different educational institutions.

Third, the training of teachers and other professionals must also create a level playing field. The main goal must be to create a training system that establishes in teachers the acceptance of the responsibility of the education for all children, and gives the experience of collaborating with other professionals. Systems that give teaching practice in the main in segregated settings are clearly not addressing the needs of teachers who might wish to work with special needs students in mainstream classrooms, or of systems that are developing an inclusive approach. The training of other professionals who work with disabled students must also take account of the inclusive context, and of the need to develop teamwork and to work constructively with other professionals.

At a more practical level, there has been much published material on how schools work. The OECD work stresses the importance of individual education programmes, but also the way in which support services work with the school. To be consistent with the philosophy that teachers have the responsibility for the education of all students, support services should have the main goal of supporting the school and the teachers, and not the students themselves. In other words, they need to be agents who empower the school, and help it to become a learning organization.

Involving parents and the community in schools is also a key element, not only for accountability purposes and funding, but also in linking employers with schools. The aim of this is to establish work opportunities and to provide realistic curricula choice.

In the international community, issues such as these are widely discussed and, through the processes described, common understandings are reached. A great deal of interest is taken in how other countries are coming to grips with these very difficult policy and political decisions. The benefits offered by collaboration of this sort are useful in helping administrators of different countries develop arguments in support of reforms.

Concluding remarks

For those working mainly in national systems, it is not always easy to appreciate the value of the work carried out in international agencies. It is only recently that the public is becoming more aware of the work carried out by organizations such as the OECD in the field of education. There is a great deal of activity involving policy-makers from many nations, who meet regularly to share experiences, and to understand the implications of agreements, such as that made at Salamanca for education reform. This process of understanding moves the policy agenda along, and relevant changes in the law may well follow.

The discussions which take place at regular intervals at the various international agencies are carried out with substantial collaboration. It is through these discussions that many national administrators and university researchers gain shared understanding and insight into new problems, and the ways in which other cultures, education and social systems function. These agencies have a critical role to play in establishing joint understanding of complex issues. They help to provide the right arguments for influencing and creating new policies that are commensurate with global agreements, and relevant to a shared view and understanding of globalization, the knowledge economy and 'the shape of things to come'.

Endnote

1. The member countries of the OECD are: Australia, Austria, Belgium, Canada, the Czech Republic, Denmark, Finland, France, Germany, Greece, Hungary, Iceland, Ireland, Italy, Japan, Korea, Luxembourg, Mexico, the Netherlands, New Zealand, Norway, Poland, Portugal, Spain, Sweden, Switzerland, Turkey, the UK, the USA.

21. Exclusion: the middle classes and the common good

Sally Tomlinson

Introduction

In modern capitalist societies, the restriction of access to particular kinds of education, and to the acquisition of academic and professional qualifications, is a dominant form of social exclusion. Increasingly, as Parkin pointed out over twenty years ago, 'credentialism is a form of closure, designed to control and monitor entry to key positions in the division of labour', or, indeed, to any position in the labour market (Parkin, 1979, p 48).

Credential inflation, once considered an aspect of education in developing countries (Dore, 1976), is now an obvious feature of developed countries. Employers use the status of qualifications, and of the place where they were obtained, to screen and exclude. There is widespread acceptance that a major and important characteristic of a modern society is that credentials must be acquired through mainstream education, to legitimate occupational success, privilege and advancement, and there is an escalating demand for more credentials, preferably of the traditional 'academic' kind. Twentieth-century democratic ideologies, which have focused on equality of opportunity for previously marginalized groups – women, manual workers, ethnic minorities and some disabled groups – have helped to swell this demand.

Governments in developed countries are grappling with a situation in which, while more people are engaged in the competitive attempt to gain qualifications and employment, large numbers are still excluded from entering the competition on equal terms. There is pressure to use education as an agency for both exclusion and inclusion. Governments want higher levels of education and raised 'standards', but at the same time they are increasingly concerned with the costs of social exclusion, in terms of crime, deviance and dependency. Liberal democracies continue to debate how far social exclusion and perceived social injustice will fragment their societies (Galbraith, 1992; Hutton, 1995).

The social and economic consequences of the increased exclusion of more vulnerable social groups are becoming well documented (Andrews and Jacobs, 1990; Commission on Social Justice, 1993; Heath and MacMahon, 1997;

Wilson, 1987, 1997), and in Britain the New Labour government elected in 1997 made inclusion into 'one nation' a central rhetorical theme. Prime Minister Blair opened a government Social Exclusion Unit in December 1997, asserting, 'At the heart of all our work…is Britain rebuilt as a nation in which each citizen is valued…no one is excluded…and we make it our purpose to tackle social division and inequality' (Blair, 1997). Although politicians agree that preparing a younger generation, through an education and training system that is notionally inclusive, is more cost-effective and less socially damaging than any alternative, governments are subject to structural forces that are difficult to control.

Whatever the rhetoric, the structure in Britain comprises a number of old and new elite groups, which feel increasingly insecure, and a larger number which, galvanized by the promise of equal opportunities, are now engaged in serious competition to gain and sustain access to a 'good life'. Competition for 'positional advantage' (Hirsch, 1977) creates the conditions for the exclusion of as many potential competitors as possible. A society in which redistributive social justice ensures that all members have equal access to education and its credentials, and to other social goods, appears increasingly utopian.

This chapter discusses the changing modes of exclusion, as middle-class and aspirant middle-class groups seek competitive advantage via the exercise of market power in education. It will look at the way young people regarded as having special educational needs are largely excluded from acquiring worthwhile credentials, and then move on to discuss how far it is possible to begin to create conditions for full social and educational inclusion. Some social theorists fear that modern societies will degenerate into exclusive enclaves and 'malignant forms of anomie' (see Ferrara, 1997), but others are more optimistic. One possibility is a 'civic republicanism' (Bellah *et al.*, 1991), which centres on a revival of institutions in which the common good of the entire society becomes a central feature.

Changing modes of exclusion

Current studies of social exclusion focus largely on the excluded groups, their circumstances, characteristics and supposed deficits. This continues a long tradition in Western societies, which have attempted to explain the poverty, deprivation and disadvantage that persist although those societies, despite recessions, restructured local and national economies and global competition, have steadily become more prosperous. The socially excluded, although a much expanded population, are similar to the groups that worried the ruling classes in Victorian England: 'Those living in urban slum conditions'…the stagnant pools of deteriorated men and women…incapable of work demoralizing their children…encouraged in their idle habits by indiscriminate and unconditional doles (Webb, 1926, p 172).

This tradition has persisted in the sporadic re-emergence of poverty and deprivation as a national public issue in the USA and European countries. It is easier to study the characteristics of those caught up in cycles of disadvantage (Joseph, 1972), cultures of poverty (Lewis, 1968) and underclass conditions (Murray, 1984), than to try to explain the macro-economic conditions that create poverty, political failures over redistributive social justice, or the strategies by which more fortunate groups attempt to ensure their 'inclusion', and connive in exclusionary practices.

In nineteenth-century Britain, education openly reinforced a class structure based on ascription by birth and wealth. 'The different classes of society, the different occupations, require different teaching' (Schools Inquiry Report, 1886). This translated into 'public' schools for the upper classes, minor public schools and a hierarchy of grammar schools for the middle classes, and elementary education for the masses. Yet, even at this time, an expanding middle class was demanding a replacement of ascription by achievement, as measured by lengthy education and the acquisition of credentials. The 1886 Schools Inquiry Report referred to 'a great body of professional men...who have nothing but education to keep their sons on a high social level' (Schools Inquiry Report, 1886, p 93). At the same time, in France an expanding bourgeoisie was demanding allocation of jobs on the basis of credentials and competence, rather than wealth, nepotism and patronage (Goldthorpe, 1996).

In the UK, the period from the 1920s to the 1970s was characterized by a shift towards meritocratic and egalitarian ideals, embodied by the slogan of 'equality of opportunity'. The idea that all would be given equal opportunity to gain access to good credentials and jobs, and that superior jobs would then be seen to be deserved, had a strong appeal for the middle classes. As cultural capital theorists have demonstrated (Bourdieu, 1977; Collins, 1979), people of this class either already possessed, or quickly developed, the strategies to ensure that their children enjoyed advantages in any supposedly equal competitive examination. However, developments towards comprehensive education in the 1960s were supported by many middle-class parents, who realized that, despite cultural advantages, their children might be displaced in selective schools by 'bright' working-class children.

Although few schools, especially in urban areas, had become truly comprehensive (see Benn and Chitty, 1996) by the late 1970s, common schools had begun to widen access to educational credentials. Consequently, the number of students leaving school with educational qualifications rose steadily. The sociological literature of the period demonstrated that the middle classes dominated selective schools, grammar streams and higher education, and became adept at searching out the best comprehensive schools, at accessing resources, and at avoiding schools attended by the poor, minorities and those with special needs.

At the same time, there was an increase in the number of students from manual working-class backgrounds who obtained a higher education, and subsequently joined the ranks of the new and aspirant middle classes. This group predominantly found employment in the expanding public bureaucracies that characterized twentieth-century modern societies.

From the mid-1980s, egalitarian ideologies began to disappear from government agendas in a number of developed countries, with education systems restructured along market lines. In the UK, an educational market was created, based on parental 'choice' of school. Competition between schools is now fuelled by the annual publication of raw scores of public examination results, and schools are rewarded via a funding formula for the numbers of pupils they select. While market forms were intended to introduce financial efficiency, accountability and responsiveness to clients, they were also intended by the political right to reintroduce social selection into education (Flew, 1987). The redevelopment of education as a 'social class sorting mechanism' has been swift, encouraged by the new left as well as the old right, and welcomed by large sections of the middle classes.

Thus, a major result of choice policies around the world has been to increase social class segregation in schools. An OECD study speculated that 'sometimes this is because more privileged groups are more active in choosing desired schools. Sometimes it is because such schools are in more prosperous neighbourhoods where residents continue to get privileged access to them' (OECD, 1994). However, it could equally result from the determination of the middle classes globally to create, or re-create, socially exclusive schools, and the ability of the middle classes to influence educational policy decisions. In the UK, the research carried out by Ball and his colleagues indicated that social class differences enabled more privileged 'choosers' to discriminate between schools, evaluate teachers and avoid schools with negative characteristics (see Gewirtz, Ball and Bowe, 1995). The competitive market situation in the UK and other countries encourages schools to reject socially and educationally vulnerable students, and to orient themselves towards meeting the perceived needs of the middle classes.

Middle-class needs

A study of the perceived needs of the middle classes will probably help to explain educational exclusion better than any study of the characteristics of the excluded. Most sociological studies of the 'new' middle classes of the twentieth-century – distinct from the 'old' nineteenth-century bourgeoisie, who based their social positions on the ownership of capital – point to the part played by education and qualifications in the emergence of a property-less middle class, and explain the commitment of this group to the education of their children (Vidich and Bensman, 1968; Vidich, 1995).

Studies also note that, although the 'middle groups' in Western societies are numerically dominant, they are by no means unitary. The middle-class segment can include highly paid managers, administrators and professionals, lower-paid semi-professionals, white-collar employees, skilled workers and the well-pensioned retired. The groups can be further sub-divided into smaller segments at various occupational, skill and life-style levels, and by gender, ethnic, racial, regional and age factors. Their common characteristic is a commitment to the social and political system which has provided them with a 'good life', or, at least, a better life than their parents, and their fierce determination to see that their children are reproduced into similar spheres.

Increasingly, all middle-class groups base their claims to status and income on 'good' education, the 'right' credentials, and either expertise, or the promise of such expertise. The expertise ranges from senior to middle management in public bureaucracies, private management, and the professions, to semi-professional and white-collar jobs with some minimum of security. Long before the advent of new technologies, middle-class groups realized the importance of access to knowledge and credentials (Burris, 1986). There has been an increase in the importance of a middle class, educated in private or privileged state schools and 'good' universities, which now dominates the communications, opinion and propaganda industries, and also the political sphere; and this group are determined that their own children will have similar access to privileged education. This entails not only using their new market power to 'choose' those schools that will equip their children with the credentials they need to move to the required courses in more prestigious universities, but also equipping their children with the right social and personal skills – described by Brown as a 'value-added curriculum vitae':

> Within the middle classes, the development of the charismatic qualities of their children is becoming as important as arming them with the necessary credentials, contacts and networks. (Brown 1997, p 744)

The needs of this segment of the middle class are less 'equality of opportunity' for meritocratic competition; rather, they seek the ensured exclusion of students who take up teaching time and educational resources, and who do not come from the required social and familial backgrounds. The less secure, lower-income middle-class groups, and aspirant groups, feel even more intensely the need for the exclusion of those who will interfere with the acquisition of good credentials. These groups do not have access to networks and contacts, their children are less likely to acquire the necessary social competences, and they are thus more dependent on meritocratic competition. Governments respond to the aspirations and fears of these groups by adopting policies of reassurance, such as ability tracking, specialist schools for those with particular 'aptitudes', and the continued exclusion of troublesome students. Such policies signal the fact that there will still be advantages for the aspirant classes.

The educational needs of the middle classes – which now include the 'need' to move away from meritocratic and egalitarian ideologies, and to exclude the disadvantaged and troublesome from interfering with their children's educational progress – can be understood as a reaction to 'conditions of modernity' (Giddens, 1993). Middle-class groups are today increasingly affected by the heightened insecurity that results from global economic competition, governments often not in full control of national economies, high unemployment, and de-layering in public bureaucracies and private business.

Although a self-interested approach is understandable, in defending their own interests, middle-class groups may be acting in ways that are detrimental to the social cohesion of whole societies. Robert Reich, a former US Secretary of Labor, has painted a somewhat apocalyptic picture of American society. He sees educational attention focusing on a small group – around one-fifth of the student population – whose class, culture and resourced background turn them into 'symbolic analysts', able to command both tangible and intangible wealth because of the value the global economy places on their skills and qualifications (Reich, 1991, p 244). The problem for Reich is that, while the economic future of that one-fifth of the population is good, four-fifths face a precarious economic future. The temptation for the fortunate few is not so much to exclude others, but to exclude themselves, withdrawing into their own schools, housing enclaves, healthcare and transport. What, he asks, do we owe to one another as members of the same society if we no longer inhabit the same economy? (Reich, 1991, p 303.)

Galbraith (1992) in the USA and Hutton (1995) in the UK have analysed their respective societies in similar terms. Galbraith defined a contented majority of middle and upper classes, with a small number of skilled workers, especially in two-income families. Governed by self-interest, they are unwilling to fund education for groups that are rapidly becoming excluded from any possibility of joining mainstream US society. Hutton described the UK as a 30/30/40 society (Hutton, 1995, p 14), with around 40 per cent of the workforce enjoying tenured employment and secure self-employment, 30 per cent in insecure or temporary employment or self-employment, and a bottom 30 per cent marginalized, unemployed or working for poverty wages. He notes that 'in Britain the growth in inequality has been the fastest of any advanced nation' (Hutton 1995, p 18).

Although Hutton argues for a principle of inclusion in public policies, his recipe for educational inclusion is to create more grammar schools and to introduce streaming in schools, 'in order to attract members of the middle class back into the state system' from private schools (p 311). This policy would not do much to improve the prospects of the excluded disadvantaged, but it would satisify the needs of a large number of the middle class, ensuring that their children had more access to free, superior teaching and academic credentials.

Some twenty years ago, Bourdieu and Boltanski noted that even the wealthier sections of the middle classes could no longer rely on transmitting capital to their children; they saw that 'an intensified use [was] made of the [state] education system by those sections of the ruling and middle class who previously assured the perpetuation of their position by the direct transmission of economic capital' (Bourdieu and Boltanski, 1978, p 198). This led inexorably to a steady inflation of academic qualifications. The 'credential society' discussed by Collins in 1979 has become more and more a reality (Collins, 1979). The acquisition of credentials becomes crucial to the middle classes, both as a legitimation for employment and as a protection against unemployment. The credential inflation, however, is premised on the assumption that academic credentials will take precedence over vocational qualifications.

The avoidance of the vocational

A major need of the middle classes has always been to avoid the relegation of their children to vocational and practical education and training. Vocational qualifications are not the 'right' credentials, and the academic–vocational divide in Britain is synonymous with a class divide. Nineteenth-century education was unambiguously designed to cater for different social classes. The middle classes received their certification via university-dominated examination boards, an upper working class took up apprenticeships or training validated by Craft Guilds, and the majority of workers went into unskilled labour or on-the-job training.

Certain strategies have been developed by twentieth-century policy-makers and professionals, in order to rationalize the continued separation of a minority into high-status academic education, and a majority into early school leaving or vocational training. Throughout the twentieth century, middle-class policy-makers have drawn on psychometric theories of intelligence and ability to bolster the self-interested belief that only a minority of favoured students are capable of abstract thought, a minority of the rest are interested in applied technical ideas, and a majority in practical activities. This was the basis of the Norwood Committee's proposals (1943) for the restructuring of post-war secondary education in Britain. Interestingly, a critic at the time asserted that 'seldom has a more unscholarly or unscientific attitude disgraced the report of a public committee' (Curtis, 1952). The post-war Labour government endorsed divided schooling and curricula, and ensured a continuation of a low-status schooling with a practical and vocational orientation for the majority. The methods by which the middle classes avoided secondary modern schools and ensured that their children obtained grammar school places were succinctly documented by Jackson and Marsden (1962).

Comprehensive school reorganization incorporated academic and practical courses into the curriculum and continued to sort pupils using criteria heavily influenced by factors relating to class, gender and ethnicity. By the late 1990s, the creation of the National Council for Vocational Qualifications in 1986, the development of the (originally) work-based National Vocational

Qualifications, and, in 1991, the school-based General National Vocational Qualifications, have led to a three-track system post-14, and this is becoming firmly embedded. The academic–vocational divide is widening in schools and colleges, despite some moves towards a unified framework, and, as always, the academic route is dominated by the middle classes (Avis *et al.*, 1996; Tomlinson, 1997). Schools and colleges can develop vocational courses for students from 14, and students will be able to leave school to study these at college (Education Act 1998). The students encouraged to leave schools and take up these courses are likely to be from lower socio-economic and 'disaffected' groups, leaving schools 'safer' places for middle-class students.

The 'A' level (Advanced Certificate of Education), a qualification originally designed as a traditional academic, subject-centred examination for 20 per cent of the 'top ability' pupils at 18, is now attempted (in at least one subject) by 50 per cent of young people at school or college. Despite rhetoric about bridging the academic–vocational divide the 'A' level route is perceived as the high-status path to higher education and the professions. Few middle or aspirant middle-class parents are satisfied with other post-16 routes. A review of 16–19 qualifications in 1996 was instructed to 'maintain the rigour' of 'A' levels (Dearing, 1996) – unsubtle code for 'keep the examination elitist'. Nevertheless, a political consensus developed across left and right to protect this route.

(It is interesting that almost all politicians, policy-makers and senior educationalists have reached their present position via 'A' levels. The view that a majority of young people should be steered towards vocational or occupational routes from 14 does not apply to their own children.)

In 1997, Tomlinson wrote that,

It is tempting to speculate that the three-track route is now becoming acceptable provision for young people post-14 precisely because it accords with the future society and economy envisaged by Galbraith (1992) and Hutton (1995). The scenario suggests a 40/30/30 society in which a contented majority (with A levels and higher education) enjoy secure jobs and a comfortable life-style; a middle group (the GNVQ group?) who even with 'applied education' to high levels, undertake contract work and insecure employment; and a bottom group, who despite NVQs are fortunate to find any kind of employment or niche in the economy. (Tomlinson, 1997, p 7.)

The three-track system is leading to a situation in which, despite assertions of inclusion, higher standards and life-long learning, young people are not being educated to be equal citizens or even members of the same economy. The needs of the middle classes are very clearly served by the domination of the academic routes. As Robinson has recently demonstrated, the middle classes are reading labour market trends correctly. The growth in employment opportunities in business, financial and public services, 'where relatively well-paid managerial, technical and professional jobs are concentrated' (Robinson 1998), has encouraged young people to acquire 'A' levels and degrees. In addition, following the use that employers make of credentials, there has been an increase in the requirement that people have higher qualifications to gain access to these jobs. Whether this credential inflation is justified or not, perceptions do justify middle-class fears; at the present time, governments are acquiescing under pressure to expand and resource higher education, rather than invest more heavily in low attainers and vocational courses. In England, it has been the 'A' level route, rather than alternative vocational tracks, which has been sought by those who rationally calculate that their chances of advancement in a competitive society lie in this direction (see Green and Steedman, 1997).

The exclusion of the non-academic

The majority of young people designated as less able, 'non-academic', or having special educational needs have always been from the lower socio-economic classes (Tomlinson, 1982). Explanations for this have usually centred around the deficits and characteristics of the individuals, their families and their social environment. An alternative explanation can be sought in the strategies the middle classes have always had at their disposal; these have enabled them to prevent their children from acquiring pejorative labels, from being excluded from mainstream schools, or from losing out on any resources that might advance their education. The exclusion of large numbers of lower-class young people from mainstream schools and colleges, and from the chance to acquire credentials; their relegation to segregated schooling, lower-level vocational tracks and courses; and their likely place in the economy, all have important implications for an inclusive citizenship.

What will be the place of those regarded as having special educational needs in economies where levels of education and training are to be raised and national targets met, but only if, individually, young people make greater efforts continually to invest in themselves? It is likely that those designated as 'special' will find it even harder than before to acquire skills and competences that can be exchanged, even intermittently, for work. A majority of them will already, through their previous school career – whether in a segregated or integrated setting – have acquired labels associated with non-competence and, possibly, an identity low in feelings of self-worth. They are likely to suffer more acutely from messages that it is their own responsibility if they fail to acquire the competences necessary to find and keep a job. 'Specials' may find that they have a particular and unenviable place in the political economy of Britain in the new century. The issues go beyond questions of training and employment, however. They are linked to government policies produced to deal with uneconomic citizens.

The disappearance of the kind of work undertaken by many of these people (without training or accredited skills and competences) has left them as part of a larger group of young people who are to be managed as a force available for work, as and when jobs need to be done. Low-attainers now compete for work formerly undertaken by those educated in special schools or programmes, but all are urged that the way to find employment is by constant investment in the self, via the acquisition of skills and competences.

In the UK, NVQs or their academic equivalents are to be collected into a national record of achievement, which will demonstrate that the government has achieved targets for a better-trained and educated workforce. The implication is that, if young people are not employable, it is because they have not invested enough in themselves, not that there is anything wrong with economic structures. Young people labelled as 'special' are likely to find it more difficult to collect meaningful skills and competences, because of acquiring 'non-competence' labels, and being more susceptible to messages that it is their fault if they fail to find or keep a job.

The British government has a poor record of promoting inclusive employment policies and those in charge of new accreditation systems have made it clear that few concessions are to be offered. For employers, any 'special' courses or labels are likely to be a way of legitimating non-employment. In the restructured vocational education and training system of the latter 1990s, those who have received a 'special education' for their learning and behavioural difficulties are likely, as in the past, to remain at lower levels, fail to acquire competences, and be reinforced in their lowly position within a low-wage workforce whose skills and competences are are, in any case, to be used only intermittently in the economy. These individuals are likely to form a large segment of Hutton's marginalized 'bottom 30 per cent', and illustrate quite dramatically Reich's assertion that developed countries are creating societies in which not all members appear to belong to the same economy.

Paradoxically, there is an exception to the use of special educational categorization as an agency of educational and economic exclusion. The upper and middle classes have always produced some children with learning difficulties. However, they were able to make private provision or deny the children's existence. Tredgold, writing in 1908, was one of the first writers to acknowledge 'upper-class dullness'. He wrote that 'throughout the country there are hundreds of feeble-minded persons, many of them gentlefolk by birth...they perform little household tasks and outdoor duties, take up simple hobbies like poker-work and stamp-collecting, and enter into the ordinary social amusements of their class' (Tredgold, 1908, p 175).

In the 1970s, Tomlinson found in a study of children being assessed as 'educationally sub-normal' that middle-class parents had a variety of strategies for avoiding this stigmatic label, and transfer to an 'ESN' school. They were, however, willing to accept that their child was 'dyslexic' and needed special help (Tomlinson, 1981). During the 1980s and 1990s, a considerable increase in the demand for 'statementing' has come from parents, who have learned that resources are available for specific learning difficulties – notably dyslexia and dyspraxia. Arguments abound about the nature and origins of specific learning difficulties, but 'dyslexia' has mobilized some powerful upper- and middle-class supporters, notably former cabinet ministers and members of the House of Lords. The middle classes are justifiably afraid that, if their slow-learning children have difficulties acquiring qualifications, they may be at a disadvantage in the new-style labour markets.

The common good

The structural situation in the UK, as in other developed countries, comprises a diverse and expanded middle class and aspirant middle class, who feel increasingly insecure, and whose 'needs' take precedence in any competitive struggles for 'positional advantage' in the society. The political reality is that these groups – whose votes are critical for governments – are catered for by the kind of educational policies that create and re-create social exclusion on a daily basis. Such policies can lead to further inequality and division, and even to social disorder, but alternative policies that threaten middle-class advantages and privileges may jeopardize their electoral basis.

In the late 1990s, the New Labour government embarked on what Muller has called 'an honourable but diminished project of pragmatic amelioration' (Muller, 1997, p 15). Echoing the New Deal workfare programmes in the USA of the 1930s in the USA, and President Johnson's War on Poverty in the 1960s, the UK New Deal of the 1990s includes Welfare to Work programmes, targeted social security payments, and Education and Health Action Zones aimed at raising educational standards and health levels in disadvantaged areas. These policies may have some effect on the well-being of the poor and disadvantaged. They will have little effect on the middle classes, however. This group will continue to ensure, more than ever, that the future status and security of their children is secured, through the acquisition of academic and professional qualifications, and the separation of their children as far as possible from those who may interfere with this aim.

Given this situation, is it possible to envisage the creation of a society in which all groups begin to espouse the idea of a 'common good'?

One approach to the common good, prominent in the UK, derives from theories of social cohesion and social capital, which build on critiques of market competition in public spheres as a major cause of social and economic inequality. In a 1997 Report on Further Education, widely discussed in government, Kennedy pointed out that law, contract and economic rationality provide a basis for prosperity in modern societies, but that these must be 'leavened with reciprocity, moral obligation, duty towards community, and trust' (p 6). Only in this way will the social capital – the feeling that people are 'joined together in a common endeavour' – take precedence over individual, familial or class self-interest. Furthermore, Kennedy sees a powerful role for education in creating social capital, 'education strengthens the ties which bind people, takes the fear out of difference, and encourages tolerance' (p 6).

Similarly, the 1993 Commission on Social Justice took the view that economic prosperity and national renewal could only come about if social justice – defined as the equal worth of all citizens, equal opportunities and life chances, and the elimination of unjust inequalities – pervaded the society and stood against 'the fanatics of the market economy' (p 19). All citizens must believe they live in a fair society, which offers them chances. The social justice report related current inequalities to social class, specifically noting that

> even in times of full employment, the UK has wasted, and continues to waste, much potential achievement through an inefficient and divisive education system...which fails to educate most youngsters to 'A' level standard, and sorts people as soon as it can into social classes where, for the most part, they stay for the rest of their lives. (p 18)

Pragmatic measures taken in the UK at the end of the 1990s have included attempts to encourage the creation of social capital by community and voluntary endeavour, particularly in health and education. However, the geographical separation of middle and working classes means that social capital building goes on in different localities, and does nothing to 'strengthen the ties that bind us' across the social class divide.

The communitarian theorists (Etzioni, 1988; Selznick, 1992; Taylor, 1989), prominent in the USA, have also influenced UK political thinking. The notion of the reconstruction of community in a wide and unitary sense, community as a kind of 'existential anchoring' (Ferrara, 1997) in a complex world, and community as an expression of the 'morality of co-operation' (Etzioni, 1988, p 247) all resonate with politicians and with the public. The reported support for increased taxation to pay for public services is quoted as an example of communitarian feelings, although it may also be due to a realization by the middle classes that they are losing the benefits they enjoyed (disproportionally) under the post-war welfare state.

Bellah and his associates (Bellah *et al.*, 1991) have defended a 'civic republicanism', in which public institutions are reinvigorated and incorporate a genuine concern with the common good. An orientation to the common good does not mean charity, or voluntary community association, but it does mean the government taking the initiative and encouraging civic responsibility:

> It is not enough to implore our fellow citizens to 'get involved'. We must create the institutions which will enable such participation to occur. (Bellah *et al*, 1991, p 15)

Creating inclusive institutions would mean 'loosening the iron grip that special interests have' – a view that is particularly relevant to education, where the special interests of privileged groups take precedence over the common

good. In the UK, it is possible to list four basic principles upon which education could be based:

1. Public policies must be based on shared understandings of the common
   good.
2. The idea of the common good needs to be re-stated. Opportunity for individuals is crucially important but opportunity for all depends on communal recognition of what is good for all.
3. All members of a society must feel that they have 'equality of conditions'
   with equal access to education and other public goods.
4. All members of a society must be convinced of the 'equal worth of all citizens', and that they are part of a just, fair society to which all can contribute.

The problem is whether communitarian philosophies of the common good
can be proposed within a class society in which conditions of inequality are
not only created by public policies, but also welcomed by the middle classes.
This group now seeks, more than ever before, to exclude potential competitors for social goods and resources, and defend and extend privileges and advantages for their own children.

References

Andrews, K. and Jacobs, J. (1990) *Punishing the Poor*, Macmillan, London
Avis, J., Bloomer, M., Esland, G., Gleeson, D. and Hodgkinson, P. (1996) *Knowledge and Na-
tion: Education,Politics and Work*, Cassell, London
Bellah, R. N., Madsen, R., Sullivan, R., William, M., Swidher, A. and Tipton, S. M. (1991) *The
Good Society*, Knopf, New York
Benn, C. and Chitty, C. (1996) *Thirty Years On: Is Comprehensive Education Alive and Well or is it
Struggling to Survive?*, David Fulton, London
Blair, T. (1997) Speech on the opening of Social Exclusion Unit, London, 8/12/97
Bourdieu, P. (1997) *Reproduction in Education – Society and Culture*, Sage, London
Bourdieu, P. and Boltanski, L. (1978) 'Changes in social structure and changes in the de-
mands for education', in S. Giner and S. Archer (eds) *Contemporary Europe: Social Structure
and Cultural Change*, Routledge, London
Brown, P. (1990) 'The "third wave": education and the ideology of parentocracy', *British
Journal of Sociology of Education*, 11, (1), pp 65–85
Burris, V. (1986) 'The discovery of the new middle classes', *Theory and Society*, 15, pp 317–49
Collins, P. (1979) *The Credential Society*, Academic Press, New York
Commission on Social Justice (1993) *Social Justice: Strategies for National Renewal*, Vintage,
London
Dearing, R. (1996) *Review of Qualifications for 16–19 Year Olds*, Schools Curriculum and As-
sessment Authority, London
Dore, R. (1976) *The Diploma Disease*, University of California Press, Berkeley
Etzioni, A. (1988) *The Moral Dimension: Towards a New Economics*, Collier-Macmillan, London
Ferrara, A. (1997) 'The paradox of community', *International Sociology*, 12, (4), pp 395–408
Flew, A. (1987) *Power to the Parents*, Sherwood Press, London

Galbraith, J. K. (1992) *The Culture of Contentment*, Sinclair-Stevenson, London

Gewirtz, S., Ball, S. J. and Bowe, R. (1995) *Markets, Choice and Equity in Education*, Open University Press, Buckingham

Giddens, A. (1993) *The Consequences of Modernity*, Polity Press, Cambridge

Goldthorpe, J. (1996) 'Problems of meritocracy', in R. Erickson, and J. O. Jonsson (eds), *Can Education be Equalized: The Swedish Case in Comparative Perspective*, Westwiew Press, London

Green, A. and Steedman, H. (1997) *Into the 21st Century: An Assessment of British Skill Profiles and Prospects*, Centre for Economic Performance, London

Heath, A. and MacMahon, D. (1997) 'Educational and occupational attainments: The impact of ethnic origin', in V. Karn (ed) *Education, Employment and Housing among Ethnic Minorities*, HMSO, London

Hirsch, F. (1977) *Social Limits to Growth*, Routledge, London

Hutton, W. (1995) *The State We're In*, Jonathan Cape, London

Jackson, B. and Marsden, D. (1962) *Education and the Working Classes*, Routledge, London

Joseph, K. (1972) Speech to Pre-School Playgroups Association, London, 29/6/72

Kennedy, Helena (1997) *Learning Works: Widening Participation in Further Education*, Further Education Funding Council, Sheffield

Lewis, O. (1968) 'The culture of poverty', in D. P. Moyhihan (ed), *On Understanding Poverty*, Basic Books, New York

Muller, J. (1997) 'Social justice and its renewals: a sociological comment', unpublished paper, School of Education, University of Cape Town

Murray, C. (1984) *Losing Ground: American Social Policy 1950–1980*, Basic Books, New York

Norwood Committee (1943) *Curriculum and Examinations in Secondary Schools*, HMSO, London

OECD (1994) *Schools under Scrutiny*, Centre for Educational Research and Innovation, Organization for Economic Co-operation and Development, Paris

Parkin, F. (1979) *Marxism and Class Theory: A Bourgeois Critique*, Tavistock, London

Reich, R. (1991) *The Work of Nations*, Simon and Schuster, London

Robinson, P. (1998) 'Measuring the knowledge economy: employment and qualifications', in D. Robertson (ed) *The Knowledge Economy*, Routledge, London

Schools Inquiry Report (1886) (The Taunton Report), London

Selznick, P. (1992) *The Moral Commonwealth: Social Theory and the Promise of Community*, University of California Press, Berkeley

Taylor, C. (1989) *Sources of the Self: The Making of Modern Identity*, Harvard University Press, Cambridge

Tomlinson, S. (1981) *Educational Sub-normality: A Study in Decision-Making*, Routledge, London

Tomlinson, S. (1982) *A Sociology of Special Education*, Routledge, London

Tomlinson, S. (ed) (1997) *Education 14–19. Critical Perspectives*, Athlone Press, London

Tredgold, A. F. (1908) *Mental Deficiency*, Balliere, Tindall and Cox, London

Vidich (1995) *The New Middle Classes*, Macmillan, London

Vidich and Bensman (1968) 'Liberalism and the new middle classes', in A. J. Vidich and J. Bensman (eds) *Small Town in Mass Society*, Princeton University Press, Princeton

Webb, B. (1926) *My Apprenticeship*, Longman, London

Wilson, W. J. (1987) *The Truly Disadvantaged*, Chicago University Press, Chicago

Wilson, W. J. (1997) 'Studying inner-city dislocations: the challenge of public agenda research', in A. Halsey, H. Lauder, P. Brown and A. S. Wells (eds), *Education, Economy, Culture, Society*, Oxford University Press, Oxford

22. Advocacy, self-advocacy and inclusive action: a concluding perspective

Jo Lebeer, Roberta Garbo, Peetjie Engels and Annet De Vroey

Introduction

This concluding overview defines what for most of those involved as theorists and practitioners within the professional field of special education has become the key component of the future 'inclusive': that in order to be regarded as full citizens belonging to society, and participating in every aspect of its social life, the way to achieve this is through radical inclusive education, right from the start. Within developing configurations of inclusive education, youngsters with disabilities and their parents are no longer seen as passive recipients of educational benevolence. Rather, it now provides a voice of equal status in determining, in partnership with professionals, the nature and organization of practices directed towards full participation in all human processes. The chapter shows some concrete utopias as they are realized in three countries, Holland, Belgium and Italy, each indicative in turn of individual involvement and group action at local or national levels in advocacy and self-advocacy.

1. Pioneering for inclusive education in Holland

In June 1997, Peetjie Engels, 19 years old, living in the south of Holland, passed her secondary exams. The achievement certificate was given to her personally by Education Minister Netelenbos, during a mini symposium, organized by the Down's Syndrome Foundation and Stibco (Foundation for the Cognitive Development). Peetjie is the first person with Down's Syndrome in Holland (and neighbouring countries) to achieve such a high schooling level. She goes to school on her scooter, takes judo lessons, and also does gymnastics, horse riding and plays the clarinet. She even wrote a paper on Down's Syndrome. Now she has registered in a school to train in the support of elderly people.

Peetjie's school career started in a special school at the age of two. Her IQ at the age of six was 60, and she was referred to a special school for very low abilities, where objectives were reduced to socialization. Her mother fought to get her into a school where she would at least learn to write, count and read. At the age of ten, Peetjie went to the international institute in increasing learning potential in Israel, to get a LPAD, while her mother studied Instrumental Enrichment. Prof. Feuerstein advised Mrs Engels to send Peetjie to a normal primary school.

Mrs Engels, a dietician and recipe-book writer, practised Instrumental Enrichment every day.

'I always felt alone,' she said. 'I had to invent everything on my own. I didn't know if I was on the right track, because everyone declared that I was mad. Prof. Feuerstein was the first one to congratulate me for the work that I did with my daughter. I was stunned.' Using 'her intelligence as a farmer', as she defines it, she transformed the school programme so that her daughter understood it.

Peetje can express herself clearly. She wants to help other families with disabled children, so that they are not treated as too childish. She found schoolwork pleasant and quite ordinary. Below is her story; she wrote it herself on the computer, in English, which is not her mother tongue.

'Hi everyone.

'My name is Peetjie Engels. I am 19 years old. I have Down's Syndrome, bad eyes and other medical problems. However, today still I am at a senior secondary school. Last year I have passed my exams and got my diploma from the secondary school.

'First I was at a day care centre. After that I had to go to a school for very retarded children, the ZMLK[1]. But my parents sent me to a school for retarded children, a MLK[2]. I didn't learn a lot. There it wasn't nice for me, because there was a lot of struggle and in the playground there was no fun. I had to go by taxi or by special bus. I came home too late, to play with other children.

'We went to Israel, to professor Feuerstein. They tested me and my mum got lessons, which she taught me. Feuerstein said, I had to go to a normal elementary school. There it was nice. I was with the children of Schinnen and Werny, my sister, was on that school too. We went together to school and I had a lot of friends. I went by bike to my friends to play, and they came to me too. I had to think a lot more, but that wasn't the trouble, because it was a lot nicer there. At home I practised every day with my mum. I was with my friends on the swimming club, on judo, in a choir and on gymnastics.

'After that I visited a normal secondary school. There I got other subjects like: math, English and German. I had a lot of home tasks. I have bad memory, and I need more time to learn than my peers. Sometimes they were jealous, because I had good marks by hard studying. Especially the last year I had to work very hard. Because I wanted to have my diploma. And I am proud to tell you I got it with very good marks.

'I think children with Down's Syndrome have to go to a normal school, if they want. That costs a lot of money for the school. I have a mentor who helps me, when I need it. Also the other teachers help me, especially when it is difficult.

'I do all things, school and clubs, integrated. That is nice, but sometimes it is also hard for me.

'At school, there is a girl who is not nice to me. She is calling me names. Maybe she doesn't like to be in the same class with me.

'In a shop it is difficult to count my money. Once a customer said: "I can pay faster", and then I was a bit embarrassed.

'In my swimming club there is one child who doesn't like to swim with me in the same group. She always says: "You swim to slow, go to another group." But I swim as fast as most of the others.

'Some people are childish, that I hate. Sometimes they help me to do things I can handle myself, such as: paying or deciding what to do. I dislike that.

'My appearance is not the same as my peers, I don't care. People are looking at me, but that isn't too bad. My tongue has been operated on. First I was afraid, but after the operation, I was glad that my tongue was shorter. With my longer tongue I was difficult to understand and I couldn't eat easily. My mouth was filled with my tongue. When my tongue was shorter, I could talk and eat easily and my face looked nicer. What I mean: other children with Down's syndrome can be operated too. For them that is a lot nicer. With my shorter tongue I am able to sing in the youngsters choir.

'People always think, I can't handle all kinds of new things. So they said: Peetjie can't read, she can't write, she can't swim. But I do all kind of things. They also said: Peetjie can't do math. Don't teach her English, she will never be able to talk English. And what do you say. "Can I handle it?"

'One professor said: A child with Down's syndrome can never handle abstract issues. But I know perfectly what is abstract and what is concrete. I can talk about my and other persons' feelings. Know how to handle various situations.

'In my view children with Down's syndrome who are less fortunate as I am, can feel sad or ashamed. I think maybe they feel sorry that they can't handle all those things. It is sad when you can't count, read or do your own shopping.

'Some people think I am to pity, but that isn't so. I have Down's syndrome, but mostly I am very happy and all my days are nice. I like to go to school and to my clubs and to play music. Of course there are sad moments too, but then I think of nice moments: a performance, a game or a party.

'I have a motor-scooter. I can drive it because I can keep my balance. I learned it on gymnastic and horse riding. I swim a lot, which is good for my muscles. I do judo to control myself. I play the clarinet, because it is good for my mouth and my tongue. With the whole family we go down hill skiing and wind surfing. In the weekend I go to a club or a pub with Were my sister and other friends. I can go with them, because my behaviour is good, I am quite the same as other youngsters. You see, for certain I am not a piteous little child.

'I am going to tell what I want when I am an adult.

'I want to live in my own house, a normal house with a garden. I want to have a dog and a horse. I will do the cleaning, cooking and shopping. I want to decide by myself what time I have to go to bed, what I do in my spare time and what I eat.

'I don't like to live alone. When there are bad moments, I don't like to be lonely. I like to live with a friend. He has to be nice and own a good spirit. I don't want a friend who makes trouble, or a person who thinks that I am only a stupid Mongol. I want a friend who understands Down's syndrome, and who accepts me. I have to accept my friend too. With everybody there can be something.

'I want to work and earn my money. I like to take care of children. I want to work in a children's-home as an assistant. The chief warden has to work alone. I don't like to work alone. I'm afraid that sometimes I might not know what to do, and then I will make mistakes. For a moment I can work alone, and as an assistant, I can always ask for help.

'Many think that people with Down's syndrome can't raise children, but I think, that isn't true. I can. I want to work with children with Down's syndrome. I will learn all kind of things to them. When they will take my glasses, I will say: "Don't do that" and then they don't. Messing around with food is only allowed when they are young. I will talk a lot with them. When they don't talk, I will teach them. Together we will stand for a mirror and make faces and then they imitate me.

'When I work with children with Down's syndrome I have to work very, very hard, to teach them to work, to talk: anyway: everything. With these children you have to be very strict, otherwise they can't learn anything.

'I have learned to think. I will teach Feuerstein's lessons to the children with Down's syndrome. As no other, I know how to do that.

'I hope other children with Down's syndrome will have the same chance as I had. That they will be as happy as I am. And that all people believe they can handle all kind of things, just as I do.

'Please, I'll ask all of you. Work with them.'

2. Starting inclusion in a country of apartheid: MENTOR, a pilot project to promote inclusive education in Belgium

The MENTOR (Modifying Environments towards better Teaching, Rehabilitation and Integration) project is a pilot project supported by the Equal Opportunities Programme of the European Commission's DGV for Social Affairs. It offers a training and support service for parents and educators, with the aim of promoting and enabling the education of children with a range of cognitive impairments within the mainstream educational system. The project is an answer to an increasing request by parents of disabled children to have their children mainstreamed; these parents often meet resistance from all sides.

Context

Belgium has the second-highest extent of special-needs education in separate environments in Europe (Pijl, Meijer and Hegarty, 1998). There are many special schools distributed geographically all over the country, and categorized into 8 types:

1. children with mild learning difficulties (type 8);
2. children with moderate learning difficulties (type 1);
3. children with severe learning difficulties (type 2);
4. children who are deaf and have language disturbance (type 7);
5. children with visual impairment (type 6);
6. sick children (type 5);
7. children with motor disablement (type 4); and
8. children with psychological disablement (type 3).

These categories frequently overlap, but they are broad enough to accommodate about 30 000 special-needs children, or 3.3 per cent of the entire children's population in the Northern Region, Flanders. Rehabilitation facilities are organized within these special schools; physiotherapist, speech and occupational therapists are available, as is psychological guidance for children and parents.

Because the network of special schools is so well established, mainstream teachers and school guidance services tend to refer children towards them at an early age. Mainstream schools tend to operate in a standard-oriented way, based on a 'normal' level of attainment. As soon as a child cannot attain these standards in school performance, s/he is referred for special schooling. There is some governmental support for 'integrated education' – children with special needs are allowed to attend mainstream primary and secondary schools and obtain the help of a support teacher for a maximum of 2 hours per week – but, in practice, due to budget limitations and standardization of curricula in mainstream schools, this is only allowed to highly intelligent and fluent-learning disabled children with hearing, visual or motor impairment, or 2 per cent of the population of disabled children. It is fair to say, therefore, that inclusive education in Belgium is not yet supported in practice by the government.

Parents who do not want their child educated in this separate system, and who want inclusive education, can have this only if the mainstream school director and team agree out of benevolence. Even if they do agree, the parents will be financially and organizationally responsible for special needs staff.

There are recent indications that this situation is changing. First, more and more parents of children with learning difficulties are requesting inclusive education; many are simply putting their children in mainstream schools, negotiating with teachers and directors to individualize a programme, and providing support teachers out of their own funds. These parents are not yet well organized, but they are becoming a pressure group. Their main motives are issues of human rights: they claim inclusion, because they are opposed to the total educational apartheid of the Belgian system, which puts disabled children in a separate environment. They claim inclusion is better for developing social relationships, and they base their arguments on United Nations declarations. Also, they dispute whether special education in a separate environment is effective in enabling the acquisition of academic skills. Indeed, the academic level obtained by moderately mentally retarded children is rather low; they hardly learn to read or write or calculate, and they are usually prepared only for a life-long protected (or 'sheltered') way of life in a separate environment.

Another small group of professionals, working on European projects, have become advocates of inclusion. Three university professors have written a report, which states that inclusive education should be introduced as the norm for all children in Belgium (Ghesquiere *et al.*, 1996). This created huge resistance from special as well as mainstream schools. The report stated that mainstream schools should allow individuality and become less oriented towards meeting national standards, and that special schools should take up a role of service centres within the mainstream. In a major breakthrough, the official Flemish Education Council, which advises the Minister, adopted a report advocating inclusion for all in principle.

The realization of full inclusive education in Belgium will, however, take years. In practice, it will be achieved only through the involvement and actions of volunteers, and the goodwill of teachers, alongside supportive and financially well-off parents who can afford it.

Project Mentor: a brief description

Project Mentor started as a response to a growing need expressed by those parents who advocate inclusive education in Belgium. The project is part of a continuing collaboration between an organization of parents of disabled children and professionals within a University Department of Medicine. It aims to challenge the existing rigidly segregated system of education for disabled children, and to improve the opportunities for the social inclusion of children with cognitive impairments. In particular, it seeks to promote their education within the mainstream system. The three-person project team includes one professional who is the parent of a child with a cognitive impairment, and one person who is visually impaired. The project comprises a number of approaches:

1. Documentation centre: A book and video library has been established, and is open to the public two afternoons each week. Written requests for information are also answered; and a computerized database of material in the centre is being developed.
2. Training: Courses and study groups for 12 to 15 parents and people volunteering to act as assistants to children attending mainstream schools, are

being held on 'Development and Learning Enhancement', 'Basic Introduction to Learning how to Learn', and 'Development and Inclusion'.
3. Other training modules and study days are being arranged for professionals (including teachers in integrated schools, psychologists and remedial therapists) on 'Learning how to Learn' (for children with intellectual disabilities); the University is associated with the International Centre for the Enhancement of Learning Potential in Jerusalem, and organizes a full training in Feuerstein's theory, and applied systems of Structural Cognitive Modifiability and Mediated Learning Experiences: 'Instrumental Enrichment' and 'Learning Potential Assessment'. Each year, about 20 people start a new 25-day professional training.
4. An International Workshop on Inclusive Education was held for professionals, parents and volunteers during a European intensive course on inclusive education at the University of Gent (28 March 1998). Speakers included disabled people and parents from the Netherlands, Italy and Belgium.

Advice on and support for inclusive education

Individual parents who want their children to be included in a mainstream school are offered advice on what action to take, and then given continuing support. Assistance is provided at initial meeting(s) with head and class teachers and supporting staff. Regular visits take place in the school to assist in meetings between parents, teachers, remedial therapists, representative of the psycho-medical social service, and assessment of the child's progress. A video is used to record the classroom situation for discussion at the subsequent meeting. Up to June 1998, 15 children, including children with autism, several with Down's Syndrome, genetic chromosomal disorders and cerebral palsy, have been helped to secure places in mainstream education.

Awareness-raising activities

In order to warm up the general public for inclusive education, a series of articles has been published in the professional press (for teachers, psychologists, general education, medical), as well as in the public press (newspapers and weekly magazines); an interview was given on the radio; and regular 'conferences' about inclusion are organized in mainstream schools.

Part of the project to raise awareness, and to promote inclusion in all aspects of society, is the organization of a dance workshop, both for people with motor impairments and for people without disabilities. The production and performance of a new dance theatre is planned in association with Warande Turnhout, a cultural centre, and Adam Benjamin from London, the founder of the Candoco Dance Company.

Political lobbying

An *ad hoc* initiative working party has been established, to get inclusive education off the ground; leading players in the field of inclusive education have
been invited, including representatives from the Ministry of Education, of
Welfare, from the Educational Authorities, from the National Education
Council (VLOR), from other parent organizations, from teachers' unions, and
from each major political party.

Outcomes

A video for parents and teachers on inclusive education will be produced, incorporating some material from the videos made during the assessment of
children's progress in school. A book for parents on their role in helping children to learn and develop through everyday experiences is also planned.

It also planned to undertake a research project on the conditions for, and
experiences of people with severe cognitive disabilities in inclusive education,
and to seek formal recognition of inclusive education and of the resource centre from the Flemish authorities.

Further information:
Annet de Vroey and Elke Willaert, KVG- Gezin and Handicap vzw, Arthur
Goemarelei 66, 2018 Antwerp, Belgium
Tel: (32) (0)3 216 29 90; Fax: (32) (0)3 248 14 42; E-mail: post@kvg.be

Jo Lebeer MD Ph.D, Department of Medicine, University of Antwerp, Building S, 5th Floor, Universiteitsplein 1, 2610 Wilrijk, Belgium
Tel: (32) (0) 3 820 25 18; Fax: (32) (0) 820 25 26; E-mail: lebeerjo@uia.ua.ac.be

3. Italy's radical choice for inclusion: a long way from law to practice

Inclusion according to the Italian law

The movement supporting inclusion in mainstream education dates back to
the end of the 1960s in Italy and has led to a complex and broadly discussed experience in the last thirty years. The strength of the movement, and, even
more than that, a general cultural bias fighting exclusion in any form (economic, social and cultural), and advocating equal opportunities in all fields,
has led to the enforcement of certain laws. Those laws stated what inclusion
meant and how it could be implemented in a progressive and consistent way.
The first formal recognition, with Act n. 118, 1971, found broader echo and
momentum in Act n. 517, issued in 1977, which officially shut down special
schools, opening the way to a 15-year experience of across-the-board inclusion. The whole process, and the expertise that had to be developed in order to

face such a radical and 'sudden' decision, led in 1992 to the enforcement of Act 104, a general legislative framework aimed at answering in a more systematic and exhaustive way the complex needs of a handicapped child and his/her family in an 'open environment'.

According to Act 104, the right of the handicapped child to education is based on the following principles:

- The handicapped child aged 0-3 may, and has the right to, attend pre-kindergarten and nursery schools.
- The right to education of a handicapped person is granted at kindergarten, in mainstream classes of school institutions of any order and rank, including universities.
- The main objective of inclusion is to develop the handicapped person's potential in learning, communication, relationships and social processes.
- The exercise of the right to education cannot be hindered by either learning difficulties or other difficulties arising from the disabilities related to the specific handicap.
- After identifying the pupil as a handicapped person and gathering the information arising from his/her functional diagnosis, a dynamic-functional profile is drawn in order to define a personalized education plan, jointly worked out by the parents, the health and education professionals and the specialized teacher in the school. These two tools – the dynamic-functional profile and the education plan – are regularly reviewed in order to monitor the effects of the different intervention programmes and the impact of school activities on the development of the child.
- In schools of any order and rank, while local authorities have the duty to supply assistance for independent working and personal communication to all pupils with sensory and physical handicap, support activities are provided by the school through specialized teachers. They provide specialized teaching in the areas indicated by the individual education plan and take part in the planning and didactic activities of the whole class. They are recognized as part of the teaching staff providing support to the class as a whole, not as the special-needs teacher dedicated solely to the special-needs child attending that class.

Inclusion and belonging: the school as an integrating background

Based on the principles outlined above, it is possible to conceptualize three aspects of inclusion, as follows:

- it is a process, as it aims especially with the disabled child to challenge his/her functions as much as possible, thereby countering the risk of regression and loss of liveliness, due to a relationship with a static, very 'simple and safe', predictable environment;

- it is a relationship, as it is precisely in the relationship with the 'other' that a person, whether disabled or not, may find opportunities and a drive towards development and education;
- it is an event, as when we switch from providing assistance to the pupil in need to providing meaning and meaningfulness in the relationship of that pupil with the human and physical environment he/she experiences, we advocate his/her dignity and right to belong in a very practical and easily-understood way.

Thus, inclusion, with the breadth of meanings it carries, may or may not materialize itself as a process, as a relationship or as an event in a number of contexts, in the different 'places' where development and education occur – the nuclear and extended family, the playing field, the neighbourhood, the school, the workplace, and so on.

As far as school is concerned, the Italian journey towards inclusion has seen a significant number of cases – according to data provided by the Ministry of Education, after the enforcement of Act 104, the attendance of 'certified' handicapped students has been over 40 000 units in secondary junior schools and over 7 000 in secondary high schools – and covered over twenty years, if Act 517, 1977, with the abolition of special schools, can be taken as the starting point of the whole process.

Such a journey, where field experience has intertwined with theoretical work and extensive research, has yielded some conceptual tools and a few tricks of the trade. These may prove to be of use when trying to make inclusion of a disabled child in a mainstream environment a success, or when trying to minimize the risk of failure. The latter is in itself a key objective, if the experience at school is put in perspective and considered as part of what life in open society may look, sound and feel like for a disabled child.

Conceptual tools

The following tools may be useful:

- favouring the integration of different contributions and elements (individual characteristics, competence, tools, languages, ways and modalities), acting as an integrating background, a broader *gestalt* in which differences can be perceived as integral and enriching parts of the whole;
- allowing for an integration of affective and cognitive components, in other words, promoting the motivation to understand and learn;
- helping to structure learning contexts, which may progressively lead to understanding and learning in broader and more complex conceptual frameworks, which are intrinsically dynamic;
- promoting the pleasure to be and to learn, generating the emotion of

learning through a co-operative integrating approach to educational processes.

Tricks of the trade

The following 'tricks of the trade' may be useful:

- structuring activities so that the disabled pupil may stay in class most of the time;
- having the specialized support teacher act as a class teacher in all respects;
- proposing the same materials and tools as schoolmates, targeting activities to specific objectives and needs, but emphasizing wherever possible the common learning experience and the participation in the process;
- helping the child to take part in the interaction as actively as possible and giving 'time' for the acquisition of social rules, even through passive participation: much is learned by watching others, and belonging to the group does not necessarily mean being actively involved all the time;
- using the class as a powerful mediator, as an opportunity for promoting meaningful learning experiences through small-group activities (co-operative learning and peer-tutoring), which give more room to sharing and active involvement;
- paying attention to key non-verbal elements, such as the use of the class as a learning space, and to the way 'distance' (physical, emotional, relational, and so on) is managed within the class.

Three stories about inclusion

Caterina

Born in 1974, Caterina starts attending kindergarten at three, with a somewhat passive attitude, which leads her teachers to have a pessimistic outlook on her development. However, language and other abilities progress fairly well during those years, and at six she goes to the elementary school where her mother works as a teacher. She is the first girl with Down's Syndrome to attend that school, which makes the experience rather difficult for everybody. In particular, the school is challenged to look for creative solutions: small-group activities are organized, while the specialized support teacher helps Caterina learn at a pace, and with the amount of consolidating practice, which fit her individual characteristics as a learner. Tests and evaluation activities are conceived always with her individualized education plan in mind; this plan is tightly geared in terms of content and rules to that of the whole class.

The five years of elementary school close with success and satisfaction (she has acquired reading and writing skills, and basic maths), but junior secondary school starts with serious difficulty and withdrawal at first. Thanks to her participation in drama, this initial lack of adaptation to a new learning environment comes to an end, opening up a second and a third year of learning and participation. At the end of these three years, Caterina can perform mathematical expressions, calculate the area of complex geometrical figures, translate short sentences from Italian into English, and answer basic questions on all subject matters. Given the encouraging results and her declared 'passion' for studying, her parents look for a high school that will welcome her and offer good learning opportunities. Given the fact that Caterina has in mind to become a teacher, like her mother, they choose a four-year private course for educators. She attends this regularly until the final exam, following the same subjects and topics as her schoolmates, but with a level of difficulty tailored to her individualized education plan.

Now 24, Caterina works part-time as a secretary in a private company. In her leisure time, she goes to modern dance, computer and English classes, and works as a volunteer in Milan.

Daniela

Born in 1977, at the age of three Daniela goes to kindergarten where her elder sister has been already for some time; she encounters warm acceptance and a lack of prejudice. Things change radically at the elementary school, where, after two years with a 'good' teacher, she bumps into a teaching team, including a specialized support teacher for eight hours a week, that shows a total lack of understanding and acceptance. Their typical comments to the family are, 'But does she really understand?' or, 'No, the problem is that she cannot possibly make it.' They do not even want to take advantage of the specialized counselling the professionals from the Association are prepared to give. As a result, Daniela enters junior secondary school with minimal reading and writing skills.

The situation in her new school is exactly the opposite. Showing maximum openness and availability, this institution offers weekly meetings with the family and the support teacher, and the rest of the teaching team. After one year devoted to 'getting to know' Daniela and her needs, the following two prove very joyful and useful and lead to a final exam in which her academic performance proves satisfactory, in relation to her individualized education plan. When the time comes to choose what to do next, Daniela goes for a very challenging option, an art high school, despite the attempts of her parents and reference professionals to discourage her from taking too steep a path. In fact, the five years spent at high school prove to be very hard, full of cognitive and emotional difficulties, marked by a lack of trust on the part of the teachers who do not see why she should be there, and what her objectives are. At the end of this period, Daniela gets a certificate of attendance – not a diploma, but an official document stating an 'education credit' – which proves useful in accessing a one-year vocational training. Here, teaching of secretarial skills is coupled with creating awareness of a new environment (the company), and the social, communication and cognitive skills needed to operate in it. After six months of in-company training, with the support and supervision of a tutor responsible for the project, Daniela, now 21, work full-time in a key financial institution.

Alessandro

Born in 1979, Alessandro has a very pleasant and fruitful time at kindergarten, but the first years at the elementary school do not prove equally positive. Alessandro works side by side (literally) with a support teacher who, right from the start, decides that he should have his own activities, regardless of what his schoolmates do, because those activities best fit his learning needs. As a result, he spends most of his energy trying to do what the class teacher does with the others, and develops a very negative attitude towards the support teacher, to the inevitable expense of overall development and academic performance, but with some success in his social relationships.

Junior secondary school brings about great change and new opportunities. Thanks to a simplified individual programme, parallel to that of the class, and to the presence of a sensible support teacher, who took turns with colleagues in order to provide support to the class as a 'learning group', rather than to 'the disabled pupil'. Alessandro gets rid of his resistance and opposition, and takes on a more responsible attitude. Using the same strategy, after junior secondary school, he attends three years of high school before passing to a EC vocational training programme. Now 19, he is still attending this programme.

One of the key features in Alessandro's story is the way in which his parents have consistently encouraged him to play an active role at school, in social life and in his personal relationships. He belongs to a family that attaches great importance to a sound value system and culture, and he likes 'good books' and poetry, and has participated actively on student committees and in political life while attending high school. He is a 19-year-old who is in charge of his own life, within the limits of his condition, age and experience.

Inclusion: an opportunity for affective and cognitive literacy

Are these success stories the norm, related to provide reasons for inclusion? No, they are unusual, describing young adults who have lived in a totally open environment, with families that have strongly advocated their right to find adequate answers to their special needs in a non-special environment. Unlike most success stories, they convey the good and bad aspects of inclusion; they demonstrate development as a dynamic process, with accelerations and Down's decelerations, with good experiences and setbacks, when a lack of knowledge and understanding is encountered. They are unusual because they are based on an idea of educational success that could be expressed in terms of affective and cognitive literacy.

What Caterina, Daniela and Alessandro have to tell us is that, having had the opportunity to share the emotion of learning – the engine capable of starting up the motivation to learn – with their schoolmates and peers, they have been able to develop a feeling of sharing and belonging to a broader group. Thanks to their presence in the class, their schoolmates, in turn, have had the valuable experience of belonging to a whole; in that whole, differences find a place and a meaning, difficulties occur and may find an answer within the class, and a human and physical environment is conceptualized in terms of integrating background. Thanks to the options provided by inclusion, the disabled pupil has been included – comprehended, understood and made part of the class, or the broader whole. He or she will, in turn, learn how to comprehend, understand and make part of him or herself other events, relationships and experiences. By the same token, his or her schoolmates have experienced first hand in their relationship with him or her that it is indeed possible to comprehend, understand and include differences, that learning in this very broad and enriched sense can be shared, regardless of the level of performance. To borrow the words used by Andrea Canevaro, one of the most enlightened pioneers of inclusion, 'The quality of inclusion for a disabled pupil is the litmus paper of the good functioning of an educational institution.'

Further information:
Roberta Garbo, Associazione Italiana Persona Down's
Tel/fax: +39 331 25 92 45; E-mail: rgarbo@logic.it

End notes

1. Dutch for 'School children with severe learning difficulties'.
2. Dutch for 'School children with moderate learning difficulties'.

References

Ghesquiere, P., De Fever, F. and Van Hove, G. (1996) Op weg naar Inclusief Onderwijs!? Elementen voor de discussie rond de hervorming van het Buitengewoon Onderwijs in Vlaanderen in functie van de internationale tendens tot integratie, Ongepubliceerd rapport, Leuven/Brussel/Gent

Pijl, S. J., Meijer, C. J. W. and Hegarty, S. (1998) *Inclusive Education – A Global Agenda*, Routledge, London

Index